The Vinyl Ain't Final

THE VINYL AIN'T FINAL

Hip Hop and the Globalization of Black Popular Culture

Edited by
Dipannita Basu and Sidney J. Lemelle

Pluto Press
LONDON • ANN ARBOR, MI

First published 2006 by Pluto Press
345 Archway Road, London N6 5AA
and 839 Greene Street, Ann Arbor, MI 48106

www.plutobooks.com

British Library Cataloguing in Publication Data
A catalogue record for this book is available from the British Library

ISBN   0 7453 1941 6 hardback
ISBN   0 7453 1940 8 paperback

Library of Congress Cataloging in Publication Data applied for

10 9 8 7 6 5 4 3 2 1

Designed and produced for Pluto Press by
Chase Publishing Services Ltd, Sidmouth, EX10 9QG, England
Typeset from disk by Stanford DTP Services, Northampton, England
Printed and bound in the United States of America by
Maple-Vail Book Manufacturing Group

Contents

*The book is dedicated to our families and loved ones
and to free and unfree hip hop lovers the world over*

Acknowledgements

The editors would like to thank all the contributors for their work on this book. As with all edited volumes, so too with this work, many people have contributed to its eventual completion. The book was inspired by a conference in 2001 organized by Basu entitled 'Hip Hop and Rap: Redefining the Black Public Sphere,' and kindly funded by the Intercollegiate Department of Black Studies (IDBS) at the Claremont Colleges, California. Of particular note were the panel participants which included hip hop heavy weight and practitioners: Craig Watkins, Mark Anthony Neal, Tricia Rose, Billy Jam, Brian Cross (B Plus), Ben Caldwell, Mark Maxwell, Todd Boyd, and Michael Eric Dyson.

Special thanks to Anne Beech, Judy Nash, Robert Webb, Melanie Patrick and Debjani Roy at Pluto Press for their support for our project and to Tom Mertes for his editorial assistance. We are also thankful to Noelle Hanrahan of Prison Radio and Frances Goldin Agency for facilitating the clearance of Mumia Abu-Jamal's speeches, Lesenyego Masitenyane at Ghetto Ruff Publishing and Licensing for clearance of lyrics for Prophets of Da City.

In addition, a number of students helped with both the conference and manuscript: Kimberley Smith, Lety Taylor, Jacqueline Dubose, Lindsey Hill, Caley Haaken-Heymann, Courtney Moffett, Coren Cooper, Salim Lemelle, Megan Daniels, and Sounun Tek.

Several institutions and foundations provided important funding assistance including Pitzer College Research and Awards Committee, the Dean's Office, Pomona College research committee and Hawley Fund at Pomona College.

Finally, we would like to express our deepest gratitude and appreciation to our families. Basu would like to thank Surinder, Sekhar, Sanjoy, and Minnie Basu, whose love and support thousands of miles away in Coventry, UK, was felt close to her heart in Claremont California. Closer to home she would like to thank Tim Perello for his constant source of inspiration, patience, and support. For Sid Lemelle, a special 'shout out' to Salima Lemelle and their children (Sean, Sabra, Immy, and Salim) who helped him appreciate the importance of hip hop culture over the years.

Foreword

Robin D.G. Kelley

Contrary to recent media claims, hip hop hasn't 'gone global.' It has been global, or international at least, since its birth in the very local neighborhoods of the South Bronx, Washington Heights, and Harlem. While the music, breakdancing, and graffiti writing that make up the components of hip hop culture are often associated with African-American urban youth, hip hop's inventors also included the sons and daughters of immigrants who had been displaced by the movement of global capital. The DJ who is said to have started it all by dropping break beats at dances and parties in the South Bronx was a Jamaican immigrant named Clive Campbell, better known to his fans as DJ Kool Herc. The first graffiti writer of note was a Greek kid from Washington Heights whose distinctive tag was Taki 183. And Puerto Ricans and other Latinos have been central to hip hop from its inception. DJ Charlie Chase (aka Carlos Mandes) started as a bass player in salsa and Latin rock bands before joining the legendary Cold Crush Brothers back in the late 1970s. Rappers Robski and June Bug released their Spanish rap single 'Disco Dreams' as part of the group Mean Machine as early as 1981. Speaking of disco, we must remember that the modern MC and DJ can trace part of their roots to disco music and culture. Disco, after all, was a marriage of Black dance music and new electronic technology that reveled in street slang, emphasized funk, and often made references to the world beyond the U.S., from Africa to outer space. In the last years of lingering Black nationalism, when Africa was still hip and Black was beautiful and chic, the big hits of the early to mid 1970s included African Music Machine's 'Black Water Gold (Pearl),' East Harlem Bus Stop's 'Get on Down,' Kool and the Gang's 'Mango Meat' and 'Jungle Boogie,' and Babatunde Olatunji's 'O-Wa.'

But the global and transnational character of hip hop's origins is not simply a matter of style. It was born global because it erupted in the midst of a *new stage* of globalization. While the economy has been global for a very long time—at least since the days of the transatlantic slave trade—we have witnessed a marked difference in scale and degree of concentration since the 1970s. Multinational corporations control 70 percent of world trade, and about one-third of this trade consists of transfers within the 350 largest global corporations. New developments in communications technology enabled corporations to move manufacturing operations virtually anywhere in the world in order to take advantage of cheaper labor, relatively lower taxes, and a deregulated environment hostile to trade unions. Good paying jobs in America's cities, made possible by decades of unionizing, began to disappear just as the Black urban population reached its apex. By 1979, the same year the SugarHill Gang released what would officially be the first commercially viable rap record, 94 percent of the profits of the Ford Motor Company and 63 percent of the profits from Coca Cola came from overseas operations. Between 1973 and 1980, at least 4 million jobs were lost to firms moving outside the U.S., and during the decade of the 1970s, at least 32 million jobs were lost as a result of shutdowns, relocations, and scaling back operations. The decline of manufacturing jobs in steel, rubber, auto, and other heavy industries had a devastating impact on Black workers. Although Black joblessness had been about twice that of Whites since the end of World War II, Black unemployment rates increased even more rapidly, especially after 1971. While the number of unemployed White workers *declined* by 562,000 between 1975 and 1980, the number of Black unemployed *increased* by 200,000 during this period. The loss of manufacturing positions was accompanied by an expansion of low-wage service jobs. The more common service jobs included retail clerks, janitors, maids, computer programmers and data processors, security guards, waitresses, and cooks—jobs with little or no union representation and very little in the way of health or retirement benefits. In 1978, 30.6 percent of Black families earned income below the official poverty line compared with 8.7 percent of White families.[1]

The jobs created by the transfer of production processes to so-called 'underdeveloped countries' did not improve the standard of living for workers in these countries. Instead, things got worse. The International Monetary Fund (IMF) and World Bank imposed austerity measures, trade unions were crushed, and undemocratic regimes gained support from corporations and countries with strong economic interests. Structural adjustment policies, state violence, economic instability, and flows of capital prompted international immigration and thus created a cheap labor pool for the U.S. and other metropolitan nations such as France, England, and Germany. Many of the new immigrants were also Black, hailing from Africa, Latin America, and the English-, Spanish-, and French-speaking Caribbean. By the early 1980s, approximately 50,000 legal immigrants from the English-speaking Caribbean and some 6,000 to 8,000 Haitians were entering the U.S. annually, about half of whom settled in New York City.[2]

It was these folks, along with native-born Blacks who were themselves descendants of migrants and immigrants, who populated the inner cities and gave birth to the cultures of hip hop. Obviously, these kids created an art form that responded to poverty and oppression, to joblessness and police brutality, to the drug wars and gang violence. But these were also the same populations who brought a lingering sense of hope and optimism to the ghettoes of North America. Living in the shadow of tremendous wealth, downtown prosperity often fueled desire for the finer things. The aerosol art movement, more than anything else, was intended to beautify, not destroy. Rapping and DJing was a way to get paid, to make a name for oneself, and, above all, to 'move the crowd' as Rakim put it. Hip hop emerged as an arts movement with the imperative to create something fresh by using technology, speech, and the body in new ways. The ancient traditions of communal and competitive dance, oral storytelling and rhyming were transformed through technology (mixers, beat boxes, tape machines, turntables) enabling DJs to create new music out of old, fracture rhythms and voice, create new sounds by scratching and sampling. And taken as a whole, breaking, writing, rapping were means by which urban youth could seize public space that had been increasingly denied them. In the pioneer days of hip hop, DJs tapped into public power sources and set up huge outdoor speakers to get the party started, turning playgrounds and parks into places of celebration and community. There were no speeches about police brutality or dilapidated housing, but their surroundings never let them forget where they lived and their memories and observations often made it into their lyrics, their samples, and their masterpieces painted on the sides of subway cars that spread their message through the city. Hip hop, in other words, was a creative means to try to escape poverty and oppression while commenting on it.

What has happened to the culture since is bigger than hip hop. As this book demonstrates, we now find hip hop in every corner of the globe, and like the South Bronx, each locale embodies a kind of globalism. The music and the art continue to embrace, even celebrate, its transnational dimensions while staying true to the local cultures to which it is rooted. In France, the Saian Supra Crew mixes hip hop with the rhythms of African immigrants of the Paris suburbs, and they speak directly to the social and political issues facing their communities. In Italy, the radical hip hop group Jovanotti advocated Third World debt relief and spoke out against conflict in Kosovo. In Hungary, Black Train uses hip hop to speak out for the human rights of the Roma and other ethnic groups. The Danish hip hop trio Outlandish, sons of Arabic, Pakistani and Honduran immigrants, frequently rap about issues affecting their lives in Denmark. There are many, many examples, as you will see, and not all of these artists can claim some kind of political agenda. Indeed, the one thing virtually all of these artists have in common is that they acknowledge their debt to those Black and Latino kids in New York who launched this global movement in the first place.

In most academic circles nowadays, acknowledging that the ghettoes of North America continue to be the primary cultural referent for hip hop around the globe will easily draw charges of 'Americocentrism.'[3] Rather than outright deny the centrality of the U.S. in the culture and distribution of hip hop culture, *Vinyl* uniquely embraces writings on the subject inside and outside of North America. Even as artists incorporate local cultural forms, language and stories that speak specifically to their experiences, the clothing styles, dance styles, vocal styles, even down to their stances and poses, mirror the styles of African-American urban youth. The content might be different, but the look and the sound of hip hop around the world shares much in common with what emerged out of the States. Japan is a case in point. Hip hop there erupted over two decades ago, sparked by the introduction of the film *Wild Style* by Charlie Ahearn. Images of kids breakdancing alongside MC battles on the playground or in underground clubs captured the imagination of many Japanese youth. Breaking became very popular, followed by crews of MCs and DJs with names such as Nitro Microphone Underground, DJ Oasis, Illmariachi, Buddha Brand, Soul Scream, Muro, By Phar The Dopest, Hill The IQ, Illmatic Buddha MCs, Lamp Eye, Rhymester, King Giddra (including Zeebra and K Dub Shine), Scha Dara Parr, DJ Krush, Tha Blue Herb, and Kick the Can Crew.[4]

Besides many of the obvious American references in their names (and the fact that the leading hip hop club in Tokyo is called Harlem, as Rhiannon Fink notes in this volume), one need only to listen carefully to the way contemporary Japanese rappers mimic features of African-American and Afro-Caribbean speech as they rhyme in their native language. African-American speech we tend to associate with hip hop is not just creative slang but syntax, grammar, accents and 'tone' or a distinctive sound that is shaped by regional and generational differences. To hear differences in tone or certain affectations in speech—pitch, timbre, and other elements that may convey social meanings—we have to be able to listen to hip hop speech with a musical rather than literal ear. For example, a particular tone or grain of the voice can convey cool or hip, or dangerous, or humor or just plain goofiness (consider the Pharcyde, Flava Flav of Public Enemy, Humpty of Digital Underground, or Eminem—the use of the nasal sound or the high-pitch whine). We all identify the gruff dancehall voice, for example, as well as the 'smoove' and sexy voice (Big Daddy Kane, Lloyd Banks). Thus, the song 'Dangerous Love' recorded by Little from the wildly popular Kick the Can Crew, featuring as guests the rap group Innocence, captures the way that regional differences in Black speech are translated into a different language. Shojin of Innocence raps with a West Coast smoothness as if he learned Japanese in Oakland. One hears a slight California-by-way-of-Texas twang where he boasts about how smooth a player he is. He is followed by Channel who appropriates the gruff voice of Jamaican dancehall style. He even affects a slight Jamaican accent![5]

Japanese hip hop also incorporates many English words because, according to anthropologist Ian Condry, the language contains no stress accents and the sentences must end with one of a few simple verb endings.[6] Indeed, there are so many unfamiliar words and phrases that many uninitiated Japanese speakers cannot understand Japanese rap (though perhaps the same can be said about rap music in the U.S.). Japanese artists got around the language limitations by incorporating and adapting several phrases from American hip hop lingo. Some notable examples include, 'chekkeracho' (Check it out y'all), 'Yo, chekki' (Yo check it), and 'Yok'kike' (Yo, kick it!—which is a pun meaning listen well).

I would hesitate to call this mimicry. African-American and Afro-Caribbean urban culture is foundational to the aesthetic, as 'swing' is to jazz. At the same time, there are historical and political reasons why the ghettoes of North America and African Americans continue to loom so large in the imaginations of hip hoppers all over the globe. Black America's inner cities have been perceived by aggrieved populations as sites of resistance. Before the proliferation of images of gangsterism as authentic representations of Black urban life, African-American popular culture was embraced from Brazil to South Africa to Ghana as a source of inspiration and liberation. Even in the early years of hip hop, groups like Public Enemy, X-Clan, Jungle Brothers, Queen Latifah, Poor Righteous Teachers, to name a few, were sometimes seen as models of libratory politics. And these same artists, in turn, resurrected traditions of Pan-Africanism and international solidarity by their willingness to address the oppression of people outside the U.S.—notably in Africa. Consider the impact of Queen Latifah's video, *Ladies First*, which opens with still photographs of Sojourner Truth, Angela Davis, and Winnie Mandela, as well as film clips of Black South African women battling police during the beer riots in Durban in 1959. Throughout the video, the camera cuts to the Queen dressed in military garb in some kind of 'war room,' pacing over a huge map of South Africa. As she studies the map she replaces replicas of White male racists with Black raised fists. Meanwhile, around the same time Latifah recorded 'Ladies First', young West Africans, West Indians, Algerians, Tunisians, and other Black and brown youth in the suburbs of Paris began to create hip hop with a similar Pan-African and 'ghettocentric' flavor. Saliha, a popular French female rapper, recorded 'Enfants du Ghetto' in the early 1990s, and Tonton David recorded 'Peuples du Monde,' in which he praised Marcus Garvey for telling the truth about Africa and being a symbol of unity and African solidarity.[7]

While Black aesthetic elements and the historical power of the Black liberation struggles help explain the continued prominence of African-American images in hip hop around the globe, these factors do not tell the whole story. Rap music, after all, is a global commodity distributed by U.S. dominated networks of production and exchange. Young people around the world are bombarded with commercial rap from the U.S.; indeed, it is largely through the exchange of cassettes, bootleg recordings, and the internet that they have access to the *underground* developments happening in the U.S., let alone anywhere else. Young people in Britain, France, South Africa, or Japan may know all the gossip on their homegrown hip hop heroes, but they probably know as much about Jay-Z, Ludacris, and 50 Cent and the whole G-Unit. The bankrupt images of gangsterism and materialism are what dominate the global airwaves, yet as some of the authors in this volume note, the 'Americocentrism' of hip hop may have tragic consequences as well as resistive urges.

As idealized and problematic as it is, the old representations of Black urban culture as a site of resistance and liberation have given way to market-generated culture bereft of any critical social or political commentary. Ironically, the political bankruptcy of commercial rap also coincides with what appears to be a political awakening of the hip hop generation, as evidenced by the well-attended National Hip Hop Political Convention in June 2004. But the fact remains that hip hop's corporate face is one that promotes raw capitalist values, violence, and extreme materialism. If these corporate forces are victorious, we have to wonder what affect it will have on hip hop globally, especially as artists from outside the U.S. create music with incredible political, social, and intellectual depth. Many artists and critics of the music are asking this question. I recently spoke with Italian hip hop scholar, artist and activist, Giuseppe Pipitone, who told me that he and other 'old heads' in Milan were struggling with young girls who wanted to be video hos and boys who thought rap music was just about being gangsta. Their understanding of the music, he pointed out, was highly influenced by MTV and similar U.S.-based video programs. What amazed me is that he is having this conversation with youth in a country where the Italian Communist Party was once one of the biggest promoters of hip hop culture![8]

These are all difficult questions and challenges that the authors in this book take up and move beyond. They deal forthrightly with the commodification of Black popular culture and explore its ambivalent and often contradictory character. Several authors refuse to limit their discussion to rap music (which has been the case with most recent critical analyses of hip hop) and extend their examination to breaking, DJing, and graffiti. Moreover, as some authors confront the proliferation of violent, nihilistic representations, the depoliticization of hip hop and the uncritical celebration of 'bling bling,' others continue to look for and find sites of opposition and resistance in places as distant as Hawai'i, France, Cuba, and Tanzania.

The Vinyl Ain't Final proves that there are no easy answers, no simple way to characterize what is at once a global social movement and a multibillion dollar industry. It ain't final simply because it ain't finished. If there is one thing virtually everyone agrees with it is that hip hop is a living culture constantly re-making itself, and it is a reflection of the concerns and struggles, hopes and desires, of at least two generations. Thankfully, like any good party, it will never be 'final' and will live on as long as the music and the culture continues to 'move the crowd.'

Hip Hop is Dead! Long Live Hip Hop!

NOTES

1. Barry Bluestone and Bennett Harrison, *The Deindustrialization of America: Plant Closings, Community Abandonment, and the Dismantling of Basic Industry* (New York: Basic Books, 1982), p. 42, pp. 25–48; Holly Sklar, *Chaos or Community? Seeking Solutions, Not Scapegoats for Bad Economics* (Boston: South End Press, 1995), pp. 5–10 and pp. 55–6.

2. See Philip Kasinitz, *Caribbean New York: Black Immigrants and the Politics of Race* (Ithaca, NY: Cornell University Press, 1992); Nancy Foner, *New Immigrants in New York* (New York: Columbia University Press, 2001); John Arthur, *Invisible Sojourners: African Immigrant Diaspora in the United States* (Westport, CT: Praeger, 2000).

3. See, for example, Tony Mitchell's introduction to *Global Noise: Rap and Hip-Hop Outside the USA*, Tony Mitchell, ed. (Middletown, CT: Wesleyan University Press, 2001), pp. 1–33.

4. The best discussion of hip hop in Japan I've read is Ian Condry, 'A History of Japanese Hip-Hop: Street Dance, Club Scene, Pop Market,' in Mitchell (ed.), *Global Noise*, pp. 222–47; Ian Condry, 'Japanese Hip-Hop and the Globalization of Popular Culture,' in George Gmelch and Walter Zenner (eds), *Urban Life: Readings in the Anthropology of the City* (Prospect Heights, IL: Waveland Press, 2001), pp. 357–87.

5. 'Dangerous Love, Part 2,' Little featuring Innocence, *Rhyme Explorer* (Ora-1029 Stereo, 2001).

6. Condry, 'History of Japanese Hip-Hop,' p. 232.

7. 'Enfants du Ghetto' and 'Peuples du Monde' are on the compilation CD *Rapatitude* (Virgin Records Fr. 30767, [1990]).

8. Giuseppe Pipitone, interviewed by author, New York City, June 16, 2004.

Introduction

Dipannita Basu and Sidney J. Lemelle

The title of this book takes its inspiration from another time and place. In the mid 1980s the young British Jamaican deejay presiding over the dance floor of the PSV club in Hulme, Manchester (UK) was not spinning the vinyl. In the Jamaican sense of the word he was toasting over a musical mélange of reggae, dancehall, and soul.[1] He introduced records, requested rewinds from the 'selecta' (the DJ who selects and plays songs) and generally hyped and 'big upped' (complimented) the ladies in the house, the massive (participants and fans of the sound system) as well as getting the audience members to respond to the music with screams, whistles, lit lighters held high, and unfettered dancing. Sporadically, his coupling of orality and rhythm over the music also spoke to the local issues that affected the dark-skinned presence in the heartlands of 'There Ain't No Black in the Union Jack' Britain.[2]

Ever since the mass immigration of Jamaicans to Britain during post-World War II reconstruction, the diaspora transported the flavor of the dancehall, the dub, the sound system, the alcohol, the patties, the goat curry, the heightened bass and drums, to the much chillier climes of another island—the British Isles. Indeed, it was the cold weather (which meant the party was inside rather than out) and the ease with which the deejay's patois effortlessly switched to a Mancunian accent that on a good night were two indicators this was not Jamaica. It was post-colonial, de-industrialized Manchester, in the mid 1980s, where the Jamaican sound system (Mobile Discotheques) was the dread and dulcet sounds of the 'empire striking back.'[3] At the end of the night the deejay finished his rhythmic enunciations by reminding us, the last song might be playing, but 'The Vinyl Ain't Final.'[4] He simply meant that just because the club was closing, it did not mean the music, interested and intoxicated parties, or avid devotees had finished their fun for that night, or any other. The venue might change (an illegal blues club, an uptown night club), and the genre might change (dancehall, lovers rock, ska, rap, house, disco, funk), but the sound clash (politics of noise) and cultural battles (performance battles, turf clashes over public space, social controls) never ended. In the spirit of the deejay's words and sentiments, our contributors reveal, that for hip hop culture too, the Vinyl Ain't Final simply because it is never a *fait accompli*.

Unlike most recent books on hip hop *Vinyl* differs in several significant ways. It bridges the gap between studies of hip hop culture and rap music

1

in the U.S. and its diasporan and global reach. Entering into the fray of one of the most exciting and expansive areas of popular culture, music, scholarship and commentary, the editors of *Vinyl* invite critical approaches from a variety of cultural 'experts' within and outside of academe. In *Vinyl*, new jack academics, old skool poets and proto-rappers, journalists as well a host of interdisciplinary scholars are bought together to comment on hip hop and rap music in recognition of the importance for 'a new architecture for producing and sharing knowledge ... [that] would increase new forms of dialogue between academics, public intellectuals, activists, and policy makers in different societies.'[5] Thus we are in agreement with the notion spelt out by Jonathan Friedman when he argues:

> The on-going history of the world cannot be interpreted as [solely] an intellectual conversation in which problems can be solved by convincing people that they have it all wrong. The absurdity of such a position is a token of the alienation of its spokesmen and women.[6]

Uniquely, *Vinyl* is not exclusively concerned with the provenance of rap music and hip hop culture in the United States ('America').[7] The roots of rap and hip hop have become (and arguably always have been) international and therefore our book looks to Africa and the African diaspora in the Caribbean for case studies, as well as 'border-crossers' in Europe, Asia, the Pacific Islands, and the United States. The contributors to *Vinyl* are not so much focused in a systematic account of hip hop or globalization, nor are they engaged in uncritical celebrations of its hybridity. They are interested in critical perspectives that recognize hip hop's location within the political economy of culture and capitalism as well as its symbolic, economic and cultural purchase, as they analyze, observe, and comment upon its everyday realities and resistive strategies. In short, we seek to extend our understanding of the social thickness and economic density of rap music and hip hop culture's positioning at the nexus of global culture and commerce in the twenty-first century—both inside and outside the U.S.

GLOBAL REACH

Rap is arguably the most predominant and commodified element of hip hop culture which originally comprised breaking or b-boying (dance), DJing (or turntablism), graffiti art, and rapping (or MCing). As Rachel Raimist reminds us, hip hop started off as:

> A group of kids sitting on the stoop, standing on the street corner, that have a lot to say ... but they don't have tools, expensive things to create art. So they started beating on the sidewalk, beating on a garbage can, telling their stories in poems and in raps, painting it on the walls.[8]

Thirty years since its inception in the South Bronx, New York City hip hop's expressive cultures, language, music, sartorial styles, dance and art has migrated across racial, ideological and national boundaries to become one of the foremost forces in youth culture globally, resulting in a plethora of mass mediated and grassroots expressions the world over. Hip hop culture and most significantly rap music has gone from its local practices of 'party and bullshit' to become what Chuck D famously describes as the 'CNN of Black people.' Over its 30 year duration the primary conduit for this cultural communicative system in the global digitalized public sphere are about 20–30 large companies consisting of webs of interlocking alliances between telecommunication companies, entertainment conglomerates, hard and software firms, and broadcasting companies.[9]

Macro critical perspectives upon globalization frequently focus on U.S. imperialism, its global hegemony and the injection of its values, lifestyles and commodities across borders into the jugular vein of national cultures. In the realm of culture the homogenization of these (particularly 'American') Western values was poised to subsume cultural differences and national identities globally, creating the 'Coca-Cola-ization' of world culture.[10] In this schema, cultural imperialism results in the 'economic and political domination of the United States ... thrust[ing] its hegemonic culture into all parts of the world.'[11] With the proliferation of media technologies, theorists such as Theodor Adorno charged that the cultural industries, such as the music industry, produced standardization in the production of music and cultural duping on the consumer end. Essentially music's composition, production, and consumption—just like any other consumer product— labored under the aegis of an assemblyline production process.[12]

Certainly the spatial reach, density and power of transnational interconnectedness between communities, states, international institutions, multinational corporations and international bodies such as the United Nations (UN) and the World Trade Organization (WTO) is well documented. Yet, such macro analyses say little of how these forces work on the micro social level. The rethinking of the macro and micro into the notion of 'glocalization' was first noted by sociologist Roland Robertson who observed that the word and idea was used in Japan by marketing experts who used the Japanese term to reference how Japanese products should be reformulated for particularistic local tastes and interests.[13] As J. Lull, a professor of communication studies, points out: 'political-economic-cultural influences do not enter cultural contexts uniform.'[14] Rather, globalization intensifies localization rather than leads to a flattening out of local cultures as a 'response to [a] desire for fixity and for security of identity in the middle of all the movement and change.'[15]

Colombia provides a good example of this change; like many other parts of the world within hip hop's global reach, there is recalcitrance and seduction to cultural imperialism.

Significant numbers of Colombian youth use hip hop's musical identities, styles, and symbolic ethnicities as engines for cultural expression and expertise; conduits for dreams and aspirations to get rich quick (in a declining economy with a rate of inflation of 20 percent), and malleable templates for renegotiating social and political identities in the face of poverty, crime, and political corruption. Although the symbolic and consumer driven language of brand names and Bentleys as the *lingua franca* does not enclose hip hop's possibilities in Colombia, it does not exclude the production of 'trade groups' such as Colombia Rap Cartel who consider a career in rap as a means of getting rich quick and riding around in Cadillacs, Californian style. At the same time the sheer love of hip hop culture and artistry compel others. Indeed:

> One of the few DJs in the Guinness Book of World Records isn't from the Bronx, or LA. He's not from the USA at all. DJ Joyman Vargas hails from the barrio of El Trebol, in Cali, Colombia. Right before Christmas back in 1997, while most of the city was partying to the 4/4 beat that earned Cali the tag, 'The Capital of Salsa,' DJ Joyman, set the world's record for the most consecutive hours mixing on the radio—122, or five full days of spinning records![16]

And for others, such as 23-year-old Colombian rapper and producer Carlos Andres Pacheco, 'hip hop speaks the language of the world's ghettos,' but with cultural twists in the music (the 3-2 salsa clave) and specific Colombian concerns. Entwined within the political economy and shenanigans of America's 'Drugs Wars' in Colombia, the young, poor, and dark skinned suffer the most in the drug ravaged and fuelled economy, and its incumbent 'War Against the Poor.' Through their lyricism, Colombian rappers often explicate and explain how this international cocaine and heroin trade is ruining their communities.

Nonetheless the existence and success of local hip hop practitioners, who have 'glocalized' rap to their own particular situations, is underscored by 'globalization's basic economic clichés: the drive for more and more markets and market niches.'[17] Nowadays the marketing strategy of 'glocalization' is more than a Japanese marketing term, it is global and companies commonly enact 'local, international and global strategies approaches ... and recognize the importance of adaptations and tailoring [products and services] in the marketplace of business activities.'[18] Within the global cultural industries,

> Music has always been the least capital-intensive of the electronic media and therefore the most open to experimentation and new ideas. US recording artists generated 60 percent of their sales outside the United States in 1993; by 1998 that figure was down to 40 percent. Rather than fold their tents, however, the five media TNCs [transnational corporations] that dominate the world's recorded-music market are busy establishing local subsidiaries in places like Brazil, where 'people are totally

committed to local music,' in the words of a writer for a trade publication. Sony has led the way in establishing distribution deals with independent music companies from around the world.[19]

Hence, rather than oppositional phenomena the local and global are relational. As Murray Forman notes:

> ... while transnational media enterprises and the global culture industries have a powerful influence over what gets circulated into world markets, there are no guarantees as to how cultural commodities will be incorporated into localized practices and the lived experiences of subjective pleasure and desire.[20]

While the localized aspects of hip hop and rap have been taken up by scholars within U.S. borders, this line of enquiry is frequently on border patrol. For many American scholars on the subject it appears that rap around the world is little more than an urban soundtrack to a 'McWorld.'[21] Often, rap music and hip hop culture's transnational reach is relegated to the historical archives of its 'roots'; ritually acknowledged then ignored; or clinically dismissed as little more than disembodied and commodified forms of global 'niggahood' the world over.[22] One groundbreaking work on the global reach of rap music is Tony Mitchell's edited book *Global Noise*.[23] *Vinyl* picks up, but expands upon Mitchell's work which

> Documents and analyzes for the first time some of the other roots hip hop has developed outside the USA, filling a vacuum in academic writing on the subject, in which the expression of local identities globally through the vernaculars of rap and hip hop in foreign contexts has rarely been acknowledged.[24]

Yet, we take issue with Mitchell's claim that

> For a sense of innovation, surprise, and musical substance in hip hop culture and rap music, it is becoming increasingly necessary to look outside the USA to countries such as France, England, Germany, Italy and Japan, where strong local currents of hip hop indigenization have taken place.[25]

This characterization and dismissal of the scene in the U.S. as a monolithic and stagnant culture appears to reflect a lack of appreciation for, and knowledge of, the immense body of cultural and academic work which also highlights the importance of space and place in hip hop and rap's African-American social history, racial configurations, and cultural practice.[26] In *Phat Beats, Dope Rhymes: Hip Hop Down Under Comin' Upper*, Australian scholar Ian Maxwell argues for the de-essentializing of rap and hip hop as an expression of 'Black,' or 'ethnic,' identification.[27] Through his interesting meditations on rap music and the culture of White Australians in Sydney he explores 'the possibility of its truth as Hip Hop without predicating that claim on a simple identification of skin color, of shared Blackness.'[28] He goes on to note there is a more generalized notion of 'otherness/ or marginalization ... racial or ethnic otherness might then be considered a special case of a more general sense of otherness, the specificity of which might take any number of forms.'[29] In *Vinyl* we find that in the United States and abroad, the contributors decouple hip hop's authenticity from a rigid fixation on its African-American roots, yet do not collapse into uncritical celebrations of hybridity, which runs the risk of reducing any regard for the Black roots of hip hop as the outmoded racial politics of essentialism, that is out of fashion in a postmodern world. Rather, we are more concerned with the geopolitical realities of uneven development and resistance to it in the spaces of the 'third world,' as well as those of 'third world' places and peoples in the 'first world.' Thus, *Vinyl* has two sides (parts). The first concentrates upon hip hop culture and rap music in the U.S. The second part takes us around the globe to Europe, Africa, Asia, and the Pacific Islands.

SIDE ONE: GROOVING TO THE VINYL STATESIDE— RAP AND HIP HOP IN THE U.S.

In Tricia Rose's seminal work on hip hop and rap, *Black Noise*, she outlines the important 1960s antecedents to rap music and hip hop culture. One of the groups she highlights is The Last Poets—often seen as proto-rappers of the civil rights era.[30] In Chapter 1 we feature the poetry of Umar Bin Hassan, one of the legendary members of the group.[31] The Last Poets was formed in May 1968 by David Nelson, Gylan Kain, and Abiodun Oyewole. It soon grew from three poets and a drummer to seven young Black and Latino artists; adding Felipe Luciano, Umar Bin Hassan, Jalal Nurridin, and Suliamn El Hadi. This New York City 'hip' group came along during the domestic change and upheaval of the 1960s. Drawing upon the radical politics of the 1960s Black Arts movement, in the early 70s their radical word play, style, delivery, and social commentary echoed the West African *Djali* or griot storyteller and foreshadowed much of hip hop's spoken word and fiery politics. To dramatize their commentary they used heavy drum rhythms and defiant spoken verse to reproach Black folks for accepting the status quo of racism and disenfranchisement, while critiquing White supremacy. The Last Poets have variously been hailed as key precursors for hip hop's revolutionary poetry and political impulses and causes by Russell Simmons, Quincy Jones, Tupac Shakur, Doug E. Fresh, and even David Bowie. With his usual acuity Mark Anthony Neal complains that it is shameful in a 'world where Ja Rule could sell 10 million copies of dribble and forefathers of hip hop like Umar Bin Hassan, Grand Wizard Theodore and Grand Master Caz remain virtually unknown to those who plunk down $15–20 for rap recordings.'[32] Bin Hassan's insistent presence in hip hop is not only as an artist but a wise and knowing elder whose activism and art continues to inform hip hop culture. He appears regularly at conferences and workshops on hip hop, poetry and politics nationwide. Most recently, he appeared with Common on his song 'The Corner.' Bin Hassan provides a much-needed voice to bridge the fractures of not only class but generation. He reminds us that history is not dead, and nor is the power of the word. He contributes three short poems—'For the People,' 'TRIBUTE,' and 'REDBONE'—which address the issues of music and beauty and their relationship to the revolutionary struggle.

The next contribution is by the internationally known political prisoner Mumia Abu-Jamal, the renowned journalist from Philadelphia who has been on death row since 1981 for allegedly shooting Philadelphia police officer Daniel Faulkner. For some he is a cop killer, but for others he is a political prisoner targeted by the state because of his political beliefs and associations with Black Panthers. He began his journalism career as the Panthers' Minister of Information for the Philadelphia chapter at age 15, writing for their national newspaper. After leaving the Panthers, Mumia became a broadcaster in local radio, eventually winning a Peabody Award for his work. Yet while Mumia was president of the Philadelphia Association of Black Journalists, he was also still a radical, and for this reason was the target of police harassment. After his questionable trial for murder he has become a *cause célèbre* and regularly broadcasts pieces on contemporary U.S. society.[33]

Luminaries such as Nelson Mandela, human rights organizations like Amnesty International, and mainstream and 'underground' hip hop artists have all taken up his case. Mumia foreshadows the political ilk of rappers such as KRS-One, Public Enemy, Poor Righteous Teachers, and X-Clan. Indeed the single 'Mumia 911' is a collaborative cut recorded for the benefit album *Unbound* featuring conscious rappers, Pharoahe Monch, Black Thought, Aceyalone, and Chuck D. Furthermore, the Beastie Boys and The Coup have played at 'Free Mumia' benefit gigs, and Project Raptivism, a collaborative effort by the Dead Prez, Chubb Rock, and The Last Poets, supports political prisoners like Mumia by pledging sales from their first album *No More Prisons* to the non-profit Prison Moratorium Project, a national campaign aimed at raising awareness about America's prison-industrial complex.

We have reproduced three of Mumia's ruminations in Chapter 2: 'A Rap Thing,' 'On Rapping Rap,' and 'Hip Hop or Homeland Security.' His pieces, particularly the often sampled 'Hip Hop or Homeland Security' (Immortal Technique), chronicle the human condition and speak to the hip hop generation of the contradictions of capital and society within hip hop culture. His words speak for themselves.

In Chapter 3, Dipannita Basu extends the critical tempo, by unmasking the social forces that shape a hip hop (Black American) generation whose aesthetic labors (music, style, language) capture disposable incomes, while their own bodies are disposed of at the helm of what Diane Gordon calls the 'justice juggernaut.' Essentially, the questions that guide her text are: Have the economic gains of hip hop gone primarily to White controlled capital? If so, what are the social costs to the hip hop generation and the broader African-American community? Although she focuses on Black men, it is important to note that Black women are also experiencing alarming and increasing rates of incarceration and criminalization. In the United States, Black women born in the 1990s are five times more likely to end up in prison or jail than if they were born in 1974, and are six times more likely to go to prison than White women.[34]

In Chapter 4, Dipannita Basu and Laura Harris's analysis of hip hop filmmaker Rachel Raimist's documentary *Nobody Knows My Name*, and the interview with the filmmaker that follows, compels us to adjust our gendered cultural lens about hip hop as a lived culture outside as well as at the periphery of the cultural industries in a different way from the previous chapter. *Nobody*, they argue, succeeds, though not without imperfections, in re-centering the communal aspects of hip hop as an organic culture and career for women of all hues. And yet the relative silence on race by the featured women of color in the documentary is palpable behind the camera. As Rachel recounts, *Nobody Knows My Name* is considered a hip hop documentary. As such, Raimist is often invited to speak during Black History Month. Upon learning she is a light-skinned Puerto Rican, conference organizers often retract their request or re-schedule her for Women's Month Events.

In Chapter 5, journalist Eric K. Arnold fashions a fast-paced, detail rich, insider account of hip hop entitled 'From Azeem to Zion-I: The Evolution of Global Consciousness in Bay Area Hip Hop.' His observations are a touchstone for this volume.

> It is no accident that the places where hip hop has thrived internationally and in the United States tend to be large urban centers with diverse, multi-ethnic populations ... One reason for this might be that the freedom of expression inherent in hip hop has been somewhat of a universal language. As such, its relevancy to the struggles of young people all over the world in their fight for their own identity and liberation from political, social, and economic oppression—by any means necessary—is undeniable.[35]

Arnold points out that the regional phenomenon of Bay Area hip hop reflects the intersection of global forces with local concerns, historical legacies with contemporary concerns, and the influences of pimps, entrepreneurs, Black radicals, Asian turntablists, rap activists, and funk doctors. The result is a complicated mix of the indigenization of rap within the particular historical and spatial configurations of the Bay Area.

The final two chapters of Side One examine how young people bind to the political and oppositional category of African-American Blackness through rap music.

In Chapter 6, 'Head Rush: Hip Hop and a Hawaiian Nation "On the Rise",' Adria L. Imada analyzes the intersection of hip hop culture and indigenous nationalism in the 50th state of the USA—Hawai'i. In contrast to the representations of Hawai'i as an idyllic tropical paradise, Imada redirects our gaze to the contested nature of nationhood by focusing on the group 'Sudden Rush,' Hawai'i's most well-known hip hop group. In her chapter she explores how Hawai'i has taken rap's Blackness as a form of dissent and 'indigenized' it in relation to the neo-colonial domination of mainland USA.

The role of hip hop's imaginative geographies forged within, around, and through the cultural histories and resistances of Afro-Asian solidarities are explored in Chapter 7, Sohail Daulatzai's 'War at 33⅓: Hip Hop, the Language of the Unheard, and the Afro-Asian Atlantic.' Daulatzai expands the genealogical and geographical referents of the work of artists such as Rakim, Mos Def, and the Kaliphz. His exploration exposes the limits of current theoretical approaches to both Islam and to Afro-diasporic thought, namely Orientalism and Black Atlantic discourses, by turning our critical gaze to the history of diasporic radicalism and internationalism through textual analysis and its socio-historic context. This is a perfect segue to part two.

SIDE TWO: RAP AND HIP HOP GROOVE GLOBALLY

On this 'side' of *Vinyl* the contributors explore individuals and places that are influenced by the development of hip hop culture. Several of the figures, groups, and genres are internationally well known, while others are not usually associated with rap music and hip hop culture. The chapters in this section explore how rap music and hip hop culture have become mediums for protest among the youth. Their new global mixtures of local linguistic, musical, and political contexts are firmly located in the dynamics of power and political economies of globalization.

John Hutnyk's Chapter 8, 'The Nation Question: Fun^da^mental and the Deathening Silence,' acerbically examines the representations and regulation of the South Asian British rappers Fun^da^mental, from their forays into copyright legislation to their representation in British hip hop music commentary. He argues hip hop media reportage too frequently reduces the band's punk Islam inflected hip hop with its emphasis on human rights activism, to mere sloganeering, and cultural exotica, or side-steps into debates about authenticity, with the U.S. as the base of comparison.

As with Imada and Daulatzai in the U.S., Timothy S. Brown investigates how Germans 'in to' hip hop culture appropriate and reconfigure it in

multifaceted ways including reinterpreting Blackness for this locality/
context. Thus in Chapter 9, Brown illustrates the multiple connotations
assigned to hip hop's cultural flows and explores some of the meanings and
uses of hip hop—and of 'Blackness' in hip hop—by Germans. In addition to
rappers such as Die Fantastischen Vier (uncritical and 'Whitebread' versions
of 'pop rap') and Advanced Chemistry, he also explores the 'Oriental hip
hop' of Turkish-German migrant rap. According to Dietmar Elflein, this
'Oriental hip hop' modeled itself along the lines of the Nation of Islam in
the U.S.; this 'artificially constructed ethnic minority which was supposedly
"Turkish" became something of an oppositional movement to German
national hip hop.'[36]

In a similar vein, Veronique Helenon analyzes the theme of 'Blackness'
and its multiple meanings in Chapter 10, 'Africa on Their Mind: Rap,
Blackness, and Citizenship in France.' As Steve Cannon notes, there is in
Afro-French rap 'a closer physical and therefore less mythical relationship of
(Black) rappers in France to the "pays d'origine" [African homeland] than
in the USA,' and despite the fact that only 6 percent of the population of
France consists of non-European immigrants, rap and hip hop have become
a vital form of anti-racist expression for ethnic minorities.[37] Helenon takes
up the ensuing contested terrain of nationhood for these Black minorities to
show that French hip hop is distinct from African-American hip hop in that
it speaks to the peculiar status of 'minorities' within the society, while being
used as a bridge to overcome national differences that often separate people
of color. Thus, rap music puts into public purview yet another meaning
of Blackness, which transcends national boundaries and fixed origins to
reference North Africa, the Caribbean, and sub-Saharan Africa.

Aside from Europe, other areas where rap music has had a tremendous
impact are the Caribbean, Asia/Pacific Islands, and Africa. Each chapter
in its own way sees hip hop culture as an expression of both consciousness
and resistance: It is an assertion of the self-expression and self-organization
of African peoples, and an expression of their resistance to Eurocentricism
and uneven development due to globalization. Yet our contributors point
to the ambiguous conjuncture of the discourses of race and class, thereby
underscoring the contradictory nature of rap and hip hop. These issues
become the primary points of departure for understanding rap and hip
hop as a multileveled, multifaceted, and constantly changing process of
self-expression and resistance, within state practices, colonial legacies, and
the political economy of the music industry.

In Chapter 11, 'Cuban Hip Hop: Making Space for New Voices of
Dissent,' Annelise Wunderlich investigates the politics of race and gender
in a changing Cuban society. She examines how both Cuban teenagers and
the Cuban government have become fascinated with hip hop. Wunderlich
explains how the latter now sees 'rap music—long considered the music of
American imperialism—as a road map to the hearts and minds of the young

generation.' She points out that in recent years, more and more youth, in particular Afrocuban youth, have started voicing their dissatisfaction through rhyming and yet there are divergences as well as similarities that exist between hip hop culture in a purely capitalist society and in a socialist country such as Cuba, which adds its own unique twists. She shows how one of Havana's most successful hip hop producers, Pablo Herrera (formerly a Professor at Havana University) works with the Asociación de los Hermanos Saíz, the cultural arm of the Young Communist Party. Yet, he also works outside the party structure in making transnational links with U.S. alternative rap artists like Dead Prez, Common [Sense] and Mos Def as part of the Black August Collective—a group of African-American activists and musicians dedicated to promoting hip hop culture globally.[38]

From the Caribbean we hip hop back to the Pacific Rim as the next two chapters (12 and 13) focus on the cultural aspects of hip hop and rap music as it migrates to the Pacific Islands and Asia. April K. Henderson contributes the chapter 'Dancing Between Islands: Hip Hop and the Samoan Diaspora.' Her narrative teases out the complexities, connectedness and contradictions of diasporic identities and practices in the nexus of race and class. Tracing the genesis of street dance forms such as 'popping' and 'locking' in Los Angeles, and 'strutting' in the San Francisco Bay Area and Sacramento through the Samoan diaspora, she provides an upclose account of b-boy 'border crossers' who are an integral part of the Californian hip hop scene.

Another report from the frontlines takes us across the Pacific to Japan where Rhiannon L. Fink's chapter 'Negotiating Ethnicity and Authenticity in Tokyo's Club Harlem' provocatively poses the question, 'is Club Harlem authentic?' In her musings she charts the negotiations of ethnicity and authenticity, as she unmasks the complicated intersections of Blackness as a popular signifier in a location fraught with 'contentions of hollow imitation' and authenticity.

Issues of Blackness are turned in another direction, in another continent as the last two chapters move from the Pacific to the Indian Ocean. In 2001, Tony Mitchell commented that there 'appears to have been little critical analysis of hip hop in Africa, apart from a 1999 master's thesis, "Tracking the Narrative: The Poetics of Identity in Rap Music and Hip Hop Culture in Cape Town," by Lee William Watkins of the University of Natal, South Africa.'[39] However, since that time, there have been a growing number of theses, dissertations, and articles on the topic. In addition, the internet has added a whole new dimension to the information on Africa and broadened the discussion. Today, one can sit in Claremont, California, and watch hip hop videos of Tanzanian Bongo Flava artists rapping in Kiswahili or Kimasai or the Senegalese rappers Positive Black Soul rhyming in English, French, or Wolof. There are several websites devoted exclusively to African hip hop in general, and site specific ones for countries where it is particularly popular—among them Senegal, Algeria, South Africa, Angola, Tanzania, and Kenya.[40]

In Chapter 14 on hip hop culture in South Africa, Zine Magubane analyzes the various ways in which U.S. rap music has been 'indigenized' or integrated into the symbolic framework of South African culture and society. Her focus is on two important issues: The political and economic conditions that shape the global production of African-American culture and the forces that shape how this global culture is received and used by local populations. To highlight these points Magubane begins her analysis with 'a brief discussion of the status of "Blackness," its complex relationship to Western modernity, and the implications this has for thinking about what we mean when we talk about the globalization of "American" or "Western" culture.'

Magubane argues, and others in Side Two of the book agree, that rap music that has become a major part of what is exported and consumed globally as 'American music culture' is a complicated mix. As a result, when it is 'indigenized' both elements become available for interpretation and incorporation. As several authors argue, rap artists transform traditions, shaping the values that have become a critical part of U.S. popular aesthetics to reflect local political, economic, and gender struggles.

In the final chapter of this volume, entitled '"Ni Wapi Tunakwenda": Hip Hop Culture and the Children of Arusha,' Sidney J. Lemelle focuses on how hip hop culture as a representation or signifier of 'Blackness' is played out in the East African nation of Tanzania. As he points out, Tanzania has a long history of adopting and adapting cultural elements and incorporating them into its identity. In this historical context these cultural aspects contributed to its rich and diverse cultures, but also reflect contradictions of class, ethnicity, language, and gender. Lemelle's chapter analyzes hip hop culture as a force that helps shape contemporary public debate and discourse on the political and economic landscape of Tanzania. As Wunderlich, Imada, Henderson, Fink, and Magubane have already done, this chapter addresses the global effects of hip hop, thereby intervening into the debate on Blackness and cultural imperialism.

Thus, in the spirit of hip hop, we have brought together a range of commentators that reflects the diversity of the music and culture of hip hop itself. As Murray Forman concludes in his introduction to the co-edited volume (with Mark Anthony Neal) on the hip hop 'canon,' *That's the Joint!*, '[it] is not the final word on hip hop scholarship'; our work falls into the same category, or as the deejay in Manchester reminds us: 'the vinyl ain't final ...'[41]

NOTES

1. Based on Basu's experience as an Asian British citizen in the UK, she uses the term 'deejay' in the Jamaican sense, which refers to the person on the 'mic (toaster). This is in contrast

to hip hop parlance, where the DJ spins records on the turntables and the person on the 'mic is the MC.

2. This title is reappropriated from the mantra of racist skinheads in Britain by Paul Gilroy in the title of his seminal work on race in Britain: Paul Gilroy, *There Ain't No Black in the Union Jack: The Cultural Politics of Race and Nation* (London: Hutchinson, 1987; published with new foreword, Chicago, IL: University of Chicago Press, 1991). Basu's experience of the transported Jamaican dancehall culture was a result of the post-colonial immigration of South Asians and Afro-Caribbeans from ex-colonies to Britain. Both post-colonial diasporas were stigmatized and barely accepted (in differing, but ultimately, for common reasons—race) in a country whose own imperial machinations put us there. A politics simply stated as 'we are here because you were there'.

3. Culled from the University of Birmingham Centre for Contemporary Cultural Studies' *The Empire Strikes Back: Race and Racism in 70s Britain* (London: Hutchinson/The Centre for Contemporary Cultural Studies, University of Birmingham, 1982).

4. In 1930 RCA Victor marketed 'Program Transcription' discs, the first commercially available vinyl long-playing record. Vinyl was not routinely used in record production until the 1960s. It was referenced as vinyl rather than records predominantly in the wake of DJ/turntablism culture in the 1980s. As a device for the recording and playback of sound, this technology and its subsequent developments changed the landscape of making music and distributing it so others could hear.

5. Arjun Appadurai, 'Grassroots Globalization and the Research Imagination,' *Public Culture*, Vol. 12, No. 1 (Winter 2000), p. 18. This comment is made within the importance of power, protocols of inquiry and their relationship to global capital and grassroots activism.

6. Jonathan Friedman, 'Global Crisis, The Struggle for Cultural Identity and Intellectual Porkballing: Cosmopolitans Versus Locals, Ethnics and Nationals in an Era of De-hegemonisation,' in Pnina Werbner and Tariq Modood (eds), *Debating Cultural Hybridity: Multi-Cultural Identities and the Politics of Anti Racism* (London: Zed Books, 1997), p. 88.

7. The authors consciously use the term U.S. instead of the generic 'America' because of the ethnocentric implications involved in such a reference.

8. Bianca Toness, 'B-girl, be you,' Minnesota Public Radio, June 2, 2005. Available at <http://news.minnesota.publicradio.org/features/2005/06/02_tonessb_bgirls/>; accessed June 4, 2005.

9. Just as globalization is a historical process which has accelerated in speed and scope in the last 30 years or so, so has the relationship between the state and private interests. In 1876 U.S. President Rutherford B. Hayes stated: 'This is government of the people, by the people and for the people, no longer. It is government of corporations, by corporations and for corporations.' Today, 52 of the world's 100 largest economies are corporations. Workers world wide who are poor, casual, working and middle class are seeing their real wages cut for longer hours, less job security, cuts in pensions, health care and insurance while the benefits and salaries of executives steeply rise. 'Globalisation—The Role of Corporations.' Available at: <http://www.heureka.clara.net/gaia/global05.htm>; accessed May 14, 2005.

10. Jonathan Freidman, 'Globalization as Awareness,' in John Benyon and David Dunkerley (eds), *Globalization: The Reader* (New York: Routledge, 2000), p. 44. See also Wayne Ellwood, *The No-Nonsense Guide to Globalization* (London: Verso Press, 2001).

11. Mike Featherstone, 'Global and Local Cultures,' in Jon Bird, Barry Curtis, Tim Putnam, and Lisa Tickner (eds), *Mapping the Futures: Local Cultures, Global Change* (London: Routledge, 1993), p. 170.

12. Theodor Adorno and Max Horkheimer, *Dialectic of Enlightenment* (London: Verso, 1979).

13. Roland Robertson, 'Glocalization: Time-Space and Homogeneity-Heterogeneity,' in Mike Featherstone, Scott Lash and Roland Robertson (eds), *Global Modernities* (London: Sage, 1995), pp. 25–44.

14. J. Lull, 'Globalization,' in Benyon and Dunkerley, *Globalization*, p. 41.

15. Doreen Massey, 'A Global Sense of Place,' in Ann Gray and Jim McGuigan (eds), *Studying Culture* (London: Edward Arnold, 1993), p. 236.

16. See Timothy Pratt, 'The Rap Cartel, World Records and Other Tales From Colombia,' *WireTap*, September 19, 2000. Available from <http://www.alternet.org/story/9819/>; accessed May 15, 2005.

17. Steven Feld, 'A Sweet Lullaby for World Music,' *Public Culture*, Vol. 1, No. 1 (Winter 2000), p. 167.

18. Göran Svensson, '"Glocalization" of Business Activities: A Glocal Strategy Approach,' *Management Decision*, Vol. 39, No. 1 (2001), pp. 6-18. The term 'glocalization' is the melding together of global forces that are adapted towards the particularities of the local.

19. Robert McChesney, 'The New Global Media: It's a Small World of Big Conglomerates,' *The Nation* (November 29, 1999). Available from <http://www.thenation.com/doc.mht ml?i=19991129&c=2&s=mcchesney>; accessed March 7, 2005.

20. Murray Forman, *The 'Hood Comes First: Race, Space, and Place in Rap and Hip-Hop* (Middletown, CT: Wesleyan University Press, 2002), p. 20.

21. Exceptions to this case are George Lipsitz, Ian Condry, and Paul Gilroy.

22. Tony Mitchell, *Global Noise: Rap and Hip-hop Outside the USA* (Middletown, CT: Wesleyan University Press, 2001). See also Andy Bennett's discussion on the origins and representations on hip hop in 'Hip-hop Culture in Two Cities,' in Andy Bennett (ed.), *Popular Music and Youth Culture: Music Identity and Place* (New York, NY: St. Martin's Press, Inc., 2000). Bennett also provides an in-depth literature review on the significance of the local and global in hip hop outside of America. He draws upon a number of music genres including dance, bhangra, as well as hip hop to examine how youth use the cultural resources of music to reformulate and articulate identities which draw upon the local context and the global scene.

23. Mitchell, *Global Noise*, p. 2.

24. Ibid.

25. Ibid.

26. The tensions and contradictions of space in hip hop and the importance of local knowledge, networks, representations, and possies are well documented by American scholars such as Tricia Rose, David Toop, Murray Forman, Greg Dimitriadis, Mark Anthony Neal, Gwendolyn Pough, and Robin Kelley amongst others.

27. Ian Maxwell, *Phat Beats, Dope Rhymes: Hip Hop Down Under Comin' Upper* (Middletown, CT: Wesleyan University Press, 2003), p. 96.

28. Ibid.

29. Ibid., p. 46.

30. Tricia Rose, *Black Noise: Rap Music and Black Culture in Contemporary America* (Middletown, CT: Wesleyan University Press, 1994), p. 55.

31. Although many believe this to be true, Gil Scott Heron was never a member of the group. The Last Poets took their name from a poem by the famous South African poet Willie Kgositsile, who posited the necessity of putting aside poetry in the face of looming revolution. 'When the moment hatches in time's womb there will be no art talk,' he wrote. 'The only poem you will hear will be the spear point pivoted in the punctured marrow of the villain … Therefore we are the last poets of the world.' Available from <http://www. math.buffalo.edu/~sww/LAST-POETS/last_poets0.html#lastpoetsbiography>; accessed May 18, 2005.

32. Mark Anthony Neal, 'Hip Hop and Beyond: Hip Hop Comes to Berkeley.' Available from: <http://www.popmatters.com/music/features/020506-hiphop.shtml> (May 6, 2002); accessed May 18, 2004.

33. Terry Bisson, 'The Case of Mumia Abu Jamal,' *New York Newsday*, 1995. Available from <http://www.terrybisson.com/mumia.html>; retrieved May 21, 2005. Mumia Abu-Jamal 'has been a resident of Pennsylvania's death row for twenty-three years. Writing from his solitary confinement cell his essays have reached a worldwide audience. His books *Live From Death Row*, *Death Blossoms*, *All Things Censored*, *Faith of Our Fathers*, and the recently released *We Want Freedom* have sold over 150,000 copies and been translated into nine languages. His 1982 murder trial and subsequent conviction have been the subject of great debate.' Available at <http://www.prisonradio.org/mumia.htm>; accessed May 21, 2005.

34. Marc Mauer and Ryan King, 'Schools and Prisons: 50 years after Brown Versus Brown, The Sentencing Project.' Available at <http://sentencingproject.org/pdfs/brownvboard.pdf>; accessed May 21, 2005.

35. p. 83, this volume.

36. Dietmar Elflein, 'From Krauts with Attitudes to Turks with Attitudes: Some Aspects of Hip Hop History in Germany,' *Popular Music*, Vol. 17, No. 3, pp. 255–65, quoted in Mitchell, *Global Noise*, p. 18.

37. Steve Cannon, 'Panama City Rapping: B-boys in the Banlieues and Beyond,' in Alec Hargreaves and Mark McKinney (eds), *Post-Colonial Cultures in France* (London: Routledge, 1997), p. 164.

38. Information on Pablo Herrera and Black August available at <http://www.afrocubaweb.com/rap/pabloherrera.htm>; accessed May 21, 2005. Also see <http://www.afrocubaweb.com/rap/Blackaugust00.html>; accessed May 21, 2005.

39. Mitchell, *Global Noise*, p. 8.

40. Undoubtedly the oldest of these websites was Africanhiphop.com, formerly named *Ruba-Kali* when it was launched in February 1997. It is a project of the African Hip Hop Foundation, a non-profit registered in the Netherlands, run by a group of volunteers from different countries.

41. Murray Forman and Mark Anthony Neal (eds), *That's the Joint!* (Middletown, CT: Wesleyan University Press, 2004), p. 7. Many critical scholars such as Homi Bhaba, Lawrence Grossberg, Stuart Hall, and Greg Dimitriadis argue that notions of knowledge and/or identity are an ongoing process.

SIDE ONE:

Grooving to the Vinyl Stateside—
Rap and Hip Hop in the U.S.

1
'For the People,' 'TRIBUTE,' and 'REDBONE'

Umar Bin Hassan

'FOR THE PEOPLE'

At ease with the source. I revel in the silent song of the breeze. The oppression that begins each moment comes to grip with the mind's eye. In the dark green density of the forest there is a place where all beings, all consciousness, all experience comes together in the flight of the wasp, in the darkness and secrets of mestizo eyes, in the torrid and raging passion of pagan rituals. All cries, all pleas, all justice, all meanings are visible to the divine in you, to the divine in me. Swept up in the anthem of human progress and the rendering of ourselves to mink coats and alligator shoes. Hoping and praying we remember where we learned to become human. In the beginning our minds are strong. Our hearts are big. We keep believing in love and kindness to our friends, to our enemies. But these values. These few pennies and dimes degenerate our sensitivity. Our soul awakens us from a dreadful sleep. She cannot feed us the rocks and pebbles that sprout from the soil. She cannot kiss us with lips protruding with disease and pollution. She cannot hold us with arms burdened by exploitation. But still we see our future in her images and symbols. In the beauty of her tapestries. In the horns and guitars. And dancing in the street. And cool breezes kissing the desert sands. And the romance of street people sincerely pleading take your time with the music, for this is for the people. Take your time with the music for this is for the people. Take your time with the Revolution for this is for the people!

'TRIBUTE'

That special place inside your smile, that belongs to the softness
   of our hearts.
The new circle is beginning. Will we be there when it ends?
The children patronize a flaming merry go round.
Many are riding the pale horse.
They nod so divinely at a lost parade.
Their ghostly playmate has left their innocence in shambles.
A whirlwind has stolen their humility.
What smile is this upon their face.
A smile that mourns the obscenity of their youth.

19

No flowers for them to smell. No grass to sing the praises of nature.
No blue skies for them to bathe their hopes in.
Trapped in the skylines of florescent charms.
Warm and timid touches being forced into unnatural acts.
While rich men dance with limp dolls in the luxury of their shame.
Their mouths foaming from dead languages, while democratic lies
 bay at the moon.
Why must the dark ages still play games with us? But righteousness
 is still standing.
Truth beckons its glory to us.
Can't you see that it's time to move on into that Special place inside
 your smile that
Has graced us with warmth and inspiration.
Blind sprinters lost in a moment of a peaceful masquerade.
Evil is an intruder. But why do we let it in?
We have no one to blame but ourselves.
Time and time again we are being harassed by spastic heroes.
Heroes who speak maggots for words. Heroes who vomit in the
 eyes of sabbath.
Heroes who unleash killer locusts upon our dignity.
Run … Run … the ocean is going to sail without us.
The stars have no sympathy of our allegiance with darkness.
The birds are not singing. They are not winging
And we can't fly! We can't fly!
Grounded with the sinister burden of free enterprise.
Bombs shatter the shrines of our independence.
But there must be struggle and striving and struggle.
And a walk to the water, every step a journey into trust.
The future needs a friend to believe in.
The truth flashes by in the trail of a comet.
The ancestors always speak in volumes.
The children are the ones we must save.
Take their hands sincerely, and walk with them in their time,
 in their rhythm, in their
Smiles, in their pushes on the swings, in their falling down and
 getting back up.
You will learn how to live and be at ease with yourself in the
 Special place inside
Your smile!

'REDBONE'

In the Sketches of Spain and the cool drama of your smile, my first breath
of fresh air was REDBONE. And I constantly began to cling to the hem

of your sacred song of never what you ... needed. But only of what you wanted to give. I happily waddled and toddled in the stutter of your name rolled off of my lips wisely and carefully as I tried to keep my distance in Manchild rebellions and the Dance of the Infidels that always seemed to find their way back to your Mood Indigo. You were the only real Africa in my clenched fist and revolutionary posturing. Your Prayers. Your whispered suggestions on the Wind kept my eye on the Prize. I was your Prince for a moment in that realm of Misterioso and the humiliation of men seeding redress for miscarriages of justice in Mississippi Juke Joints and the Lullabys of Birdland. You nurtured my soul with Responsible dreams and hopes for the future of your words ... became mine to be confused, but concise. Troubled, but seeking. Somewhat exaggerated, but always loving inspirations to write poems for REDBONE women like you.

With Captain Morgan's Spiced Rum in one hand and trust in the other we ran naked through Public parks opened late at night for private lap dances and strip poker in the real ... Garden of Eden inside of me and inside of you ... were my first love in the Big City of Country Boys who became small town memories and fading Neon flickers of moving too fast to slow down. Slow down ... you said as you straddled my young, strong ... hard country grind while guiding it into soft and lingering romantic adventures. And as I slide into your welcome Brass and Rhythm sections converge on our senses. You seriously begin to exercise your imagination while tempting and teasing my perversions. The warmth and wetness of your greeting overwhelms my inhibitions as they stroll the broad and shaded avenues of your pleasure. Your tongue. My tongue. Become one. Become bandits. Explorers in Dark, exotic and uncharted territories. Together we taunt and provoke the pristine and the passion in me could not contain the passion in you knew ... how to open and close those sumptuous and sculptured thighs as soft teeth and warm tongue came to reside in places of eternal gratitude and the Divine intervention of the Living God of Voo doo legends and Creole mamas in my face. Their masterpieces entrusted to my artistry as my street culture rises ... to meet their high ... art of snapping and popping that Coochie in my mind. You were my partners in crime. My walks in the Rain. My tuna noodle casseroles and Nights in Tunisia of forever experiencing and embracing poems for REDBONE women like you.

Laid back in the music of the Dells. The Impressions. The Temptations in a mellow mood. You came heavily armed. And as the Gardenias of Lady Day smiled down on you ... snatched me from demons trapped in squared circles mathematically opposed to my resurrection on the third day I became one with you again in kinship, in familiar traditions, in the sibling rivalry we once shared in the line of fire. In the sincerity of your loud gestures and Tenor Madness of trying to save life. I lived with you. Fought with you. And then humbled myself to your patience and unconditional love took me back to the beginning. To the Projects. To the snow cream on very bad days ... To a father who kept whizzing past us in three dimensional time. To sucking off of each other's laughter in order to survive the sizzle of crack pipes and temporary insanity runs in our fears, runs in our dreams, runs in our families should be more like you are the TRUE ... sisters of the Church and the Temples at Memphis and the Candaces of Moroe strong and revered warriors from the banks of the Nile and radiant smiles ... and hands on healing ... placed on wide hips of subtle and gracious insinuations challenging and imploring me to keep writing poems for REDBONE women ... like you.

2
'A Rap Thing,' 'On Rapping Rap,' and 'Hip Hop or Homeland Security'

Mumia Abu-Jamal

'A RAP THING'[1]

'You remind me of my jeep. I wanna wax ya baby ... remind me of my bank account. I wanna spin ya baby.' That's from 'You Remind Me of Something' by R. Kelly. The song is smooth with a funky bottom and a sexy lead vocalist. Why does it grit my teeth every time I hear it. Well it's not because I'm, as one of my sons put it, an old man who just can't interpret the young whipper snappers. That said, I must admit, I'm more at home with R&B with the soft significance of an Anita Baker, or even Brown Stone. Singers like Sade, and yes ya' all—Whitney. I also enjoy much of rap for its vitality, its rawness, its irreverence, and its creativity. Rap is an authentic descendant of a people with ancient African oral traditions. From griots who sang praise songs to their kings. To bluesmen who transmuted their pain into art. For a generation born into America's chilling waters of discontent, into the 1970s and 80s, into periods of denial, cutbacks, and emergent White supremacy. One must understand how love songs sound false and discordant, out of tune with their gritty survivalist realities. When their mothers and fathers were teenagers, Curtis Mayfield sang, 'we are winners, and never let any body say that you can't make it, cuz when people's mind is in your way, were movin' on up.' Earth, Wind, and Fire—in exquisite harmony, 'Keep Your Head to the Sky' and Bob Marley and the Wailers thundered over rolling baseline, 'get up stand up, stand up for your rights.' The hip pop generation came into consciousness on Tina Turners—What's love got to do with it or an egocentric mix that glorified materialism like Run DMC's my Adidas about a pair of sneakers or Whodini's friends how no one can be trusted. Their parents grew up in the midst of hope and Black liberation's consciousness. The youth grew up in a milieu of dog eat dogism, of America's retreat from its promises, of Reaganism, and White, right-wing resurgence. In that sense, rap's harshness merely reflects a harsher reality of lives lived amidst broken promises. How could it be otherwise? At its heart though, rap is a multi-billion dollar business permeating America's commercial culture and influencing millions of minds. It is that all American corporationism that transforms rap's grittiness into the gutter of materialism—a woman, a living being, reminds a man of a thing, a car. That to me is more perverse than the much criticized—bitches and ho's comments. This is especially objectionable when one notes than in America in the last century, in the eyes of the law, Blacks were property, chattel, things like wagons owned by Whites. That a Black man, some three generations later could sing that a Black woman, his god given mate, his female self could remind me of my jeep, amazes me. This isn't nor could it be a condemnation of rap. The late Tupac Shakur's 'Dear Mama' and 'Keep Your Head Up' are shining examples of artistic expressions of loving oneness with one's family and people. Creative, moving, loving, funky, angry and real are that late, young man's works, as is a fair amount of the genre. Like any art form in America, it is also a business with the influences of the marketplace impacting upon its production. The more conscious its artists, the more conscious the art. Keep Your Head Up. From Death Row—This is Mumia Abu-Jamal. (Sound of prison door shutting)

'ON RAPPING RAP'[2]

'Let me write the songs of a nation, and I care not who makes its laws.'
Daniel O'Connell, Irish Nationalist (1775–1847)

The recent Rap Summit in New York (2001), organized by hip hop entrepreneur Russell Simmons, and supported by leading industry, political, academic, and cultural figures speaks volumes, not so much of the music, as of the people who make the music, and what role they play in American (and increasing, global) society. One does not have to look long nor hard to perceive the criticism launched at the rap music genre. It is, in part, this very criticism, coupled with political threats, that made such a Summit necessary. It's helpful for us sometimes to look at history to see more clearly where we are today, and why. You don't have to crack a history book to find the first example. (Talk to your mom, pop, or grandmom, grandpop.)

In the 1970s and 1960s when rock music and rhythm and blues were emerging, it was heavily criticized by adults, who called it 'noise.' Southern racists and segregationists called it '##### music,' or 'jungle music,' and organized events to burn such records, or even bulldoze piles of such materials. What was happening then was an historical echo of what was happening before, in an earlier era. When both jazz and the blues emerged from Black culture, these artists were severely criticized for making music that was seen as 'immoral.' The late, great jazz trumpeter, Miles Davis, bore the hatred of small-minded cops in Philadelphia and Manhattan, and could easily predict harassment, a jail cell, or a beating when he performed in either venue.

Black feminist scholar, Angela Davis, in her book *Blues Legacies and Black Feminism* notes that both Whites and bourgeois Blacks regarded the blues as 'lowly,' 'vulgar,' or 'bizarre' musical forms. Today, the same artists who were criticized and demeaned as 'low,' 'vulgar,' or even drug addicts, are remembered as musical geniuses, and icons, whose work is revered for its scope, depth, power, and brilliance. Imagine how dry American music would be without John Coltrane, Miles, Bessie Smith, Billie Holiday. Or Bob Marley, Peter Tosh, Chuck Berry, etc ...

What is happening with rap?

Every generation of Black America creates its own music form, to speak to their place in national life. Rag-time and blues were the first musical forms made outside of the church, and as a secular form, was condemned by African-American religious and community leaders. It caught on with working class and poor Blacks though, because it spoke to their lives in a false, hypocritical 'freedom,' which was really blue.

Similarly, rap has been criticized for its violent misogynistic (means the hatred of women) character. That violence, misogyny, and materialism arises from a national characteristic that is profoundly American. America is easily one of the most violent nations on earth, and has a barely suppressed hatred of women. Materialism is almost a pre-eminent American trait. Much of the criticism leveled at rap was at one time directed to other Black art forms, and usually had more to do with the policing of Black sexuality than anything else. Nothing so disturbs the twisted labyrinths of White supremacy than Black creativity, artistry, and productivity. Think of it this way: what other music form draws the scrutiny of the corporate press like rap? I have heard heavy metal that was so steeped in violent imagery, of death, torture, and dismemberment, that it made my nose bleed. It was so misogynistic that it gave me a headache. But these were White artists, who are presumed to be free. Rappers are allegedly 'free' to say what they wish, but they are profiled by the state, in the same way Miles was 40 years ago. The cops didn't think he should be driving an imported car, so they busted him on Broad Street in Philly.

How little things have changed.

'HIP HOP OR HOMELAND SECURITY'[3]

To think about the origins of hip hop in this culture and also about homeland security is to see that there are at the very least two worlds in America. One of the well to do and another of the struggling. For if ever there was the absence of homeland security it is seen in the gritty roots of hip hop.

For the music arises from the generation that feels, with some justice, that they have been betrayed by those who came before them. That they are at best tolerated in schools, feared on the streets, and almost inevitably destined for the hellholes of prison.

They grew up hungry, hated, and unloved and this is the psychic fuel that generates the anger that seems endemic in much of the music and poetry, one senses very little hope about the personal goals of wealth, to climb above the pit of poverty.

In the broader society the opposite is true, for here more than any other place on earth wealth is so widespread and so bountiful that what passes for the middle class in America could pass for the upper class in most of the rest of the world. Their very opulence and relative wealth makes them insecure and homeland security is a governmental phrase that is as oxymoron as crazy as say military intelligence, or the U.S. department of Justice.

They are just words that have very little relationship to reality. Now do you feel safer now? Do you think you will anytime soon? Do you think duck tape and Kleenex and color codes will make you safer?

From death row, this is Mumia Abu-Jamal.

NOTES

1. Taken from Mumia Abu-Jamal's commercial CDs, *All Things Censored*, Vol. 1 (1998); available from <http://www.prisonradio.org/maj/175_progess.html>.
2. Column written June 19, 2001; available from <http://www.iacenter.org/majessay.htm>.
3. Recorded February 20, 2003; available from <http://www.prisonradio.org/maj/175_progess.html>.

3
Hip Hop: Cultural Clout, Corporate Control, and the 'Carceral Cast'[1]

Dipannita Basu

INTRODUCTION

Visual and aural representations of hip hop play a prominent role in shaping the public's imagination and perceptions of Black youth. The much celebrated hype of rap moguls and artists livin' large in baronial splendor is deeply engrained in the fabric of hip hop's ghetto fabulous mythology. I argue that this myth of music industry uplift for Black males is overstated, and runs the risk of becoming a weapon of mass distraction to the continuing significance of racialized relations of those that not only rise because of hip hop's entrepreneurial dynamic, but fall.

My starting point and impetus for the chapter comes from the experiences of two 'invisible' working-class members of what Kitwana Bakari calls the hip hop generation: Lil' Slim and T-Bone, two native Angelinos who the music industry left behind and California's prisons and jails welcomed.[2] By extrapolating from their micro-experiences, this chapter provides a critical exploration of racialized (colonized) relations, state interventions, market economies, and machinations of White supremacy to unmask the broader social forces that underscore the making of hip hop culture (especially rap music) and the rapacious 'taking' of the hip hop generation as prisoners.[3]

LIL' SLIM AND T-BONE: CULTURAL CLOUT AND SOCIAL VULNERABILITY

My motivation and point of departure in this chapter is the 'invisible' yet real lived experiences of Lil' Slim and T-Bone. They are testimonies to a society that takes the fear and fascination of 'Blackness' to new heights in terms of its profiteering, policing and fetishism of Black culture, communities and bodies.[4] Their singular tragedies and shattered dreams reflect the *broader* perils of 'race' and power for members of the hip hop generation at the nexus of a '... contradictory position[ing] of social vulnerability and cultural clout.'[5]

In the early 1980s and 90s, Lil' Slim and T-Bone were representative of other low-key African American go-getting entrepreneurs in Los Angeles whom I met through my field work on hip hop entrepreneurs.[6] For them, working in the rap music industry was a route out of the economic cul-desac of their working-class/poor Black neighborhoods while retaining their stylistic, social, and existential roots in it. Against the upsurge of West Coast rap's popularity in the late 1980s and early 90s their 'ghetto pass' authenticated with one or two strips (Black/felonious) is not just a ride to the pen or the road to the ruinous informal economy. It is a ticket into the rap music industry.

T-Bone was employed in the artist and repertoire (A&R) department of an urban music division in a record label in Los Angeles. By parlaying his love of hip hop with his knowledge and networks of DJs, club owners, local crews and rappers, this subcultural capital became a competitive advantage for record labels scouring the 'streets' for the next big hit. During the same period, Lil' Slim operated a marketing and promotions company that specialized in street promotions and advertising for hip hop/R&B/Urban acts. He was self-employed but hired staff (his 'street' team) on a regular but *ad hoc* basis.

In 2000, the music industry made $14.3 billion and hip hop music sales accounted for 12.9 percent of all domestic record sales. That year Lil' Slim and T-Bone were situated in another thriving sector bursting with a 'captive' Black market in what Mike Mauer calls America's 'race to incarcerate' where one out of 15 of its citizens is incarcerated. Like numerous others of their generation, Lil' Slim and T-Bone were behind bars for non-violent offences, borne out of necessity—no money, no job, no prospects—rather than unmitigated malice, avarice, or violence. Indeed, in California, four out of five former inmates return in alarming numbers 'not for the commission of new crimes but for violating the terms of their parole.'[7] As more African-American youth are condemned to states of confinement and detention, the market increasingly appropriates their cultural production.

In 2004, one in eight Black males between the ages of 25 and 29 can be found incarcerated on any given day. (This is nine times the number in 1954, the year of the historical *Brown v. Board of Education* decision.[8]) In the same year, hip hop's musical muscle meant it sold more records than the staple number one selling genre for decades, rock.[9] Of course, music is just one element of hip hop's cultural clout. As the hip hop generation is overly branded as *de facto* criminal, hip hop culture is branded for the blandishments of marketplace. In the first rap song to hit the top 40 in the U.S., SugarHill Gang name-checked the Lincoln Continental and the Sunroof Cadillac in 'Rapper's Delight.' Ever since, rappers have playfully converting shout-outs to profitable endorsements that can deliver companies with the audience demographics that will sell their products. The media and marketing company, Simmons Lathan Media Group (SLMG), which is in partnership with hip hop mogul Russell Simmons, estimates that hip hop's potential customer base is approximately 45 million people aged between 13 and 34, of which 80 percent is White.[10]

At the nexus of hip hop culture's cultural clout and social vulnerability, Lil' Slim and T-Bone are members of a hip hop generation who are: 'unwanted as workers, underfunded as students, and undermined as citizens, minority youth [particularly Black] seem wanted only by the criminal justice system.'[11] As their disposable bodies overcrowd prisons, holding cells, jails, half-way houses and youth custody centers, their cultural expressions and aesthetics capture the disposable incomes of youth globally. Against this context, their experiences compelled me to think about the similarities that existed between their time working in the hip hop industry and their passage to 'doing time'— an experience that befalls one in eight Black women and puts one in three Black males under the auspices of an American prison system whose rate of incarceration exceeds that of even South Africa under Apartheid.

By extrapolating from their *individual* experiences as working-class members of the hip hop generation 'done good' working in the rap music industry, and as 'bad boys' in the criminal justice system, to the *broader* social forces in America's racial cartography, I am guided by some key features of Robert Blauner's internal colonial perspective to explore the following questions: Are there similar organizing principles between their experiences in the music industry and the criminal justice system? Have the economic gains of hip hop gone primarily to White controlled capital? If so, what are the costs to the hip hop generation and broader Black community?[12]

In sociology, the critical framing of racialized relations in America by the radical sociologist Robert Blauner countered much of mainstream sociology's ethnicity based theories of 'race' relations that dominated sociology in the late 1960s and 70s.[13] His colonial analogy countered the prevailing sociological paradigms in which the political and economic dimensions of 'race' were largely absent. In distinguishing the experiences of ethnic groups such as Italians, Poles, and the Irish, Blauner argued that 'communities of color in America share essential conditions with third world nations abroad: economic underdevelopment, a heritage of colonialism and neocolonialism, and a lack of real political economy and power.'[14] Within this framework, he characterized urban 'riots' in America to similar impulses as those of revolutionary struggles against colonial powers around the world.

Although the machinations of the music industry and crime and punishment may seem far removed from each other, I suggest that similar operating principles function in both realms to the detriment and cultural/social death of the expressive culture and the young people whose creative energies gave rise to it in the first place. In this regard, key themes in Blauner's characterization of the relationship of oppression, domination, and exploitation of Black Americans guide my enquiry. They include: the restriction of Black people's movement—from job mobility to policing methods that continue to keep Black people 'in their place'; economic exploitation; the transformation, denigration, and destruction of Black cultural and social organizations; the governance, control, and management of Black culture and people outside of their communities; and the prevalence of anti-Black racism and White privilege that is economically, psychologically, and socially imposed by a group who consider themselves superior.

I begin by discussing the experiences of Lil' Slim and T-Bone in the production of rap music to explore the broader regimes of restricted occupational movements that operate in the music industry. Here, normalized beliefs about the inferiority of Black expressive cultures and cultural workers are examined in tandem with the structural and cultural privileges of Whiteness. Next, the differences in Black and White consumption patterns highlight the stark diverging social realities of Black and White fans of hip hop in the realm of policing. I then go on to explore the broader social context of hip hop as a commodity and as a generation.

Robert Blauner noted early on what most Black folks already know, and what more recent scholars and critical observers of America's 'dilemma' have turned their attention to—the notion of White privilege as a system of historically entrenched 'head starts.' This perspective is useful because it troubles the current public culture in which 'race' no longer matters over and beyond its situational and symbolic identity and consumption.[15] Under this racial rule, hyper-successful and visible Black capitalists in the rap industry suggest opportunities for uplift are inclusive and colorblind, even for those who flout the dictates of middle-class propriety (from Suge Knight, Luther Campbell, and Eazy-E to 50 Cent). This is a positioning I trouble, by locating Black capitalist success within the intersections of globalization, state policies/ideologies, and 'free' market principles. By drawing the reader's attention to the emergence of America's prison-*industrial* complex, the high rates of incarceration of Black Americans are also located within an understanding that crime and punishment in America is tied up to racial ideologies, money, and markets.

I bleakly conclude by pondering the future of the hip hop generation in a society where the 'deadly symbiosis' of prison life with life in the ghetto simultaneously provides many artifacts for consumption and fashion (baggy trousers, cornrows, tattoos, prison slang, and other elements of prison/gang/ghetto culture are bought to us from the 'big house' to our house, mediated daily by hip hop culture on our TV sets, radios, iPods, computers, magazines, video games, and cinema) yet renders invisible the routine machinations of the 'carceral caste' where 'the obsolescence of the ghetto as a device for caste control and the correlative need for a substitute apparatus for keeping (unskilled) African Americans in a subordinate and confined position—physically, socially, and symbolically'—becomes prison.[16]

BLACK ENTREPRENEURSHIP: RESTRICTIVE LEGACIES AND CURRENT CONSTRAINTS

Lil' Slim operated in a realm of hip hop entrepreneurship that is a far cry from the rap moguls the public are familiar with. In the lower echelons of rap music's entrepreneurial orbit, he skillfully combined pleasure and leisure as a competitive advantage in starting his own business. Coupled with low start-up costs, access to a ready labor pool (subcontracted 'street' team), and his own alliances and connections with the interpretative communities in rap music, his business provided for his economic and existential needs and paid for his modest wants. Lil' Slim's business was essentially a small, disaggregated marketing unit that did promotions and parties for rap and R&B music labels and management companies. As the business environment became more aggressive, Lil' Slim faced minor hiccups to financial upheavals. Eventually he was faced with financial disaster and business failure. When he was a subcontractor for a large promotion project (posting posters on billboards, handing out flyers in clubs, records stores, working with club promoters, DJs, and so on), his compensation went unpaid after frequent stalling tactics. The contractors owed him money not only for the project, but also for his staff and per diem expenses (gas, printing, transportation) which left him fiscally stranded. He thus faced the ire of his workers (who demanded their pay regardless of his situation), and the scorn of his bank (the terms and conditions of a bridging loan were in essence prohibitive). Since losing his business, his dire financial circumstances were compounded by a personal blow. He received a three year jail sentence for robbery.

When the exigencies of financial fall out (following the non-remuneration for contracts he completed) put a stranglehold on his operations, his ability to obtain financial resources from his bank was untenable due to their prohibitive restrictions in the form of the terms and conditions of the loans he applied for. Failure to obtain a bridging loan for his business led him to attempt to raise money by remortgaging the family house. He was subject to intense scrutiny about his past credit, even though his ratings were good. Ultimately the terms and conditions of the remortgage offered to him were so high that they were restrictive in themselves.

The obstacles to business development are socially scripted and speak to more than contemporary lending structures of banks. Even as hip hop entrepreneurs flout the structural constraints of small business ownership, by leveraging their subcultural capital of 'Blackness' they often cannot escape its ultimate largess. Although more African Americans have entered into the middle-class fold in the last 40 years, their mobility into suburbia is routinely restricted as they are systematically 'steered' to Black middle-class enclaves in the opposite direction of economic growth. Depressed home values in what sociologists Nancy Denton and Douglas Massey call (in their acclaimed sociological study) 'American Apartheid', means it costs more for Blacks to buy homes.[17] Having a home in the Black belt means it is worth less than a similar property in a White neighborhood, which in turn stifles the ability in accessing favorable or equitable terms for loans.[18] In contrast, higher levels of intergenerational wealth and more valuable property of Whites means they have an easier chance of getting ahead in small business.

In short we can situate Lil' Slim's experienced within the broader socio-political system of White supremacy. Charles Mills explains:

> The blocking of black entrepreneurs from access to white markets; the denial of start-up capital by white banks; the higher prices and rents for inferior merchandize and housing in the ghettoes; the restricted access of blacks to state and federal services that whites enjoyed; the federally backed segregation and restrictive covenants that diminished the opportunities for most blacks to accumulate wealth through home ownership.[19]

On the one hand Lil' Slim chased the American Dream through the provenance of culture, both entrepreneurial and hip hop. Despite exploitative relations, his insistent worldview was that he was getting paid for something he loved. He worked with dignity and pride and his business was immeasurably better than the alternatives. Yet accumulative disadvantages accessing sources of wealth and equity meant that even as he ran a successful business he continued to live in a less desirable residence with worse environments, schools, and public services. For Lil' Slim this essentially means that his subcultural capital (insider knowledge, organic roots in local hip hop scenes, etc) was an integral competitive advantage in his rap marketing business even as he paid a 'Black tax' on it.[20]

IT'S HARD TO ROCK AND RAP:
RESTRICTIONS AND PROHIBITIONS WORKING IN THE MUSIC INDUSTRY

In T-Bone's case, biased cultural evaluations in the music industry about Black cultural worth and ability reduced his musical knowledge to 'street' knowledge which confined him to working in specific genres and departments. This reflects broader institutional practices and cultural assessments which regulate Black occupational positionings and progress.

In the mid 1990s, restructuring at T-Bone's record label hit the Black division the hardest and he was downsized. His concerted efforts to find similar or even lesser jobs within the music industry were unsuccessful. There was too much competition in other Black (urban, R&B, rap) music departments. He was not even a consideration in other (White) pop/rock departments. Other job opportunities were limited. Working as a telephone marketer was out because he sounded too 'Black' and the same barrier, but visually enacted, kept him from waiting tables. His reluctance to hustle in the narco-economy, his inability to get a minimum wage job, and the recurrent hurdles posed by the Department of Social Services in processing his welfare claims conspired to make a living wage untenable without some form of subsidy from the informal economy. He was sentenced to three years for receiving stolen goods (clothes and shoes).

Even before T-Bone was downsized, his efforts to work with rock music were met by lackluster responses by Black and White senior staff alike. Both were united in their unwillingness to train, mentor, or encourage him in this direction. T-Bone's frustration about his situation was in part centered upon the evaluations of his capabilities by others, who consistently deemed his skills and abilities as unsuitable for enactment outside of Black 'Urban' music departments. The restrictions imposed on T-Bone in terms of his career trajectory that aspired to work with rock, rather than rap, is located within a spatial and organizational designation of rap music as 'street,' which places it within a particular understanding of its cultural impetus and its commercial prospects. Keith Negus locates this restrictive coding in the distinction between the 'street' and the 'suite,' in which the former operates as a metonym that is routinely deployed to restrict rap music and staff outside of the corporate 'suite.'[21] Within this institutional understanding T-Bone's utility is relegated and reduced to 'street' knowledge, which not only affects ascendancy up the corporate ladder, but movement between departments. A cultural logic based on a degraded historical memory.

Indeed, T-Bone's ire was equally fired up by the colorblind ahistoricism on which his suitability outside of rap music was premised. Black and rock are not mutually exclusive as anyone familiar with the Black Rock Coalition or a fan of Muddy Waters, Chuck Berry, Jimi Hendrix, Ike Turner, Bad Brains, Living Color, Lenny Kravitz, Tamar-Kali, Rage Against The Machine, or Sista Grrrl Riot knows. Today rap/rock collusions and crossovers stretch from the DJ in the heavy metal band Slipknot to Jay-Z jamming with Linkin Park. Yet whether they—or earlier rappers such as Run DMC, The Beastie Boys, or Ice T—spontaneously merge, strategically deploy, or are made to conform to the tastes and formats of White suburban audiences, the assimilatory impulse is based upon a double standard between Black and White artists. Essentially Black artistry and talent is orientated towards White consumption and pleasure. For example, the 'crossover' tactics at rap's inception moved its alliance with disco (gay, Black, Latino) to rock (White, suburban).[22] Undeniably this brought rap to wider audiences of all colors, but rap's crossover to

A sizable white teen audience can therefore also be seen as a discursive process in which the socially invested values of rock and rap were articulated toward each other in such a way that they suddenly made sense to white teen listeners, who may have had only a passing familiarity with the genres based on the occasional crossover of single hits.[23]

Norman Kelley describes the process as colonial-like, where the raw materials of producing hip hop (styles, songs, aesthetics, vernacular) and labor (Black entrepreneurs, artists) are reoriented outside the 'colonies' (ghettoes) to meet the demands for consumption in wealthier (suburban) areas. The attraction of Black urban culture to consumers in a broad spectrum of markets turns into further marketing opportunities for major advertisers wishing to use its cultural cachet to sell more products, brands, and services.[24]

It should come as no surprise that the racial myopia of the music industry in which T-Bone operated, grew out of an industry where Black records were entitled 'race records' in the 1930s and promptly relegated to second-class citizenship. Jazz critic and historian Frank Kofsky, for example, notes the cultural denigration that accompanied the colonial dynamic of treating Black music as subordinate to Whites'.[25] While Western classical music was often subsidized by record labels, jazz was left to fend for itself. Jazz musicians were even encouraged by their labels to 'cross over' to other more popular genres so as to augment the sales of their records—a cultural corruption never asked of those working with Western classical music.

In 1980, the year when Kurtis Blow, the first rapper to be signed to a major label (Mercury Records) sold a million copies of 'The Breaks,' the eminent Black psychologist Kenneth Clark noted that African Americans in corporate America were occupationally restricted and tracked into areas such as 'community affairs.' Rarely were they found in line positions concerned with developing or controlling production, supervising White staff or competing equally with them for promotion and opportunities for mentorship. Sixteen years later, in 1996, T-Bone was working in the rap industry; Bone-Thugs-N-Harmony took the record for the fastest rising single from the Beatles' 'Can't Buy Me Love' with their single 'Tha Crossroads'; and the 1996 Harvard Consultation Project report surmised that Black record executives 'are constantly relegated to positions with grand titles, with duties that amount to little more than being a talent scout.'[26] The trickle-down economics adversely affects rap artists who have to make do with departments with less cultural clout and economic resources for music and video production, marketing, and promotion.

Hip hop scholars such as Norman Kelley, Nelson George, Mark Anthony Neal, Murray Forman, Keith Negus, and Yvonne Bynoe critically engage with the racialized relations and its incumbent effects on the institutional processes of genre-making, the star-making system, social and spatial stigmatization of the music, and the relegation of Black workers to secondary labor market positions. They variously note that Black artists and their music are systemically viewed as less durable, less sustainable, and less serious than White artists. Success is routinely treated as an outcome of their 'natural' talents as artists and performers, rather than their hard labor and discipline in the face of fewer resources. This recalls the 'closeness to nature' put upon Blacks by Whites, when discussing their suitability for hard labor, or their 'natural' (racial) ability to sing and dance so effortlessly. This cultural logic becomes an institutional self-fulfilling prophecy (if it is natural, its success requires less effort, time, money, and resources to make good) which leads to further forms of labor exploitation.[27]

At both ends of the production–consumption spectrum, the love of Black music (for profit or pleasure) is frequently enjoyed without their physical presence. Wendy Day, a female rap advocate, activist attorney, and founder of the Rap Coalition, describes her White privilege, even in the hard nosed patriarchal architecture of the music industry's corporate structures:[28]

> There are a lot of places that my skin color [White] got me into and a lot of situations that my color gets me into. Someone from Atlantic Records is much more comfortable negotiating a deal with me than some one who doesn't look like him or her.[29]

While musical crossover has historically set the limits of Black modes of musical expression, the crossover of Black executives and staff into pop or rock departments, or departments concerned with international and global scope, is also paltry. Administratively, Black staff and executives in the music industry are routinely circumscribed by industry-wide perceptions that they are best suited to local or regional markets, and knowledge and tastes. Yet the disembodied cultural clout of the 'street' in expansive marketing strategies is bluntly stated by the VP of Black Music Marketing for BMG distribution. 'The end result is that when you talk about "the street" what you really want is it on radio and … MTV.'[30] The end result all too often being:

> For Whites brought up in suburbia or in affluent, homogenous urban neighborhoods, the biggest, nastiest, lustiest most uninhibited edge they can find in their nearly all White experience is dressing up 'Black,' talking 'Black,' walking 'Black' even if their 'Black' is a distorted MTV version.[31]

The implications of this are addressed below.

DIFFERING REALITIES IN BLACK AND WHITE: FROM STYLE WARS TO WARS ON BLACK YOUTH

Hip hop culture is prime pickings for advertising corporations which 'lead the way in their attempt to theorize a pedagogy of consumption as a means for appropriating postmodern differences among youth in different sites and locations.'[32] bell hooks critically assesses the colonial prerogative:

> … wherein whatever difference the Other inhabits is eradicated, via exchange, by a consumer cannibalism that not only displaces the Other but denies the significance of the Other's history through a process of decontextualization.[33]

As the decontextualization of 'difference' continues apace, so does its cultural congealment with White desire, fetishism, stereotypes, and even virtual masquerades of 'Blackness.' David Leonard notes that video games such as *Grand Theft Auto* allow for suburbanites to 'live in your world, play in ours' (the advertising motto of Playstation II) and enables them to move '… away from the safety of White suburbia to a place where you can shoot a pimp, plant a bomb, or sleep with a prostitute … [which] reflects the power and racialized fantasy of contemporary video games.'[34]

Hip hop inflected fantasies of gangs, guns, and ghettoes underscores a socio-spatial reality in which White privilege protects White youth from the very 'outlaw status' that compels many of them to hip hop in the first place. Even as White youth (the most avid purchasers of hip hop according to SoundScan) copiously consume a 'knowable' Black culture, it is mostly in the physical absence of African Americans themselves and with differing constructions of social reality.[35] A recent Gallup poll survey in 2004, found that 76 percent of Whites, including nine out of ten aged under 30, thought Black Americans are now being treated very fairly or somewhat fairly. Only 38 percent of Blacks agreed. As Nick De Genova reminds us, gangster rap 'provides a very different kind of "therapy" for those who live its nihilism, than the shock treatment it provides for those who live in mortal terror of it.'[36]

Robert Blauner spelled out the importance of White skin racial privilege in the colonial relationship of Blacks to White America as a system of 'unfair advantage' with 'preferential situations' or systematic 'headstarts' for Whites in every sphere of life—even for life itself (most apparent in the disparities of those condemned to death row). White definitions, institutional processes, and evaluations are imposed on Black lives. In the labor market Whiteness defines employment opportunities; in the music industry it defines what will be well resourced and widely disseminated; in the welfare system it defines who gets welfare (corporations) and who appears to get welfare (Black single mothers); in schools it defines deviance and disruption, excellence and methods of tracking; in the criminal justice system it defines what is a crime and which groups and locations should be criminalized.[37] Within this social construction, Black lower-class youth are commonly perceived as perpetuators of crime and criminal miscreants (never victims). Consequently they are systematically treated as if they are deserving only of detention centers, jails, holding cells, and prisons—even in schools.

For too many Blacks in America's public schools, frequent frisking and pat-downs are as routine as pop quizzes are for others more fortunate and fair. Amidst the physical decay of many inner city schools, there is physiological damage as 'minority' schools are disproportionately equipped with metal detectors and holding cells (rather than books and educational resources). Consistent with the increasing number of Black adults in prisons, poor Black children are increasingly subject to intrusive systems of surveillance and social control as childish antics become criminalized and 'zero tolerance' policies turn many public schools into training grounds for prison with punishment rooms called anything from the 'jailhouse' to the 'dungeon.'[38] The encounters and differences between Blacks and Whites once in the criminal justice system is spelt out by Jerome Miller, the former head of the department of youth services in Massachusetts. He learnt

> ... very early on that when we got an African-American youth, virtually everything from arrest summaries, to family history, to rap sheets, to psychiatric exams was skewed ... The White teenager was more likely to be afforded competent consul and appropriate psychiatric and psychological testing, tried in a variety of privately funded options, and dealt with more sensitivity and individually at every stage of the juvenile justice processing.[39]

When Lil' Slim was hanging out in a park with more than three reputed gang members dressed in a blue Pendleton with 'dickies' (trousers), in the late 1980s, his Black body and blue clothing voided any ambiguities about his gang affiliation in the eyes of the LAPD (Los Angeles Police Department) gang Intel. Lil' Slim was never given a chance to explain what he was doing that afternoon. He had resigned himself to the fact his particular location, his clothes, his 'attitude,' his color, and his associates together signaled only one possibility to the police, a *de facto* signifier of gang membership, never simply fashion, friendship, or street-wise fraternity.

His resignation and indignation is well founded. Former Californian state senator Tom Hayden explains that this dragnet approach classifies 'known' gang members (Black and Latino youth) on the basis of: associating with gang members, being identified by another police agency, having tattoos, writing graffiti or wearing gang clothing (certain sports insignia, 'baggy' clothing), as well as admitting membership.[40] Despite the unreliability and arbitrary nature of gang rosters, they are used to trigger sentence enhancements and conduct 'sweeps' by LAPD gang Intel.[41] For Lil' Slim, clothing choice, neighborhood, and guilt by association secured his alleged membership in a gang, in what the American Civil Liberties Union (ACLU) calls a Black List.[42] In turn this triggered a sentence enhancement when he was convicted of aiding and abetting two others in stealing clothes from a department store in the late 1980s.[43]

The police are 'key agents' for maintaining the colonized status of Black Americans: stopping Blacks in White neighborhoods is keeping Blacks 'in their place'; criminal intent and suspicion is based on skin color as probable cause; and tardy response times to Black victims of crime, contrasts with the occupational forces that over-police the movement (be they sudden or spatial) of the triple threat—Young, Black, and Male. In this regard sociologists Joe Feagin and Harlan Hahn argue:

... police officers represent accessible agents of government that directly link the black public to the highest levels of governmental decision-making. Policemen are the extended arm of the government, and blacks probably have more contact with law enforcement officers than with any other political representatives. For many, therefore, abstract concepts of governance are personified more by the cop in the police car or on the street than by elected leaders.[44]

Sociologist Darnell Hawkins posits that a key factor in the colonial-like relations of the criminal justice system stems from the sense of threat posed by Blacks. In this schema when a Black person kills a White person, they are offending against more than the victim; they are challenging White control of social order. The killing (or neutralizing) of Black people, particularly the young, is systematically legitimized and excused as a rational, pre-emptive strike in maintaining law and order. In *Makes Me Wanna Holler: A Young Black Man in America*, Nathan McCall recalls how he was faced with two felonies with very different outcomes:

I shot and nearly killed Plaz, a black man, and got a thirty-day sentence; I robbed a white business and didn't lay a finger on anybody, and got twelve years. I got the message. I'd gotten it all me life: Don't fuck with white folks.[45]

This form of governance and control is class blind and color conscious.

In the song '41:19' Chuck D of Public Enemy asks 'What you got?' The response is 'Ratatat-ta-tat,' a sonic missive mimicking the 41 shots fired at a young African immigrant Amadou Diallo, in the vestibule of his own home, in the Bronx in 1999. Amadou's sudden movement as he reached into his pocket for his wallet to get his driving license was the putative cause. The officers received no sentencing under the jury's verdict of the killing as justifiable homicide. During their trial, the police officers stated that their interest in Diallo peaked because he fit the description of a serial rapist which read 'Young, Black, Male.' In the wake of the tragedy, Reverend Al Sharpton clearly articulated what Black communities already know. African Americans are not all pro-crime or anti-police. They do however strongly object to the racist operations that manifest themselves as under-policing on the one hand (slow response, tardiness in investigations, treating the victim like a suspect, failure to keep victims informed, or follow-up on all leads), and over-policing on the other (racial profiling, extra-judicial killings, paramilitary policing).

Historically and currently, solving 'Black on Black' crime or the paltry prosecuting of police brutality and extra-judicial killings by the police is of little concern to the prerogatives of serving and protecting the property imperatives of White rule and maintaining an oppressive social order. Even swollen wallets, a desirable residential address, or cadres of White friends and associates cannot put to rest past regulations of social place and physical space. Decades ago Miles Davis used to phone the Beverly Hills Police Department to inform them that a Black man in a nice car would be driving around in their 'hood when he left his home in that zip code.[46] Claims that hip hop artists and associates are scrutinized by police and federal authorities surfaced in the press in Miami and New York and was the subject of intense interest by cyberspace hip hop heads and their websites and blogs.[47] While the police deny targeting rappers and their associates specifically, the point remains that despite these well-resourced police operations to capture rap-related criminals and drug cartels, there have been no arrests in connection with the murders of iconic rappers such as Biggie Smalls, Tupac Shakur, or Jam Master Jay.[48]

In the popular imagination, many mainstream members of society associate robbery, violence, unnatural death, and murder with 'street' level crime, as the peculiar domain of Black folks, especially the young. This is both misguided and malfeasant. According to the U.S. Bureau of Census, in 2002, approximately 13,000 Americans were murdered yet 56,000 died from occupational diseases ranging from black lung to asbestos poisoning, while others died from unnatural deaths through hospital malpractice to hazardous consumer products. The FBI (Federal Bureau of Investigation) estimates that burglary and robbery cost the United States $3.8 billion a year, while auto car fraud costs $30 billion and health fraud costs about $400 billion a year. The fallacy and irony of this situation, and its parallels to hip hop corporatization, are underscored by Nelson George's observation:

> A family can go from criminal activity to the White house in one generation (from bootlegger Joe Kennedy to President John Kennedy) ... [and by] creating subdivisions and joint ventures a major corporation can often distance itself from the more disdainful activities of its subsidiaries—the kind of deniability that presidents love.[49]

WHO IS THE HNIC?
THE CONTROL AND GOVERNANCE OF BLACK TALENT IN THE MUSIC INDUSTRY

'Black visibility is not Black Power.'[50]

At the high-end of Black entrepreneurship in the rap industry, the commonly understood meaning of a 'triple of threat' is subverted and deployed to describe hyper-visible rap entrepreneurs. P. Diddy (Bad Boy Entertainment), Jermaine Dupri (So-So Def), Damon Dash and Jay-Z (Roc-A-Fella Records), Master P (No Limit Records), Lil' Kim (Queen Bee Records), Missy Elliott (Gold Mine Records), Mos Def and Talib Kweli (Good Tree Records), Suge Knight (Tha Row Records, formerly Death Row Records), Bryan and Ronald Williams (Cash Money), and Dr. Dre (Aftermath Records), amongst others can variously rap, produce, star in films, comedies, TV shows, and display tremendous entrepreneurial acumen. Even though they are immensely well off, they are nonetheless tied to the colonial yoke, as their rap labels are integrated by the organizational structures of major record companies that have annexed them through mergers, joint ventures, distribution deals, or complete buy-outs.[51]

Four major record labels dominate the recording industry currently. Universal Music Group, Sony BMG Music Entertainment, Warner Music Group, and EMI Group. Together the big four hold over 75 percent of the musical market share where Black-owned labels are headed up by what Ellis Cashmore quips are 'titular CEOs.'[52] For instance, Russell Simmons' legendary Def Jam roster is a subsidiary of the Universal Group. Labels such as Murder Inc. (Ja Rule, Ashanti) and Roc-A-Fella Records, alongside artists such as Eminem, Stevie Wonder, G-Unit, and 50 Cent, are all under the aegis of this parent company.

The strident sense of limitless possibilities in the extraction of hip hop to commercial imperatives is 'closely related to colonial discourse that renders marginal or "lesser" cultures as easily accessible sites for capitalist intervention and commercial exploitation.'[53] The hip hop generation provides the bulk of the labor and raw materials (creativity, talent, networks, aesthetic orientations) for *producing* the music. Yet, the real power lies in its marketing and distribution—getting the music/artist seen and heard in record stores, on video rotation and radio, and ensuring exposure and promotions in prominent places such as retail outlets, billboards, and magazines.

Hence, the music industry is controlled by media conglomerates with predominately White upper-class men at their helm.[54] They control the vast apparatus of the music industry, and hence rap music, in a corporate arena where copyright, publishing, merchandizing, touring, political clout, collection of royalties as well as record sales constitute the bedrock for culling profit from musical production. As Ben Bagdikian, the award-winning journalist, author and scholar notes:

> ... no small group, certainly no group with so much uniformity of outlook and as concentrated in power as the current media corporations, can be sufficiently open and flexible to reflect the full richness and variety of society's values and needs.[55]

Thus the framing of hip hop to the masses, of shaping its cultural course and global imagery, is troublingly beholden to commercial interests and professionals whose social perceptions and ethical codes have an ignoble history of representing 'Blackness' in the worst possible ways, often with the complicity of Black folks themselves. Yvonne Bynoe notes for example, how middle-class Black executives are not averse to urging lower-class rap artists to 'keep it real' by nurturing a 'disdain [for] education, self-improvement, public decorum and personal responsibility.'[56]

The complicity of Black artists and entrepreneurs in degrading and reducing rap music to mainstream stereotypes of hyper-sexual, bodacious, gang-banging, hummer-riding, gun-toting, strip-club going, rapacious and 'patriotic' consumers of brands and big 'booties' is about personal preference, gain, and aspirations. It is also grounded in broader historical contingencies. 'Colorblind' ideology requires intermediaries and symbols of success by the Other to reaffirm the level playing field of a multiculturally (racially) available American Dream in the absence of one. In his book *The Black Culture Industry*, sociologist Ellis Cashmore concludes that one of 'the most significant value[s] of Black culture may be in providing whites with proof of the end of racism while keeping the racial hierarchy essentially intact.'[57]

Nelson George noted decades ago that when hip hop spread from the urban underground to White suburbs, 'Breakthrough black superstars made more money than ever in history—most of it helping to subsidize multinational corporations that reconfigure black artistry into reproducible formulas.'[58] In 2005, heavy weight rapper Jay-Z made *Time* magazine's list of the top 100 Americans even though a year earlier he told *Vibe* magazine that in comparison to the late 1980s and 90s

> Now, no-one makes an album anymore. As soon as they walk into their label's office, executives are asking for a single ... A rapper will do their 'girl' song, the club song, and then their 'gangsta' song ... It's not about the music anymore. It's about reaching for the numbers.[59]

And reaching for the numbers, profits, markets—is also intimately linked to the sphere of crime and punishment.

AND STILL COUNTING: MUSIC, MONEY, MARKETS, PROFITS, AND PRISON

If we are to understand the scope of outside control and governance of Black culture and bodies in the new millennium, it is significant to note that the 'invisible hand' of the market works in the sphere of music *and* crime and punishment. Making hip hop music and warehousing the hip hop generation into prison are, to differing degrees and outcomes, interrelated to elite bureaucratic, political, and economic interests in the face of the sweeping epochal changes in the 1970s. During that time, technological innovations allowed the free flow of money around the world in a matter of seconds. The subsequent impact of technological changes, global flows of capital and flighty investments, resulted in massive downsizing, deregulation of markets, disaggregated forms of production, concentrated forms of ownership (mergers), and de-industrialization. These shifts in society were due to technological changes *and* the ideological, political, and economic shifts from 'public' and state to 'private' and market as the basis of economic growth.[60]

In the telecommunications industry the deregulation of markets essentially 'freed' corporations from state imposed rules, regulations, and regulatory bodies so as to ease up the 'natural' machinations of the market.[61] Government legislation such as the benchmark 1996 revision of the 1934 Telecommunications Act 'deregulated' (or as critics argue, yielded to the privatization of) regulation. This piece of legislation hugely favored large corporations and essentially devolved the government's role in regulating the digitalized public sphere by creating favorable market conditions that eased massive mergers and buy-outs. This legislation has particularly adverse effects on Black and other 'minority' owned radio stations. Clear Channel Communications expanded its ownership from 40 radio stations prior to the 1996 Act to over 1,240 afterwards and bought out US Radio, the largest Black-owned broadcast company in America. In contrast 3.8 percent of commercial broadcast facilities were owned by 'minorities' despite constituting 29 percent of America's populace. And even in this restricted market segment, Black radio stations are routinely regulated to ghettoized airways on AM frequencies, away from the top 50 Arbitron ranked radar.[62] This means fewer listeners, less advertising revenue, less control of programming content, and more brain drain as larger companies hire away their most talented staff.

The alleged benefits of competitive broadcasting facilitated by the deregulation, is not just about numbers. The political economy of the opportunity structure expresses itself culturally. White controlled capital impacts radio programming, streamlines output, squeezes out diversity and local programming. It frequently replaces local programming with national and syndicated programming. This compromises the democratic potential and artistic diversity of a traditional digitalized Black public sphere-Black radio. It can regulate the terms and conditions of debates and political viewpoints (in a community always considered amongst the most radical and outspoken in the nation), where transgressions are professionally risky and economically sanctioned. For example, Eric Arnold reported that after Clear Channel Communications took over the Bay Area's KMEL hip hop activist David-D Cook was fired after airing an interview with Representative Barbara Lee and the Coup's Boots Riley in which they objected to the War on Afghanistan.[63]

In 2000, Viacom bought out the former Black-owned TV cable company BET (Black Entertainment Television) from Robert Johnson, gaining a niche market (of primarily African-American viewers) estimated at $469 billion consisting of 62.4 million households.[64] In 2001, Robert Johnson executed a colorblind market-led policy as he announced that Viacom's CBS News division would provide daily reports on BET's news shows, using CBS-owned correspondents as a synergetic cost-cutting strategy.[65] As local and Black inflected perspectives on community, cultural affairs, and news is displaced by remote corporate news anchors, the risks of representation from a 'White is right' perspective in Blackface is enmeshed in a history of

White distortions, omissions, and stereotypes—from news reporting to the types of rap songs and videos on rotation.[66]

Under Viacom's control and governance, MTV (also owned by Viacom) deleted the words 'White man' from Kanye West's song and video 'All Falls Down,' in which he describes how the 'Man' gets paid off Black Americans who consume anything from crack cocaine to expensive sneakers. Conversely, there is little compunction to censor semi-pornographic videos (except that it is on 'after hours') such as Nelly's 'Tip Drill.' The artists' own predilections and preferences cannot be ignored (or decontextualized from the misogyny and patriarchy in society generally). Nor can the corporate context, which consistently frames the acceptable limits of Black expressivity on unacceptable terms. White controlled systems of 'publicity' (dissemination of the music through radio, video, retail stores, etc) means the act of sliding an ATM card between the cheeks of a Black woman (on Nelly's 'Tip Drill' video) bent over, is a more acceptable form of rap's cultural expressivity than a rap on the machinations of White supremacy.

ECONOMICS, POLITICS, AND BLACK BODIES: THE PRISON INDUSTRY COMPLEX

At the *fin de siècle* Lil' Slim and T-Bone were incarcerated in California's burgeoning prison-industrial complex, whose control and governance concerns itself with those of any capitalistic venture—wage control, economies of scale, capture of state laws, and policies to harvest colossal profits.

Lil' Slim and T-Bone commonly commented on the intrusions of capital in their lives in 'lock-up,' ranging from: the private transportation companies that moved them between courtrooms and holding cell; the exorbitant fees charged by private telecommunication companies that levy a 'penal tax' on phone calls to the 'outside'; and the availability of jobs inside prison not so available on the outside.[67]

Angela Davis, Christian Parenti, Eric Schlosser, Eve Goldberg, and Linda Evans as well as a slew of prison activists and civil rights organizations highlight the race and class dynamics of an *industrial* sector where disproportionate numbers of Blacks constitute the bedrock for 'captive' markets, job security, tax breaks, and lucrative architectural and construction contracts for other social groups and businesses.[68] This interrelated set of bureaucratic, political, and economic interests encourages increased spending on imprisonment, regardless of the actual need.[69] It has given prison construction in the United States an unfettered momentum, at the cost of social policies that tackle the roots of crime, such as poverty and poor education. As Lil' Slim and T-Bone were growing up, affirmative action programs for Black males to attend college rapidly declined, while 'favored' placements into the back of squad cars and jail cells peaked. Between 1980 and 2000, about 39,000 African-American men were added to California's prisons, while those in higher education declined by about 3,800.[70] Alarmingly, if incarceration rates and racial disparities continue at their current rate, female members of the generation growing up in the 1990s will be five times more likely to go to prison than the generation that came of age in the 1970s.[71]

During the late 1970s and 80s the political climate of neo-conservatism was in ascendancy. During this period the state withdrew its interventions in providing basic services such as transportation, affordable housing, health care, adequate schools, police and fire services, by adopting a legislative and bureaucratic 'hands-off' approach based on the principles of 'free' markets and low trade barriers.[72] By adopting this private enterprise model, local, state and federal governments imposed massive cutbacks in public spending, while market-led solutions could be used to solve public social problems. Hence corporations profit from taxpayers' money—even in the realm of law and order and crime and punishment. Private companies in this industrial complex have received inordinate amounts of public resources such as: 'cheap land, tax breaks, and discounts in sewage and utilities charges, making prison companies a major beneficiary of corporate welfare,' with little public scrutiny, accountability, or interaction.[73] In a 1996 interview in the *Los Angeles Times*, Robert Verdeyen of the American Correctional Association hints at the private, public, and political interests in ensuring 'captive' markets through the letter of the law. He explains:

> A lot of the construction boom has to do with changes in our criminal statutes—minimum mandatory sentences, Three-Strikes and you're out, the end of parole … Any time you start changing the laws and making penalties stiffer, you're going to drive your population up.[74]

Lil' Slim served time under California's 'Three-Strike' law where the third strike (third felony) conviction results in a mandatory sentence of 25 years to life.[75] Theoretically he could earn two more strikes and be locked up for 25 years to life for stealing golf clubs or $150 of videotapes from two different stores.[76] The low-level nature of many of the crimes prosecuted under 'Three-Strikes' is routine not rare, and is particularly 'excessive' in its breadth of criminalization and anti-Black focus. The mutually reinforcing relationship between the criminal stigmatization of Blacks and racial subordination, through such stiff laws, makes it easier to legitimize increasingly stringent measures in the criminal justice system as Blacks become criminalized. Hence bolstering the common-sense notion that 'Blacks deserve prison, not redress.'[77] Within this context, Corrections Corporation of America (CCA), the largest private penal conglomerate in the world, does not hold out false promises as it boasts 'If we build them, they will come.' A strategy peculiarly poised to capture Black 'captive' markets for profits while rendering many to cruel and unusual forms of penology.[78]

THE 'CARCERAL CAST' AND THE HIP HOP GENERATION

In accounting for the high rates of incarceration amongst lower-class Black males, Loïc Wacquant argues that rather than a 'crime and punishment' paradigm,

> Vestiges of the dark ghetto and the expanding prison system have become linked by a triple relationship of functional equivalency, structural homology and cultural fusion, spawning a carceral continuum that entraps younger black men rejected by the deregulated wage-labor market.[79]

He traces the transformation of the communal ghetto up until the 1960s (with its Black communal and social institutions, businesses, and mixtures of classes) to the emergence of today's 'hyper ghettos' to: class segregation which overlays racial segregation; the loss of Black labor's positive economic functions (in the face of global forces and de-industrialization); and the shift of state institutions from public welfare policies to the disciplining, punishing, containment and conformance of all aspects of Black social, public and private life—from schools, street corners to public housing— premised on a 'carceral continuum.' The result? A society where lower-class African Americans 'now dwell, not in a society with prisons as their White compatriots do, but in *the first genuine prison society* of history,' where punishment does not end with prison.[80] Instead the 'carceral cast' extends further than 'doing time' to post-detention supervision, post-prison supervision and the general 'prisonization' of public housing and schools in poor inner city areas. Depressingly, this framing of America's penology best fits the social location of Lil' Slim and T-Bone, as it does younger and younger members of their generation.[81]

On the couple of occasions I spoke to T-Bone and Lil' Slim about their experiences locked up, both variously noted the conditions as: worse in county jail than prison, filthy, rife with heated racial tensions and gang rivalries, living with the immanent threat of violence, and a volatile mix of offenders locked up in overcrowded conditions with those who are drug addicted, mentally ill or just homeless. After serving their time, Lil' Slim and T-Bone face post penal punishment. They face post penal state bureaucracies of control and regulation (parole, probation) as well as diminished opportunities for work. They can be denied forms of state entitlements such as housing benefits, food stamps, and other forms of assistance such as business licenses and loans, because they are felonious.

In Robert Blauner's explication of the ghetto rebellions in the 1960s, he viewed the race 'riots,' such as Watts in 1965, as political expressions of Black urban proletarian protest and resistance to White domination, facing off with the foot soldiers of the state—the police. They were not simply instances of 'rioting and looting' or the aftermath of the actions of a few prejudicial police officers. Rather, they were *visible* political protests against the structures of White supremacy and subordination that garnered attention world-wide and generated publicity, public debate, and political responses in addition to a host of scholarly articles, books, and media coverage. In 1992, the global coverage of the Rodney King video and the ensuing Los Angeles uprisings also ensured that the 'fire this time' was emboldened in the public's conscious, and (paltry and often regressive) public policy responses ensued, as did books, scholarly articles, and documentaries.

In the twenty-first century, the growing global neo-liberalism, bolstered by anti-Black racism intersects on Black lives to strengthen and merge the length, breadth, and powers of the 'invisible' hand of the market (in the prison and in the music industry—and indeed every industrial sector) with the 'iron fist' of law. The sheer devastation of this raced and classed system does more damage than 'cannibalize' hip hop culture; it wages outright war on a generation, a social group for whom previous Wars ('War on Drugs,' 'War on Gangs,' 'War on the Poor'—rather than on poverty) were just warm-up battles.

Within Wacquant's schema of the 'merging of prison and ghettos,' for those like Lil' Slim and T-Bone, at the center of the 'commoditization of social relations,' and the 'devolution' of the state's social policies, Gil Scott-Heron's proto-rap 'The Revolution Will Not Be Televised,' written decades ago, is eerily prophetic today.

Wacquant argues that by surveying, monitoring, neutralizing, imprisoning, and depoliticizing Black populations 'recalcitrant or superfluous to the new economic regimes …,' ghetto rebellions will disappear from the public sphere.[82] Instead, they are increasingly becoming contained within states of confinement. In prison, urban 'riots' transmute into prison 'riots' which are *invisible*, pitted against different subordinate racial and ethnic groups or gangs (rather than at symbols of the dominant order), and are responded to internally (and sometimes privately) by administrative responses that are silent and severe (secure housing units, supermax facilities, and 'lockdown' are becoming the new normalcy, rather than reserved for incorrigible or violent offenders as in previous times). This foreshadows the ultimate tragedy and irony. In the nascent years of the twenty-first century, the 'Black noise' (as Tricia Rose titles her seminal book on rap) that brought representational ruckus nearly three decades ago by bringing 'publicity' to hitherto invisible sections of America's poor Black youth, through rapping, DJing, graffiti art, breakdancing, beat boxing, and entrepreneurialism, is increasingly sequestered and restricted within the confines of an omnipresent 'carceral cast' while their abstracted culture enjoys the principles of a global 'free' market economy.

RAPPING UP

In his 1896 *Plessy v. Ferguson* dissent, Justice John Marshall Harlan stated that 'the law regards man as man, and takes no account of his colors.' At the height of the civil rights movement, Dr. King's dream was that people should 'not be judged by the color of their skin but by the content of their character.' Yet, for the hip hop generation, the collision of color and class produces a reality far removed from the 'I have a dream' aspirations of the civil rights generation, as well as the excesses of conspicuous consumption in the midst of diminishing opportunities for decent schools, colleges, and health care. The chimerical images of ghetto fabulous rappers getting one over on the 'Man' are more 'reel' then real. Some rap moguls may hang out at the Hamptons, and 'bling bling' their way through the criminal justice system (even as they are surveilled by authorities). But for many 'invisible' Black entrepreneurs in the music industry, and other everyday Black youth, working conditions (when they can be found) are exploitative and racist, and brushes with the law are more kiss the pavement than kiss my arse. T-Bone and Lil' Slim can testify to that.

NOTES

1. The term 'carceral cast' is culled from Loïc Wacquant's article, 'Deadly Symbiosis: When the Ghetto and Prison Meet and Merge,' *Punishment and Society*, Vol. 3, No. 1, 2001.
2. I met Lil' Slim and T-Bone as part of a broader study on Black entrepreneurs in the hip hop music industry conducted during my post doctoral fellowship in 1992/93 at The Center for African American Studies at UCLA, California. To maintain their confidentiality their names have been changed. See Dipannita Basu, 'Rap Music, Hip Hop Culture, and the Music Industry in Los Angeles,' *The Center for Afro-American Studies Report*, Vol. 15, Nos. 1 & 2 (1992), pp. 20–2. When I first met them, their sheer enthusiasm and commitment to their rap industry livelihoods was compelling. When I last spoke to them from prison their despair and depression overwhelming. Their spirit and their experiences guide this chapter's exploration rather than a scholarly ethnographic study (since I knew them first as a researcher, and subsequently as friends). By 2003 I had lost contact with both of them while they were still locked up, and I was out of the country for several months. This chapter is a dedication to them, and all those like them, whose 'invisible' labor and incarceration are submerged as our attention on rap and hip hop culture is constantly drawn to rich, famous, and infamous rappers. The danger of this focus becomes that blithe celebrations of hyper-visible rap moguls valorize a We-Are-The-World multiculturalism that subtly suggests the hip hop generation culls equitable economic returns on its cultural interpellations globally, and where the 'criminally minded' lyrics, posturing and slippage between art and life of rappers reinforce the public's perceptions about the criminal nature of Black men as America's Public Enemy Number One. When, in reality, the majority of the hip hop generation are sent to prison for rap sheets far more mundane than many a criminally minded rap song.
3. I use the terms the hip hop generation interchangeably with Black Americans to reference two generations of African Americans growing in the post-1965 civil rights era. I am particularly concerned with poor, working-class, males of this group. In contrast, the 'hip hop nation' comprises people of all races into rapping, breakdancing, DJing, graffiti art, and other aspects of hip hop culture such as language, style, knowledge, and street

enterprise. The U.S. Census Bureau reports that Black Americans constitute about 13 percent of the U.S. populace. In 2002 the unemployment rate for Blacks was more than twice that for non-Hispanic Whites (11 percent and 5 percent respectively). Of the 32.9 million people living below the poverty line the poverty rate for Black Americans is 23 percent compared to 8 percent for non-Hispanic Whites, with Black children feeling the real nub. Of those in poverty under the age of 18 years the rate is three times higher than that for Whites.

4. By focusing primarily on Black male members of the hip hop generation, I am not suggesting a racial, ethnic, gendered, or cultural exclusivity to the origins and practices of hip hop, or to the ethnic differences between African Americans and other Black diasporic communities. Cultural mixing and borrowing are common characteristics of Black diaspora. Nor am I denying that there is an enormous range of experiences, identities, and subjectivities that constitute the term 'Black.' Rather, I am extrapolating from the peculiar experiences of Lil' Slim and T-Bone to understand the wider social forces that shape their generation (especially the lower classes and the poor) as their aesthetic labors (making/producing hip hop/street marketing) are commoditized and their Black bodies hyper-criminalized. Both in its percentile increases in capturing mass markets for music, and for 'lock up' in America's prisons, jails, and other forms of detention, the presence of African Americans reveals a marked difference from other 'minority' and racial groups. Lyricsworld.com reports that in 1975, the percentage of Black recording artists that made the top 40 was 9 percent, in 1985 it was 13 percent, and in 1995 it was 34 percent. Figures quoted from Linda Holtzman, *Media Messages: What Film, Television, and Popular Music Teach Us About Race, Class, Gender and Sexual Orientation* (London: ME Sharpe, 2000). In tandem, the rates of Black male incarceration have also increased with much cause for concern. America's prison population has increased sixfold from 1972 (the year T-Bone was born) to 2000. By 2002, 12 percent of African Americans in their twenties were in prison or jail.

5. Tricia Rose, *Black Noise: Rap Music and Black Culture in Contemporary America* (Middletown, CT: Wesleyan University Press, 1994), p. 184.

6. They are two entrepreneurs amongst an unprecedented number of the hip hop generation who have staked out a living with the ascendancy of West Coast rap in the late 1980s and early 90s. They include the self-employed, business owners, and casual or subcontracted workers. Their activities range from 'independent' record label owners and staff, to working as publicists, journalists, make-up artists, stylists, clothing designers, sound engineers, producers, graphic artists, and public-relations and marketing firms. See Dipannita Basu, 'What's Real About "Keeping It Real",' *Post Colonial Studies*, Vol. 1, No. 3 (1998), pp. 371–87.

7. David Newman, *Sociology: Exploring the Architecture of Every Day Life* (California: Thousand Oaks, 2002), p. 174.

8. The Sentencing Project, 'New Incarceration Figures: Growth in Population Continues.' The report culls its figures from the U.S. Bureau of Justice Statistics, 2004. It noted that there are over 2.1 million people in jails and prisons in America, an increase of 2.6 percent from the previous year. Available from: <http://www.sentencingproject.org/pdfs/1044. pdf>; accessed March 13, 2005.

9. Rap and R&B enjoyed a 7.6 percent growth to 162.2 million units, up 12 million from the previous year, coming ahead of rock. Ed Christman, 'US Music Sales Break Losing Streak.' <http://www.abcnewsorg.com/Entertainment/wireStory?id=394258>; accessed January 13, 2005.

10. Julie Watson, 'Rapper's Delight: A Billion-Dollar Industry.' February 2, 2004, <http://www.forbes.com/2004/02/18/cx_jw_0218hiphop_print.html>; accessed March 10, 2004.

11. George Lipsitz, 'We Know What Time It Is: Race, Class, and Youth Culture in the 90s,' in Andrew Ross and Tricia Rose (eds), *Microphone Fiends* (New York: Routledge, 1994), p. 19.

12. In the 1960s and early 70s, at the height of Black Power, (at the other end of the integrationist impulses that characterized the civil rights movement and emerging Black middle classes) many activists and academics built upon the internal colonial perspective to describe the process of domination and exploitation in America's ghettoes, reservations, and barrios as internal colonies with similarities to the relationship between European colonizers and their colonies. This scholarly perspective, idea, and rhetoric of the U.S. as an internal colony has historical links to international anti-colonial revolts in the 'third world' and stretches from Frantz Fanon, Harold Cruse, Malcolm X, W.E.B. DuBois, Frederick Douglass, the Black Panther Party, Mumia Abu-Jamal, to prototype rappers such as Gil Scott-Heron, The Last Poets and rappers such as KRS-One, Rass Kass, Immortal Technique, Paris, and Boots Riley of the Coup. The perspective of internal colonialism understands the United States' racial landscape as an internal colony with systematic forms of White oppression that incorporate economical, cultural, and political subordination. In this schema, trapped in urban ghettoes, Black people live under segregated conditions where educators, the police, social service workers, and other arms of the White-controlled state institutions enact a system of White supremacy and Black oppression. The Black ghetto depends on small and large capitalist enterprises, which are controlled by Whites for jobs and services. Residents under-sell their labor and buy necessary commodities at inflated prices from White-owned enterprises. Loans and access to finance and other forms of economic development are available at high interest rates. Local Black politicians and other intermediaries have little power or serve the needs of those residing outside of the ghetto community.

13. Robert Blauner, *Racial Oppression in America* (New York: Harper and Row, 1972). As sociologist Stephen Steinberg reminds us, Blauner laid the sociological foundation for the sociology of 'race' in the post-civil rights era that was informed, by his own admission, from what was happening in the 'street' rather than moribund theories from the citadels of academia. His analysis formed an alternative paradigm for understanding the structural conditions of Black Americans and other 'minority' communities in the U.S., in contrast to mainstream sociology which characterized race relations as little else than issues of assimilation and prejudice. Many of the foundational characteristics of internal colonialism are echoed in later critical sociological and race writings on the importance of Whiteness, colorblind ideology and institutional racism in contemporary society. See Eduardo Bonilla-Silva, *Racism Without Racists: Color Blind Racism and the Persistence of Racial Inequality in the United States* (Boulder, CO: Rowman and Littlefield, 2003).

14. Blauner, *Racial Oppression in America*, p. 72.

15. Herbert Gans, 'Symbolic Ethnicity: The Future of Ethnic Groups and Cultures in America,' *Ethnic and Racial Studies*, Vol. 2, No. 1 (1979), pp. 1–20.

16. Wacquant, 'Deadly Symbiosis,' p. 95.

17. Melvin Oliver and Thomas Shapiro, *Black Wealth, White Wealth: A New Perspective on Racial Inequality* (New York: Routledge, 1997). Despite the increased numbers of Blacks in the middle-classes, they earn 70 cents for every one dollar earned by the White middle-classes, and only 15 cents for every dollar of wealth possessed by Whites.

18. See for example, Joe Feagin, *Racist America: Roots, Current Realities and Future Reparations* (London: Routledge, 2000).

19. Charles Mills, 'White Supremacy as a Sociopolitical System,' in Ashley Doane and Eduardo Bonilla-Silvia (eds), *White Out* (New York: Routledge, 2003), pp. 43–4. White supremacy refers to a system of social and economic privilege of White Europeans at the expense of other racial groups, and does require conscious racist attitudes.

20. Thomas Shapiro, *The Hidden Cost of Being African American: How Wealth Perpetuates Inequality* (New York: Oxford University Press, 2004).

21. Keith Negus, *Music Genres and Corporate Cultures* (New York: Routledge, 1999).

22. Greg Dimitriadis argues that Run DMC's second album, *King of Rock*, LL Cool J's 'I Can't Live Without My Radio,' the Beastie Boys' 'Fight for Your Right to Party,' and Run DMC and Aerosmith's 'Walk this Way' signaled a more rock and MTV-orientated rap. This contoured the 'outlaw' status of Black music and beats to the 'cock-rock' prerogatives of White male suburban audiences (aggressive, dominating, boastful). Greg Dimitriadis, *Performing Identity/Performing Culture: Hip Hop as Text, Pedagogy, and Lived Practice* (New York: Peter Laing, 2004).

23. Murray Forman, *The 'Hood Comes First: Race, Space, and Place in Rap and Hip-Hop* (Middletown, CT: Wesleyan University Press, 2002), p. 153.

24. Norman Kelley, 'The Political Economy of Black Music,' in Norman Kelley (ed.), *Rhythm & Business* (New York: Akashic Books, 2002). Rappers consistently make the number one position in the Billboard Top 20 and the American Brandstand charts. The latter is a chart which tracks the number of brands mentioned in the songs of those in the Billboard Top 20. In 2004, rappers topped the charts in referencing consumer brand names (judged by the numbers of 'shout-outs' and name-checks). Kanye West came in at number one (ironically with a critique of consumption) and Twista, Lil' Jon, Chingy, and Ludacris were also top 10 chart contenders. Cadillac cars, followed by Hennessy, Mercedes, Rolls Royce, and Gucci got the most mentions in their raps. Available from: <http://www.agendainc.com/brand.html>; accessed March 2005.

25. Frank Kofsky, *Black Nationalism and the Revolution in Music* (New York: Pathfinder Press, 1970).

26. Harvard Consultation Project 1996, 'Harvard Report on Urban Music,' Harvard Law School, quoted in Forman, *The 'Hood Comes First*, p. 287.

27. There are undeniably some very successful Black music executives such as Jean Riggins, Hiriam Hicks, Ronald E. Sweeney, and Michael Mauldin, who head up predominately Black music divisions. Yet this state of affairs echoes broader trends. Over time, the earnings of Blacks relative to Whites improved more between 1940 and 1960, than it did between 1970 and 1990. In 2004, the Urban League's annual report on Black America found that the mean income for Black males is 70 percent of White males ($16,876 gap), and for Black females the mean income is 83 percent of White counterparts ($6,370 difference). The Urban League, *The State of Black America 2004: The Complexity of Black Progress.* Available from <http://www.nul.org/news/2004/soba.html>; accessed March 15, 2004.

28. Wendy Day founded the Rap Coalition, a not-for-profit organization. According to its website, 'It protects rappers, producers, and DJs, from this hostile environment, and provides artists with a place to turn when they need help or support, at no cost to them. We are an artists' advocacy group dedicated to the support, education, protection, and unification of hip hop artists, similar to a union.' Available from <http://www.rapcoalition.org/>.

29. Wendy Day and Norman Kelley, 'Wendy Day: Advocate for Rappers,' interview by Norman Kelley, in Kelley (ed.), *Rhythm and Business*, p. 257.

30. Negus, *Music Genres and Corporate Cultures*, p. 99.

31. Yvonne Bynoe, 'The White Boy Shuffle.' Available from: <http://www.urbanthinktank.org/whiteboy.cfm>; accessed August 15, 2004.

32. Henry Giroux, 'Doing Cultural Studies: Youth and the Challenge of Pedagogy.' Available from <http://www.gesis.ucla.edu/courses/ed253a/giroux/giroux1>; accessed December 3, 2004.

33. bell hooks, *Black Looks: Race and Representation* (South End Press, 1992), p. 31.

34. David Leonard, 'Live in Your World, Play in Ours,' *Color Lines*, Vol. 5, No. 4 (Winter 2002/03). Available at <http://www.arc.org/C_Lines/CLArchive/story5_4_04.html>; accessed January 13, 2005.

35. In 2000, the metropolitan area of Los Angeles had an *index of dissimilarity* of 69. This essentially means that either 69 percent of the White or 69 percent of the Black population

would have to move from one census tract to another to produce an even distribution across census tracts. Post civil rights segregation was prompted in the 1970s by White (people, services, and businesses) estrangement from cities through the processes of suburbanization, exurbanization, annexation, gated communities, and the mobility of global capital. See David Theo Goldberg's excellent analysis between the old 'activist' segregation and that of the post civil rights era: 'The New Segregation,' *Race and Society*, Vol. 1 (1998).

36. Nick De Genova, 'Gangster Rap and Nihilism in Black America: Some Questions of Life and Death,' *Social Text*, Vol. 13, No. 2 (1995), p. 116.

37. My point is not to deny the moral culpability of those involved in crimes, such as gang violence or selling drugs, that abuse and victimize other poor people in their neighborhoods. Rather it is to note how the socio-spatial and socio-economic context of these crimes is developed in ghetto conditions that are themselves deeply anti-social and overly punitive. The social constructionist characterization of crime does not suggest that crime does not exist. It does, and those most at risk from it are the least protected by it. Rather it is the recognition that the labeling of deviancy and crime is an uneven social phenomenon heavily weighted in favor of claims-makers (the media, moral entrepreneurs, politicians, and interest groups) about deviancy, crime, and criminals, as well as the political, social control, and property imperatives of White ruling elites who craft the nation's laws.

38. Adamma Ince, 'Preppin' for Prison,' *Village Voice*, June 19, 2001.

39. Jerome Miller quoted by Vincent Schiraldi in 'The Juvenile Justice System in Black and White.' Available online from: <http://www.buildingblocksforyouth.org/issues/dmc/schiraldi.html>; accessed October 6, 2004. The quote is taken from his book, *Search and Destroy*, where Miller describes his experience with race and the juvenile justice system when he headed up the department of youth services in Massachusetts. Building blocks for youth is an 'alliance of children and youth advocates, researchers, law enforcement professionals and community organizers that are seeking to reduce overrepresentation and disparate treatment of youth of color in the justice system and promote fair, rational and effective juvenile justice policies.'

40. For incisive studies of Black youth, hip hop, gangs, and the police in Los Angeles see Mike Davis, *City of Quartz: Excavating the Future in Los Angeles* (New York: Vintage Books, 1992); Robin D.G. Kelley, 'Kickin' Reality, Kickin' Ballistics: Gangsta Rap and Postindustrial Los Angeles,' in William Eric Perkins (ed.), *Droppin' Science: Critical Essays on Rap Music and Hip Hop Culture* (Philadelphia: Temple University Press, 1996); Brian Cross, *It's Not About a Salary: Rap, Race, and Resistance in Los Angeles* (New York: Verso, 1993).

41. Jeff Chang and Ryan Pintado-Vertner, 'The War on Youth,' *ColorLines Magazine*, Vol. 2, No. 4 (Winter 1999/2000). Ryan Pintado-Vertner, 'How is Juvenile Justice Served?' *San Francisco Chronicle*, February 27, 2002. The LAPD has a number of gang units known as CRASH (Community Resources Against Street Hoodlums). A major scandal and investigation broke in 2000, over the Rampart (a division of the LAPD) gang Intel, as accusations of corruption, brutality, and false testimony by police officers resulted in the review of hundreds of criminal cases in which suspects were wrongly convicted.

42. Even for middle-class Black youth 'the interaction of popular culture with the economic and spatial realities of the Black middle-class (and of course the Black poor) imbues the "gangsta" image with more serious repercussions for Black youth.' Mary Patillo McCoy, *Black Picket Fences: Privilege and Peril Amongst the Black Working-Class* (Chicago: University of Chicago, 2000), p. 16. Clothing selection for Black males and their concerned parents is not simply based on individual preferences. It is a site for playing with their 'Blackness' and often involves strategic decisions in clothing which are important for psychological and even physical survival. Ann Arnett Ferguson, *Bad Boys: Public Schools in the Making of Black Masculinity* (Ann Arbor: University of Michigan Press, 2001).

43. Lil' Slim was charged even though the security camera showed that he was not involved in the stealing of any of the garments, but was accompanying those caught stealing.

44. Joe Feagin and Harlan Hahn, *Ghetto Revolts: The Politics of Violence in American Cities* (New York: Macmillan, 1973), p. 157.

45. Nathan McCall, *Makes Me Wanna Holler: A Young Black Man in America* (New York: Vintage Books, 1995), p. 150.

46. See for example, David Harris, 'The Stories, the Statistics, and the Law: Why "Driving While Black" Matters,' *Minnesota Law Review*, Vol. 84, No. 2 (1999), pp. 65–326.

47. The New York Police Department (NYPD) compiled a six-inch dossier on a league of well and lesser known rappers and their associates. South Miami Police surveilled rappers and their associates in airports, hotels, and clubs; and police exchange interstate 'intelligence' and monitor radio stations and lyrics for information on new rap rivalries. Evelyn McDonnell and Nicole White, 'Police Secretly Watching Hip Hop Artists,' *The Miami Herald*, March 9, 2004.

48. Recently, Cedric Muhammad from BlackElectorate.com interviewed Congresswoman Cynthia McKinney on her crafting of legislation to open government files on Tupac Shakur's murder. He reported that the statement was issued at the end of a long meeting, featuring, amongst others, Paul Robeson, Jr. (son of the legendary actor) and Afeni Shakur, Tupac's mother, and former Black Panther member. Robeson talked about his own father's opposition from the FBI and CIA files, the surveillance efforts of intelligence agencies on Jimi Hendrix and Bob Marley were also discussed and Afeni Shakur detailed her first-hand perspective with COINTELPRO, the FBI's counterintelligence programs to repress political dissent in the United States.

49. Nelson George, *Hip Hop America* (Penguin, 1999), p. 140.

50. Stokely Carmichael and Charles V. Hamilton, *The Politics of Liberation* (New York: Vintage, 1967), p. 47.

51. In joint ventures the major record company is essentially a bank, which deducts its costs (overheads, costs in distribution, and manufacturing cost) before sharing the profits with the 'independent.'

52. Ellis Cashmore, *The Black Culture Industry* (London: Routledge, 1997).

53. Forman, *The 'Hood Comes First*, p. 225.

54. When *Black Enterprise* recently announced its list of the 75 most powerful African Americans in corporate America, there were more women (three female CEOs) and there had been a 300 percent increase from six CEOs in 2000 to 18 such positions in 2004. Yet the founder and publisher of *Black Enterprise*, Earl G. Graves, both praised and opined these figures. He noted: 'it is also true that African Americans still hold less than one percent of the tens of thousands of senior-level, corporate posts at America's largest public corporations.' Kenneth Meeks, 'Meet 75 Executives Who Hold Tremendous Clout in the World of Business, Including the 18 Who Earned CEO Positions,' *Black Enterprise*, February 2005. Available from <http://www.blackenterprise.com/Pageopen. asp?source=/archive2005/02/0205-39.htm>; accessed March 15, 2004. The list draws from the 1,000 largest domestic and international corporations traded publicly on the U.S. equities markets.

55. Ben Bagdikian, *The Media Monopoly* (Boston: Beacon Press, 1997), p. 9.

56. Yvonne Bynoe, 'Money, Power, Respect: A Critique of the Business of Rap Music,' in Kelley (ed.), *Rhythm and Business*, p. 232. Some industry insiders evoke 'Black on Black' crime in reference to Black businesses/people ripping other Black people/businesses off.

57. Cashmore, *The Black Culture Industry*, p. 2.

58. Nelson George, *Buppies, B-Boys, BAPS & Bohos: Notes on Post-Soul Black Culture* (New York: HarperCollins, 1992), pp. xi–xii.

59. Shawn Carter, 'Hova and Out,' *Vibe Magazine* (January 2004).

60. Stuart Hall, 'The Centrality of Culture: Notes on the Cultural Revolutions of Our Time,' in Kenneth Thompson (ed.), *Media and Cultural Regulation* (London: Sage Publications, 1997).

61. Robert McChesney reminds us that 'free' markets are not created solely by economic forces. They are a product of political decisions made by government in collusion with business elites that affect the conditions of competition in the marketplace. Multinational music/entertainment companies seek to liberalize regulations on competition by lobbying the government for favorable market conditions in areas such as: supporting copyright inspectors, lobbying to license music in an increasing number of public spaces, and lobbying for 'intellectual' property laws such as criminal prosecutions of cyber bandits. Prior to the 1980s, national media systems were predominantly owned by national industries. In the twenty-first century, the media is a global oligopoly just like oil and automotive industries were earlier in the twentieth century. Writing in 1999, Robert McChesney notes the major transnational corporations that monopolize the industry were: Viacom, Time Warner, Seagram, General Electric, AT&T/Liberty Media, Disney, Sony, News Corporation, and Bertelsmann. Robert McChesney, 'The New Global Media: It's a Small World of Big Conglomerates,' *The Nation*, November 29, 1999.

62. 'Changes, Challenges, and Charting New Courses' (2003). Available from <http://www.ntia.doc.gov/opadhome/mtdpweb/01minrept/mtdpexecsum.htm>; accessed March 3, 2004.

63. Clear Channel also provides (mostly poor public) schools with 'free electronic equipment' to the tune of $50,000 as dwindling state support for education signals a lucrative corporate business opportunity, with minimum outlay for a monopolized audience. Schools receive the funding provided they broadcast ten minutes of current events and two minutes of commercials. Cultural Studies scholar Henry Giroux notes that an estimated 80,000 students are exposed in school urinals to advertisements for Footlocker, Starburst, and Pepsi.

64. It also made Johnson immensely wealthy. His 1.6 percent of Viacom shares makes him the second-largest individual shareholder after Chairman Sumner Redstone.

65. Brett Pulley, 'The Cable Capitalist,' *Forbes Magazine* (August 10, 2001).

66. In the realm of crime reporting for example, one study found that between 1990 and 1998 the coverage of homicides declined by 38 percent yet their coverage increased 473 percent on network news and young Black males received 30 percent of more band width than others. 'Off Balance: Youth, Race, and Crime in the News.' Executive Report for the Building Blocks of Youth Foundation. Available at <http://www.buildingblocksforyouth.org/media/>; accessed March 5, 2004.

67. Ironically, the California Department of Corrections sought markets in Japan for its convict-made 'Gangsta Blue.' Victoria's Secret, MCI, Motorola, and Microsoft are some of the private corporations which alongside state operated businesses, such as UNICOR, use prisoners as cheap captive labor.

68. For example, influential Wall Street firms and investment banks such as American Express and Smith Barney pour billions into supporting prison bond issues, construction, and the privatization of prisons. Prison stocks were some of the best investment options in the 1990s.

69. Eric Schlosser, 'The Prison-Industrial Complex,' *Atlantic Monthly*, December 1998.

70. Since 1985 the general fund spending on colleges in California has dropped by $1 billion, while corrections spending increased by $3 billion. Vincent Schiraldi and Rose Braz, 'Cut Prison Budgets, Not Education' (2003), <http://news.pacificnews.org/news/view_article.html?article_id=af339ecad558634b2fa92aaea26c3221>; accessed December 3, 2004.

71. Marc Mauer and Ryan King, 'Schools and Prisons: 50 years After Brown Versus Brown,' *The Sentencing Project*. Available from <http://sentencingproject.org/pdfs/brownvboard.pdf>; accessed August 11, 2004.

72. In the same period, Reaganism mobilized coded and implicit references to Black criminality ('law and order') and pathology (Black family structure) in which Black men, women, and communities were cast as internal threats to the nation's moral fabric, its social security, and its economic future. By mobilizing implicit references to Black pathology and White victimhood, politicians blamed Black people for their own problems and simultaneously developed a rhetoric and discourse which cast social policies, such as affirmative action, as 'preferences' for Black people with Whites as the victims of state social policies. For an excellent account of the criminalized crisis scenario of Black youth see Craig Watkins, *Hip Hop Culture and the Production of Black Cinema* (Chicago: University of Chicago Press, 1998). See also Robin D.G. Kelley, *Yo Mama's Dysfunctional: Fighting the Culture Wars in Urban America* (Boston: Beacon Press, 1997).

73. Julia Sudbury, 'Celling Black Bodies in the Global Prison Industrial Complex,' *Feminist Review*, Vol. 70 (2002), p. 62.

74. In a recent study by the Justice Policy Institute co-author Erik Lotke stated: '"Three-Strikes" is turning California's prisons into a purgatory for "minorities".' According to 'Racial Divide: An Examination of the Impact of California's Three-Strikes Law on African Americans and Latinos,' in Los Angeles County, 10 percent of the population is African American and African Americans are 29 percent of those arrested. They represent 56 percent of those serving life sentences under 'Three-Strikes.'

75. Under 'Three-Strikes' the most common third-strike offenses are robbery and first degree burglary (both are considered violent or serious offenses) followed by possession of a controlled substance, second degree burglary, and possession of a weapon. Legislative Analyst's Office paper on October 14, 1997 at the Assembly Committee on Public Safety in Los Angeles. Available from <http://www.facts1.com/ThreeStrikes/Stats/#Nearly>; accessed August 26, 2004.

76. In 2003, the Supreme Court upheld two sentences from the state of California bought up under mandatory sentencing. One was a felon who stole $150 of videotapes from two different stores and was convicted of two felonies. He was sentenced to two consecutive terms of 25 years. The other was by a felon who stole some golf clubs. In 2003, the Supreme Court issued two rulings upholding California's Three-Strikes law. The cases were *Lockyer v. Andrade* and *Ewing v. California*.

77. David Cole, *No Equal Justice: Race and Class in the American Criminal Justice System* (Monroe, ME: Common Courage Press, 1999), p. 177.

78. According to CCA's official website, its 'mission is to provide quality corrections at less cost to the taxpayer, in partnership with government.' The 'Black tax' in penology are White sources of economic and political advantage. As early as 1901, W.E.B. DuBois traced the history of the convict lease system and the strategic enactment of 'Black Codes' as an economic and social control. The convict-lease system entrapped African Americans into a criminal justice system which returned them in a state of bondage, as free labor for southern White landowners, thus helping them to maintain their power and privileged status. Today locking up poor and 'minorities' generates wealth for corporate interests and jobs and overtime for prison guards. Calvin Beale, a senior demographer with the U.S. Department of Agriculture, describes rural prisons as a 'classic export industry' that is drawn disproportionately from the ghetto and poor inner city areas. Mainly rural White communities benefit from their penal presence and their political disenfranchisement. Prisoners are counted as part of the local population in which the prison is located not as displaced prisoners from their home address and communities, thus, White rural areas which predominately house prisoners, disproportionately benefit from the bolstered Census counts (hence resources divvied up by the government). And even with the 1965 Voting Rights Act signed into law, African Americans are still being kept away from the vote, with 1.4 million Black felons in 2002 unable to vote. Eric Lotke and Peter Wagner,

'Prisoners of the Census,' *Pace Law Review*, Vol. 24, No. 2 (Spring 2004). Available from <http://www.library.law.pace.edu/PLR24-2/PLR218.pdf>; accessed May 5, 2005.

79. Wacquant, *Deadly Symbiosis*, p. 95.

80. Ibid., p. 121.

81. Most social psychologists agree that the socialization and physiological processes of maturing are not fully realized by 14 to 17 years of age, yet California's Proposition 21, the 'Gang Violence and Juvenile Crime Prevention Act,' passed by voters in 2000, assumes the contrary. Proposition 21 makes it easier to prosecute juveniles as adults. It significantly restricts juvenile probation and has much harsher sentencing procedures. It also increases penalties for gang related violence and sets up a gang registration process. Disproportionate numbers of 'minority' youth are imprisoned under this legislation. Mike Males and Dan Macallair, 'The Color of Justice: An Analysis of Juvenile Adult Court Transfers in California.' Available from <http://www.buildingblocksforyouth.org/colorofjustice/coj.html>; accessed January 29, 2004. Catherine Campbell, a civil rights attorney from Fresno, provides an unabashed critical assessment of the juvenile (in)justice system: 'A lot of it begins with putting the kids of poor parents into foster care. That's how authorities inspire hatred, anger, frustration and feelings of worthlessness. It's the "I don't give a fuck zone," and with only a few months of that, most kids are pretty much destroyed. They are "criminalized" when their behavior crosses over the almost unavoidable line of criminal behavior'; quoted in Alexander Cockburn and Jeffery St. Clair, 'Remember Those "Super-Predators"?' *Counterpunch* (December 2000). Available online: <http://www.counterpunch.org/youth.html>; accessed May 20, 2005.

82. Wacquant, *Deadly Symbiosis*, p. 97.

4
'Nobody Knows My Name' and an Interview with the Director Rachel Raimist

Dipannita Basu and Laura Harris

INTO THE FRAY: GIVING PUBLICITY TO B-GIRLS

Nobody Knows My Name (1999), directed by Rachel Raimist, remains one of the few documentaries about women in hip hop, within a culture where movies and documentaries are integral elements that define the genre. In hip hop's formative years, hip hop documentaries such as Tony Silver and Henry Chalfant's *Style Wars* (1983), Tony Silver's *Style Wars* (1981), and Charles Ahearn's *Wild Style* (1982), as well as films such as Stan Lathan's *Beat Street* (1984), cast men as central figures. Nearly two decades later, during the period over which *Nobody* was conceived and executed, documentaries such as John Carluccio's *Battle Sounds* (1997), as well as documentaries with wider distribution such as Peter Spirer's *Rhyme & Reason* (1997) and Brian Robbin's *The Show* (1995), once again foreground the male presence and performance. Against this context, Raimist documents the routine operations of hip hop in the lives of everyday b-girls in the subcultural spaces of Los Angeles, New York, and San Francisco. *Nobody* features T-Love and Medusa (MCs, poets, rappers), Leschea (hip hop artist), Lisa (mother and b-girl), Asia One (breakdancer), DJ Symphony (turntablist) and Nikke Nicole (record producer) in their homes, on their couch, on stage, in the studio and as talking heads. *Nobody*'s power resides in its subjects' capacity to articulate in everyday terms critical positions on the contested terrain of hip hop as they negotiate hip hop as a cultural experience distinct from, yet impacted by, mainstream representations and economic demands of making ends meet.

Like any precious gem in raw form, *Nobody* is rough on the exterior but full of promise and treasure on the inside. Between the tears and heartaches, joys and epiphanies of the featured b-girls, this promise of hidden treasure is found in the documentary's richly content-driven, under-produced, gritty aesthetics. Its representation of and dialogue on hip hop culture seductively, but not sexually, disrupts the gendered and raced assumptions that hip hop is mainly about Black men, mics and mainstream markets.[1]

Raimist brings directorial 'wreck' to the screen, as do the documentary's subjects.[2] *Nobody* gives name, vision, and voice to everyday b-girls in a variety of hip hop's interpretative communities (DJing, MCing, graffiti, producing beats, b-girling), as an absorbing visual counterpoint to the routine practices of 'undermining, deletion, or derogatory stereotyping of women's creative role in the development of minority cultures.'[3] Kyra Gaunt reminds us that even more is at stake in this unfaltering focus on the male presence in hip hop culture: 'the ideological power of maleness in a mass-mediated [hip hop] culture … makes it so difficult to fully appreciate African-American women's creative and expressive participation as anything other than subsidiary to men's.'[4] *Nobody* counters this. It clearly engages the viewer with the idea that it is not only the presence of women in hip hop's multiple public spheres, but their role in shaping those sites.[5]

In the year of *Nobody*'s release, Lauryn Hill won an unprecedented five Grammies for *The Miseducation of Lauryn Hill* and Eminem's best-selling missive of misogyny *Slim Shady* topped the charts.[6] Both Raimist's documentary and Hill's songs challenge the reductive, degrading imagery of women. Though far less distributed than Hill's multi-platinum CD, *Nobody* gets 'play' nationwide through college conferences, libraries, and independent film festivals.[7] Despite the 'expert' locations of its primary circulation, *Nobody* departs from much of academic or public intellectual claims on hip hop. *Nobody*'s initial scenes briefly introduce each subject making an 'expert' statement about her specific gendered relation to the culture as they perceive or experience it. Its exploration of the everyday subjugated knowledge and practices of females in hip hop renders the b-girls in the documentary as 'cultural experts.' This inclusion of performers, audience members, music makers, and casual critics extends the legitimacy of permissible expertise and cultural critique beyond male and mainstream scholars or public figures.[8] For this reason *Nobody* has the potential to capture the interest of devout fans, Black feminists, cynical leftists/cultural conservatives, as well as curious newcomers to hip hop. Furthermore, by capturing the struggle to survive and thrive in the fluid but distinct spaces of the digitalized public sphere (radio, studio), the local community (Medusa runs the club 'Nappy at the Roots' in Los Angeles; Asia One performs in a dance crew; and DJ Symphony spins in a variety of clubs and competitions), as well as in the home (Lisa is a hip hop mother), *Nobody*'s expansive treatment of women in hip hop allows them to come into public view not for their celebrity status, but for their more mundane but no less meaningful contributions to the culture's ever evolving idioms and practices.

When b-girl T-Love tells the viewer in a talking-head shot that she loves hip hop unconditionally and emphatically, she succinctly explains its highs and lows: 'It makes me broke, but I cannot help it cuz I love this shit.' Her singular proclamation situates hip hop as a love and life. It functions as a collective sentiment of the featured women by focusing on female subjects who are not pre-fabricated or famous. While a segment of *Nobody* certainly pays tribute to female rappers from Roxanne Shanté to Queen Latifah and MC Lyte, the film goes beyond a simple account of this popular legacy of

Black women's contributions to hip hop to vividly reframe the importance of hip hop culture, female expressions, and the passion for the genre as one largely unseen by the mainstream's public and marketing gaze.

Nobody represents the hip hop nation. It expands hip hop's racial dynamic to a focus upon gendered perspectives and local multicultural practices. On film, we meet Asian, Latina, Black, and mixed heritage b-girls for whom hip hop is (as Raymond Williams famously quips) 'a way of life,' a performance, assiduous practice, and even a means to turn 'play to pay.'[9] For the women featured, gender is an overarching issue with a range of concerns from: talent versus appearance, hip hop community building versus individual recognition, public hip hop visibility versus domestic hip hop invisibility, and economic disparities versus creative opportunities, to name a few gendered realities of hip hop which *Nobody* details for its audience. Whatever their specific gender issues, their involvement in gender roles, and their approach and understanding to gendered work are distinct, varied, and far more complex than much of the public gives them credit for.

PERFORMANCE POLITICS

The idiosyncrasy of this film is that it offers a diverse range of voices in constructing b-girl womanhood in hip hop. Yet, it rarely disrupts popular notions of gender in hip hop by subverting or playing with sexual identities and sexualities. Often it does so by skirting issues of sexuality that are central to the work of hip hop feminists who have made valuable insights into the sexual politics of hip hop (from its role in courtship rituals and as an expressive arena for public displays of female freedom and sexuality which work against traditional methods of regulation and self-regulation). While a problematic tactic in terms of crucial gains made by feminist scholars in the terrain of female sexualities, it does however offer a counter-dialogue, a distinct voice, to studies that primarily, and necessarily, cast their critical gaze on the cultural politics of sexuality of female performers.[10]

Medusa (the lyrical seducer) makes it clear she is wholly disinterested in any complicated analysis of mainstream hip hop/rap since her critical model, arising out of her artistic practice, suggests the economic equation between gender, hip hop, and sex is over-determined by bitches/ho/sleezer tropes she is simply not interested in recuperating. In *Nobody*, these women are clearly intent on a representation of themselves as serious, committed, talented artists. Yet this appears to have a silencing effect in terms of their discussion, or lack thereof, of sexuality in relation to their artistic performance. This absence can be read as a restrictive propriety that recalls a modern day rendering of the 'culture of dissemblance,' which purposively presents Black women in the public sphere as 'respectable,' and necessarily stripped of any signs of overt sexuality.[11] It is enacted in large part to overturn the reformulated stereotypes of Black women circulating elsewhere in hip hop's digitalized public sphere (radio, MTV, BET, etc). Or perhaps the representations of sexuality in *Nobody* are rendered illegible to most viewers (trained to see 'female sexuality' as per the mainstream) outside of a subcultural insiderism that operates in the different social spaces of local hip hop communities and consumers. For example, Medusa attracts a substantial feminist and queer audience to her performances in the Los Angeles area. Except for Medusa's unavoidable sexual charisma in the documentary, indeed one that unavoidably riffs off 1960s Black Power movements, 1970s Blaxploitation images, and contemporary queer recuperations of non-normative female sexualities, *Nobody* focuses intently on artistic skills, not sexual appeal, in reaction to the images of women in hip hop prevalent during the time of its production and release which persists to this day.

Nobody foregrounds women's reflections and narratives of their experiences in an array of hip hop's foundational cultural constituents (MCing, producing records, DJing, dancing, and singing) in both public and private spheres. We encounter Medusa, for example, via inserts of interviews and footage, as an LA underground MC, poet, and actress who scats, spins and freestyles, in an array of hair styles and fashion statements (from full Afro and Afro-queen garb to casual b-girl style). Asia One is shown sitting on her living room sofa as well as spinning on her head as she puts it down for dance in hip hop's expressive styles and leisure driven disciplines. Leschea lets the viewer know that hip hop stretches beyond genre conventions or street and industry prerogatives of authenticity. Singing in the assumed conventional genre of R&B, which Leschea ardently maintains is hip hop, she challenges the dominant and socially constructed categories of rap, hip hop and R&B, when she tells the camera, 'I don't get it, you have to rhyme to be hip hop? I dress, talk, and sleep it. Every thing about me ... everything about Leschea is hip hop.'

Lisa is a hip hop mother. For her, gender discourse is not primarily a public spectacle debate but a daily private negotiation. She is a wife and mother of a hip hop artist/family. We see her sitting in her house, following her two children, cheering her younger son and husband when the former desires to rap and the latter is doing so. Her gender issues are less about her own artistic path but more in relation to the recognition of the importance of the domestic (nurturing, voluntary not estranged) role in the cultural production of hip hop—a gender role she revises as equal in power to her husband's MCing. She challenges the audience to consider the role of women in hip hop not only in terms of sexual politics, but in terms of their hard graft, their labor behind the scenes. In so doing the audience comes away with the role of wives and mothers in hip hop as something much more than invisible, marginal or worse, parasitic. Facing the camera, she demands her gendered function to be valued as a role of respected assertion and artistic influence over the final product. Her presence and narrative dents the cultural trope of separate spheres—the differential authority and respect given to the activities and labor carried out in the private (feminine) and public (masculine) realm. Her presence reminds the viewer that the reproduction and nurturing of hip hop emanates from the domestic realm as well as from public performances and the cultural industries.

GENDER AND POLITICAL ECONOMY

Nobody pushes the envelope of the observation that most female rappers have to foreground their sexual appearance even if their style and the weight of its substance impresses. It suggests that masculinist perspectives and evaluations of marketplace worth accorded to female artists goes deeper than the hotly debated and much maligned misogyny of the male protagonists of hip hop culture. The viewer is left with a deeper understanding of the gendered political economies that are embedded in the social constructions of authenticity, success and popularity, as well as looks.

Singer Leschea describes the effects on her artistic endeavors as a hip hop artist in a cultural field where 'authenticity' reads 'male.' Early on in her career, she was informed that she would be perceived by industry logic as a fragile market product, redeemable only if she added a male to her music (known, recognizable, authentic rapper). This rests on the assumption she is weak, or even if she is strong, she is not strong enough without the bolstering effects of a male. Such cultural understandings stretch from street-driven notions of authenticity to industry-wide practices. Women's experiences in the industry are historically and predictably formulaic: female vocal and performative styles are frequently dismissed as lacking the agility, mastery, requisite tone, or sheer force and command of their male counterparts.

Nobody reveals that male mentorship is both opportunity and constraint. Within the context of male-dominated crews and posses in hip hop, mentorship to an established name accesses wider networks and opportunities and provides a chance to become a recognized name. Leschea recounts a story where an artist and repertoire (A&R) executive for Warner Brothers heard her on an unnamed tape, and wanted to find out who was singing on it. Fortuitously, as staff listened, someone recognized the male vocals of Master Ace's rhymes. His fame was her fortune, because she now had a name, and as a consequence could be reached as Warner Brothers' interest in her piqued. Yet Master Ace's patronage was not without conditions. He was instrumental in providing a valued artistic apprenticeship by letting her come on tour with him. He did so however, on the proviso she sang not rhymed. The necessity of male patronage, and the conditions of performance for industry success, recalls women's particular positioning as handmaidens servicing male success and visibility in the public domain, which is historically poised to grant success, market exposure, and contracts to Black women based on limited readings of their gendered worth or cultural capabilities. A cursory glance at some of Black music's female songstresses and rappers reveals a system of patronage where successful female artists are under the highly visible tutelage of a male presence on the mic or as manager or mentor. Stretching from Berry Gordy and Diana Ross; Tommy Mottola and Mariah Carey; Missy Elliott and Timbaland; Lil' Kim and Biggie; Eve the First Lady of the Ruff Ryders; Aaliyah and R. Kelly to Ashanti and Murder Inc.—male patronage can also take less obvious forms.

In the tradition of Roxanne Shanté's 'Roxanne's Revenge,' *Nobody Knows My Name* invokes the aesthetic of Black female call and response to this explicitly gendered economy. Shanté's rap responded to and 'dissed' on UTFO's popular 'Roxanne, Roxanne,' a typical male-driven rap about desiring a neighborhood 'shorty.' As popular accounts frame it, in 'dissing' UTFO with Queensbridge ghetto attitude, Shanté gave birth to the '[G]angsta bitch as we know it. Like the Coffys and Cleopatra's of Blaxploitation screen fame, Shanté was simply not having it.'[12] In *Nobody* the memory and image of Shanté is invoked to situate the documentary within hip hop performance history. However, while the memory of Shanté's attitude is reverently invoked, the film resists the legacy her attitude produced as its subjects offer what is, in fact, a direct critique of the gendered political economy out of which it arose. Indeed, 'Roxanne's Revenge' was not Shanté's self-developed vehicle but her producer's, Marley Marl. Of interest is that he was also UTFO's producer (with whom he was reportedly annoyed for missing a gig). This defining moment in hip hop culture—raw public gendered dozens—was also one that was embedded in a power dynamics based on male prerogatives, resources, and institutional structures beyond the genre.

Under these restricted but always resisted conditions, other interviewees also enquire: What about our artistry, our innovations, our differences, and our history? Asia One, b-girl breakdancer, articulates her position as one of not competing with men but about building her own b-girl community, particularly one that is not reliant upon or looking for male patronage. As Asia One succinctly phrases it, 'We shouldn't expect them to do our shit for us.' From yet another perspective DJ Symphony, the only female member of the World Famous Beat Junkies, relates her position as: 'I don't spend hours a day practicing to be pretty or to be cute on the turntable. I practice to be a DJ. I practice skills. I'm not there to be looked at, I'm there to be listened to ... [At parties] these girls will come up to me ... Can we speak to the DJ? And I will be like, I am the DJ!' DJ Symphony's insistence on community evaluation based on her technical knowledge versus her gender embodiment disrupts a DJ culture where men are assumed to inherently embody the musical knowledge and skills, an assumption arguably produced via a gender ideology. Central to DJing is an artistic dynamic in which the archiving and technological wizardry of the techniques and technology of making music in turntablism (outside the natural voice) is highly gendered. Masculinist DJ cultures allow for geeks and techno freaks to be the leading proponents of dance music's appropriation in archiving and producing musical knowledge

(as opposed to the more feminine traits of hoarding and consuming)—
perhaps a sublimation of the geek's *impossibility* of getting laid. On the other
hand, for women in hip hop the impossibility of *not* getting laid is an issue.
We are reminded of the words of old skool graffiti artist Lady Pink, 'As a
female writer your sexual reputation is run through the dirt. Boys will not
tell each other that a girl said no to them. People were saying crazy things
about how I wasn't doing my own pieces and so on.'[13]

DIFFERING TAKES ON SUCCESS

Cheryl Keyes distinguishes four overlapping but distinct categories of female
rap artists based upon the constructions of an interpretative community
which she observed via recorded performance and personal interviews.[14]
She describes them as: 'Queen Mother' (Queen Latifah, Sister Souljah,
Yo-Yo), 'Fly Girl' (Salt-N-Pepa, TLC, Missy Elliott), Sista's with Attitude
(Roxanne Shanté, Lil' Kim, Foxy Brown), and 'Lesbian' (Queen Pen).
Nobody troubles this useful feminist typology to forward the insights of
those who are rejected by such marked typologies. As one of the women
in *Nobody* recounts, 'When a male group goes to an A&R person, he asks
what do they sound like. With a female group he asks for a picture.' This
cursory and casual control of women's performance style is a common
practice of industry executives who do not even entertain a 'hearing' or
'look-in' to female recording artists unless they are looking good, in a style
that is currently fashionable/marketable.

As Medusa recounts, female rappers who refuse any marketplace typology
are too often marginalized or simply deemed 'unmarketable.' Medusa reports
that 'While they [record executives] say they can feel it or understand it, they
knew no-one else would.' On the one hand she is rendered marginal within the
broader digitalized public sphere of the music industry, despite, or because
of her 'raw' and uncompromising talent. By music industry executive logic
Medusa is unsuccessful, not as a result of any lack of talent, but because her
style is too sublime to fit into the current marketing modes. That may certainly
be the case, but as Medusa points out why don't they 'at least put it out there
so the people can decide for themselves?' On the other hand, populist notions
of the direct correlations between gender and authentic talent are undermined
in the documentary by Medusa's variegated performances off and on stage.
As she scats, sings, raps, introspects, and acts, the viewer is convinced that
considerations other than raw talent and hard work figured into the music
industry's cultural calculations of her 'worth.' The viewer comes away
skeptical of the industry and in no doubt of her multiple talents.

The figure of Medusa, as well as others in *Nobody* who have achieved
minor commercial success or local followings, re-inscribe hip hop's gendered
ideals of authenticity and success by finding their status via subcultural
celebrity or an elevated sense of self, identity, and community through their

love and labor for hip hop. What Brian Cross intimates in his brilliant book on rap and resistance in Los Angeles entitled *It Ain't About a Salary*, Medusa brings to life on the screen. She reminds the audience that success cannot be measured in purely quantitative terms, as she describes the unmitigated pleasure she derived from a large mural of her, put up without her knowledge (but not permission), on the main drag of Hollywood Boulevard. Medusa viewed this as a success on a collective and personal level. One not registered by cash machines or units sold, yet not exclusive from them either. The politics of her success reveals both territorial and historical coordinates. The mural pays historical homage to strong Black women via the politics of her big Afro, a recognizable marker of Black power in a place of public prominence where the White symbolic space of Hollywood Boulevard (and its markers of measurable, global success) is over-determined, while providing a tribute to her own place in LA's hip hop subcultural spheres. In other words, while traditional Hollywood wouldn't recognize a 'strong Black female' iconography so prominently and music industry executives would not finance a Hollywood billboard for her, she, through her subcultural clout, gets to occupy the space anyway.

Record producer Nikke Nicole, proudly, though not boastfully, informs the viewer that her skills as a hip hop producer have earned her a living since 1989 (ten years). A success, not of the magnitude of say Missy Elliott, but noteworthy given the masculinist evaluations of women's abilities in technical, precise, and rationale work, such as producing or engineering music. As rap became the most commodifiable constituent of hip hop, performance went from face-to-face interaction in parks and clubs to producer based technologies in the studio. As Tricia Rose explains,

> Young women [are] not especially welcome in male social spaces. Today's studios are extremely male dominated spaces where technological discourse merges with a culture of male bonding that inordinately problematizes female apprenticeship ... [having] a serious impact on the contributions of women in contemporary rap production.[15]

As Rachel Raimist gives voice to her subjects, we now turn to give Rachel her voice by ending this chapter with her own thoughts on the possibilities of hip hop culture to carry oppositional weight in its art, practices, representations and performances against the homogenizing, hyper-masculine and half-hearted versions of hip hop too frequently in wider circulation.

INTERVIEW WITH RACHEL RAIMIST, JANUARY 2005

In your documentary you chose to explore not only the role of the MC, as many hip hop analyses focus upon, but the major components of hip hop including the domestic sphere. Please discuss how this was a conscious choice or not.

Raimist: The idea for the film went through many manifestations. Initially, I wanted to make the film about women in hip hop tracing the history of women, across elements, and filming as many women nationally and internationally as I could gain access to. Funding was low, both of my parents were dying of cancer, and I became pregnant, all during the process of filming and trying to edit *Nobody*. So I made some hard choices and decided that I would feature the women who I felt shared their stories most honestly and intimately. I wanted to represent a woman from each element— rapping, b-girling, DJing and graffti art—but I had difficulty accessing graffiti artists who would or could (because of the legal issues involved) share their story. I also consciously chose to focus on women like Lisa, the hip hop wife and mother, who most people wouldn't necessarily claim as 'a woman in hip hop.' I interviewed a woman who was the girlfriend of a famous DJ, I interviewed women label reps and radio hosts, but chose to share Lisa's story because it was a model for hip hop mothering that I had not yet seen, and was seeking myself because I was pregnant while making the film. I did have access to more mainstream, commercial artists. I filmed Foxy Brown performing at the House of Blues in Los Angeles, and I filmed Lauryn Hill doing radio and in-store appearances on the day her Miseducation album came out. I had access and was often paid to film famous rap women, but in all of that work I only saw prepared 'my album shows I've really grown as an artist' type answers. I felt there was something plastic and performative, even rehearsed, about their responses. I felt it was much more important to tell the stories that don't make it onto BET and MTV. I chose to tell stories that I had not heard told publicly outside of my circle of friends in New York and LA underground hip hop scenes.

Please speak about the intersections of being a Puerto Rican woman, a filmmaker in the hip hop genre, and a producer concerned with the distribution and reception of your documentary at venues such as the Hip Hop Film Festival. What happens in these community settings, if anything, in terms of Nobody's *gendered perspective?*

Raimist: I see identity politics as strictly tactical. I deploy facets of my own identity in particular spaces to work for my larger goal of feminist praxis moving toward a more just society. I was born to a Puerto Rican mother and a Russian Jewish father. I am not Jewish and speak only in broken Spanglish. I have experienced many instances of the assumption of me being Black (via email and telephone requests for Black History Month events) because hip hop is often considered Black culture. When the requesting organizers hear my response of being Puerto Rican with light skin privilege, the offers are often withdrawn or re-scheduled for Women's Month events. At the same time on panels different Black activists like Davey D claim Puerto Ricans as part of the African and Afro-Caribbean diasporas. On a panel at the University of California, Berkeley he said, 'Rachel, you're

Puerto Rican and you're Black, I claim you.' It is an important move within hip hop to document the contributions of Puerto Ricans who were part of the foundation and ongoing contributions to hip hop culture. New York Ricans from the *Hip Hop Zone* by Raquel Rivera and *From Bomba to Hip Hop* by Juan Flores are important contributions to work about Puerto Ricans in hip hop. Both fortunately and unfortunately, *Nobody* has become the one token film about women. In the hip hop film festival circuits as well as at Women's Studies and feminist events, *Nobody* functions as the token women's film or the token 'women-of-color' film. It is important to have women represented in hip hop's larger cultural sphere, but why is a film made a number of years ago still one of the few hip hop films about women's experiences? While I am pleased to have my work included and appreciated in many spaces, it seems difficult to move past the additive tokenism models, still today. I believe that it is important to state that this is not the all-encompassing film about women in hip hop and it was not meant to be (except in its initial conception in my brainstorming phase). I hope instead that it continues to be a springboard for women who want to make movies, despite any obstacles they face. I hope that more films are produced that discuss women's experiences and contributions in hip hop. I often get emails from women with ideas for films but rarely do I ever get copies of finished material. There are so many reasons for this—funding limitations, access to resources, skill level, confidence, and many others. If I, a broke, pregnant college student with a credit card and a dream can do it, anyone can.

Nobody *focuses on a specific subcultural sphere in relation to gender while generally dismissing other potential forms of gendered resistance such as artists negotiating the mainstream that often forms the topic of hip hop feminist analyses. This could be seen as a prescriptive feminist model, one that rejects the direct manipulations of sexuality by female artists at work in a different cultural sphere, and even suppresses women's sexuality overall in a manner similar to the feminist movement's battles around women's sexual agency. What do you think of feminist work which reads for feminist agency in mainstream hip hop/rap? How do you understand the relation of that public discourse to the community discourse reflected in* Nobody?

Raimist: I didn't set out to make a film about women in hip hop as a necessarily 'prescriptive feminist model,' I simply wanted to see my life and my experiences represented on-screen. The women in *Nobody* don't necessarily consider themselves feminist, which I do (now). I am in a Feminist Studies PhD program trying to sort out what that really means. Honestly, on many days I'm frustrated by the discipline—about who and what counts as feminist, what is considered 'good' or 'useful' feminist theory; and what it means to have a degree program in Feminist Studies. Considering the racism within women's movements and in academia today, it becomes even more

frustrating. I find that with time many programs and departments struggle
with the professionalization of Women's Studies as a field of study. The
whole system of academia—the acceptable ways of producing knowledge
(printing only in 5-star refereed journals that count for tenure, etc) seems to
gate-keep what types of knowledges and what kind of knowledge producers
'count.' Every day I find that I fight and resist being disciplined by the
discipline. While I understand and see the value in 'feminist work which
reads for feminist agency' in mainstream rap, I do find it problematic that
the only mainstream rap woman that has named and claimed herself as a
feminist is Lil' Kim (in a *NY Post* article). Most mainstream rappers can
only be concerned with sales, marketing and image, that is the nature of
being a mainstream, commercial artist. It is valuable to seek readings of
feminist agency, but it also needs to be considered why most hip hop women,
including those in my film, do not name and claim themselves as feminist.

*What about female sexuality in this subcultural sphere, it is a topic conspicuously
absent from* Nobody *except to reject its popular manifestations, is this
purposeful or not, why or why not? How do the artists of* Nobody, *if they do,
conceive of their sexuality in relation to their artistry? How did you perceive
it as the filmmaker?*

Raimist: I made a conscious choice to exclude sexuality from the film. At
the time the film was made the Lil' Kim/Foxy empowering or embarrassing
arguments were the most frequent discussions about women in hip hop.
Similarly, the rumors about the lesbian rappers that still prevail today were
the means by which many within the hip hop community would discount
and discredit women rappers. I wanted to share some stories of hip hop
womanhood that aren't necessitated on sexual preference or sexuality. The
film was shot at a time where strippers and pimp culture began to dominate
industry functions. At least one of the main characters in the film is bi-sexual,
worked for many years as a stripper, and has hosted adult parties, but the
same way the L-word gets deployed to discredit commercial rappers, many
do the same to this woman. I didn't want her to be the 'sexually deviant'
example; I wanted her to shine for her artistry. This film was made for hip
hop women like me—women who have loved and lived hip hop. I wasn't
concerned with meeting the needs of feminist theorists or assisting with
feminist readings of hip hop, but rather, to tell my own story without turning
the camera on myself. I worked in the hip hop industry as a videographer
and photographer, and with my daughter's father, ran a street marketing
and promotions company. I was disgusted by the atmosphere at industry
functions, namely the way to get a record played on the radio—to entertain
radio DJs at strip clubs, and the eye candy dominating the stages at rap
concerts and in rap videos in heavy rotation. My goal was not to expose or
interrogate something that was already overexposed and continues to be, but

rather my desire was to simply share stories of women in hip hop who live hip hop not for money or fame but because it is what flows in their blood.

We state that your film is 'richly content-driven, under-produced, [with] gritty aesthetics.' Why is this the case? To reflect the aesthetics of organic communities and individual stories on the screen? Or more practical considerations such as production costs etc?

Raimist: *Nobody Knows My Name* is a no budget documentary, financed on credit cards, shot entirely hand-held by a pregnant woman who balanced the camera on her stomach. I chose to film hand-held because aesthetically I wanted it to look 'real' and in opposition to the flossy, glossy images of Hype Williams and MTV rap videos. I chose to conduct interviews by myself or with one friend in the room to reach as intimate conversations as possible. I chose to not use effects or special titles. I especially didn't want fake graffiti titles, what I feel is a constructed MTV aesthetic. I had no budget and no frills, but I feel like I shared a lot of truth and honesty.

Was the decision to have a segment on the business of hip hop a forethought or something that emerged from the interviews themselves? What is your experience as a cultural producer in an industry that is notorious for its racialized and gendered relations, in both production and representation (i.e. the politics of making this film for you: finance, distribution, contract, editorial control)?

Raimist: Including women working in the music business was always part of the vision for the film. I conducted extensive interviews with female label executives but I did not feel like I could get past the mask of performance, meaning, 'I developed this marketing plan,' 'I helped X artist sell records.' I cut those to a minimum. They are included in a limited way because they help to structure and explain what is at the background of every discussion about hip hop, the commercialization and commodification of the culture and its practitioners. As a woman who had literally been living behind an industry man (my daughter's father and partner of ten years worked for Jive Records), running his street marketing and promotions company, managing his street team, writing proposals and retail reports. I did all of this while trying to go to school and make my films. I felt tired of being a nameless woman, called 'his girl' or 'the girl with the camera' but never known by name. I've found, in my ten years of hip hop industry work that behind every 'successful' artist (rapper, b-boy, poet, artist), there is always someone, typically a woman (a wife, girlfriend, mother, sister or cousin), who is running the show. Whether as mother-manager, as head of the day-to-day household raising the children, or as the one who handles the paperwork, most hip hop operations have a woman that no one sees or hears, literally running everything behind the scenes. Many audience members responded, 'Who is she? She isn't a woman in hip hop,' but I absolutely disagree. It is the stories of the most overlooked, most discounted and the most ignored, that I am most interested in sharing with the world. I chose to distribute the video with Women Make Movies, a feminist educational distributor, rather than a large DVD distributor that could sell the film in nationwide chain retailers. I was offered a substantial deal by a very large distributor who actually joked with me about the irony of a company like his signing a deal for a film like mine. The acquisitions VP said, 'I think your hip hop women work is really important and I will put it out, but let's be real, it's no money-maker, and it's funny that it is the profits from my porno department that will fund this.' I declined that distribution deal, and a number of others. Instead, I went back to school getting a PhD in Feminist Studies at the University of Minnesota. Even though financially I am not rewarded, I find much value in getting film to hip hop community and students, and feel a sense of accomplishment when I get my sales statement that says that Harvard, Berkeley, Stanford, NYU, and many, many other colleges and universities have purchased my film.

If you were to make the film today what would be different and why in terms of representation, images and financing/distribution. How much of that is your own artistic development, and how much is it because of hip hop's position in a different historical moment?

Raimist: I would love to make another film about women in hip hop having each woman keep video diaries and share footage they shoot or have had shot of their lives. I think it would be really interesting and valuable to see how each tells their stories and what they deem important. I would still do interviews with each to intercut, but only after I've viewed the footage they've shot of themselves. It would also be nice to have a gathering—a dinner, discussion, and performances—of the women together. *Nobody* really sparked a lot of community building and connective spaces for me, for women in the film, and among audience members. I think it would be beautiful to see this element represented within the film as well. Now that I've traveled extensively with the film, I've been connected into this larger community of hip hop women artists, activists, journalists, and scholars. People like Cristina Verán, Toni Blackmon, the Anomalies Crew, Kuttin' Kandi, Sisterz of the Underground, Mystic, Bahamadia, and Jean Grae, would all be included if I were to shoot the film today. Maybe some 'larger,' more mainstream artists would be included, if and only if they would shed some of the layers of masks they wear for mainstream audiences. For example, I would love to film Rah Digga, the only female member of the Flip Mode Squad, who has a baby with Young Zee of the Outsiderz (a less commercially successful rapper). If she were to allow me into her home, to see her as a mother and as a girlfriend, in addition to sharing stories about her music career, I would love that. All in all, if I did it again, I would still tell the stories of the struggling, underrepresented, and the unknown women in hip hop.

NOTES

1. Men tend to dominate each element of hip hop's constituent cultural practices of MCing, breakdancing, graffiti writing and DJing, but women have always been part of the culture's creative dynamic. In its earliest days, women were central to the public performance of not only rap but hip hop culture. Women graffiti artists included Lady Pink, Lady Heart, Charmin, Barbara 62, Eva 62, and Stoney. Female rappers stretched back to the late 1970s and early 80s from Real Roxanne, Baby Love, Jazzy Joyce to Roxanne Shanté. In 1980, Lady B's 'To the Beat, Y'All' was the first rap recording by a solo female. The Sequences were the first female group to record. After Salt-N-Pepa gained unprecedented mainstream success in the mid 1980s, they have been followed by, amongst others: MC Lyte, Queen Latifah, Yo-Yo, Da Brat, Boss, Eve, Mary J. Blige, Lil' Kim, Foxy Brown, Sarah Jones, Rah Digga, and Missy Elliott. See: Nancy Guevara, 'Women Writin' Rappin' Breakin',' in William Eric Perkins (ed.), *Dropping Science* (Philadelphia: Temple University Press, 1995). Tricia Rose, *Black Noise: Rap Music and Black Culture in Contemporary America* (Middletown, CT: Wesleyan University Press, 1994); Gwendolyn Pough, *Check It While I Wreck It: Black Womanhood, Hip Hop Culture and the Black Public Sphere* (Boston: North Eastern University Press, 2004).

2. Gwendolyn Pough uses the rhetoric of 'bringing wreck' to examine how Black women's discourses and practices in hip hop have troubled dominant masculine discourses, given publicity to women in the public sphere, and even influenced the broader U.S. imaginary.

3. Guevara, 'Women Writin' Rappin' Breakin',' p. 51. B-girls were initially girls and young women who breakdanced. In more recent parlance it refers to a broader social and cultural allegiance to 'represent' hip hop as a lived culture.

4. Kyra Gaunt, 'The Musical Vernacular of Black Girl's Play,' in Murray Forman and Mark Anthony Neal (eds), *That's the Joint!* (New York: Routledge, 2004), p. 261.

5. See Mark Anthony Neal's exhaustive study of the Black musical counter publics. Mark Anthony Neal, *What the Music Said: Black Popular Music and Black Public Culture* (New York: Routledge, 2002). See also Pough's extensive corrective to the silencing and invisibility of Black women's voices in hip hop which is important because 'Black women's speech and expressive culture have been limited in the public sphere due in part to circumstances ... such as maintaining community, promoting Black manhood at the expense of Black womanhood, and constantly vindicating Black women against misrepresentation'; *Check It While I Wreck It*, p. 79.

6. The title *The Miseducation of Lauryn Hill* riffs off a searing critique of race in America, Carter G. Woodson's *The Mis-Education of the Negro* (Washington, D.C.: Associated Publishers, 1933; reprint, Trenton, NJ: Africa World Press Inc., 1990). The title, *Nobody Knows My Name* culls from the experience and song of one of the featured subjects, rapper T-Love. As she explains in the documentary, after being dropped from her label, everyone who was previously 'jocking' her suddenly acted like she had no name. The title also recalls James Baldwin's collection of essays *Nobody Knows My Name* (1961) whose subjects range from racialized relations in the United States to the role of the writer in society.

7. Raimist is a hip hop feminist filmmaker, scholar, and activist whose work on award-winning feature length documentaries include: *Freestyle* (Best Documentary, Urban World Film Festival, 2000; Best Soundtrack, LA Independent Festival, 2001; and Best Documentary, Woodstock International Film Festival, 2000), *Nobody Knows My Name* (South by Southwest Film Festival selection and Best Documentary, Denver Pan African Film Festival), and *Garbage, Gangsters, and Greed* (Best Documentary, Santa Cruz Environmental Film Festival, 1999). As a rap activist Raimist parlays her academic skills to agitate publicly for social change. She has been featured in *Spin*, *LA Weekly*, *The Village Voice*, and *60 Minutes*, and has written articles in *Urb*, *Source*, and *BLU* magazine. She is

currently working with Melissa Riviere on 'GIRL BE: A Video Survey of Women in Hip-Hop' which is an ongoing film project about the impact and contributions of women to the hip hop movement. The 'B-Girl Be History of Women in Hip Hop' website compiled by Rachel, Miranda Jane, Monalisa Murray and Desdamona is an excellent resource to online magazines, websites and articles featuring women in hip hop: <http://www.intermediaarts.org/pages/programs/b-girl_be/resourcepage.htm>.

8. Cheryl Keyes, 'Empowering Self, Making Choices, Creating Spaces: Black Female Identity via Rap Music Performance,' *Journal of American Folklore*, Vol. 113 (Summer 2000), pp. 255–69.

9. To use Robin Kelley's poignant quip of hip hop's economic engine.

10. In the realm of music, the cultural politics of sexuality in blues has been studied by Hazel Carby and Angela Davis. Carolyn Cooper has turned her acerbic critical gaze to dancehall, and Tricia Rose, Gwendolyn Pough, Joan Morgan, and Cheryl Keyes amongst others, to hip hop.

11. As Pough notes, the burden of representations in the Black community has led to recuperative and remedial forms of stereotypes replacing bad with good ones. In the case of Black women's sexuality she refers to Darlene Hine Clarke's characterization of a 'culture of dissemblance' whereby Black women developed a culture of silencing public displays or discourses about Black women's sexuality in order to counter the stereotypes of them in the general public. The classed and assimilatory impulses of respectable Black womanhood also factor into this orientation.

12. Vibe Books, *Hip Hop Divas* (New York: Three Rivers Press, 2001), p. 18.

13. Pamela Oliveras, 'Women in Graffiti'; available at <http://www.verbalisms.com/content/archives/000019.php>; accessed March 30, 2005.

14. Keyes, 'Making Choices, Creating Spaces.' She bases the emergent categories on interviews by Black women, audience members, and music critics, as observed through recorded performances and interviews. Greg Demetrius argues that to perceive rap music as peculiarly and profoundly misogynist distracts from other hyper masculine and misogynist tropes such as 'cock rock,' where 'performers are aggressive, dominating and boastful, and they constantly seek to remind the audience of their prowess, their control.' *Performing Identity/Performing Culture: Hip Hop as Text, Pedagogy, and Lived Practice* (New York: Peter Laing, 2004), p. 24.

15. Rose, *Black Noise*, p. 58.

5
From Azeem to Zion-I: the Evolution of Global Consciousness in Bay Area Hip Hop

Eric K. Arnold

WELCOME TO OAKLAND

It seems a little ironic to be writing an essay celebrating the positivity and diversity of the Bay Area's hip hop scene at a time when newspaper headlines are reporting somberly on the rising murder toll in Oakland, which had reached 110 by December 29, 2002—and will likely escalate before 2003 is more than a few hours old.[1] Looking at a piece of black and white newsprint decorated with the faces of the recently departed—some wide-eyed with hope, others downcast and sinister—it's impossible to escape the fact that the majority of the deceased were young Black males.

These poor souls were born into the hip hop generation and died amidst a background of all things ghetto—drug deals gone bad, dice games turned ugly, innocent bystanders caught in drive-by shootings, and cases of mistaken identity. Included in each brief obituary is a recounting of the circumstances that led to every murder, or at least as much information as the police were willing to provide to reporters. One 16-year-old was allegedly murdered after one of his friends tried to bum a cigarette from an unidentified man who reacted to the request with gunfire; another man in his 30s was shot to death for asking motorists speeding in a residential district to slow down. Sometimes, the epitaphs are vague and sketchy. Alongside a photo of a dreadlocked fellow who earned a listing as homicide #29, it is said, 'police were not sure what the dispute was about.'[2] All we know of this individual is his age (21) and the fact that he lived on 55th Street in North Oakland— ironically, the same neighborhood once occupied by Merritt Junior College, where the Black Panther Party had been founded, 26 years earlier.[3]

Occasionally, the newspaper clips have provided some details on the areas where the murders took place. One West Oakland 'hood, called Dogtown, is described as 'an area known for its heavy concentration of drug dealing.'[4] Other killings happened on street corners, outside liquor stores, in parked cars, and in one instance, via shots fired into a family home during a holiday party. While the homicides were fairly well-spread out throughout the city, the heaviest concentration of killings in 2002 took place in the inner city turf of East Oakland, a low-income, predominantly Black-and-Latino area with a hard knock reputation. Back in 1995, Oakland rap group Black Dynasty described the ghetto lifestyle in the song 'Deep East Oakland'[5] where the 'deep east' is described as the 'killing fields' where the informal economy of drug dealing undergirds the local economy of the 'block' in 'cokeland.'

As seen through the eyes of Black Dynasty, life in East Oakland represents the underside of the so-called 'ghetto fabulous' lifestyle espoused by mainstream rappers and marketed wholesale to suburban America. But there's nothing too fabulous about living in an economically depressed area whose residents are both severely under-educated and severely under-employed. Casual drug use comes with the territory, as do violent conflicts over control of drug turf and incarceration. In this socio-economic context, desperation begets crime, often resulting in tragic consequences. It's an eye-opener to realize that for the victims of the Oakland streets, their participation in the public sphere, Black or otherwise, has been reduced to a meaningless statistic. It's even more unsettling that even as BET and MTV videos show gangstafied ballers cavorting with skimpily clad hotties, it's much more probable that the pursuit of thug life will lead not to platinum plaques and 'hood riches, but to unsolved case files and mournful funerals.

Like most similar inner-cities in the United States, if not the world, East Oakland is a veritable parade of ethnic and social stereotypes—there you will find ghetto superstars, crack whores, and welfare recipients, along with single parents, families with children, and elderly homeowners. It may not be surprising to some to learn that East Oakland was also the infamous patrol zone of 'The Riders'—disgraced police officers fired amidst allegations of falsifying arrest reports and widespread brutality. But that's not to say nothing positive has come out of East Oakland. In the last two decades, the region has served as a breeding ground for numerous hip hop artists—metaphorical roses that grew through the cracks in the concrete, to paraphrase Tupac Shakur.

This artistic push coming from the bowels of the ghetto has many parallels to the phenomenal cultural movement that took place in the South Bronx, hip hop's folkloric birthplace—a place not unlike East Oakland in character and appearance. In the intro to *Yes Yes Y'all,* Nelson George writes, 'The Bronx ... became the symbol of all that ailed us.'[6] He goes on to note the median family income in the South Bronx was 40 percent less than the rest of New York; that there were 6,000 abandoned buildings and 13,000 suspicious fires in 'one pivotal year' (1975) which earned landlords over $10 million in insurance settlements while leaving 10,000 people homeless; and that drug dealing and crime were as common as baby formula and diapers. George also points out that the South Bronx was the home of drug kingpin Nicky Barnes, who served as inspiration for the Nino Brown character in the film *New Jack City*—as did Felix Mitchell, Barnes' East Oakland counterpart.

Just as the South Bronx produced the youth-oriented culture which would become hip hop, East Oakland's indigenous inner city birthed a local music scene, inspired by criminal-minded street life, which would become a blueprint for the sub-genre known as gangsta rap. Over the years, East Oakland has been identified with lyrically explicit artists like the Luniz, Dru Down, Richie Rich, and Keak the Sneak, individuals who literally grew up on street corners. The area was also the stomping grounds of all-world graffiti icon Mike 'Dream' Francisco—a prolific, talented Filipino-American graffiti writer, muralist, and tattoo artist who was tragically murdered in Oakland in 1999.[7]

The most celebrated hip hopper to come out of East Oakland, however, is Todd Shaw, aka $ir Too $hort, who as of this writing has accumulated more gold and platinum recordings than any other rap artist in history. Shaw started rapping in the early 1980s, not long after the SugarHill Gang's influential 1979 single 'Rapper's Delight' became the first rap song to break nationwide. As a teenager growing up in East Oakland during the first wave of what became the crack cocaine epidemic, Shaw was surrounded by drug dealers, playas, and ballers. Graduating from midnight recording sessions in his basement, Shaw and his cohort Freddie B began making personalized rap tapes for the local clientele, singing their praises like ghetto griots.

In an interview conducted for *Source* magazine in 2001, Shaw recalled, 'We just went down to one of the little drug turfs where they sell the dope and started selling (tapes) ... We'd do a customized thing for you, where we'd put your name in it and talk about your neighborhood, your car, your kid, or your girl, whatever you wanted in it, and we'd put in there for you.'[8]

The environmental backdrop against which Shaw's rap sagas were played out was, to paraphrase Kurtis Blow, as tough as the local NFL football team the Oakland Raiders.[9] Organized drug gangs ran the streets, leaving behind an all-too-familiar wake of dead bodies, broken promises, and cracked-out dreams. During the course of three successive Republican Administrations in the 1980s and early 90s, Oakland homicides 'hovered around 150,' peaking with a record 175 killings in 1992, before declining during the Clinton years, according to the *San Francisco Chronicle*.[10] Yet in the midst of all the violence being enacted on the streets, an indigenous Oakland rap scene spearheaded by Too $hort inspired artists in other cities within a 50-mile radius of Oakland to follow their example and make their own self-produced, self-distributed variations on hip hop.

Shaw's 1985 single 'Girl (That's Your Life)' wasn't the first rap song to come out of the Bay Area—an obscure dude by the name of Motorcycle Mike is usually given credit for that—but for all intents and purposes, $hort's debut on wax ushered in a new era of independent Bay Area rap artists, who were influenced by the world around them as much as by hip hop coming from other regions. Five years after Too $hort released 'Girl,' an underground hip hop scene had germinated, it seemed, in every Bay Area city with a large Black population. Everywhere you looked, people were putting out their own rap music, selling tapes 'out the trunk' à la Too $hort or on consignment at indie-friendly retail outlets like T's Wauzi in

Oakland or Leopold in Berkeley. In 1990, one could count Vallejo's E-40, the Click, Khayree and The Mac; Richmond's Calvin T and Magic Mike; San Francisco's I.M.P. and Paris; Hayward's Spice One; and Oakland's MC Pooh, Digital Underground, and MC Hammer among the many Bay Area artists who were putting out successful singles, tapes, EPs, and albums on independent labels.

By and large, originality has been the engine that powered the Bay Area indie hip hop scene. For instance, E-40's influences include Too $hort and Calvin T, but his unique rapid-fire slang expositions are all his own. Similarly, all three of the Vallejo 'Macs' produced by Khayree—The Mac, Mac Dre, and Mac Mall—sounded different from each other. And while San Francisco rappers Paris and RBL Posse both took a hardcore approach to rap, their rhymes sounded nothing alike. Paris spoke of political conspiracies and referenced the Black Panthers, while RBL outlined the struggle for survival in the inner city and celebrated marijuana use as a cure for ghetto ills.

Interestingly, San Francisco, the most populous city in the region, didn't really develop its own hip hop identity until the mid 90s. Although Paris notched a gold record with 1990's *The Devil Made Me Do It*, the Frisco rap scene didn't really take off until the underground funk of RBL Posse and JT the Bigga Figga and the smooth playa-isms of Rappin' 4-Tay rose to prominence. 'As far as San Francisco, there were other people doing it, but we were the first outta Hunters Point,' RBL's Black C recalled in an interview. At first, he says, 'Everybody was happy with somebody just saying Hunters Point on the mic.' Yet RBL's unexpected success—they sold over 100,000 copies of the single 'Don't Give Me No Bammer Weed' and over 200,000 units of the album *Ruthless by Law*, both of which came out on Oakland indie label In-A-Minute—inspired others around San Francisco and the Bay to do their own thing. According to Black C, when ''94–'95 came, you started seeing a lot more independent record companies coming out ... the independent thing was popping.'[11]

However, the biggest concentration of Bay Area underground rap artists have been clustered around Oakland, which has remained at the center of the region's hip hop scene as it has developed into what it is today. The hardcore environment of the inner city ghetto played a role in shaping Oakland rap, but the city's remarkable multicultural diversity was also a factor. Although San Francisco is generally thought of as more international than its cousin across the Bay Bridge, over 57 languages are spoken in Oakland, which has long been home to a melting pot of Asian, African, Hispanic/Latin, and European communities.

High murder toll or not, it would be a misconception to label all Oakland hip hop as gangsta-oriented. By 1993, the Oakland sound included the playaristic rhymes of Too $hort, the inner city blues of Spice One, Digital Underground's engaging mix of party-oriented material and social commentary, MC Hammer's rated-PG MTV anthems, and the ultra-lyrical approach of the

Hieroglyphics crew. The Oakland urban music scene also stretched into R&B territory, with acts like En Vogue and Tony Toni Tone updating vocal styles gleaned from the Black church and juke joints with the modern big beats ubiquitous to hip hop. Since then, Oakland artists have branched out into almost every urban subgenre imaginable, from the conscious sentiments of Zion-I, the Coup and Company of Prophets to the neo-punk alternative hip hop of Anticon to the urgent emotion-grabbing material of neo-soul acts Goapele and D'Wayne Wiggins to Cat 5's laptop electronica and the new school turntablism of DJ crew the Oakland Faders.

As Oakland hip hop has embraced cultural diversity, so too have hip hop artists in other Bay Area cities. While you can still find people making music today similar to what was coming out of the region ten or 15 years ago, it is no longer possible to easily characterize the Bay Area as possessing just one type of hip hop or urban music sound. Nowadays, cities like Richmond are home to both the street-level observations of Lil' Ric and the socio-political commentary of Rico Pabon (Prophets of Rage); San Francisco hip hop includes rappers from the blood-stained streets of Fillmore and Hunters Point, as well as the innovative progressive jazz trio Livehuman, who add DJ Quest's turntables to a drum and upright bass combo. It's fairly evident that throughout the Bay Area, rap is no longer just a Black thing: thugged-out Caucasian rapper Woodie hails from the sleepy North Bay suburb of Antioch, Filipino turntable legend Q-Bert resides in Daly City, and Berkeley is the home base of multicultural crew Bay Area Art Collective. As Oakland rap legend Richie Rich told *Source*, 'you could have two (people) that live next door to each other, but they don't dress the same. Everybody be on they own little shit, but they all represent the Bay that's in 'em.'[12]

THE MUSICAL ROOTS OF BAY AREA HIP HOP

The evolution of the Bay Area hip hop sound didn't happen overnight. In fact, the region has always had its own distinct cultural flavor, going back to the Barbary Coast days of the late nineteenth century. From a musical standpoint, much of the early Bay Area hip hop differed from the jazz fusion and James Brown breakbeats typically identified with old school New York rap. Instead, the Bay Area's emphasis was on minimalist funk with hard snares and heavy bass, basically music that sounded fresh emanating from car stereos. Regional variations existed from city to city as well. The slow-rolling, Parliament-influenced beats of Too $hort's producers Al Eaton and Ant Banks differed from the somewhat more uptempo, keyboard-saturated 'mobb music' made by Vallejo architects Khayree Shaheed, Mike Mosley, and Studio Ton. Other variations on Bay Area hardcore rap were created in cities like Richmond, East Palo Alto, and San Mateo.

In the Bay Area, the practice of sampling was certainly less extensive than on the East Coast, whose hip hop sound leaned heavily on SP-1200

digital sampling units and 808 drum machines. In 1988, Al Eaton replayed
the riff from Average White Band's 'Schoolboy Crush' for Too $hort's 'Life
Is ... Too $hort,' a break which had previously been sampled on records
by NY rap groups X-Clan and Eric B & Rakim. Eaton's track ended up
sounding distinctly different—it's arguably 'warmer' and funkier—from the
other songs which had looped the same break. Other Bay Area producers
experimented with both sampling and live music, honing their own signature
sound in the process. Vallejo-based producer Khayree, for instance, looped
Prince's 'D.M.S.R.' on The Mac's 1990 single 'The Game Is Thick,' and
snagged a snippet of Chaka Khan demanding 'tell me something good' on
Mac Dre's 1992 boulevard anthem 'Too Hard For The Fuckin' Radio.' Yet
a scant year later, he was crafting tracks laid with original guitar, keyboard
and bass parts, like Mac Mall's 1993 hit 'Sic Wit Tis.'

The judicious use of live instrumentation, along with the distinctive
Bay Area slang phrases that found their ways into the mouths of rappers,
suggested that the region wasn't just imitating what was coming out of
New York, but putting its own twist on hip hop. And while East Coast hip
hop became more homogenized as major labels got into the game, because
the Bay Area was dominated by independent labels, it was subject to fewer
pressures as to how it should sound, which resulted in widespread creativity
and innovation. The practice of utilizing live musical instrumentation, both
in the studio and in concert, continues to be a staple of Bay Area hip hop to
this day, even if it's since become more identified with more commercially-
successful artist-producers like DJ Quik and Dr. Dre and Grammy-winning
Philadelphia group The Roots.

Speaking of roots, it's fairly significant that two of the mainstays of the
early Bay Area hip hop scene, Khayree and Eaton, both started out in the
West Coast funk bands of the late 1970s. Eaton was a guitar player known as
'Big Baby Jesus' who often appeared on stage wearing a diaper (an obvious
nod to P-Funk's Gary Shider). Khayree, on the other hand, jammed with
various local funk groups as a bass player and was an apprentice of Felton
Pilate, the musical director of Vallejo outfit Con Funk Shun, before playing
a seminal role in two pioneering Bay Area rap labels: Strictly Business and
Young Black Brotha.

The Bay Area's funk legacy, a tremendous stylistic influence on the region's
hip hop sound, goes all the way back to the late 1960s, when Sly and the
Family Stone paved a new direction in Black music. Sly's mix of rock,
boogaloo, soul, R&B and even White-identified pop music (he covered Doris
Day's 'Que Sera, Sera') helped to create what would later be called funk and
reportedly inspired both Herbie Hancock's *Headhunters* (who recorded a
song called 'Sly') and Miles Davis' visionary, prescient *On the Corner* LP.
Besides Sly, some of the more notable Bay Area funkateers included Larry
Graham, the inventor of the 'slap' bassline; Shuggie Otis, the composer of
'Strawberry Letter 23' and a big influence on Prince; Con Funk Shun; and

Tower of Power, a multiracial East Bay-based group remembered for their powerful horn section and the local anthem 'Oakland Stroke.'[13]

EVERYBODY STROKE

With its solid Black community, anchored in Oakland (at the time one of the largest predominantly African-American cities in the country) as well as San Francisco's Fillmore district, the Bay Area was a huge market for national acts like Parliament, Roger Troutman and Zapp, the Ohio Players, Lakeside, and L.T.D., who could count on enthusiastic audiences whenever they toured. Throughout the 1970s, less-heralded local funk bands could also be found in every corner of the Bay Area, jamming at dive bars and clubs that had originally served the thriving blues scene of the 1940s, 50s, and 60s.

In a previously unpublished interview, Khayree recalled:

From '72 to '78 was the era of funk bands. So you had cities like Oakland, Vallejo, San Francisco. San Francisco had Grand Theft, Vallejo had Con Funk Shun, of course, earlier than that, (there was) Sly Stone. You had individuals that were musicians, sort of how you have MCs today. Their craft was the drums or the congas or singing or the bass guitar or the guitar. This was right before hip hop, when all the clubs would have live bands.[14]

Years after the fact, politically conscious Oakland rap group the Coup paid tribute to the 1970s funk era by sampling a live recording of Parliament singing 'Oakland, do you wanna ride?'[15] on the Bay Area classic 'Me and Jesus the Pimp in a '79 Grenada Last Night.' The song is as good an example of hip hop storytelling as anything Slick Rick has released. It also represents a discernible link between Oakland's legendary pimp culture, funk music, and the hip hop generation, symbolized by Boots Riley's narrator, an impressionable youngster whose mother is said to be Jesus the Pimp's 'number one hoe.'[16]

The groove-oriented dance beats and futuristic image of funk music also resonated with the many West Coast poppers, lockers, and boogaloo crews of that time, whose role in the region's emerging urban youth culture was not unlike the b-boys who danced to Kool Herc's breakbeats in the old school days of East Coast hip hop. Years before 'Rapper's Delight' would initiate hip hop's recorded era, Parliament's 'Flashlight' inspired teams of boogalooers to create routines based around the seemingly mechanical movements of the 'robot' dance—a West Coast phenomenon which became an essential element in the pop-locker's bag of tricks. This background came in handy during the early 1980s, when Afrika Bambaataa's 'Planet Rock' and the Jonzun Crew's 'Space Is The Place' followed George Clinton's 'Atomic Dog' in quick succession. Although nominally an R&B record, 'Atomic Dog' was built around a techno-funk beat, which made it a stylistic precedent for what would become hip hop. Similarly, 'Planet Rock' and 'Space Is The Place' were uptempo electro-funk jams that followed the P-Funk mothership into the rhythmic cosmos.

For whatever reason, these early hip hop and proto hip hop songs enjoyed tremendous popularity among West Coast teenagers. Young Blacks, Asians, Latinos, and even those of Caucasian ancestry gravitated toward the electronic drums and slickly syncopated rhythms, in the same fashion that teenagers in the 1950s went crazy over rock'n'roll. The electro-funk records of the early 1980s quickly led to a regional variant created by California-based groups like the Egyptian Lover, Uncle Jamm's Army, the World Class Wreckin' Cru (featuring a young, sequin-suit wearing Dr. Dre) and Newcleus, whose biggest hit, 1984's 'Jam On It,' mixed sped-up vocals with (at the time) state-of-the-art beats while telling the story of an erstwhile funk-o-naught named Cosmo D who, like the SugarHill Gang, battled Superman on wax.

Yet with a few notable exceptions—like MC Hammer's massive 1986 club hit 'Ring 'Em,' which clocked in at a cardiac-pumping 120 beats per minute—Bay Area hip hop preferred it slow and low over fast and furious. A few uptempo numbers can be found among Too $hort's early material, but the song that pushed him to national recognition, 1987's 'Freaky Tales,' was molasses-paced, the better to hear every salacious rhyme and absorb the full impact of every bottomless bass boom. The song was an unrepentant ghetto anthem replete with 'freaky tales. The song also captivated middle-class kids, some of whom hid their Too $hort cassettes under their beds so not to raise the ire of their morally concerned parents.[17]

THUG MARTYR: TUPAC SHAKUR

In 1990, Digital Underground, a hip hop collective lead by rapper/pianist Shock G who had scored a Richter scale-shaking hit a year earlier with 'The Humpty Dance,' introduced a young artist who would go on to become the singularly most influential rap icon the world has ever seen. The young artist's name was Tupac Shakur.[18]

Tupac, of course, would go on to multiplatinum success and introduce the phrase 'thug life' before being tragically murdered in Las Vegas in 1996. Many essays, books, and documentaries have analyzed the rapper's impact on popular culture, but they all seem to agree on one point: In many ways, Tupac symbolized the young Black male of the 1990s. At times confused, angry, emotional, and troubled, at others brilliant, prolific and intense, Tupac's inner turmoil reflected what African-American men between the ages of 16 and 30 as a whole were going through, speaking volumes about the state of American society in the process.

It's well known that Tupac, who was born in New York, but moved to the Bay Area while a teenager, came from a family who had been deeply involved in the Black Panther Party. For all his gangsta bravado, Tupac was well-steeped in the revolutionary ideologies of Huey P. Newton, Bobby Seale, Eldridge Cleaver, and Fred Hampton, a connection that many of his gangsta contemporaries did not share. Parallels can also be drawn between Tupac and Lil' Bobby Hutton, a member of the Oakland Black Panthers shot to death by police in 1969.[19] Lil' Bobby Hutton never made it out of his teens—he was only 18 when he died—while Tupac never saw his 30s. Yet each was committed to being a soldier in the struggle for survival, Tupac's 'Ambitions As Ah Ridah' aside.

Tupac was far from the only rap artist to be inspired by the Panthers—a list that includes everyone from N.W.A.'s Eazy-E to Paris to Boots Riley of the Coup to Public Enemy's Chuck D to KRS-One—but he was one of the most resolute when it came to self-determination. While Chuck D symbolically relived George Jackson's ill-fated, controversial escape attempt[20] and N.W.A. shouted 'fuck the police,'[21] Tupac flung himself headlong into armed confrontations with cops, showing that he was a man of action as well as rhetoric.

Since his death, Tupac has become an international martyr, a symbol on the level of Bob Marley or Che Guevara, whose life has inspired Tupacistas on the streets of Brazil, memorial murals in the Bronx and Spain, and bandanna-wearing youth gangs in South Africa. Tupac also unwittingly charted the course for the mainstreaming of thug rap, via act-alikes like Ja Rule, DMX, Master P, and Krazy, whose Soundscan tallies owe much to Tupac's distinctive cadences and his 'down for whatever' attitude. Few, if any of these artists have the depth of character or the poignancy of Tupac, but that's another story.

But while Tupac and similar gangsta-themed artists have dominated rap on both an underground and commercial level in the last five years, thugs, playas and hustlas present only one dimension of Bay Area rap. The other side of the cultural coin, as it were, draws its inspiration from such sources as literate, middle-class bohemianism, japanimation, children's fairytales, grassroots activism, spoken word poetry, and artistic improvisation.

'Dank,' the potent strain of cannabis indica that originated in the Bay Area, remains a visible link between thugged-out Bay Area crews and those of a more intellectual variety. However, it would be inaccurate to assume that every member of the hip hop generation in the Bay Area can be found spinning doughnuts at illegal sideshows in the streets of Deep East Oakland. For example, Tajai Massey, a member of Souls of Mischief (one of the groups under the Hieroglyphics umbrella) worked as a teacher before he had a record out and has remained involved in education, even while pursuing an entertainment career.

Currently a substitute teacher in the Oakland public school system, Massey feels that the lack of consciousness in much of today's rap music has contributed to the social ills besetting Oakland's Black community. He goes so far as to speculate that the situation could be part of a wider conspiracy.

> Why is the murder rate increasing? All the hip hop now is not educating you. When we came out, there was (the) Stop The Violence (movement). In the Bay Area, you gotta look at it, like, ever since the Panthers was here, it's been a conscious effort to destroy the Black community out here. How is it that we're in a city of 300,000 people and we got a murder rate like this? How is it that crack comes from here? I can go get a fully automatic weapon right now, know what I'm saying?[22]

However, Massey remains optimistic about the possibility that hip hop could be a solution to poor attendance and declining test scores at the elementary school level. According to Massey, 'The problems are deeper than what hip hop can fix, but hip hop can play a part' in reaching students deemed unreachable by the education system.

Teren Jones, aka Del tha Funkee Homosapien, another Hieroglyphics crew member, happens to be the cousin of LA gangsta icon Ice Cube, and penned the fan favorite 'A Gangsta's Fairytale,' from Cube's first solo album, *Amerikkka's Most Wanted*. He currently lives in East Bay suburb El Cerrito, but grew up in Oakland, which would seem to make him no different from the legion of 'game-related' O-town rappers. Yet over the course of four solo albums, a Hieroglyphics group album and two well-received alternative hip hop-themed projects with producer Dan 'The Automator' Nakamura, Jones has eschewed being 'hard,' instead carving out his own unique style of abstract imagery, often influenced by science fiction and Japanese animation.

Jones appeared as alter-ego Deltron-Z, a cybernetic rhyme-sayer living in a post-apocalyptic thirtieth-century world, on 2001's *Deltron 3030* album, a project which appealed not only to hip hop fans, but also to aficionados of other alternative music genres, including rock and electronic music. The album bespoke a global, universally relevant consciousness light years away from the predictable bang-bang shoot-'em-up themes which have made the gangsta genre predictable and repetitive. Deltron-Z could easily be a character from a manga (Japanese graphic novel) or anime video; his rhymes are rendered with extreme vividness as he maneuvers around the Automator's techno-futuristic soundscapes, battling computer viruses while reflecting on what it's like to be a robot with a brain.

In an interview, Jones said,

> I get phrases from anime, cause I'm hella into language. Phrases or concepts that I think are interesting. Comic books are good for that too … It stimulates my imagination,

reading comic books, watching cartoons, playing video games, stuff like that. It makes me think a little more imaginatively ... more creatively.[23]

Apart from the Hieroglyphics crew, there are many other examples of clever creativity at work within the Bay Area's underground hip hop scene. Blackalicious, a group composed of MC Gift of Gab and DJ-producer Chief Xcel, existed for almost a decade as an independent outfit, releasing albums on the Solesides and Quannum Projects labels, before signing a major label deal with MCA and putting out the brilliant *Blazing Arrow* album in 2001. To call the album critically-acclaimed would be an understatement; music writers held *Blazing Arrow* in such reverence that it appeared on numerous critics' Top 10 lists in both 2001 and 2002. Such staying power suggests the album's hype was well-deserved, especially in an era where many commercial rap projects sell strongly in their first two weeks of release, then plummet down the charts rapidly.

Almost two years before *Blazing Arrow*'s release, Chief Xcel explained in an interview why to him, underground is just a state of mind.

For us, independent just means economy. Always being in the driver's seat of our own car, being able to make the kind of records we wanna make at will. In terms of underground, we don't even like to get into that terminology. When it comes to our music, we're just trying to make good music, period. I think underground, commercial, to a large extent those are just political terms. Our whole thing is just make good music and let the music speak for itself.[24]

Another example of the diversity of talent and creativity coming from the Bay Area is Azeem, a nationally recognized slam poet who emerged out of the region's burgeoning spoken word scene. After cutting his teeth as a featured MC in the group Spearhead, Azeem has been one of the region's most prolific rappers, releasing two solo albums on different labels and appearing on numerous side projects, including DJ Zeph's self-titled LP and the *Funky Precedent Volume 2* compilation, in a two-year period between 1999 and 2001. Azeem's spoken word background is evident on thoughtful, spiritually conscious songs like 'God's Rolex,' which affirms the existence of the Almighty while satirically commenting on the evils of materialism. The stripped-down track is perhaps closer to the Last Poets than contemporary mainstream artists like Ja Rule or Nelly, who for some represent symbols of rap's commodification. On several other songs, Azeem fearlessly addresses rap's stereotypical cliches, taking stabs at ignorant gangstas and 'boring' abstract rappers alike with a level of irony bordering on genius.[25]

Similar socially-aware modes of thought have been employed by groups like Zion-I, who have commented on the dangerous mentality prevalent among at-risk youth, who may not realize the consequences aspiring to be a 'boss baller' or 'shot caller' can have. On the song 'Karma,' MC Zion tells a modern-day fable about an individual—who could easily be numbered among Oakland's murder victims—whose violent rage was fueled by images provided by American pop culture such as videos, TV, action heroes, and Robert DeNiro.[26] The song's chorus reveals its message in no uncertain terms, i.e. that everything you do will someday come back to haunt you.

It might be hard for some to understand how the Bay Area, the home of turf-derived thug rap, could also be a center for conscious hip hop. One reason might be because Bay Area hip hop has been forced out of circumstance to be an industry of itself—not a single major record company has offices in the Bay. As a result, many artists, especially those in the East Bay, have developed strong ties with grassroots-based community organizations, who have often called on local hip hop groups to perform at benefit shows promoting activist causes. For example, Boots Riley of the Coup has at various times, been a member of groups the Mau Mau Rhythm Collective and the Young Comrades, and is currently a consultant at the School for Social Justice, a non-typical continuation school which has developed an alternative curriculum utilizing hip hop as an educational tool. Other youth organizations who have promoted hip hop as a form of education and spreading political and social awareness include Third Eye Movement and Underground Railroad, both of whom were active in the campaign against California's Juvenile Crime Initiative in 2000, which critics derided as a thinly veiled war on youth.

Inevitably, the wealth of both conscious and thug-related rap coming out of the Bay Area was bound to overlap. The Black Panther Fugitives' debut album, *All of Us*, released at the tail end of 2002, brings Bay Area rap not only full circle—back to the turf-oriented music of its Golden Age—but full cycle—all the way back to the community-based ideology of the original Black Panthers. Fittingly, the group records for Black Panther Records, a label owned by onetime Panther chief of staff David Hilliard. In an interview with *Murder Dog* magazine, they described their lyrical approach as 'conscious set-trippin'—a state of mind which allows them to be thugged-out intellectuals, down to ride for revolution. If this latest example of Bay Area hip hop doesn't represent 'the next level of the game' (to paraphrase Oakland rap group the Whoridas),[27] this writer doesn't know what does.

THE BAY AREA AND THE RISE OF GLOBAL HIP HOP

Bay Area hip hop has played a significant role in the developing worldwide hip hop movement currently taking place. The region's artists have perhaps lent themselves to embracing different cultures more than might normally be the case, due to the fact that touring internationally is a major source of income for independent label acts. Groups like Zion-I, Hieroglyphics, Blackalicious, Mystik Journeymen, Triple Threat DJs, and the Invisibl Skratch Picklz have connected with hip hop fans in places like Germany,

Brazil, the Philippines, and Australia, while Japanese-born MC Shing02 is a fixture in the Bay Area's local hip hop scene.

One example of the impact the Bay Area has had on the evolution of global hip hop consciousness is the Colma-based International Turntablist Federation, which within five years of its founding in 1995, boasted 30 chapters in 17 countries around the world. The ITF's hip hop-centric, grassroots approach to DJ competitions corresponded with an upsurge in the beat-juggling, scratching, and production techniques of budding turntablists around the world and contributed to the notion of manipulating records being an artform in and of itself.

Another indicator of a larger social trend has been the diversity of the Bay Area club scene, which revolves around not only American popular music genres, i.e. hip hop and house, but also Nigerian Afro-beat, Cuban *batucada*, UK garage, Jamaican dancehall, Middle Eastern dub, Indian bhangra, and other forms of electronic music which speak to a global awareness.

The fact that all these genres can exist simultaneously in the Bay Area is nothing less than a blueprint for what the world might sound like in ten or 20 years. Already, you can find mixes of traditional Arabic songs and hip hop at *souks* in Marrakesh, Morocco, and warehouses full of classic rap singles in Shibuya, Japan. Bay Area independent labels have been at the cutting edge of this worldwide trend, which has been furthered not only by progressive dance music released on imprints like Six Degrees, Om, and Ubiquity, but also by Bay Area underground hip hop-identified labels. San Francisco-based Bomb, for instance, have put out albums by Australian beatbox crew Metabass'n'Breath, Germany's the Kreators, and Spain's Skratch Commandos. All of this might well suggest that the Black public sphere is expanding across the globe the way it has already done in the Bay Area, with hip hop at the forefront of a youth-centered movement branching off into various cultural subgenres and categories—music, art, film, and dance being just some of them.

At the same time, the grim murder rates of ghetto youth—not just in Oakland or San Francisco, but worldwide—are symptomatic of a growing crisis, one that lies at the essence of a global hip hop perspective. It is no accident that the places where hip hop has thrived internationally and in the United States tend to be large urban centers with diverse, multi-ethnic populations. For instance, sprawling low-income neighborhoods in Paris and London have been among the most prolific contributors to the expanding roster of international hip hop artists. One reason for this might be that the freedom of expression inherent in hip hop has been somewhat of a universal language. As such, its relevancy to the struggles of young people all over the world in their fight for their own identity and liberation from political, social, and economic oppression—by any means necessary—is undeniable. While Afrocentric hip hop has become a played-out term in the United States, global hip hop is on the rise in every continent save

Antarctica—although there have been unconfirmed reports that the folks down there are cold chillin'.

NOTES

1. Joshunda Sanders, 'The Faces Behind the Numbers,' *San Francisco Chronicle*, December 29, 2002.
2. Ibid.
3. Eric Arnold, 'Keeping the Flame,' *East Bay Express*, October 8, 1999.
4. Sanders, 'Faces Behind the Numbers.'
5. Black Dynasty, 'Deep East Oakland (OG Mix),' Another Hit Records, 1995.
6. Nelson George, 'Introduction,' in Jim Fricke and Charlie Ahearn (eds), *Yes Yes Y'all: Oral History of Hip-Hop's First Decade* (Cambridge, MA: Da Capo Press, 2002).
7. Mike Dream represented Oakland and the Bay Area as a member of the Irie Posse, Hobo Junction, and the TDK (Teach Dem Knowledge/Those Damn Kids) Crew.
8. Eric Arnold, 'Pop Ya Colla,' *Source* magazine, November 2001.
9. Lyrics for 'Tough,' written by J.B. Moore, L. Smith, R. Ford, R. Simmons, 1982.
10. J. Herron Zamora, 'Oakland In Flux,' *San Francisco Chronicle*, December 29, 2002.
11. Eric Arnold, 'Black C on Hunters Point and S.F. Hardcore Rap,' *San Francisco Bay Guardian*, May 2, 2001.
12. Arnold, 'Pop Ya Colla.'
13. Lyric for 'Oakland Stroke,' written by Stephen Kupka, Emillio Castillo, David Garibaldi/ Tower of Power, 1974.
14. Khayree Shaheed, interview by author, 2001.
15. This sample, recorded in Oakland, originally appeared on Parliament's *P-Funk Earth Tour*, Casablanca Records, 1977.
16. Lyric for 'Me and Jesus the Pimp in a '79 Grenada Last Night,' written by R. Riley, 1988.
17. See Lyric from 'Freaky Tales,' written by T. Shaw, 1987.
18. It seems like poetic justice that Shakur made his debut on 'The Same Song,' a ditty whose message is nothing if not universal. See lyric from '(All Around the World) The Same Song,' written by G. Jacobs, R. Brooks, T. Shakur, 1990.
19. Eric Arnold, 'Keeping the Flame,' *East Bay Express*, October 8, 1999.
20. Public Enemy, 'Black Steel in the Hour of Chaos,' Def Jam Recordings, 1988.
21. N.W.A., 'Fuck the Police,' Priority Records, 1988.
22. Tajai Massey, interview by author, 2002.
23. Eric Arnold, 'Del Tha Funkee Homosapien speaks on anime,' *Murder Dog*, Vol. 9, No. 3, 2002.
24. Eric Arnold, 'Underground is a State of Mind,' *San Francisco Bay Guardian* (January 2000), p. 26.
25. Lyric for 'Simple Ting,' written by I. Azim, 2001.
26. Lyric for 'Karma,' written by S. Gaines, A. Anderson, 2002.
27. Lyric for 'Shot Callin' and Big Ballin',' written by the Whoridas, 1995.

6
Head Rush: Hip Hop and a Hawaiian Nation 'On the Rise'

Adria L. Imada

On August 12, 1998, I joined hundreds of people at 'Iolani Palace to protest the U.S. annexation of Hawai'i one hundred years ago. 'Iolani Palace was the seat of Hawai'i's government before it was illegally overthrown by White missionary descendants collaborating with U.S. Marines in 1893. After the overthrow Lili'uokalani, the deposed queen of Hawai'i was imprisoned in the palace for eight months by the new pro-American regime. The palace remains a powerful symbol and sacred site for Native Hawaiians, especially those rallying for Hawaiian self-determination today.[1] At high noon, the Hawaiian flag was raised to the top of the palace and reverential forms of hula and Hawaiian music were performed in honor of Lili'uokalani. The audience sat and watched these performances politely.

However, another kind of performance proposed a radical future from the past and got the crowd to its feet. An interactive play called *Forever Protest Annexation* revisited the annexation and rewrote Hawaiian history. Rather than watching helplessly as American soldiers stormed the royal palace, Hawaiian men disarmed them and proclaimed their resistance to U.S. annexation (see Figure 1). The play invited us to speculate: what would Hawai'i be like if it were still a sovereign country and not the fiftieth state? We began to see alternative futures in which we may all participate. The Hawaiian actors exhorted the audience to yell 'Kū'ē!' which means 'resist, oppose, stand different' in Hawaiian. They proclaimed, 'It's never too late to kū'ē!' and the bass started pumping. The young men on stage—members of the Hawaiian hip hop group Sudden Rush—broke into their signature song, 'Kū'ē,' from their eponymous second album:

> Back in 1893, the U.S. military dethroned and imprisoned my queen Lili'uokalani. All of these problems stay in my brain, I don't wanna, wanna go insane ... Feeling the pain ... 'Cause in 1997 ain't a damn thing changed.[2]

Many in the audience immediately started dancing: children, sovereignty activists, even American tourists (see Figure 2). The first person I saw dancing was a *kupuna*, a Hawaiian elder, who looked like she was well into her seventies. Sudden Rush transformed the sacred steps of the palace into a space of Hawaiian hip hop/techno-culture with heavy beats, rapping in

Figure 1 Sudden Rush in *Forever Protest Annexation* at 'Iolani Palace, August 12, 1998 (photograph by Adria L. Imada)

Figure 2 Hip hop at annexation protest, August 12, 1998 (photograph by Adria L. Imada)

the Hawaiian language, and a generous sampling of traditional Hawaiian chanting. The first hip hop group to craft rap lyrics in the Hawaiian language, Sudden Rush explicitly promotes resistance to U.S. annexation and the continued occupation. As the cultural critic George Lipsitz writes, 'Culture enables people to rehearse identities, stances, and social relations not yet permissible in politics … Popular culture does not just reflect reality, it helps constitute it.'[3] Rather than being regarded as disrespectful, Sudden Rush moved people to dance, experience pleasure, and celebrate survival in Hawai'i. Through these performances we could enact, however provisionally, an improved future.

Hawaiians are arguably disempowered in their own land, where they comprise 20 percent of its population. Hawaiians suffer from the lowest life expectancy, highest cancer mortality rates and incarceration rates, and are the least likely to complete four years of college.[4] Nearly 50 percent of incarcerated juveniles are Hawaiian.[5] Meanwhile, Hawaiian entitlements are continually subjected to political retrenchment on local, state, and federal levels. White and Asian residents of Hawai'i, backed by conservative organizations in the continental United States, have challenged Hawaiian institutions and legal claims in state and federal courts.[6] The Hawai'i State Admission Act of 1959 gave the state government of Hawai'i control of 1.4 million acres of 'ceded lands,' or Hawaiian Kingdom Lands that were 'ceded' to the U.S. government after the 1898 annexation. The state was obligated to hold these lands in trust and use them to benefit Native Hawaiians. However, historically the state has violated this trust agreement by not regularly allocating land-use revenues to the semi-autonomous Office of Hawaiian Affairs.[7]

In the 1980s, Hawaiian sovereignty groups began rallying for Native self-governance and today several organizations propose different models for self-determination. One group, Ka Lāhui Hawai'i, which was most prominent in the early 1990s, calls for a nation-within-a-nation model similar to that of Native American tribes; The Nation of Hawai'i and the Hawaiian Kingdom Government, are pro-independence groups that favor complete independence from the United States.[8] The sovereignty movement has gained widespread support among Native Hawaiians and non-Native locals in Hawai'i over the past two decades, but activists face an uphill battle.

Sudden Rush's hip hop activism has emerged from this self-determination and nationalist movement, and in turn, their music has enlarged the terrain of political resistance in Hawai'i. As Hawai'i's most prominent hip hop group, Sudden Rush has become known in the islands for their activist, youth-oriented 'island music.' Taking a musical form most often associated with urban Black experiences and dissent, Sudden Rush has indigenized hip hop. They mix U.S. hip hop, reggae, and contemporary Hawaiian music into their own brand of 'versa-style' hip hop, offering forceful critiques of Hawaiian history and U.S. neo-colonialism. While encouraging young people to enjoy their lives, Sudden Rush also wants to empower a Hawaiian nation 'on the rise.' Their music, both defiant and hopeful, allows new publics to envision and work toward more just political futures in Hawai'i.

On the east coast of the island of Hawai'i, in the town of Hilo, three young Hawaiian men—Shane Veincent, Caleb Richards, and Don Ke'ala Kawa'auhau—began performing Hawaiian hip hop in the early 1990s. With a population of 38,000, Hilo is more geared toward the production of macadamia nuts and coffee beans than cutting edge music. Twenty-eight year old Shane Veincent grew up here, not far from Pane'ewa Hawaiian Homelands, the residential areas for Native Hawaiians that are administered by the state of Hawai'i.[9] A rebellious teenager, Veincent spent ten years with his uncles and cousins in Pane'ewa beginning at the age of 13. In the family house he listened to Hawaiian slack key guitarists like Gabby Pahinui as well as American musicians like Roy Orbison. Veincent received an introduction to hip hop in the early to mid 1980s through popping and breaking. Every day he arrived at his intermediate school with a stereo and favorite piece of cardboard. His love of crowds and public performance led him to rapping and singing in high school. After putting rhymes together, he battled his classmates at school and house parties. Eric B and Rakim were his favorite rap artists, and he enjoyed hip hop as 'party music.'

Veincent recalls first meeting Caleb Richards at a house party. 'I'd been in different rap groups. Caleb came to this party. "You rap, huh?" I asked him.' Veincent then challenged Richards, 'Bust a verse.' Sufficiently impressed with Richards' skills, Veincent decided to hook up with him. They became friends, meeting up after school to write their own rap songs with instrumentals. The duo won a talent show at a county fair in the early 1990s. Preferring to surf and make music, Veincent did not graduate from high school.

After performing for about a year, Veincent and Richards met up with their classmate's older brother, Don Ke'ala Kawa'auhau. Two years older than Richards and Veincent, Kawa'auhau is 'Da Rappa Nui' ('The Big Rapper' translated from Hawaiian Creole English) and the 'head man' of the group. Kawa'auhau also shares eclectic musical influences. Regardless of genre, Kawa'auhau liked musicians who were good storytellers. He admired Bruce Springsteen for telling empathetic narratives, but Kawa'auhau also remembers the impression that the local song 'Hawai'i '78' made on him. A mournful ballad by the late Hawaiian artist Israel Kamakawiwo'ole, it highlights the demise of the Hawaiian monarchy and the transformation of Hawai'i into a tourist playground. These were subjects Sudden Rush later would address forcefully in their music.

Throughout his Catholic school education, Kawa'auhau played 'ukulele, guitar, and took piano lessons. His approach to hip hop was more studied than Veincent's love of spontaneous live performance. While in high school Kawa'auhau used his first paycheck from Waldenbooks to buy his first rap tape, Sir Mix-a-Lot. With every new paycheck, he bought more rap—MC

Hammer, Heavy D, Run DMC, Ice-T—'even guys like Young MC, guys that people used to diss.' He ended up accumulating 'hundreds of tapes people never heard of.' He appreciated the flexibility of rap: 'You can fit a lot of stuff into one song. You're not stuck with verse, chorus, four lines here, four lines there.' Most importantly for him, however, rap allowed him to 'say exactly what you feel,' and as he would discover, it was a form that could also accommodate the Hawaiian language.

Kawaʻauhau joined Sudden Rush in 1993, which was the hundredth anniversary of the U.S.-backed overthrow of the independent Hawaiian Kingdom. In January 1993, thousands of nonviolent protesters gathered at the royal palace, galvanizing public support for Hawaiian sovereignty and inserting Hawaiian rights into the public consciousness. Kawaʻauhau had begun studying ʻōlelo Hawaiʻi (Hawaiian language) at the University of Hawaiʻi-Hilo and was inspired by the recent surge in Hawaiian political activism. He painstakingly composed rap lyrics first in English, then in Hawaiian. He listened to a beat, then wrote a line with Hawaiian words that rhymed. The result was the song 'Oni Paʻa' (Steadfast):

Hoʻohui, hoʻohui mai hoʻolohe i ke aupuni/ Makemake lākou i kekahi aupuni/ I hea? Ma Oʻahu. Ua lohe ʻia./ Ma hope o ka wāwahi ʻia ʻana o ka heiau./ Hewa loa kela, mālama i ka poʻe, Mālama iā kākou.

Unite, unite! Don't listen to the government/ They like build another street/ Where?/ On Oʻahu. 'Ass what I heard/ After they destroy a heiau (Hawaiian temple)/ Listen, that's what's wrong./ Take care of the land, take care of the people, Take care each other.

ʻŌlelo Hawaiʻi has only eight consonants, and when rapped very quickly with thick beats in the background, as it is in this song, the sound is both staccato and heavy on the vowels. When Kawaʻauhau got up at the mic at a party and received an enthusiastic response, he thought, 'This could actually turn heads. People could either like it for the message, or like it for the music and hear the message. You can win more ways than one.' Veincent and Richards soon heard about Kawaʻauhau's skills as a rapper, and after a session, the three clicked as a group in 1993. Kawaʻauhau brought his knowledge of Hawaiian issues, while Veincent and Richards supplied the street credibility.

Sudden Rush cut their first album, A Nation on the Rise, in 1994, working with their producer Rob Onekea. A friend who owned a hip hop clothing store sponsored the album, which cost about $2,000 to produce. Hawaiian music played with slack key guitar, steel guitar, and ʻukulele has usually been prized for its link to Hawaiian musical traditions. But Sudden Rush used the most alienating materials of modernity and post-industrialism—mechanical beats, digital sampling, urban technology—to declare Hawaiian resistance.

A few songs on their first album critiqued the U.S. colonization of Hawai'i, including the song 'Oni Pa'a': 'We're living on very land that was stolen. The first amendment is the freedom of speech. But what can we say when they're stealing our beach. Oh say can you see, America's a thief.' They also called attention to the growing Hawaiian sovereignty movement: 'By any means necessary, said one brother. Hawaiians say sovereignty one way or another.'

But many of the songs—'Cruisin,' 'Wreck Shop,' 'Bouncin'—tended to be derivative of mainstream U.S. hip hop from the period, like House of Pain, Cypress Hill, and the Fu-Schnickens, with an emphasis on a distinctly Hawaiian party lifestyle. *Nation on the Rise* received minimal airplay in Hawai'i. Producer Onekea felt that Sudden Rush's music fell into a gap between contemporary Hawaiian music and mainland hip hop and did not fit easily in local radio programming. There is no dedicated 'urban' or 'hip hop' station in Hawai'i, and U.S. hip hop can be heard only occasionally on a few top 40 stations.

Despite the lack of airplay, by 1997 the group had put together their second album, *Kū'ē*, which was another low-budget garage project featuring a large dose of Hawaiian rap lyrics. They called Hawaiian language rap '*nā mele pāleoleo*': *mele* means song, and *pāleoleo* is talking loudly. For thousands of years, Hawaiian genealogy and history was passed down orally through chants, for there was no written language until the arrival of Christian missionaries in the 1820s. Hawaiian rap can be thought of as a continuation of Hawaiian oral culture. The group, however, also relied on a cheap karaoke machine to record lyrics over instrumentals and beats. They then sent the samples to Onekea on O'ahu, who remade the beats.

The album included hip hop tracks, a couple of 'Jawaiian' (hybrid Jamaican and Hawaiian) songs, and a few pop songs. Well-known Hawaiian musicians Guy Cruz, Willie K, and Keali'i Reichel contributed to the album without compensation. By this time the group had developed its own sound, which Veincent describes as 'versa-style'—a fusion of reggae, traditional Hawaiian chanting, U.S. hip hop, and R&B. For example, the song 'Kanakas Unite'[10] references Marvin Gaye's 'What's Going On': 'Mother, mother, there's too many of you crying ... Hawaiian brother, brother, brother, there's too many of you dying.' Songs on the album might pull from Bob Marley, swing to the Hawaiian chanter Keali'i Reichel, and then drop a generous sampling of beats and idioms from mainland hip hop.

This time Sudden Rush hit the airwaves of Hawai'i and went into heavy rotation on contemporary Hawaiian music stations. *Kū'ē*'s success was in part due to its hard-hitting critique of Hawai'i's neo-colonial status. The deposed Queen Lili'uokalani is pictured on the album cover along with Sudden Rush members who hoist an upside down Hawaiian flag, a symbol of Hawaiian resistance (see Figure 3). Coinciding with a period of economic crisis, *Kū'ē* offered locals a way to understand the hardship that surrounded

Figure 3   Cover of Sudden Rush's second album, *Kū'ē* (courtesy of Sudden Rush)

them. Tourism, the largest industry in the state, had nearly halted due to the Asian financial crisis in the islands. Local businesses went bankrupt daily and many Hawaiians and local Asians faced homelessness in one of the most expensive real-estate markets and militarized zones in the world. *Kūʻē* reminded audiences about Hawaiians who were dying as they waited to receive homestead land from the mismanaged Department of Hawaiian Home Lands. On the song 'Think About It,' they paid homage to Kahale Smith, a Hawaiian man who burned himself and his house down rather than be evicted from his land.

Having grown up on Hawaiian Homelands or in Hawaiian communities, the men of Sudden Rush knew firsthand the perils faced by Hawaiians, but Kawaʻauhau became the formal student of the group. After taking Hawaiian language and Hawaiian Studies classes at the University of Hawaiʻi-Hilo, Kawaʻauhau decided to change his major to Hawaiian Studies. The Hawaiian language had been banned in Hawaiʻi's public school system since 1896, a few years after the U.S. takeover of the islands. But thanks to an activist-oriented Hawaiian language program, more young people like Kawaʻauhau were learning the language. He began talking to teachers outside of the classroom, reading websites and books about Hawaiian traditions, and listening to Hawaiian sovereignty activists like Haunani-Kay Trask on public access television. Eventually, Kawaʻauhau became a Hawaiian language teacher at an immersion preschool and at a local Hilo high school. He also shared what he had learned with Veincent and Richards.

'I learned so much about our struggle [as Hawaiians] since performing as a group,' relates Veincent. In order to make the music they wanted to, the group realized that they had to teach themselves more history. They each had assignments on Hawaiian history. One of Veincent's first book reports was on Queen Liliʻuokalani. Sudden Rush also screened videos about Hawaiian legal issues, including *The Tribunal*, a documentary that placed the U.S. and the state of Hawaiʻi on trial for crimes committed against indigenous Hawaiians.

Although they consider themselves performers first, the members of the group belong to a distinguished genealogy of Hawaiian cultural activism. I loosely define 'cultural activism' as the self-conscious deployment of culture for political ends. Influenced by the civil rights movement on the continental U.S., the 'Hawaiian Renaissance' emerged in the 1960s and 70s. Mobilized by the U.S. naval bombing of the island of Kahoʻolawe and the eviction of pig farmers in Kalama Valley, young Hawaiians and local Asians became conscious of Hawaiʻi's colonial history of land dispossession and racism. This period of political and cultural activism featured multi-ethnic social protests, the Hawaiian re-occupation of U.S. naval bombing sites, and the assertion of Hawaiian performance and language. Young Hawaiians who had never heard Hawaiian at home or in school found elders to teach them their language. Hula troupes no longer called themselves 'hula studios' but *hālau hula* (hula academies) and began teaching styles of hula performed with indigenous instruments and Hawaiian chant.

The Hawaiian musician George Helm emerged from this renaissance. A 26-year-old entertainer known for his sweet falsetto, Helm was a member of Protect Kahoʻolawe Ohana, an activist organization that re-occupied the island used by the U.S. Navy for bombing practice. During an attempt to cross the waters to Kahoʻolawe in 1977, Helm and another young activist disappeared. They were presumed either drowned or killed. Sudden Rush refers to this incident in the song 'Think About It,' suggesting that the activists were murdered by the U.S. military or government.

Although traditional Hawaiian music was frequently championed in Hawaiʻi during the 1960s and 70s as the soul of the people, it was blended freely with other forms of trans-local music. In the 1980s musical group Hoʻaikane and singer Butch Helemano called themselves 'Jawaiian' (Jamaican-Hawaiian) and explicitly identified with the struggles of colonized Blacks in the Caribbean and the African diaspora. Helemano adopted long dreadlocks and his album covers were splashed with red, yellow, and green, the colors of Pan-African liberation.[11] These artists forged Jawaiian music to construct a larger collective political identity. This music features reggae beats and affected 'Rastafari' accents at times, but its lyrics assert the importance of Hawaiian land and experiences. 'Jawaiian' artists took a product from outside of Hawaiʻi and made it something that local people in Hawaiʻi could enjoy.[12]

Just as Jawaiian musicians forged a globalized music by drawing on reggae, Sudden Rush has done so by indigenizing American hip hop. They have incorporated Hawaiian politics and youth culture into music associated with urban Black experiences. While capitalism often values people of color more as consumers of Nike and Tommy Hilfiger products than as respected workers and community members, Sudden Rush deliberately consumes commercial culture and spits it back out in the form of hip hop. Like their Jawaiian contemporaries, Sudden Rush deeply identifies with African Americans and other people of color who have suffered under racial capitalism. In the song 'True Hawaiian' from *Kūʻē*, lyrics flow about 'Uncle Sam's grand larceny' from the Atlantic to the Pacific:

I can't believe how can we follow a government that chooses to
　　deceive its own people
They tell us that we're equal
But if you look at history we're just another sequel
Started with America, go from desecration
They called Indians savages and threw them on the reservation
Then they took the African man from the motherland to this
　　other land to work for the master's plan

That wasn't enough they had to cross the big blue and when
   they saw Hawai'i, yeah they took that too
They saw the hula and they called it paganist but they didn't
   think, question it was ripping the Pacific

But they are also careful to make historical distinctions between African Americans and Hawaiians. In the song 'Message to the Wannabes (Be Hawaiian)' from *Nation on the Rise*, they point out:

> The Black man was taken from his homeland
> Taken to another land
> Forced to work for another man
> But they survived, they overcame
> To the Hawaiian people, it is somewhat the same.
> Not saying we were slaves, don't get me mistaken
> To us, it's not the people but the land that was taken.

By making connections with other colonized and indigenous people, Hawaiians became part of a global political struggle and resisted the construction of themselves as isolated dots in the Pacific Ocean. Through a global medium Sudden Rush has created a politics of attachment. Hip hop and rap can help because of its power to communicate a people's struggle, as Kawa'auhau explains:

I'm not Black. I never wanted to be anything else than who I am. But if they [rappers] can make you almost feel what they went through, to me, that's cool. I don't know what it is to be this guy, but I can almost feel what he's saying. That's what we try to do. We don't want to make you want to be Hawaiian. But if you can understand us and feel what we're saying, then we're doing our job.

Onekea, who got his start in the music industry remixing hip hop music, was initially wary of producing Hawaiian rap. He recalled, 'When I first met them, I thought they were another bunch of local boys trying to rap. But when I heard them start getting into their flow, it kind of tripped me out. There was something different about them.' He thinks of Sudden Rush as the 'Hawaiian Public Enemy' for their ability to cut to the quick of contemporary Hawaiian life and amplify a message about social justice. Chuck D was Onekea's role model, a 'modern day Robin Hood.' He asserted, '*It Takes a Nation of Millions to Hold Us Back* [was] one of the best hip hop albums ever … I was just always into what they [Public Enemy] stood for. The way you treat Black people is wrong.' He added, 'I'm not an activist. I don't know how to debate in public, but I can make phat beats that make people listen, and the boys can put together lyrics that are catchy enough to remember.'

Because of their adoption of hip hop idioms and forms, Sudden Rush felt some apprehension over their reception by African-American audiences. Would they be censured for being 'wannabes' or adopting a style of music identified with Black people? When Sudden Rush first performed at a Honolulu nightclub whose audience was mostly African-American military personnel, Kawaʻauhau recalled, the crowd booed them because they were not on the flyer. 'After they heard our songs, though, they cheered for us. Someone after the show compared me to Heavy D, Caleb [Richards] to Onyx, and Shane [Veincent] to a guy from the Fu-Schnickens,' said Kawaʻauhau, laughing. 'One guy even said, "It was dope!"'

There is ample reason for Hawaiian men in particular to identify with young African-American men. African-American and Hawaiian men share a similar relationship to the state; both groups have been racialized in the social imagination as violent, oversexualized, and deviant. Since the arrival of Christian missionaries in the islands in 1820, Hawaiians have been constructed as a people unable to exercise self-control or prove themselves worthy of self-governance.[13] In contemporary Hawaiʻi, Hawaiian men are frequently discussed in the media as hardened criminals, drug addicts, and welfare cases, with infrequent analysis of the neo-colonial context of contemporary Hawaiian struggles for land and sovereignty. Many of Sudden Rush's songs address young people, particularly men, and assess Hawaiian self-destruction as a consequence of government policies. Veincent put a personal face on this larger battle while dealing with drug addiction. He briefly withdrew from the group until he completed a rehabilitation program.

Sudden Rush's intervention offers another view of Hawaiians as people who care about their families and communities. The song 'True Hawaiian' reminds listeners of the values that make a 'true Hawaiian,' such as haʻahaʻa (humility), haʻaheo (pride), and lōkahi (togetherness). They exhort Hawaiian youth to stick together and learn as much they can. Veincent reveals, 'The main reason why I do our music is to tell the story of our people to my generation and the generation to come. You can go to school, but music is how people really listen.' Despite their impassioned critique of U.S. colonization and the cannibalizing tourist economy of Hawaiʻi, Sudden Rush is not demanding that Hawaiians kūʻē violently. George Lipsitz asserts that the oppositional power of hip hop and its utility for contemporary global politics lies precisely in its 'desire to work *through* rather than *outside* of existing structures.'[14] Indeed Sudden Rush does not encourage young people to kill cops who have assaulted Hawaiians or attack U.S. military personnel who occupy Hawaiian lands. Nor do they promote burning down multinational hotels that exploit the labor of Native Hawaiians and locals. Instead their rap lyrics emphasize Hawaiian pride, unity, and respect for one's elders.

Locals of all ethnic backgrounds and ages grooved to their message. Although their music is geared primarily to a local guy hitting the beach with his surfboard, *Kū'ē* had something for everyone—a mix of political songs and 'party songs.' Sudden Rush does not want to merely preach. They are firm believers of the pleasure principle. In the single 'Polynesian Party,' different groups of Pacific Islanders revel in each other's company at a celebratory Oceanic house party: 'Yo, whatcha going to do right now, the Maori in the house? Paaarty! Whatcha going to do now, Fijians in the house, paaarty!!!' The inexorable and insistent beats urge you to move your body and have fun while you oppose. Maintains Veincent, 'We want people to hear our music but also have a good time.' 'Polynesian Party' became the most popular single of the second album and garnered the group more commercial attention and a larger audience. People who liked the song were pulled subsequently into the denser, more political songs on the album.

Kū'ē sold between 20,000 and 25,000 copies, an impressive number for a locally produced rap release. While 'Polynesian Party' became Hawai'i's youth anthem of the late 1990s, *kupuna* (Hawaiian elders) also perked up when Sudden Rush performed at community concerts. *Kupuna* approached Sudden Rush members, thanking them, 'We don't like rap music, but we like what you're doing.'[15] As they traveled throughout the islands performing, the members of Sudden Rush listened to the stories of *kupuna*, whose homegrown wisdom is sampled on *Kū'ē*.

In addition to performing, Sudden Rush wants to set an example for the youth of Hawai'i. Besides doing concerts and nightclub performances, they participate in benefit concerts for Hawaiian language immersion programs and various Native Hawaiian sovereignty groups. None of the members is involved in a particular sovereignty group, mainly due to their reluctance to choose sides in what often seems like a contentious and personalized battle between different political camps. But if approached by a Hawaiian activist group, they lend their *kokua* (cooperation). Promoting unity instead of dissension, they are contributing to 'a nation on the rise, blowing up your tape deck.' Regardless of the current political reality of sovereignty organizations, in their minds a true Hawaiian nation already exists: it is a community of Hawaiians working together for social justice. Peace can also be found in one's family and community. The song 'Paradise Found' intentionally inverts the paradigm of Western 'discovery' of the Hawaiian Islands, with Hawaiians who discover paradise in one another: 'When I open my eyes, I see I found my paradise in my family, and in the eyes of all the *kamali'i* (children).'

Sudden Rush are just as moved by their music as their audience, and they savor their connection with live crowds. Veincent remembers performing in Las Vegas for a large audience of Hawaiians who had relocated to the desert. Vegas is sometimes referred to as the 'ninth island' by Hawai'i residents because of widespread emigration to Vegas for jobs and affordable homes. Thousands of miles away from home and receiving aloha from diasporic islanders, Veincent broke down and cried on stage. The group dreams of performing across the U.S. continent and on other Pacific Islands, especially with the release of their third album, *Ea*, in 2002.

However Veincent, Kawaʻauhau, and Richards do not see themselves abandoning life on the islands. They would like their music to spread far and wide, but their home is Hawaiʻi. 'I believe certain people belong in certain places,' Kawaʻauhau said. 'When you go other places, that's okay, but that belonging, I feel that with Hilo.' Onekea's production company, Way Out West, reflects the group's sensibility. Sudden Rush wanted to put the West (i.e., the Pacific) on the international hip hop map with their music. Yet hip hop artistry alone cannot sustain a livelihood in the islands. After teaching Hawaiian language at a preschool and high school for five years, Kawaʻauhau is now a DJ at an 'island music' radio station in Hilo. Veincent is a tattoo artist in Hilo, while Richards works two jobs at a restaurant and a bar in Honolulu.

'Hawaiian rap music, is this the wave of the future, or is this just a fluke?' Sudden Rush mused in an interlude on their second album. Sudden Rush's newest album, *Ea* (loosely translated as sovereignty) was almost five years in the making. While this album, like *Kūʻē*, makes explicit reference to Hawaiian resistance, it is even more anti-colonial and critical of the United States than their previous release. Their music continues to imagine a future where Hawaiians are taking their bodies back from the modern statist project of tourism and global capitalism, a system that uses Hawaiians as tour bus drivers and hula dancers while paying a mere $8 an hour. Reappropriating your own body can be a political act; Hawaiian bodies are not simply instruments for others' profit or wage labor.

'If we could do for the Hawaiian people what Public Enemy did for Afro Americans as far as awareness and making people think, I would be pretty stoked,' said Onekea. Sudden Rush envisions a Hawaiian nation where Hawaiians are enjoying their *ʻāina* (land) and everyday lives. The beats of their music are moving islanders into new forms of collective action like those produced at the 1998 ʻIolani Palace protest. They may be 'Way Out West,' but Sudden Rush has already convinced some people to make paradise in Hawaiʻi a permanent reality—not for tourists or the U.S. military—but for themselves and their families.

NOTES

1. Following modern Hawaiian orthography, I use diacritical marks—the *ʻokina* or glottal stop and the *kahakō* or macron—for Hawaiian words and names (e.g., Hawaiʻi). I use 'Hawaiian' and 'Native Hawaiian' to mark any person of indigenous Hawaiian background, not to indicate residence in Hawaiʻi. Thus in my use 'Hawaiian' is *not* analogous to the term 'Californian.' Instead I use 'islander' or 'local' to reference people born and raised in Hawaiʻi who are not necessarily indigenous Hawaiians.
2. All lyrics cited with permission by Sudden Rush.
3. George Lipsitz, *Dangerous Crossroads: Popular Music, Postmodernism and the Poetics of Place* (New York: Verso Books, 1994), p. 137.

4. For statistics on Hawai'i life expectancy from 1910 to 1990, see Table 2.10 in *State of Hawai'i Data Book 2004*. For cancer mortality, see *Hawai'i Cancer Facts and Figures*, 2003–04, pp. 12–13. For incarceration and education attainment, see *Native Hawaiian Data Book 2002*, pp. 29 and 24.

5. This figure is based on statistics analyzed between 1995 and 1999. Hawai'i State Department of the Attorney General, Crime Prevention and Juvenile Assistance Division, *Incarcerated Juveniles and Recidivism in Hawai'i*, Vol. 2 (February 2001).

6. Freddy Rice, a fifth-generation *haole* (Caucasian) resident of Hawai'i, challenged the state's process of having Hawaiians elect Office of Hawaiian Affairs (OHA) trustees. In 2000, the U.S. Supreme Court ruled that Hawaiian-only OHA elections constitute a racial voting restriction in violation of the fourteenth and fifteenth amendments. After the Rice ruling, other legal cases opposed the constitutionality of Hawaiian entitlements. The federal case *Arakaki v. Lingle*, was filed in 2002 and challenged the legality of the Office of Hawaiian Affairs, the Department of Hawaiian Home Lands and other government agencies that support Native Hawaiians. Plaintiffs argued that these programs were race-based and discriminated against non-Hawaiians, but a federal judge dismissed the case in January 2004.

7. In 2001 OHA took the state of Hawai'i to court, seeking a moratorium on the sale of Hawaiian ceded lands to private owners. Four individual Hawaiian plaintiffs also filed suit against the state. See *Honolulu Star-Bulletin*, November 18, 2001 and November 21, 2001. OHA also introduced state legislation in early 2004 to prevent the alienation of ceded lands by the state and ensure that payments of ceded land revenue are fully reinstated. See <http://www.oha.org>.

8. See <http://www.hawaiiankingdom.org>, the official website of the Hawaiian Kingdom Government. Many of these independence groups have gained membership from among those who oppose a federal Native Hawaiian recognition bill (also known as the 'Akaka Bill') that would make Native Hawaiians domestic wards of the federal government and subject Native Hawaiians to U.S. congressional plenary power. See <http://www.stopakaka.com> for more on anti-federal recognition activism.

9. The federal Hawaiian Homes Commission Act of 1920 sought to 'rehabilitate' some Hawaiians through a government homesteading program. The act defined a 'native Hawaiian' as someone with at least 50 percent Hawaiian blood quantum, and the same quantum subsequently applies to all applicants for homestead lots. Today almost 30,000 Hawaiians are on a waiting list for residential or agricultural lots.

10. In Hawaiian '*kanaka*' means 'man' but it has come to refer to Hawaiians generally as a people.

11. Sudden Rush also emphasizes those identifications by using Jamaican dancehall on 'Run' about 'rudeboy' Hawaiians running from guns, police, drugs, and domestic violence.

12. Andrew N. Weintraub, 'Jawaiian Music and Local Cultural Identity in Hawai'i,' in Philip Hayward (ed.), *Sound Alliances: Indigenous Peoples, Cultural Politics, and Popular Music in the Pacific* (London: Cassell, 1998), pp. 78–88.

13. See Noenoe K. Silva, 'He Kānāwai E Ho'opau I Nā Hula Kuolo Hawai'i: The Political Economy of Banning the Hula,' *The Hawaiian Journal of History*, Vol. 34 (2000). Nineteenth-century Christian missionaries in Hawai'i associated hula with Hawaiian debauchery, idleness, and sexuality. They sought to ban the practice, believing that it made Hawaiians unproductive workers in the emerging capitalist economy of Hawai'i.

14. Lipsitz, *Dangerous Crossroads*, p. 34.

15. Rob Onekea, interview by author, typescript, May 2002.

7
War at 33⅓: Hip Hop, the Language of the Unheard, and the Afro-Asian Atlantic

Sohail Daulatzai

As the thieves of Baghdad that now sit in the political heart of the Empire scatter like roaches to justify and contain the impact of the tortures of Iraqis at Abu Ghraib, it is difficult not to see the brutal images of naked men being abused by American soldiers with ropes, punches, and attack dogs as part of a larger Euro-American fascination with the Muslim body. As a clear product of a Western will to power that has also shown a similar fascination with the Black body during and after slavery, these most recent images only confirm the massive institutional power and policing that is being exacted upon the Muslim Other on a global scale. And while Vice-President Dick Cheney has referred to the 'War on Terror' as the 'New Normalcy,' there is in fact very little that is new or normal, as 9/11 has only provided the political, diplomatic, and ideological cover for further domestic repression and violent foreign aggression.

In the United States, the current threat to the domestic space of the nation has been constructed around the Immigrant Muslim Other, as the xenophobic imagination that has been part and parcel of American nation building continues to racialize immigration flows and views them as fundamentally challenging the political, economic, and cultural stability of the United States. In this chapter I want to explore the cultural and political history of African-American Islam, which has had a tremendous impact in not only re-imagining the politics of race and identity—as it has been a powerful space for the expression of global anti-colonial poetics and Afro-diasporic consciousness—but that has also had a tremendous impact upon Black creative genius, particularly in the world of hip hop culture in the United States and in Britain. In doing so, I hope to map a new kind of imaginative geography forged around and through the cultural histories of Afro-Asian solidarities[1]—overlapping diasporas and histories that share experiences around racism, slavery, and colonialism.

This exploration of Afro-Asian poetics has tremendous possibilities, as it commands a serious interrogation of the minefield that is racial categorization and the fortresses of belonging that are cemented by the power of the modern nation-state. In revealing the ways in which pan-racial and trans-racial identities are forged, Afro-Asian Islam places race within a transnational framework that opens up the categories of race to

include alliances between Black, Asian, and Arab constituencies—creating a
multi-racial, anti-racist tapestry of resistance.[2] In revealing these histories of
alliance and solidarity I also suggest that globalization is not a uni-directional
process moving from center to periphery or North to South, but is instead
omnipresent in its impact. The movement of Black and Brown bodies that
have forged new forms of community and diasporic consciousness have
done so in the face of larger globalizing forces of colonialism, slavery, and
migration—giving shape to new forms of glocal resistance.

These histories of resistance that bring together the violence of slavery
and the migrations of colonialism also reveal the limits of current theoretical
approaches to both Islam and to Afro-diasporic thought, namely Orientalism
and Black Atlantic discourses. Because Orientalism as a system of thought
is anchored to European colonial history and geographically rooted within
the Islamic worlds of North Africa, the Middle East, and South Asia,
exploring the history of African-American Islam remaps these conventional
understandings not only by examining Islam in the West (i.e. the United
States), but also by configuring Blackness into a discursive equation that has
for so long been predicated upon an 'exotic,' 'Eastern,' Other whose supposed
excess and decadence differs immeasurably from the vulgar Enlightenment
constructions of Blackness as depraved and devoid of history. In addition,
the history of both African-American Islam and British Asian Islam also
suggests a reconsideration of Black Atlantic discourses that do not account
for the histories of Afro-Asian Muslim traffic within and between Europe
and the United States. The complex diasporic connections that are made
within and between African-American Muslims and British Asian Muslims
with Africa, Asia, and the Middle East, suggests more of what might be
called an 'Afro-Asian Atlantic'—a multi-hued transatlantic resistance to
modernity that has not been accounted for within the conventional narratives
of the Black Atlantic.

This mosaic of resistance is addressed in the chapter by exploring the
relationships between the Islamic worlds and Blackness in the United
States—placing these struggles around identity within the larger context
of post-World War II American politics and culture, its relationships to the
re-emergence of Black liberation struggles during this same period, and the
anti-colonial movements taking shape throughout the world. In critically
exploring the work of artists such as Rakim, Mos Def, and the Kaliphz, I
will place their work within the debates around identity and power, as these
artists use hip hop culture as a platform from which to speak truth to power
against the violent crucible of racial terror while also poetically linking
themselves with larger communities of resistance that transcend the limiting
structures of the modern nation-state. In forming complex ideological
hybridities that bring together South Asian anti-racism, Black Nationalist
radicalism, and African-American Islam, these cultural activists mobilize a

new kind of identity politics and global humanism that critically interrogate the relationships between race and nation, being and belonging.[3]

BLACK ON BOTH SIDES (OF THE ATLANTIC)

While the intersection of Islam and hip hop culture has been the most recent expression of Black humanity and rage, previous eras have seen similar artistic expressions embody the diasporic longings and collective memories of Blackness in the United States. Jazz music had been the site for previous explorations of the intersection of Blackness and Islam, as numerous jazz musicians such as Ahmad Jamal, Yusef Lateef, Art Blakey, and many others creatively forged new kinds of consciousness and new aesthetics of being that fundamentally altered conventional ideas about Blackness and its relationship to American national identity. In addition, the Black Arts movement of the late 1960s also employed Islam and Islamically themed symbols and ideas in their radical Black cultural practices of the time. According to Melani McAlister, 'the Black Arts movement defined political struggle as cultural struggle; this cultural struggle required a new spirituality. In literary circles, Islamic symbolism and mythology were incorporated into the self-conscious construction of a new black aesthetic and a revolutionary black culture.'[4] Amiri Baraka's play *A Black Mass* was based upon the Nation of Islam's myth of Yacub, and was one of the primary proponents of incorporating Islam into the Black Arts movements, for Baraka believed that Islam offered 'what the Black man needs ... a reconstruction ... a total way of life that he can involve himself with that is post-American in a sense.'[5] As with these two previous significant cultural movements, Islam came to play a part in imagining and re-imagining ideas about race in general and Blackness specifically.

In her book *Epic Encounters*, Melani McAlister looks at the role of the Middle East within African-American political history—particularly beginning in the middle part of the twentieth century when the anti-colonial movements were erupting throughout the globe and the Middle East came to play a more prominent role in the geopolitical interests of the United States. As the Arab–Israeli conflict grew in importance to leaders in Washington, African-American leaders, intellectuals and activists who were being influenced by the anti-colonial movements taking place in Africa, Asia and the Indian subcontinent, began to also look at the Middle East as an emerging battleground upon which to negotiate their own political identities, affiliations, and agendas.

For African-American Christians, the religious narratives of Exodus, slavery, and suffering were powerful tropes and analogies for translating Biblical histories into contemporary struggles around racism—creating and forging ties to the Middle East through religious narratives of liberation and redemption. But while it was important to understand the emotional and spiritual power of the Middle East to African-American Christianity and the burgeoning civil rights movement, Islam also laid claim to the region and its histories—including but not limited to Islam's holiest sites, Mecca and Medina. As such, as the Nation of Islam began to emerge as a powerful force within African-American liberation struggles that complemented and often countered the rhetoric of the Christian dominated civil rights movement, there was a concomitant rise in the role and place of ancient Egypt, Arab nationalism, and Islamic history within the discourses of African-American political culture after 1955. And as the struggles around racism and the politics of race began to escalate during this period, Islam came to be seen as an alternative form of radical Black consciousness that was quite distinct from the integrationist goals of African-American Christianity—a consciousness that was internationalist in nature and one that more clearly reflected and aligned itself with the political currents of anti-colonialism and revolutionary nationalism that were overtaking the Third World in its struggles against imperialism and colonialism.

Increasingly, Christianity came to be seen as inadequate to the political aspirations and spiritual needs of African-Americans. In 'Letter From a Region in My Mind,' published in the *New Yorker* in 1962, James Baldwin openly questioned the role and place of Christianity within African-American public life and the increasing popularity of Islam as a force within African-American liberationist thought and struggle. According to Baldwin, 'the Christian church itself ... sanctified and rejoiced in the conquests of the flag, and encouraged, if it did not formulate, the belief that conquest, and the resulting relative well-being of the Western population, was proof of the favor of God.' Baldwin continues by saying that 'God had come a long way from the desert—but then so had Allah, though in a very different direction. God, going north, and rising on the wings of power, had become white, and Allah, out of power, had become—for all practical purposes anyway—black.'[6]

It is instructive to underscore the claims being made by Baldwin regarding race and power as it relates to God/Allah. For him, and to many other African Americans, God—via Christianity—came to be associated with not only Whiteness, but also with the powerful imperialist aggressors of the Western world, including the United States. Allah—via Islam—however, was 'out of power,' and was understood as Black. In this way, Baldwin openly questioned the efficacy of Christianity for Black liberation—a critique that also challenged Black identifications with, and allegiances to, the United States. Similarly, Malcolm X urged African Americans to move beyond the physical and ideological borders of the United States in seeking redress and social justice for Black people in America. In a speech entitled 'The Ballot or the Bullet,' Malcolm says:

> We need to expand the civil rights struggle to a higher level—to the level of human rights. Whenever you are in a civil rights struggle, whether you know it or not, you are confining yourself to the jurisdiction of Uncle Sam. No one on the outside world can speak out in your behalf as long as your struggle is a civil rights struggle. Civil rights comes from within the domestic affairs of this country. Uncle Sam's hands are dripping with blood, dripping with the blood of the black man in this country ... Take it to the UN, where our African brothers can throw their weight on our side, where our Asian brothers can throw their weight on our side, where our Latin American brothers can throw their weight on our side, and where 800 million Chinamen are sitting there waiting to throw their weight on our side.[7]

As a Muslim, Malcolm employs the rhetoric of 'civil rights' and 'Uncle Sam' to suggest the clear link for him between the Christian-dominated civil rights movement of Dr. King and its appeals and accommodations to the power of the United States for African-American liberation. For Malcolm, the entrenched nature and violent history of White supremacy in the United States demands that African Americans take their struggle to an international level (the United Nations) where other people of color could more fairly and justly determine the legitimacy of Black claims to human dignity. In rhetorically linking the civil rights struggle, Christianity, and the United States, Malcolm powerfully revealed a deep fissure within African-American politics of the time. According to McAlister, whereas Black Christians continued to seek brotherhood and solidarity with Whites despite the continued violence by White Christians against non-violent civil rights activists, 'Islam offered an alternative, a basis for a black nationalist consciousness that was separate from the civil rights goals of integration into a white dominated and oppressive nation.'[8]

These struggles over race and Black identity in the late 1950s and early 60s coincided with the broader currents of anti-colonial struggles against racism and colonialism. By the 1950s, as the Nonaligned Movement was gaining momentum throughout the world, leaders such as Kwame Nkrumah of Ghana, Jawaharlal Nehru of India, Fidel Castro of Cuba, and Gamal Abdul Nasser of Egypt, among others, came into global consciousness due to their strident critiques of colonialism and its cancerous corollary: White supremacy. This kind of global racial consciousness led to the 1955 Afro-Asian Conference in Bandung, Indonesia where 29 countries from Africa, Asia, and the Middle East converged to renounce both White supremacy and the false choice—between the United States and Russia—being offered to newly liberated countries throughout the world. As a clear challenge to White world supremacy and American–Russian dominance in a post-colonial world, these countries created a defiant platform of resistance at Bandung that resonated throughout the Third World. The momentum of this momentous occasion continued throughout the 1950s and into the 60s as anti-colonial movements and national liberation struggles intensified around the world—creating tremendous feelings of affiliation and solidarity across borders and between peoples of color. For African-American anti-colonialists, and particularly with the emergence of the Nation of Islam in the United States, this was the beginning of a transformative period in Black political culture—one that would literally and metaphorically remap Black identity and struggle.

Gamal Abdul Nasser of Egypt was one of the key figures during this period as he not only attended Bandung, but he was also instrumental in hosting the follow-up event in Cairo in 1957 called the Afro-Asian People's Solidarity Conference. More importantly, he also weathered the Suez Crisis of 1956 where he defiantly stood up against France, England, and Israel—thereby solidifying his place as an anti-colonial hero both here in the United States and throughout the world. For African-American Muslims, Egypt was not only the center of African civilization and proof of Black historical greatness, but it was also now a Muslim country. In linking Black greatness and Islam, Nasser came to represent Black and Arab resistance to White supremacy—a powerful synthesis of Black radicalism, anti-colonial defiance, Arab resistance, and African-American Islam that was to have a profound impact on Black identity in the United States.

In addition, Muslim immigrants from South Asia also had a tremendous impact on the development of Islam within African-American communities, particularly with the Nation of Islam and Malcolm X. While Gandhi and the Indian nationalist struggle against the British had a powerful influence on African-American political culture that was crystallized with Dr. Martin Luther King and the non-violent civil rights movement, South Asian Muslims such as Mufti Muhammad Sadiq, Mutuir Rahman Bengalee, Bashir Ahmad Minto, Muhammad Abdullah and Abdul Basit Naeem also had a tremendous impact on the formation of Afro-Asian solidarity amongst African Americans.[9] In forging an internationalist identity between African Americans and other people of color throughout the world, Sadiq and Bengalee, by the mid 1950s, had established 'the most influential community of African-American Islam,'[10] one that was multi-racial in its composition as they saw themselves as part of a larger global movement that was resisting Western imperialism and control. Through their newspaper *The Muslim Sunrise*, there were repeated stories made about the linking of racial struggle here in the United States with those that were taking place throughout the colonized world. And from the 1950s into the 60s, Abdullah and Abdul Basit Naeem had influential roles in the formation and transformations of the Nation of Islam under Elijah Muhammad and Malcolm X, engaging with them on various theological discussions and political debates that led to further support from the Nation for 'Arab and Pakistani causes.'[11]

This complex grammar of resistance centered on Islam as the focal point for the refashioning of a new Black identity. The Nation of Islam had built upon earlier periods of Black anti-colonial sensibilities that saw

African Americans as part of a larger Pan-African diaspora. But while the Nation of Islam was clearly a 'Black nationalist' group, its vision of Black liberation must also be viewed in relation to the organization's constant and insistent transnational affiliations with the larger Islamic world—affiliations that traded upon the fact that Islam was a major world religion that was transnational in scope. For though the Nation of Islam often advocated a racial separatist vision in the United States, it sought to expand the geographical referents of Black identity beyond the exclusivity of the continent of Africa to include much of the non-White world. According to Richard Brent Turner,

> the Nation of Islam's political ideology focused on the political, economic, social, and technological uplift of African-Americans, making them aware of their cultural and historical connections to Africa and the effects of Western imperialism and colonialism on all the areas of the world where people of color lived.[12]

This more expansive vision of an alternative Black genealogy centered on Islam and sought to connect Africa with other parts of the Islamic world where anti-colonial and anti-racist movements against Europe were taking place. As a result, numerous rhetorical strategies were employed to help to define Black identity within and against the United States, as well as in relation to the expanded definitions of Blackness central to the Nation of Islam. The constant and consistent deployment of terms such as the 'Asiatic,' 'Asian black nation,' 'Afro-Asiatic Black Man,' or the 'Asiatic Black Man' were used to provide an alternative genealogy for Black people in America, one that respatialized African-American identity without exclusively looking at Africa as the site for the exploration of Blackness or the recuperation, recovery, and reconstitution of Black history. Central to this vision of Blackness was the role of Islam within its constitution, as a broader geography was employed that included the Middle East (referred to as part of 'Asia') within a construction of Black identity. As Elijah Muhammad says of Black people in America in his seminal text for the Nation of Islam entitled *Message to the Black Man*, 'we are descendants of the Asian black nation … the rich Nile Valley of Egypt and the present seat of the Holy City, Mecca, Arabia.'[13]

This expanded genealogical and geographical referent for Black people in America had clear resonances with the anti-colonial defiance and resistance that was evinced at the 1955 Asian-African Conference at Bandung and the 1957 Afro-Asian People's Solidarity Conference in Cairo. In building upon the rich resource of anti-colonial defiance and anti-racist solidarities that were part and parcel of the era, a complex fabric of resistance was created that brought Black Islam, Arab and South Asian anti-colonialism, and African-American radicalism together in a powerful offensive against White world supremacy. In expanding the geographical referents of Blackness,

African-American Islam in general and the Nation of Islam in particular also reconceptualized and even rejected any connection between Blackness and Americanness—as Muhammad Ali said in 1964, 'I'm not an American. I'm a Black man.'[14] Instead of mapping Black identity and the potential for Black liberation onto the domestic space of the American nation, African-American Islam imagined a very different kind of community that was non-national in character and diasporic in its consciousness. In this way then, 'the community it envisioned provided an alternative to—and in some sense a fundamental critique of—the nation-state. [For] African-American Muslims could claim a symbolic counter-citizenship, an identity that challenged black incorporation into the dominant discourse of Judeo-Christian Americanness.'[15] Through this complex and textured history then, African-American Islam forged a new aesthetics of selfhood that was at once individual and collective, as it inserted itself into various sites of contestation with an ideological hybridity that commanded a renewed understanding of the relationships between the citizen and the state, and the local and the global. And in the post-World War II era, it has been through the cultural spaces of jazz, literature, sports, theater, and now hip hop that these relationships have been constantly negotiated and contested as the struggles around Blackness have sought to confront power in creatively enduring and compelling ways.

THE AFRO-ASIAN ATLANTIC

Like jazz and the Black Arts movement before it, numerous cultural activists in the history of hip hop have used the art form as a platform with which to forge new kinds of alliances, communities of passion, and ways of being around Blackness and Islam that have had a profound impact on Black identity, history, and struggle. Some of the hip hop movement's most significant artists have reconstructed their identities around Islam, including Brand Nubian, Poor Righteous Teachers, Paris, Public Enemy, Ice Cube, Nas, the Wu-Tang Clan, A Tribe Called Quest, Rakim, Pete Rock and CL Smooth, Digable Planets, The Roots, Common, Black Star, Akbar, Divine Styler, Jurassic 5, Mos Def, and others as well. There is a vast canon of songs that reflect the multiplicity of ideological positionings forged by the intersections of Blackness and Islam within hip hop culture—whether it be the bourgeois nationalism of Public Enemy, the bohemian blues of Black Star, the street swagger of Gang Starr, the cosmic chaos of the Wu-Tang Clan, or the Eldridge Cleaver-like revolutionary street theory of early Ice Cube. And while this body of literature is almost overwhelming in its scope and complexity, commenting as it does on race, power, and the American nation-state, I will explore some of the work of both Rakim and Mos Def, as well as the British group the Kaliphz, to explore the manner in which these artists reveal a profound and passionate desire to speak truth to power in the face of racial violence and historical oppression.

Rap's reigning poet laureate and hip hop's natural mystic Rakim has artfully combined a poetic realism with an elevated street consciousness unrivaled in hip hop. Numerous songs of his have invoked his Islamic humanism from 'Know the Ledge' to 'The Mystery (Who is God?)'—as he poignantly articulates his theistic vision for collective redemption. In one of his most brilliant songs, entitled 'In the Ghetto,' Rakim uses the metaphor of birth to signify on the power of the word as a weapon against historical racism and the politics of place. By invoking personal memory and mind travel, Rakim taps into the deep well of Afro-diasporic collective memory, fusing together a complex history of ancient Egypt and Black greatness with his travels to Islam's two holiest sites—Mecca and Medina. In doing so, Rakim identifies as 'Asian,' further underscoring his Afro-Asian Islamic identity as he powerfully suggests that the transcendence of place and secular suffering can be achieved by harnessing the power of both individual and collective pasts to remedy the injurious impact of contemporary racism.

And while 'In the Ghetto' uses personal reflection as a vehicle for collective protest, his 1992 song 'Casualties of War' uses social realism to critically comment on American imperialism and its history of slavery, as Rakim takes on the persona of a United States soldier in the midst of the first Persian Gulf War. 'Casualties of War' is an incredibly vivid narrative about race and belief, slavery and imperialism, national allegiance and international belonging, and individual redemption and agency in the face of horror and war. Considering the current historical juncture where the invasion and occupation of Iraq persists, 'Casualties of War' is prophetic protest poetry that again clearly suggests the vital necessity for understanding and engaging the enduring power and sophisticated ideological discussions concerning race, history, and power that have been, and continue to be, expressed within hip hop culture.

In the song, Rakim vividly describes the conditions of war, as he then links the violence in the Persian Gulf with the violent, war-like circumstances that exist in impoverished neighborhoods in the United States that continue to go unaddressed by the American nation-state. Rakim's linkage of these two social traumas—war abroad and violence at home—is a poignant critique of the powerful political and economic forces in the United States that contribute to both of these terrors. In connecting American aggression with the senseless violence that occurs in the urban centers of New York, 'Casualties of War' suggests that the complex web of race, class, and nation forces people of color from violent impoverished urban centers to serve in the United States military in its imperial aggressions abroad—the racialized frontier where the frontline and color line meet.

Throughout 'Casualties of War,' Rakim defiantly expresses his disillusionment and rage against the tyranny of American political, economic, and military hegemony. While Rakim critically elaborates on American blood thirst and his own training for torture, he openly rejects his position as a member of the United States military and the corrupted ideals of its war agenda. And while this defiant self-realization of American demagoguery compels him to stop firing at the Iraqis, it is his moral and critical consciousness—one that reflects a more nuanced sense of Black identity and national belonging—that is the basis for his resistance and ultimately his redemption.

For instead of empowerment and self-actualization coming from military service and nationalism, Rakim invokes 'Allah' as his sole protectorate and not America, and then proceeds not only to provide a powerful critique of modernity itself—as he links the history of slavery with American imperial aggression in Iraq—but he also suggests an alternative vision of Black identity that expands the geographic referents of Blackness to include people from Africa, Asia, the Middle East, and America. In rejecting American notions of community vis-à-vis individual identification with the national collective, Rakim instead realizes a new kind of belonging that is transnational in scope, but locally specific as he mobilizes a recurrent trope within African-American Islam that is informed by a diasporic Black consciousness. In not only asserting his affinity and solidarity to the Islamic history of Iraq and its people, Rakim also defiantly asserts that this place—what he refers to as Asia—is where he (Rakim) came from. In referencing the trope of the Afro-Asiatic Black Man, Rakim taps into a rich legacy and resource within African-American Islam that has been used to not only expand the definitions of Black identity that do not center exclusively on Africa, but that has also served to connect Black people in the United States with other peoples of color throughout the world against White supremacy.

Rakim's identification and signification as Afro-Asian, and his epiphany regarding his origins and broader racial identity within the song's narrative, links him with the Iraqi people who are seen as the victims of Euro-American imperial aggression while at the same time rhetorically and literally rejecting any identification with the American national body. While he rhetorically rejects 'Americanness' and its racially coded Whiteness, he also begins to fire his weapon at the agents and symbols of Americanness and American aggression—namely, his general and the sergeant. What underscores the racial component of Rakim's embrace of his 'Asiatic' roots, his rejection of America, and the shooting of United States military officers, is the historically informed reference in the song to John Hawkins, whom Rakim asserts is responsible for bringing him (Rakim) to the United States—as Hawkins is responsible for initiating British involvement in the slave trade in 1562, which was the beginning of the establishment of the institution of slavery for the British empire. In using individual experience to inform collective history, Rakim's cultural pedagogy of the oppressed forges a powerful and poetic linkage of the past and present, the local and the global, slavery and contemporary imperialism into a complex grammar of resistance that critiques not only the American nation-state and its bloody history, but also any bounded sense of Black identity.

With his powerful use of language in speaking truth to power, Rakim highlights the contested nature of the relationship between Blackness, Islam, and the American nation-state. In expanding the geographical referents of Blackness and aligning himself with other peoples of color—particularly in the Islamic world—Rakim makes a powerful statement about race, resistance, and a diasporic consciousness in a world still firmly under the boot of White supremacy. In fighting state repression with a song of insurrection, Rakim's 'Casualties of War' is a testament to the enduring power of the word to inspire hope, raise consciousness, and reveal truth.

Prior to the opening track of Mos Def's album *Black on Both Sides*, Mos Def recites what is commonly uttered by Muslims prior to beginning any endeavor. In beginning his album this way, Mos Def foregrounds Muslim belief and his complex Afro-Islamic identity—a powerful testament clearly meant to inform and underscore the cultural politics of his art. The opening song 'Fear Not of Man'—which is one of the most historically rich, culturally layered, and politically complex songs in recent times, immediately follows this recitation. Using the opening track as an opportunity to discuss and describe the state of the hip hop union, Mos Def participates in one of hip hop's most common tropes, that of the self-reflexive critique of the genre and its current status. But rather than aiming his lyrical sights at other MCs who somehow dilute or damage 'the game,' Mos Def instead uses the song as an opportunity to meditate on hip hop's possibilities by advocating for the power of self-realization and individual upliftment in the face of social control and post-industrial decline. In doing so, Mos Def creatively and brilliantly employs a multiplicity of strategies that reflect a complex ideological hybridity rooted in an anti-racist, Pan-African, Black Nationalist, and anti-colonial Islamic critique of contemporary cultural and geopolitical realities.

In beautifully expressing his position in 'Fear Not of Man,' Mos Def does so over a pulsating and insurgent beat that is sampled from a 1977 song entitled 'Fear Not For Man' from the legendary and incendiary king of Afro-Beat, Fela Kuti. Fela was and is arguably one of the most radical cultural spokespersons from within the history of popular music, and who recorded numerous albums from the early 1970s until his death in 1997. Influenced by James Brown, Curtis Mayfield, Stevie Wonder, and the Black Power movement in the United States, Fela's music was a hypnotic blend of Nigerian rhythms, jazz and funk over which he would sing some of the most politically charged anthems of anti-colonial dissent and Pan-African hopes and dreams. In invoking the spirit and soul of Fela Kuti, Mos Def's song is an ongoing dialog with Fela's vision—though Mos Def's song, entitled

'Fear Not *of* Man' is a slight, but significant, recontextualization of the Fela original.

In his 'Fear Not For Man,' Fela quotes Kwame Nkrumah—who Fela refers to as the father of Pan-Africanism—and asserts that 'the secret of life is to have no fear.' Fela and his band then, driven by the beautiful percussion of Tony Allen, proceed to unleash an intoxicating rhythm of resistance. In invoking the revolutionary Ghanaian leader Kwame Nkrumah, Fela admonishes Black people to continue the struggle of those who came before, and to do so without fear—despite the repressive political environment that permeates the lives of those who Frantz Fanon called the wretched of the earth. In the throes of the post-colonial misery that has viciously and violently characterized the post-liberation moment for far too many decolonizing nation-states, Fela's 'Fear Not For Man' is meant as an inspiration towards collective solidarity—suggesting that 'Man', as the gendered representative of humanity, will prevail despite the men who create and perpetuate injustice and inequality. As an empowering ode to a utopian vision in dystopic times, Mos Def's sampling of the Fela original creates a compelling conversation between two revolutionary cultural movements: Afro-Beat and hip hop.

In sampling Fela's song and slightly modifying the title, Mos Def artfully places his piece in the context of a diasporic Black radical imagination that is rooted in history and in collective memory.[16] In *Black Noise*, Tricia Rose suggests that sampling and inter-textual reference in hip hop is a powerful weapon for the weak that foregrounds and affirms Black social and cultural history by rearticulating it and making the past present, creating what she calls 'communal counter-memory'—a strategy of resistance against forgetting and the silencing by dominant White society of Black voices, ideas, and sounds.[17] For Mos Def, by invoking the memory of Fela Kuti (through the sample and song title) and in turn Kwame Nkrumah (whose quote informs the philosophical basis for Fela and therefore Mos Def's song), Mos Def creatively connects the contemporary struggles of African Americans specifically and people of color generally, with the insurgent, anti-colonial history of both Nkrumah and Fela Kuti. This kind of cultural history and critical archaeology not only reflects the transnational dimensions and ideological reach of Mos Def, but it also serves to re-imagine Black identity both within and beyond the borders of the American nation-state—forging a diasporic consciousness that is rooted in a specific anti-racist critique of American society.

But whereas Mos Def connects racial and cultural struggle transnationally by invoking Fela Kuti and Kwame Nkrumah, 'Fear Not of Man' also invokes the locally specific yet historically informed politics of Black Nationalist struggle within the United States by referencing hip hop's elders, the legendary Last Poets—the groundbreaking spoken word collective formed on Malcolm X's birthday in 1968. In describing a world dominated by surveillance technology and filled with satellites, cameras, televisions, and societies and governments who are, according to Mos Def, trying to be God, Mos Def then refers to the Last Poets and asserts that they must have been right when they (Last Poets) claimed that a certain group of people have a God complex. In invoking the Last Poets, Mos Def makes a scathing critique of race in general and Whiteness in particular by referencing the Last Poets' classic song 'White Man's Got a God Complex'—where Mos Def assents to the Last Poets' powerful assertion regarding the machinations of White supremacy, as his silence on naming who these 'certain people' are becomes not only a deafening critique of race, power, and surveillance, but also a prescient and even prophetic insight into our contemporary moment in the post-9/11 era.

In addition, being that the song is a meditation on the power of the divine, or at least the relative powerlessness of man ('Fear Not of Man'), Mos Def's employment of the Last Poets' 'White Man's Got a God Complex' also serves to mobilize the history of Black resistance to—and understanding of—the racialized claims regarding the Whiteness of God/Jesus/the divine, thereby also subverting the dominant racial logic and hierarchy of White supremacy in America. In addition to this subtle critique of the intersection of race and belief, Mos Def's 'Fear Not of Man'—in evoking the Last Poets—is also suggesting the historical connection and political possibilities between contemporary hip hop culture and the radically poetic spoken word tradition that it emanates from, which includes the Last Poets, Amiri Baraka, and others.

In linking past and present, memory and place, culture and resistance and ultimately, hope and redemption, Mos Def's 'Fear Not of Man' fundamentally remaps conventional understandings of Black identity. While Malcolm X modeled his Organization of Afro-American Unity (OAAU) on Kwame Nkrumah's Organization of Africa Unity (OAU), Mos Def—by implicitly invoking Nkrumah's memory—creates the cultural equivalent of Malcolm X's political ideal, a vision of Black liberation that reconstitutes our understanding of the local and the global, the national and the transnational. In viewing anti-racist struggle—both political and cultural—as globally interlinked and contingent, Mos Def tells the histories of those who—according to Jose David Saldivar—have 'local frames of awareness' but who are 'situated globally.'[18] In envisioning himself and Black liberation struggle beyond the borders of the American nation-state, Mos Def in 'Fear Not of Man' weaves together a powerfully compelling narrative that links slavery and imperialism, race and colonialism, politics and culture in an artful and poignant expression of Afro-Islamic diasporic consciousness.

While Islam and Blackness in the United States have made compelling critiques of race, power, and place (particularly the American nation-state), the globalization of hip hop culture and its impact throughout the world foregrounds hip hop's own mythologization of 'place.' Be it Mos Def in

Brooklyn, the Wu-Tang Clan in Staten Island, or Nas in Queensbridge, the recurrent trope in hip hop of claiming place becomes transformed as hip hop is increasingly globalized. Just as the politics of place within hip hop in the United States is imbued with the larger powerfields of race, class, and gender, and all of the policing that this entails (both literal and rhetorical), hip hop within a global terrain can also amplify the politics of place, as the global landscape for migrants, exiles, and refugees makes questions of place and belonging highly contested and politicized. In considering the cultural politics of global hip hop, it is important to ask: How does hip hop's allegiance/homage to place empower these cultural producers—who themselves are subjects of colonial history and postcolonial displacement, and whose sense of place is so contingent and fleeting—to create political and cultural identities that are at once oppositional, insurgent, and locally specific, but also globally aware and transnationally constituted? For many, just as in the United States, the racialized matrix of modernity and globalization has had profound implications for the movements of people due to the history of slavery, colonialism, and its aftermath—and just as it is woven into the fabric of hip hop culture in the United States, hip hop in Britain also reflects the politics of race and place.

As South Asian Muslims from Pakistan (and former subjects of the empire), the Kaliphz specifically express the politics of lower class Asian existence in Britain, as they also provide searing critiques of British racism that are both creative and complex. In a song entitled 'Asiatic Static,' they rap about Asian unity in Britain between Hindus, Muslims, and Sikhs, as they encourage Asians to embrace their history as a collective struggle against British racism. This collective sense of struggle seeks to rally descendants of the Indian subcontinent around a shared and collective history, admonishing them to wear their turbans in the urban environment, reclaim their pasts, and bring their Asian identities to the streets of Britain as a resistance to their marginalization in a racist society that has shunned and even repressed Asian expressions of that history. In addition, their use of the term 'Asiatics' in both the title and the song is compelling, particularly when, in the one verse, they rap 'terrorize the jam like troops from Pakistan.' In doing so, the Kaliphz are not only serving notice of an empowered genealogy and reminder that they hail from Pakistan—locating their own histories in relationship to the British empire. But the line is also a reference to a classic song from one of hip hop's greatest albums—'Protect Ya Neck' from the Wu-Tang Clan's *Enter the 36th Chamber*. In referencing this song (where Inspectah Deck raps the exact line) as well as the Wu-Tang Clan's own complex ideological positionings regarding Islam and an Afro-Asiatic identity, the Kaliphz call on other 'Asiatics'—though this time a reference to (South) Asians in Britain—to upset the status quo in England by standing proudly and defiantly against social inequity and historical exclusion. But in invoking the Wu-Tang Clan and their own expanded and broadened definitions of the Wu's own Black

identity vis-à-vis Islam and an 'Afro-Asiatic' identity, the Kaliphz cleverly
and creatively connect themselves as Muslims, as 'Black' people in Britain
(where 'Black' has historically referred to non-White groups), and as Asians
(Asiatics) to the complex history of Islamic-centered notions of Afro-Asiatic
identity amongst African-American Muslims.

And while 'Asiatic Static' is an empowering ode through the language of
hip hop to South Asians in Britain, the Kaliphz have also been vocal critics
of the racial violence in Britain against Black/Asian youth—particularly
from racist groups such as the BNP (British National Party) and the National
Front.[19] In a song entitled 'Hang Em High'—which references the 1968 Clint
Eastwood film in which the main character is unjustly victimized only to
then exact his own revenge—the Kaliphz appropriate the notion of vigilante
justice as a commentary on the failure and even complicity of British law to
put an end to the attacks of White supremacist groups against Black/Asian
communities. In the song, the Kaliphz defiantly resist White supremacist
violence with a powerful and potent description of self-defense against
British racism, as they also deliver a rich text with which to interrogate
Black/Asian identity in Britain. In the song, the Kaliphz dispel any possibility
that they are timid or pacifists—a strong and misguided stereotype rooted
in Orientalist notions that has plagued South Asians in Britain and served
to further marginalize them. By explicitly distancing themselves from
Gandhi's pacifism, the Kaliphz instead implicitly embrace the militancy of
South Asian revolutionaries such as Bhagat Singh as they defiantly assert a
self-defensive posture against racist skinhead attacks that have claimed the
lives of numerous Black/Asian youth in Britain. But this vivid narrative of
resistance that critiques White supremacist violence in Britain also connects
it to the Ku Klux Klan in the United States—as the Kaliphz suggest the
historical connections and relationships between Britain and the United
States that have fostered racial terrorism and White supremacist violence.
In doing this, the Kaliphz also draw parallels between the history and legacy
of African-American racial violence at the hands of the Ku Klux Klan
and institutional racism in the United States and their own conditions as
historical and contemporary subjects of British colonialism and racism.
In linking place (Britain and Tennessee), race (Black/Asian and African-
American with Whiteness), and history (colonialism and slavery) through
hip hop culture, the Kaliphz have provided the possibilities for powerful and
empowered forms of identity that embody the politics of the glocal—as they
are diasporic in scope, yet also rooted in a critique of the White supremacist
undertones upon which the British nation-state is based.

THE REBEL'S SILHOUETTE

The complex mosaic of Afro-Asian resistance that has been woven together
by the overlapping histories and shared territories of struggle as a result of

slavery and colonialism should engender a fundamental reconceptualization of traditional understandings of race, identity, and the nation-state. In forging a complex redefinition of being and belonging, Afro-Asian Islam should be placed within the long and prolific history of diasporic radicalism and internationalism, as it puts forth powerful expressions of anti-racist struggle that redefines race within a broader global configuration of solidarity— enlarging the scope of social struggle and re-imagining individuals not as national minorities but as global majorities. And while the rich and textured history of diasporic Muslim thought in the twentieth century has not yet been fully explored,[20] my brief interrogation into the political and cultural history of Afro-Asian Muslim solidarity through hip hop culture seeks to give shape to this kind of diasporic radicalism that is situated somewhere between the nation and its fragments, art and politics, word and speech, and the visible and the unseen. As their drums reveal what power conceals, these artists stand at the tattered edges of the modern nation-state, creating what revolutionary writer and poet Aimé Césaire has called 'poetic knowledge,'[21] as they forge new ways to truth tell, soul search, and bear witness to being and believing in new forms of global humanism that fundamentally challenge the Enlightenment project and its dogmas that claim freedom, democracy, and individual liberty.

NOTES

1. There is a substantial political history behind the term 'Afro-Asian' as my discussion that follows will reveal. And while I am clearly invoking this history, I am also including within 'Afro-Asia' what is commonly referred to as the 'Middle East'—a term that not only problematically uses Europe as its point of reference, but also a term that refers to a region that has also been called West Asia. Theoretical interventions such as Edward Said's *Orientalism* links these seemingly disparate regions—as both Area Studies and Asian-American studies have been influenced by Said's work. And while Islam and Muslim history clearly link these regions, the term is far from perfect in illuminating and clarifying the slippage inherent. As will become clearer below though, African-American Islam has also referred to this region as Asia, as it has mobilized numerous tropes to highlight its own fundamental reconceptualization of geography—embracing the term 'Afro-Asian' as a strategic device to forge solidarity and belonging.

2. There has been considerable scholarship and debate within Islam regarding what exactly its 'true' nature is. The multiple meanings that can and have been associated with Islam—by Muslims and non-Muslims alike—are the source of deep conflicts as different societies and cultures throughout history have attempted to connect it to some materiality. I do want to emphasize that Islam is not monolithic—that its meanings are shifting and contested depending upon individuals, societies, cultures, traditions, and histories. Any attempt to understand the dynamics of the various parts of the Islamic worlds—with its almost 1 billion inhabitants spread mostly throughout Asia and Africa—can only be undertaken by engaging this profound diversity. This is no less true when exploring African-American Islam—forged as it is out of the history of slavery and racial apartheid in the United States. The ideological differences and influences between the various expressions of Muslim belief within African-America—whether it be Sunni Islam, Five-Percent Nation, The Nation of

Islam, the influence of the Ahmadiyyas (both Qadian and Lahore branches) and others, reflect similar debates that continue to exist in other parts of the Muslim worlds.

3.   In exploring hip hop culture as a site for the intersections of race, nation, and Islam in the United States, it is important to recognize the profound and significant contributions made by the intersection of Islam and Blackness to the history of hip hop, be it the work of Rakim, Brand Nubian, Poor Righteous Teachers, The Roots, Public Enemy, Gang Starr, Common, A Tribe Called Quest, Mos Def, Ice Cube, the Wu-Tang Clan, Jurassic 5, and numerous others. This presence has not been critically interrogated for the manner in which these cultural formations not only express complex political lexicons of diasporic radicalism, but they also suggest new ways of constructing alternative forms of Black identity and its relationship to American national belonging in the late twentieth century.

4.   Melani McAlister, *Epic Encounters: Culture, Media, and U.S. Interests in the Middle East, 1945–2000* (Berkeley: University of California Press, 2001), p. 104.

5.   Marvin X and Faruk X, 'Islam and Black Art: An Interview With Leroi Jones,' *Dictionary of Literary Biography: Black Arts Movement*, ed. Jeff Decker (Detroit: Gale, 1984), p. 128.

6.   James Baldwin, *The Fire Next Time* (New York: Dell Publishing, 1977), p. 46.

7.   Malcolm X, 'The Ballot or the Bullet,' *Malcolm X Speaks: Selected Speeches and Statements*, ed. George Breitman (New York: Pathfinder, 1965), pp. 34–5.

8.   McAlister, *Epic Encounters*, p. 93.

9.   See Richard Brent Turner, *Islam in the African-American Experience* (Bloomington: Indiana University Press, 1997) for an excellent history of African-American Islam.

10. Ibid., p. 138.

11. Ibid., p. 196.

12. Ibid., p. 159.

13. Elijah Muhammad, *Message to the Black Man in America* (Chicago: Muhammad Mosque of Islam, 1965), p. 31.

14. Robert Lipsyte, 'Cassius Clay, Cassius X, Muhammad Ali,' *New York Times Magazine*, October 25, 1964, p. 29.

15. McAlister, *Epic Encounters*, p. 93.

16. See Robin Kelley, *Freedom Dreams: The Black Radical Imagination* (Boston: Beacon Press, 2002).

17. Tricia Rose, *Black Noise* (Middletown, CT: Wesleyan University Press, 1994).

18. Jose David Saldivar, *Border Matters: Remapping American Cultural Studies* (Berkeley: University of California, 1997).

19. For more information on both historical and ongoing racist violence in Britain, please visit the Independent Race and Refugee News Network at <http://www.irr.ok.org>. The racist attacks on Blacks/Asians such as Stephen Lawrence, Satpal Ram, Ricky Reel, and numerous others tragically continues, particularly in light of the ideological cover that has been provided by 9/11 and the 'threats' posed to the nation-state by the 'Others.'

20. This article is a 12" single from my larger full-length project in which I hope to map the complex cultural and intellectual history of diasporic Muslim thought in the twentieth century through jazz, literature, cinema, sports, and hip hop culture as anti-colonial and anti-racist movements have reshaped global power realities and alliances.

21. See Aimé Césaire, *Discourse on Colonialism* (New York: New York University Press, 2000).

SIDE TWO:

Rap and Hip Hop Groove Globally

8

The Nation Question: Fun^da^mental and the Deathening Silence

John Hutnyk

The politics of the group Fun^da^mental is the politics of hip hop, crossed with a punk Islam that morphs increasingly into interventions around race and representation, the war of 'terror,' and a radical version of human rights activism. This chapter charts an intertwined story about the journalistic reportage that surrounds the band, the record company from which they come, and the role of commentary and critique of the cultural politics, in a National register, that is their chosen milieu. In Britain, should it surprise us, the lyrical-rhythmic production of this Nation Records' outfit has led to a terse relationship with the mainstream. Much of the music industry press and the critical comment that has been addressed to the band, and to their left-oriented takes on racism, imperialism, women and war, has betrayed itself as inadequate through distortion, condemnation, and hostility.

It is by now a commonplace that hip hop often suffers a bad press, but when it comes in the guise of Islam-oriented South Asians from the North of England, mixed up with a militant New York sensibility and an intolerance of intolerance that takes on world historical political issues, this is exacerbated. I want to argue that a new angle on Fun^da^mental might be due, though it is not for me to say that the language of the music press or academic convention is always wrong and to be rejected. It is rather that I favor the possibility of additional, even complementary, reorientations in an experimental set which hopes to open ears and minds. So, as the spotlight is moved to a different part of the stage, it might be plausible to look more carefully at the concepts and codewords involved. Thus: cue the master of anti-colonial ceremonial, Aki Nawaz, aka Propa Gandhi. The 'fun' and the 'mental' in fundamentalism is unleashed with a cascading mantra: 'There shall be love, there shall be resistance, there shall be expression, there shall be defense, there shall be peace, or ... there shall be war.'[1]

Conventional discussions of hip hop in Europe begin with ritual acknowledgement of the derivation of the form from the United States, soon followed by equally ritual insistence that local versionings of hip hop have their own character and autonomy. Without minimizing or forgetting variations in the regional reach of the music, I am tempted to argue that insistence on the similarity and difference of European hip hop(s) is little more than a two-step cultural cringe, masquerading as a boundary demarcation, but in all cases subject to forces of complicity, co-option, commercialization, and enclosure. If hip hop in Europe is marked by the same issues of articulation and institutionalization that afflict U.S. variants, it may be that a more interesting analysis would address something other than provenance or autonomy, and not repeat the formulaic recitations of the music press and cultural-industrial complex.

Global hip hop is of course institutionalized. It is a part of the music industry as *industry*. Here it is useful to remember Adorno's insistance that we examine the mass production process of the cultural. Routinization is engraved into the grooves of records that are played over and over,[2] and which are now played all over the place in an industry grafted onto a cultural form that activates a vast apparatus. Systematically integrating creativity, performance, distribution, sales; image, fashion, consumption and design; record stores, nightclubs, fashion shoots and parties; journalists, A&R (artist and repertoire), style mags and sweatshirts; spray cans and raybans, turntables and tablas; junglist-reggae feedback loops of extravagance and power; mad sonic digital fx, old school, nu skool and codes from back in the day ... even the language of hip hop conforms minds to its ways. Yet as an industry, hip hop commands and demands a range of responses and potentials to rival other contemporary media forms.

This industry has reach. 'Hip hop ... has become a vehicle for global youth' says one commentator,[3] just as he narrates the routine of a move from the 'adoption to an adaptation of US musical forms and idioms.'[4] This historical and progressivist model does acknowledge that there is now a universal hip hop language, and notes that attention is also due to its forms outside the United States. But by insisting on this attention, I suggest a telling concession is made to pride of place in a way that betrays the origins and the sentiment of hip hop as it is made and lived by practitioners, rather than as documented by music press commentators and academics.

A vast culture industry. That much is true, we all know hip hop comes with its own parallel commentaries and a reach that goes beyond the expectations of the 'under-assistant west-coast promo-man.' Within the apparatus of this chapter I want to examine the role of commentary and critique in a political light. Discussions of hip hop in Britain continually address the diversity, reach, and extension of the cultures of hip hop. This is why Fun^da^mental are worth considering here. They exemplify the scene's eclectic mix. Should we talk about the music first, or the make up of the band? Fun^da^mental hail from the Nation Records label and album to album produce a repertoire of music that has drawn an unprecedentedly wide range of comment and comparison. They have been characterized as among the first UK rap acts; they are known popularisers of the devotional Sufi music form Qawaali; they can produce lyrical Bollywood-hip hop crossover like 'Sister India';[5] or mad loud metal distortion lyric chaos like 'GoDevil';[6] they effect a hardcore punk aesthetic (impresario Aki Nawaz was formerly a drummer in the Southern Death Cult); and with a diminutive inflection, they have been marked as the Asian Public Enemy.[7] The 'Global Sweatbox' night that was a feature of the turn of the millennium London dance scene was a Nation initiative, and the label, which Nawaz co-owns, has consistently worked in an international register. Acts as diverse as Prophets of Da City from South Africa, Aziz Mian from Pakistan, Asian Dub Foundation[8] from the East End as well as Transglobal Underground and Loop Guru (from some other planetary domain) have been brought together in debate and exchange. Unlike conventional world music marketeering however, Nation and Fun^da^mental have a political project that underwrites their involvement.

Ted Swedenburg has noted that 'among the manifold responses of European Muslims to Islamophobia has been hip hop activism.'[9] This is also important in terms of the specificity of hip hop in the UK. If we want to chart this specificity, including its variant idioms and associated forms (jungle, trip-hop, grime) we might begin by noting how it is marked variously by nation, race, and class. This is relevant not only in terms of practitioners and audiences, but also in relation to wider public characterizations of hip hop as street music or club music—somehow dangerous and linked to crime and drug violence, by Government ministers no less (in Britain this is illustrated with the So Solid Crew incident in January 2003, see below). That a race and class analysis requires more than noticing *where* those who produce the sounds come *from* should be self-evident (even if those who produce the sounds are 'originally' out of some version of a so-called 'ghetto,' their incorporation into the culture industry does not guarantee a general social uplift). Keeping in mind the workings of racism and imperialism, that hip hop carries the burden of demonization alongside drugs, cars, trainers, and guns, has not insignificant consequences for the systemic impoverishment of Black peoples of whatever social status in multi-racial Britain, and across Europe as a whole.

THE TAME PRESS

In this context an 'overreverential attitude towards US rap' in British hip hop[10] is something to be questioned. While it is true that the 'variety' and 'diversity' of hip hop in Europe is often attested to, and offered as criteria for, the maturity and autonomy of the European market in itself, a cursory glance through any of the music press commentaries will confirm the ways this diversity is conflicted. Britain's premiere hip hop magazines, for example, continually carry articles, interviews, and reviews that frame evaluation in terms of whether or not UK hip hop has 'come of age.' To be reassured that there is 'a healthy UK scene,' as we are with *Knowledge* magazine in an article comparing drum and bass with hip hop, is indicative.[11] In a staged debate ('Clash of the Titans') between Rodney P and Skitz in the magazine

HHC,[12] Rodney P rails against 'All this big "UK rap is so fucking great"'
and thinks that the requirement to support UK acts without criticism is
'nowhere.' Skitz agrees, but argues that the 'foundation' has to be strong
and has to be sustained by people working on their quality, and he goes on
to say 'A bit of investment in the scene wouldn't hurt as well.' Rodney P
counters with a comment about how 'this ain't no UK rap thing; it's a hip
hop thing. It's got to be looked at as global. It's a big fucking market place
and you've got to stand up.'[13] Later in the same magazine Skeme is reported
highlighting the broad base of influences behind British rap, and then the
reviews section repeats similar refrains, though with more attention to the
global: for example 'Australian hip hop suffers the same fate that UK hip
hop did ten years ago. People keep focusing on the origins rather than the
music.'[14] The opposition between national source and quality in the global
market clearly occupies minds and pages.

What then of a group that falls over itself to transgress these conventions
within the belly of this beastly apparatus? Fun^da^mental formed back in the
early 1990s with their first single, 'Janaam'[15] and were widely praised for their
album *Seize the Time* in 1994. The Bobby Seale–Huey P. Newton reference
of the title was just one among the many influences that have stayed with
the band through numerous line-up changes and mutations—the silhouetted
figure of the Black Panther Party leader adorns 'There Shall be Love.'[16]
Consistency. *Seize the Time* also included the controversial (for MTV, who
refused to play it) anti-racist, self-defense anthem 'Dog-Tribe'—provoking
debates about vigilantism and militancy amongst community youth.[17] That
the track and video are still known despite commercial veto[18] indicates the
relevance of a more explicit and nuanced agenda within UK hip hop—one
that is engaged with local, and not necessarily just musical, concerns. What
is more, Fun^da^mental have presented, and acted out, their politics as
an engaged and revolutionary practice, with rallies, campaign work, and
activism supplementing the sounds. What the work of Fun^da^mental
means, I think, is that there is scope for an elaborated hip hop politics
that goes beyond banal slogans and imported posturings. This is not to
dismiss the musical adventures of the Rap Revolution tour party sampler
of 2002, on which Rodney P and Skitz also appear, and which is dedicated
to 'the brave Sikhs of the Punjab and all other real revolutionaries out there
fighting for change.'[19] But taking into account issues of local activism and
engagement, the tendency of commercial media to only focus upon the
slogans of revolution as a sensation or as a kind of exotica is something to
be guarded against. Sloganeering will minimize and subsume the politics
of hip hop in favor of commerce if it does not come with what used to be
called a 'programme.'

It is my argument that the work of Fun^da^mental explores their own
emergent idiom in a way that can be included within a broad category of hip
hop only if we acknowledge that the notion of hip hop creatively expands

according to who and where the forms are deployed. Hip hop inflected through Qawaali and the rhythms of the subcontinent owes much less to that derivative labeling of early Fun^da^mental as the 'Asian Public Enemy,' than to adventurous and committed engagement with what is interesting and inspiring, for Nawaz and Watts, in varieties of music not necessarily tuned into the Bronx or South Central. In their survey of the provenance of hip hop and its arrival in the UK, Hesmondhalgh and Melville stress that derision of early efforts by UK rappers was due to a high value being placed 'on authenticity above all else.'[20] As the 1980s wore on, the determination to 'keep it real'[21] and an allegiance to U.S. models of Afrocentric politics, meant British hip hop struggled to find, but eventually did find, ways to make a mark. That this happened in terms of skills—scratching and mixing—and an influence on other genres is identified by commentators as the source of a more diverse and creative musical spectrum (breakbeat, soul, jungle, trip-hop). But this is perhaps less important than the idiom that bands like Fun^da^mental found for their own expression. My argument is that slavish and almost parodic imitation of forms of hip hop commentary which are also promoted by the culture industry surrounding hip hop ('the music, the music') has singularly failed to comprehend this idiom in a *political* way.

How does this work in the music press? In Britain the music industry is served by a number of generalist glossy magazines, which used to be 'inky' broadsheets of the type that left thumbs stained after reading, and a number of specific niche market hip hop magazines that cater for a select audience. That is, there are specific genre mags and there are the wider music market specials like the *New Music Express*, or *NME*.[22] The ways these magazines address 'politics' is itself of interest—often the broader based papers will offer a general survey of political positions for the 'uninitiated' or general reader, while the specialist genre press sometimes can have something of a 'preaching to the converted' tone. 'Preaching' is a major sin for the *NME*, and it indicates a disdain of any political position that stays too far to the left of mild liberal sentiment. Thus Fun^da^mental have sometimes run foul of their journalism, and sometimes amusingly run rings around their journalists providing good copy that can show, for example, how the exoticist sensibilities of an enthusiastic but naive journalist might be exposed by the more nuanced anti-racist politics of a hip hop outfit. It is exactly their sustained challenge to any subsumption or dilution of their race and class politics that makes the rap of Fun^da^mental crucial, and critical. Their attitude entails a refusal to compromise that matters in a way that compares favorably with the way most hip hop acts are discussed in the trade papers and in academic commentary. Here the business-as-usual debate between music and culture distorts into reruns of the U.S. scene—where the imported categories of comprehension polarize between gun-culture and social uplift.

The absurdity of politicians condemning British hip hopers So Solid Crew for valorizing weaponry in lyrics and claiming this leads to deaths such as those of two teenagers at a new year's party in 2003, for example, is matched only by certain populist hip hop acts promoting themselves as the calming and healing influences in a counter-intuitive photo opportunity. In the midst of the flash bulbs and self-congratulatory awards, the socio-economic conditions that encourage gun crime remain firmly off stage, as are the more astute messages of bands like Fun^da^mental. Here the discussions of the hip hop press are also found wanting. When *Knowledge* magazine does pay attention to the political pedigree of hip hop, this is often in a denigrating or tokenistic way. Contradictorily cognizant and dismissive of the 'origins' orientation, and equally impatient with 'preaching,' the tone is one that nods up front to an 'underground spawned from an urban landscape' but quickly resorts to discussion of 'the music' in a way difficult to distinguish from the press release platitudes of a marketing operation. The paraphrase of press release should be no surprise I guess; a magazine is ultimately also an item up for sale. But the character of the scene and the flavor of an 'urban landscape' is mocked when politicized terms appear in the texts, names, and discussions, without any actual or acknowledged political content. Consider for example the deployment of notions of what it means to 'Reprezent,' or of the importance of 'knowledge' and education in the Full Cycle 'camp,' the idea of a 'campaign' group[23]—all this reinforces the undercurrent of hostility towards 'preachery' politics that ensures that the diversity and commitment of hip hop does not translate onto the global market registers. A critical observer might ask just what is the 'campaign,' 'representation,' and 'knowledge' all about if industry investment and market share are the primary foci. This might be called complicity.

Before any new preaching starts then, it should be noted that complicity is also complex for Fun^da^mental, primarily because they have long recognized and articulated the credo of Rakim. The necessity and justice of getting paid for cultural production in a cultural economy cannot be doubted. Fair dues are due to all concerned. Aki Nawaz asks, 'Where is the payback? I want to see the payback' on *Erotic Terrorism*,[24] but he has in mind a return investment on hundreds of years of global plunder, not just a royalty check today. Fun^da^mental have always articulated this in a double engagement that to my mind seems honest to ideas of a hip hop ethic. The music industry is a platform. For example, to take another of the key words in the repertoire of culture commentary, 'visibility' is a means to express a perspective that would otherwise be ignored. Visibility itself is much discussed by academics in relation to Black people in the media. It is enough to quote Sanjay Sharma who pointed out, at the launch of a cultural studies think book called *Dis-Orienting Rhythms: The Politics of the New Asian Dance Music*, that 'it used to be you'd see Sheila Chandra on *Top of the Pops* and go "oh look, Asians on the telly." Now it seems we are visible everywhere.' The burden of *Dis-Orienting Rhythms* was that this visibility was still very much complicit with and subsumed under the commercial imperatives and fashions of the media. New Asian music, of which Fun^da^mental were the primary exponents, was suddenly cool, diversity was in, difference and *desi* dominated the airwaves.

In London, throughout the late 1990s and especially in 2002, the fascination for things South Asian was unprecedented, exceeding even the 1960s hippy times. Superstores like Selfridges celebrated Asian commerce, TV stations like Channel Four presented an 'Indian Summer' of Asian cultural programming (never mind that Asian and India are not exact equivalents, that Pakistan, Sri Lanka, Nepal, not to mention China, Japan, Malaysia et al. are occluded in British use here); musical stage shows such as Andrew Lloyd Weber's *Bombay Dreams* attract sell-out audiences; the National Film Theatre reruns Satyajit Ray in the ImaginAsia cinema series; the Barbican weighs in with the films of Ritwik Ghatak and Mrinal Sen; and many more examples. Curious then that all this 'visibility' coincides with massive racial conflict in the areas of South Asian settlement in Britain (Oldham, Bradford); there is resurgence of far right anti-immigration politics, both with fringe groups like the British National Party winning council seats in Burnley, and with the former Home Secretary David Blunkett's attacks on, and deportation of, asylum seekers. This is not even to question yet the obvious hypocrisy of a general interest in Asian music, culture, and food (PM's consort Cherie Blair wears a 'vote-winning' sari to a government function supporting the 200 richest businessmen in England) just as other Asians in Afghanistan are obliterated in a bombing campaign of unprecedented excess. Never was the moment of 'origin' of Asian visibility in UK rap so revealing as when the political 'content' of Fun^da^mental's anti-racist message was occluded under a fear of 'militant Islam.' We have been here before—the duet of exotica and fanatica as the projected fears of White supremacy, castigating Black culture as dangerous and other; on the one hand strangely alien or 'ethnic,' on the other a threat. Scare mongering and cultural 'hybridity' are emphasized together—the racist agenda of marketing diversity within limits is locked and loaded.[25]

Along the way, the notion of 'hybridity' has become a safe way to categorize difficult cultural matter. Hybridity, as cultural fusion, covers anything that has not managed to fit neatly into the middle-England aspirations of the commissars of cultural industry propriety. Under the sign of the 'hybrid,' Fun^da^mental's project can be dismissed as a consequence of cultural clash and the teething problems of an immigrant population—and its 'youth element'—yet to assimilate to British ways. That this kind of delusion would be rejected by Fun^da^mental is a matter of course, but along this line media stereotypes of a very familiar vein have often been deployed.[26] An example gleaned from the weekly press as I write, Britain's serious liberal broadsheet *The Guardian* announces a 'special investigation' into the activities of Asian youth gangs in Oldham and Bradford, where Nawaz's family lives. In the course of a sensationalizing story, the paper characterizes members of these 'gangs' in a way that owes as much to Hollywood and MTV fantasies as it does to the UK scene: 'Asian role models' for our *Guardian* correspondent are described as: 'gold chain wearing drug traffickers with their new BMW cars, souped-up hi-fi systems and latest designer sportswear.'[27] Blatantly, this is a scare story, calculated to deploy stereotypes as counterpoint to government activity in other areas—a new war on drugs, anti-crime hysteria, anti-immigration feeling. The few anecdotes offered as evidence are of course misleading by any standard of examination of the activity of South Asians in Britain. And yet, the same may be said in Brixton and in Glasgow. There is, at least, a long and critical evaluation of this replication of pathologies of youth culture in the media by way of Black academic critique of scare-stories about graffiti, fights at clubs, gangs and, of course, gun culture.[28] There will always be some exceptional recourse to bad apple stories, but these stories are exceptions and almost always a consequence of playing to the crowd, usually on the part of tabloid journalists, but not in all cases. In Oldham and Bradford the agenda also serves as justification of the harsher than expected sentences (of up to five years) handed down to Asian participants in the 'disturbances' of 2001.[29] The more difficult reporting that would challenge template editorializing and conservative stitch-ups, requires more considered work, perhaps even a new investigative methodology. Credible mainstream media would be welcome here, but expectations of adequate and sympathetic reporting of Black experience, or hip hop culture cannot be high. Let us turn to the music press again—where despite the promise entailed in a political heritage unrivaled by any other artistic form ('Hip hop as Black people's CNN' etc), it is also unusual today to find serious and sustained political commentary in the hip hop press, beyond the occasional guest spot rant from a founding father.[30] I looked in vain for commentary on Bradford, the platitudes of New Year 2003 gun deaths were predictable. How commercialism tones down social criticism and encloses and contains it within restricted boundaries is illustrated yet again in the magazine majority focus on technology, fashion, and product reviews. In the final mix, the nether pages of the magazines offer a dark inverse of the political action that Chuck D, or Fun^da^mental, exhorts—instead the mantra of purchase, buy, and consume. Motives become motivations to market.

SIMON SAYS: THE HEGEMONY OF MARKET POWER

The demonization of Islam was established in the wake of Soviet Communism's collapse. The early moves that manufactured a new enemy have now been replaced by the crusading 'war on terror,' which targets Asians of all stripes within and beyond national borders and the rule of law, and irrespective of any consideration of allegiance to peace, civic life, evidence, coherence. With this context in mind, we might consider skirmishes of the music market as little more than incidental. But politicized motivation was never more explicit than in the response of Paul Simon to Fun^da^mental's 'crossover' efforts on the album *Erotic Terrorism*.[31] The reconstructed world music impresario's follow-up album after *Graceland*[32] was called *The Rhythm of the Saints*.[33] It used recordings of a town square performance by the Brazilian percussion ensemble Olodum, which were taken back to New York where Simon 'improvised music and words over them and added other layers of music.'[34] Taylor adds that it is Simon who profits; his position in a powerful economic center—the United States, a major corporation—means that he cannot escape his centrality, despite his assertion that he works 'outside the mainstream.'[35] It is then curious to compare the moment of appropriation—another key misleading term—with a parallel incident. When Fun^da^mental recorded a version of Mr. Simon's song 'The Sounds of Silence' for inclusion on *Erotic Terrorism*, their request to clear copyright for the sample was refused. Asked for permission once again, Simon was offered the publishing rights for the new version, with an additional backing vocal, but Mr. World Music again said 'no,' citing legal precepts and refusing further discussion.[36] Noting the power of some musician-entrepreneurs to own and control, and the cap in hand reliance on name stars and gatekeepers for those who might want to breach the conventions of music industry protocol, the track was renamed 'Deathening Silence,' sample removed. The retelling of these conjoined tales about Mr. Simon is not to make an equation between the selfish, or rather self-interested, conceits of copyright legalese and the more serious debacles of racism, anti-Islamic profiling, and the anti-people pogroms of the state machine. But who would be surprised if someone did equate such 'cultural' power with the way the war on terror legislates special rules that permit detention without charge or trial in the U.S., the UK, Australia, Malaysia, etc? Even though such a connection was anticipated in Fun^da^mental's ironic album title reference: 'Erotic Terrorism.'

Thinking of the detention camps in Afghanistan and Iraq, certainly there is some credence to Fun^da^mental's pre-September 11, 2001, prophecy that 'America Will Go to Hell'—in their anti-war anthem EP release from the same period as 'Deathening Silence.'[37] The use of hip hop to express a critique of American (and United Nations, NATO, or British military) imperialist activities makes Paul Simon's legal enforcement of silence something less than neutral and this conjunction surely also indicates a more nuanced relationship between politics and content than the unidirectionalist historians of hip hop might warrant. The 'deathening silence' here is not only a comment on record industry ownership of lyric and melody, but also references the ways commercial imperatives sanction quietude about the politics of so-called anti-terrorism and the inadequacy of romantic and liberal anti-racism. No mere hybridity, Fun^da^mental's call is to fight against the seductive terrorisms of complicity and conformity, the manipulation of market and law, the destruction of culture and civilization in pursuit of oil.

What kind of change in the apparatus of the culture industry would be required to orient attention away from the industrial-military-entertainment complex? What would displace the ways people in the music press and mainstream academic community consistently deploy categories that are far removed from the actualities articulated in the Fun^da^mental discussion? These critics appear deaf to ideas. I think it is clear that many misconceptions come from well-intentioned deployment of arguments around terms like 'visibility,' 'appropriation,' 'complicity,' and 'commerce.' That it is no surprise that intentions and their effects are readily undone is almost a platitude. The solution is not to insist on the correctness of an alternate interpretation[38] and it is equally not the case that insistence on fidelity to the source material will redeem all (but a listen to the albums and a check of the websites is worthwhile—combating sanctioned ignorance advanced through media bias is an obligation we must all take up[39]). These are probably the predictable moves that others have already made, but if raising questions about complacency in commentary adds impetus to the work of showing where a critique of unexamined complicity and marketing zeal restrict possibilities, then the opening is important.

Does Fun^da^mental offer something altogether different to this sanitized music industry version of hip hop that I am castigating as the conventional press release and expectation-driven cringe of European b-boys with a culture complex? My interest is to consider why a group like Fun^da^mental, that has been, however precariously, aligned with UK rap over many years, must be portrayed as a group whose activities fall outside the interests of the music industry coverage of conventional material. Am I prejudiced in insisting that activities that are excess to music industry convention make hip hop more interesting than the trade papers and academics would tell us? And paradoxically, does this indeed make Fun^da^mental an 'Asian Public Enemy,' more akin to U.S. based hip hop proselytizing of Chuck D, or a Michael Franti of the Disposable Heroes of old, railing against injustice—perhaps even the spirit of the Last Poets, who should get a mention here (but this White man got a god complex too[40])? It is the case that the old routine accusations of compromise and conformity to token 'rebellion' must be ones that wear thin for performers who have sustained political engagement for so long. The drone of the old 'sell-out' formula of recent arrivee purists must be annoying. Witness, for example, the necessity of Nawaz making statements that the politics of the album—'There Shall be Love'—could be taken as too complicated to explain without seeming 'anal.'[41] How did it come to pass that an album that moves across borders in a political and cultural exchange dedicated to resistance and creativity should *not* be discussed as such?

Instead of demanding Aki explain all, it might be worth looking to a few words of Chuck D himself on the 'origins,' where he insists on keeping in mind the need to respect those who did the work that made hip hop a crossover export culture in the first place—the global reach of hip hop now extends across all borders and includes massive 'non-Black' support.[42] The respect called for here has cultural characteristics too, it is respect for the cultural forms, its innovation *and* its political ethic—it is no surprise that the legend of the urban streetscape starts with 'making something outta ashes as Bam and Herc did within a depleted NY school system in the 1970s.'[43] The co-ordinates here are politically and not immediately market oriented. The global extension of hip hop culture follows suit in a way—it is thankfully not always the case that every time someone mentions the fact that hip hop is global that the global marketing of hip hop as industry is what they have in mind. Conversely, in the music press it is nearly always the case, since journalists in the sway of commerce think 'market' where the diversity and spread of culture is concerned. They do seem less alive to the problematic politics of the cultural and with their platitudes seem often to elide, deflect, or misconstrue sharp conflict in the interests of a kind of variety store orientalism. They focus on hip hop as the end product of an assembly line machination, rather than as culture, politics, or struggle.

Does it seem naive to think attention to the politics of hip hop in its global formations might offer a further development of critical perspectives? Is there no chance of indicating where we might see things differently than the way we do through already given and unexamined categories? It may be my particular reading, but I want to ask just why almost every essay on music starts by acknowledging Adorno's critique of the regression in listening only to then go on to ignore that critique in order to redeem contemporary music? Too many complementary albums perhaps? It seems to me that a music locked into routines formularized as origins is a music of limits, and this is just what Adorno warned against when he railed against obedience to the rhythm. Predictable innovations that are nothing but variants, the standardized performance or the oppositional stance. Against this, the secret omnipresence of resistance in hip hop might be that hip hop which breaks continually with the conventions of origins. Qawaali, Bengali, Mahgreb, Palestine—the continued promiscuity of hip hop as an inclusive creative local political movement outweighs the considerations of an historian's protocol. For what is important in hip hop? Is it two turntables, scratching, the cross fader and the MC? All of these technical innovations would amount to nothing but sales graphs for Technics and stores that sold two copies of each piece of new vinyl to Herc, where once they might have sold just one. No, what is important in hip hop is its expressive content, in terms of culture, politics, social response, and diversity. Hip hop is nothing if it does not reach from Public Enemy and N.W.A. to ADF, the Prophets of Da City and Fun^da^mental, et al. We should always be suspicious of arguments that assert technology as the means and motive of change. For several reasons such views are faulty—from the progress narrative ever so compatible with consumer marketing to the Heideggerian notion of enframing—the critique of technological determinism is well grounded, though often ignored. Herc may have used the turntable as developed by Technics, but he had to get up and use it—hip hop was as much born of creative street-level innovation as technological progress and the content and context of the music was as important as the sounds. The absolutely crucial context for understanding hip hop today is the struggle against imperialism abroad and racism at home. There is no other way to make sense of the mix.

So this is the justification for why I focus upon these extra-curricular activities of Fun^da^mental in a chapter that should be about 'the music.' No doubt, the discrepant activities of Fun^da^mental are worth examining in themselves, but for me it means more as part of a musical tradition that exceeds art and cultural industry conventions to be a part of lifestyle and politics. By this focus I believe we recapture what is specific to UK hip hop as well as that which translates and equates that hip hop with respect for the originary forms from the U.S. The music-industrial complex, its institutions, record execs, and admen are not the arbiters of the limits and character of hip hop's global appeal—this process, this form, is more than the trade papers say. It means more—and less. Hip hop is the vehicle of an idiom that rejects global terror refracted through the racism of the empire, and Fun^da^mental are among the forefront of those articulating this sentiment despite the ideological saccharine of the various presses. Of course by focusing on political work open questions remain—least of all that adequate political interventions cannot be made by a pop group alone, but rather require at the very least a mass mobilization of trained and disciplined cadres ready to assault the state where they live. What is required to rebuild civil society torn asunder by the revenge opportunism of George W. Bush and his appeasing Foreign Ambassador Blair? What is required to recharge a redistributive project of a radical democracy? These are hard questions. Nevertheless, in the absence of disciplined cadres, attention to these questions in place of the sweet lullabies upon which the music press would most times rather dwell, may expose the alibi-lullaby for what it is—time to wake up and Fight the European Power too. Fun^da^mental have been doing so for years.

The discrepant politics of Fun^da^mental has been consistent in this regard. The primacy of the politics has never been compromised before the necessity of commercial engagement. The media circus has not become an enclosure for them. Nawaz speaks at the music carnivalesque rallies of the anti-racist left, performs at the conferences and seminars of the Socialist Workers Party (note—speaks at a music festival, performs at a political meeting, this itself is contrapuntal in a good way). Apologizing not at all for transgressions, he is invited onto television programs as a musician and leaves as an orator, or is edited out as an angry young man. He writes: 'All the political statements have been made and we stand by every one ... there is and will always be those people who have no interest in bringing people together, who have no enlightenment or ambition to see from different perspectives, who will always say the most ridiculous and be entertained by the most powerful.'[44] With a constant web presence as well, distributing a range of commentaries on contemporary issues from September 11 and Palestine to Bradford and Oldham, the political exceeds the enclosures of the cultural industry category of 'music' and demands more—and this is just what hip hop at its best also strives to achieve.

Paul Simon on the other hand, acts as a classic mercantile imperial plantation master. His cultural property—'Sounds of Silence'—can be protected by law while he can happily sample Olodum at one moment and prevent Fun^da^mental from sampling him at another. Vexed questions about appropriation and ownership here, with many worries about the association of sound and culture—is music a cultural property? Is there a UK hip hop? Is the notion of 'Asian' music coherent? Is crossover a misrepresentation of the authentic? If, as is often recognized in academic discussion, everything is hybrid and there is no 'pure' source, it becomes clear that only in the weird and privileged world of commerce can anyone 'own' music. Much ink spilled. There is obviously a world of difference between the lawyer-protected borrowings of Mr. Paul Simon (inc.) and the politics of creative mixing. Appropriation itself is not the worry, expropriation and profiteering are. It's not what you take, it's who you take it from, what you give in return, and what you do with it. This is the context for understanding the efforts of Fun^da^mental to contrast the sounds of silence with the deafening injustice of theft, violence, and death meted out with regular and calculated fury by the rich and well-connected upon the poor. This understanding is too often left unheard.

RECKONING WITH THE TERMS

If we consider the implications and consequences of rethinking the way culture commentary deals with the politics of hip hop in the UK, there needs to be a radical change in the role of writing and commentary. Hip hop sensibilities might be useful here, but also a more informative and sustaining political journalism would be required. There would be good reason to have journalists listen and learn from the extensive documentation in hip hop lyricism of the crimes of the police, deaths in custody, stop and search etc, and then to ask where, for example, a journalism that deals with police crime could be printed.[45] At what point would it be considered legitimate for a hip hop magazine to publish detailed investigations of the oppressive asylum and immigration, or various anti-terror legislations being rushed into law across so much of the planet? Michael Franti again, with Spearhead and the album

Stay Human, attempted something like this around campaigning against the death penalty. A few interviews and feature articles aside, Franti's departure from the commercial mags to the more interactive writing engagement of webzines and the internet was almost inevitable.[46] This prompts questions about writing on the web as a mode of immediate discussion that breaks with corporate publishing. But no, web-based commentary seems to take up product-review culture anew when it comes to discussions of 'the music'; alongside an astonishing mobilization of alternative and diverse opinion against 'the war.' Here a critical approach developed by showing what was wrong with the everyday banality of press release driven commentary is the only possible way to avoid the crushing disappointment that commercialized life entails (when getting paid turns into being under-paid by the ultra-arrogant west-coast promo-men).

An alternative to this bifurcated world of hype on the one hand, mostly silenced alternatives on the other, would require a music criticism that engaged complicity, visibility, and the market with an uncompromising attention to the political. Is it merely expectation or habit, or is it an irrevocable *demand*, that we evaluate music in terms of music industry criteria? Isn't this a limiting factor in analytic work that should always be challenged? The musicological discipline at one end, and the commercial press release routinization of the sales pitch at the other—two sides of a broken appropriation that together cannot yet add up to appreciation. Of course practitioners and commentators (like me) are always so caught up in these routines that complicity often goes unremarked in the nooks and crannies of the vast hybridizing machine. Why write on music when death and destruction rain from the sky? It's probably not such a great alternative to approach music first as political since no doubt the corralling effects of market segmentation ensure that maneuver has been anticipated, but that such approaches are so often excoriated in the press and the institutions suggests a lacuna that deserves airplay so audiences can choose a different view. Otherwise, why so much grief?

And why is this significant for Europe? Why has there been all this worry about the source? (Is it only an anxiety about authenticity, or does the essentialism of roots run too deep?) It would do, to disorientate, just to consider what hip hop would look like if thought about and rewritten with a 'center' located outside the conventional 'home' locations—instead of New York and LA, say Newcastle or New Delhi perhaps, Sydney, or somewhere in Malaysia. And the first moves are not the be all and end all of this—there is no reason to look merely to the Black Atlantic[47] or to Black Paris[48] to disrupt all too easy versionings. What could we make of a music form delivered by satellite alongside, and reinterpreted by, Bollywood playback, Qawaali mystics and satellite TV VJs, that took up the political border-crossings of Fun^da^mental and made music and message mean again?[49] Against the war, the planetary mix is becoming ever more visible in hip hop with recognition that there are British, Italian, German, Australian, Asian, and Fijian forms (etc) at the same time that the form is universal. Unity in diversity. But visibility is only a moment of a process, necessarily reified, the dialectical character congeals around identity at a standstill.[50] To stop at the visibility of diversity is only one part of a process, the visible is only a platform, a first stage. Complicity is the next target in the deceptions of the market, thence appropriation and articulation. It is important to recognize that names, images, visions, myths are snapshots of something that moves; something that cannot be so readily enclosed unless the terms of enclosure are accepted within.

Against the terminology of an unexamined complicity, mere visibility, rainbow hybridity and jealous appropriation, what chance is there for public recognition—written and published, widely discussed—of the engaged Fun^da^mental hip hop sensibilities of practitioners and audiences? What about the concerns of the hip hop public itself, are they not of greater significance? It is the deathening silences that commercial imperatives impose upon the coherence (the sounds and the politics) of hip hop that seem the most ideological here; not censorship so much as failure of vision, blinded by complicity, unable to participate in the heterogeneity of life, stuck with defending—intentionally or unintentionally—a bland homogeneity. Can't we hope for, work for, a commentary that reports condemnation of the stupid war on drugs which criminalizes pleasure while providing alibis for the mass chemical poisonings of the street quality lottery; opposition to the imperial ambitions of Bush and Blair, there being little desire or interest on the part of most people in their oil-fueled deadly geopolitics on behalf of corporate empire and the armaments industry; reconfiguration of the space of political participation and community involvement instead of the pseudo-democracy of balloting and riot cop crackdowns on dissent; dreams of freedom; creative science; conscious poetic militancy; free-form riotous thought-crime joy; respect and communication instead of patronizing market segmentation; insight and meaning and enthusiasm and spirit; redress and recompense and unemployment for all (not just the idle rich); radical redistribution and enhanced quality of liveliness, planetary and large. All this is in the music, why not in the industry press reportage? Some may call it romantic Fun^da^mentalism, but it takes the globalization of billions to hold us back. This is an obvious reminder of what commentary on hip hop might be—it could be much more—this still is not the film, the revolution is not yet televised, the medium is not the message. These few notes are not yet a programme.

DISCOGRAPHY

Asian Dub Foundation, *R.A.F.I.*, Diffusion (1997)
Fun^da^mental, 'Janaam,' Nation (1992)

Fun^da^mental, 'Sister India,' Nation (1993)
Fun^da^mental, *Seize the Time*, Nation (1994)
Fun^da^mental, 'GoDevil,' Nation (1996)
Fun^da^mental, 'Why America will go to Hell,' Nation (1999)
Fun^da^mental, *Erotic Terrorism*, Nation (1999)
Fun^da^mental, 'There Shall be Love,' Nation (2001)
Rap Revolution Tour, *Party Sampler*, Titan Sounds (2002)
Paul Simon, *Graceland*, Warner Brothers (1987)
Paul Simon, *The Rhythm of the Saints*, Warner Brothers (1990)

NOTES

1. From the EP 'There Shall be Love,' Nation 2001.
2. Theodor Adorno, *Sound Figures* (Stanford: Stanford University Press, 1999), p. 2.
3. Tony Mitchell, *Global Noise: Rap and Hip-Hop Outside the USA* (Middletown, CT: Wesleyan University Press, 2001), p. 1.
4. Ibid., p. 11.
5. Fun^da^mental, 'Sister India,' Nation Records 1993.
6. Fun^da^mental, 'GodDevil,' Nation 1996.
7. Paul Gilroy made this connection at Goldsmiths College some years ago, Simon Frith did the same at Keele University in 1995.
8. That ADF picked up hip hop influences in France (arguably the largest market for such music outside America) and that Fun^da^mental influenced and were in turn influenced by, among many, hip hoppers from South Africa, as well as Qawaali from Pakistan, should not go unremarked. The map of hip hop creativity and diffusion does not in every case lead back to nodes in America. English rapping graphed over inner London Bengali rhythm guitar makes it big in Paris and in Japan. The old tale about Herc in the Bronx is honored but no longer an immediate ancestor here.
9. Ted Swedenburg, 'Islamic Hip Hop Versus Islamophobia: Aki Nawaz, Natacha Atlas, Akhenaton,' in Mitchell (ed.), *Global Noise*, p. 56.
10. David Hesmondhalgh and Caspar Melville, 'Urban Breakbeat Culture: Repercussions of Hip Hop in the United Kingdom,' in Mitchell (ed.), *Global Noise*, p. 87.
11. *Knowledge* (August 2002).
12. *HHC* (July 2002).
13. *HHC* (July 2002).
14. Review of Hilltop Hoods' 'Left Foot, Right Foot,' *HHC* (July 2002).
15. Fun^da^mental, 'Janaam,' Nation 1992.
16. Fun^da^mental, 'There Shall be Love,' Nation 2001.
17. See Sanjay Sharma, John Hutnyk, and Ashwani Sharma, *Dis-Orienting Rhythms: The Politics of the New Asian Dance Music* (London: Zed books, 1996).
18. MTV 'banned' the video, but were happy enough to use the opening refrain of the song—'what's the thing that makes a Black man insane ... primitive ... primitive'—as the soundtrack to a 'Pulse' fashion show special on Black hair styles. This is extensively discussed in chapter 3 of John Hutnyk's *Critique of Exotica: Music, Politics and the Culture Industry* (London: Pluto Press, 2000).
19. Rap Revolution Tour, *Party Sampler*, Titan Sounds, 2002.
20. Hesmondhalgh and Melville, 'Urban Breakbeat Culture,' p. 92.
21. For a detailed discussion of the industrial dynamic of this overloaded term, see Dipa Basu, 'What's real about "Keeping it Real"?' *Postcolonial Studies*, Vol. 1, No. 3 (1998).
22. Famously, at an academic music conference some years ago, a European colleague was puzzled by a seminar presenter's condemnation of the *NME*. Not quite getting the nuance

of the abbreviation, but in a revealing insight in any case, the questioner wanted to know just who was this 'enemy' and if there had been sufficient precautions taken to ensure they would not attack the conference (personal communication from Dave Hesmondhalgh, then organizing the International Association for the Study of Popular Music).

23. 'The Wordplay/Full Cycle Campaign,' *Knowledge* (August 2002).

24. Fun^da^mental, *Erotic Terrorism*, Nation 1999.

25. There are numerous sources of comparable material addressing U.S. versions of this same routine. First and foremost among these I think is Vijay Prashad's admirable study: *Everybody Was Kung Fu Fighting* (Boston: Beacon Press, 2001). See also *The Karma of Brown Folk* (Minneapolis: University of Minnesota Press, 2000) and the 'Satyagraha in America' issue of *AmerAsia Journal* (Biju Mathew and Vijay Prashad (eds), 'Satyagraha in America,' *AmerAsia Journal*, Vol. 25, No. 3 (1999/2000)). A volume specifically devoted to music and politics in Asia that deserves attention is Allen Chun, Ned Rossiter, and Brian Shoesmith (eds), *Refashioning Pop Music in Asia* (London: RoutledgeCurzon, 2004) and the special issues on 'Music and Politics' in the journals *Theory, Culture and Society* (Vol. 17, No. 3, 2000) and *Postcolonial Studies* (Vol. 1, No. 3, 1998) should be consulted.

26. Though stressing the 'productive syncretism of diasporic cultures' and deploying an uncritical notion of 'new ethnic identities,' Hesmondhalgh and Melville are among the few critics wary of the term hybridity as a description of hip hop 'adapted for use in very different performative and institutional circumstances from those found in the USA.' See Hesmondhalgh and Melville, 'Urban Breakbeat Culture,' pp. 86, 87.

27. 'Deadly Asian heroin gangs carve up lucrative new trade,' *Guardian*, July 14, 2002.

28. For an up-to-date review, see Stuart Hall, Charles Critchner, and Jefferson Tony et al., *Policing the Crisis* (Basingstoke: Palgrave Macmillan, 1978) and Clare Alexander, *The Asian Gang* (Oxford: Berg, 2000).

29. See Virinder Kalra, 'Balance of Law?: Riots or Rebellion and the Tariffs of Racist Policing,' *Oldham Red Notes*, 17, (2002).

30. Chuck D editorials for example, *HHC* (July 2002).

31. Fun^da^mental, *Erotic Terrorism*, Nation 1999.

32. Paul Simon, *Graceland*, Warner Brothers 1987.

33. Paul Simon, *The Rhythm of the Saints*, Warner Brothers 1990.

34. Interview with Bob Edwards, quoted in Timothy Taylor, *Global Pop: World Music, World Markets* (New York: Routledge, 1997), p. 64.

35. Taylor, *Global Pop*, p. 203.

36. Author interview with Aki Nawaz.

37. Fun^da^mental, 'Why America Will Go To Hell,' Nation 1999.

38. See Virnder Kalra and John Hutnyk, 'Music and Politics'—special section, in *Postcolonial Studies*, Vol. 1, No. 3 (1998) and Sanjay Sharma and John Hutnyk, 'Music and Politics'—special section, in *Theory, Culture and Society*, Vol. 17, No. 3 (2000).

39. The term 'sanctioned ignorance' is from the always insightful Gayatri Spivak. See Gayatri Spivak, *Critique of Postcolonial Reason* (Cambridge: Harvard University Press, 1999).

40. 'Koushik Banerjea, Ni-Ten-Ichi-Ryu: 'Enter the World of the Smart-Stepper,' in Raminder Kaur and John Hutnyk (eds), *Travel Worlds: Journeys in Contemporary Cultural Politics* (London: Zed Books, 1999), pp. 14–28.

41. This for a primarily non-English vocals album. See Kalra, 'Music and Politics' on the politics of necessary translation.

42. Chuck D, *HHC* (July 2002). It is also worth noting that Chuck D has initiated his own South Asian–British crossover adventure, coming to London to perform on stage with ADF in summer 2004, in support of the West Indian cricket tour no less.

43. Chuck D, *HHC* (July 2002).

44. Fun^da^mental, 'There Shall be Love,' Nation 2001.

45. This, I'm afraid, is personal as I have now a collection of 19 rejection letters from publishers who, with Anandi Ramamurthy, Ken Fero, and Tariq Mehmood, I had offered

a book of essays and the shooting script of the controversial film on deaths in police custody, *Injustice* (directed by Ken Fero and Tariq Mehmood). No one wants to touch it because of the accusation in the film that the officers who arrested Brian Douglas were murderers. Screening details and more on the film is available at <http://www.injusticefilm. co.uk/>.

46. But see *Get Rhythm* (May 2001).
47. Paul Gilroy, *The Black Atlantic: Modernity and Double Consciousness* (London: Routledge, 1993).
48. Benetta Jules-Rosette, *Black Paris* (Urbana: University of Illinois Press, 1996).
49. Or what to make of crossover as massacred (a subjective, but legitimate view I think) by a Portuguese-Malay nightclub singer in an obscure tourist trail club on the west coast of the peninsula. Big up to the outstandingly surreal Bobby Fernandez at Malacca's 'Loony Planet,' Malaysian residency, April 2002.
50. Theodor Adorno, *Aesthetic Theory* (London: Athlone Press, 1970/1997), p. 176.

9
'Keeping it Real' in a Different 'Hood: (African-)Americanization and Hip Hop in Germany

Timothy S. Brown

In the spring of 2003, a young Turkish-German filmmaker, Neco Celik, released his first film, *Alltag* ('Daily Life'). It tells the story of troubled youngsters on the mean streets of the Berlin district of Kreuzberg, aka 'Little Istanbul.' This neighborhood, long a stronghold of punk and other 'alternative' subcultures in Germany, is also a traditional home to families of Turkish *Gastarbeiter* (so-called 'guest workers' invited to Germany in the 1960s and 70s to help make up for the post-war labor shortage).[1] The German-born children of these immigrants occupy a place between the worlds; neither fully Turkish nor fully German, they identify more with the specific culture of their own neighborhood than with either of their two 'parent' cultures. But the neighborhood culture itself, as Celik shows, is a mixture, not only of Turkish and German cultures, but of U.S. culture—or perhaps more accurately, African-American culture. It is little surprise that the filmmaker with whom Celik is most often compared is Spike Lee; the culture in which he grew up, the culture of street-wise youngsters of Turkish-German Kreuzberg, is one fully enthralled by the sounds and styles of the U.S. ghetto. All the elements of the 'hip hop' lifestyle—rap music, graffiti, breakdancing, gangs—find full expression here, and Celik, himself a former gang-member and graffiti artist, makes no bones about the U.S. influence on youth culture in Kreuzberg. 'Everything has to do with American movies,' he explains. 'There's also the Turkish culture and our group mentality, but mostly it was American movies ... In the 1980's, everybody saw "Scarface," and everybody here called himself Tony Montana' (the name of the drug lord portrayed by Al Pacino in the movie). If Pacino's big-screen anti-heroics were—for Kreuzberg gansta 'wannabes' as for many of their U.S. counterparts—an irresistible parable of the self-made man of the streets, even more important for Kreuzberg hip hop, according to Celik, were the children of U.S. soldiers stationed in Germany who 'showed up as rappers at hip-hop parties' in the neighborhood.[2]

Celik's comments on hip hop in Kreuzberg are more than just interesting asides from a young filmmaker—they are a report from the 'front lines' of a broad process of social and cultural change in post-war Europe that often goes by the name of 'Americanization.' U.S. military and economic dominance after World War II—the argument goes—allowed it, among other things, to practice a sort of 'cultural imperialism' that overwhelmed local cultures with a flood of products and ideas, erasing old traditions and replacing them with new ones.[3] Yet however much the massive U.S. imprint on post-war Europe might resemble what one scholar has dubbed 'Coca-colonization,'[4] the cultural imperialism model is inadequate for understanding the subtleties of the process by which something like hip hop finds a new home in a foreign culture. Few scholars seriously dispute anymore that the consumers on the receiving end of the U.S. 'culture pipeline' are intelligent enough to pick and choose, to bend U.S. culture to their own uses and give it new inflections.[5] Mass audiences are, of course, constrained by the choices made available to them by the corporate culture industry. But artists and underground music fans—note that the two are frequently one and the same—are nothing if not discriminating in their ability to choose elements of imported culture that have the greatest potential in their new setting. They are, in scholarly parlance, 'active' audiences, and those among them who—as in the case of Turkish-German rappers in Kreuzberg and elsewhere—take up microphone and beatbox, do so because they see an opportunity to create new identities for themselves out of the raw material of globalized culture.[6]

Scholars have used terms like 'indigenization' and 'hybridization,'[7] 'reterritorialization,'[8] 'localization,'[9] and 'selective osmosis'[10] to describe the active element in this transfer of culture from one setting to another. John Clarke, in a well-known work on subcultural style, coined the term 'recontextualization' to denote the process by which cultural objects which have been borrowed from different contexts are integrated in a new social context—thus: re-contextualized—and thereby given new meanings.[11] This is as good a term as any for what Germans do with hip hop—they take something created in a different time and place, with a meaning all its own— and give it a new meaning relevant to their own time and place. But why Black American culture, and why hip hop? Scholars disagree about whether there is an essential 'Blackness'[12] that is communicated through cultural forms like rap music, and there is little doubt that hip hop in particular represents a fusion of cultural perspectives and productive techniques.[13] Nevertheless, hip hop can be said to be 'affectively Black,' in that in its predominant and original iteration, it is strongly expressive of the African-American experience. The important point is that whether or not hip hop represents some kind of authentic Blackness, the perceived 'Blackness' of the form is one of its chief selling-points for fans and performers. The question is: why? What use is this 'Blackness' to the kids who embrace it? What makes it so attractive, for example, to the Turkish-German kids of Kreuzberg? What makes it, for that matter, so attractive to German kids generally? Because Turkish-Germans aren't the only Germans who love hip hop. Hip hop is *huge* in Germany; and that means it is huge among ethnic Germans,[14] and not just among some undifferentiated mass public of Germans that buys into whatever sounds—'gangsta rap' or Michael Jackson—that are foisted on them by the major record labels. Some of the most articulate and innovative rap in Germany is the product of ethnic German or multi-racial underground crews dedicated to rap for both artistic and political reasons, the latter having to do, among other things, with resistance to racial discrimination and anti-immigrant sentiment. The term 'African-Americanization' in the title of this chapter is therefore not just clever word-play: Germans who love hip hop are responding not just to a different national (U.S.) culture, but to the culture of a racial and ethnic *other*. In hip hop, where the 'Blackness' of the form is fore-grounded as a form of resistance that ranges itself not only against 'adult' culture and society—as all youth cultures do—but often against 'White' society as well, a whole range of potential meanings become available. The purpose of this chapter is to explore some of these meanings, and to examine the various uses of hip hop—and of the 'Blackness' in hip hop—by Germans.

BEGINNINGS

Hip hop culture began to come to Germany as early as 1983. The influence of film was critical on German hip hop's early development, leading to a strong emphasis on the more heavily visual aspects of the culture like graffiti-art and breakdancing. Nearly every contributor to a recent collection of first-hand accounts by German hip hop artists and producers cites the influence in particular of two films: *Wild Style* (1983) and *Beat Street* (1984).[15] One consequence of the importance of film was that hip hop was able to penetrate both capitalist West and communist East Germany at around the same time. *Beat Street* was of particular importance in the East, where, as Opossum from the Leipzig group Zoo Sound explains, it was meant to illustrate for young people the evils of capitalism. Predictably, it 'had exactly the opposite effect.'[16] In contrast to many West German rappers, who (to their credit) recognized that as educated, middle-class Germans they enjoyed a position of privilege that gave them little in common with oppressed Blacks in the U.S.,[17] East German rap fans tended to see a real parallel between ghetto life and their oppression as citizens of a communist dictatorship. As Joy of Zoo Sound observes: 'We felt almost exactly like [the people portrayed in *Beat Street*]. Of course we had cash for a doctor, and here it didn't rain [through the roof of] the apartment, and we didn't have any gangsters on the street, but our life was just as dreary.'[18]

The 'first wave' of German hip hop initiated by these films around 1983 died down rather quickly, but the hardcore hip hop fans who remained after the breakdance craze faded from the media were central to the further development of hip hop in Germany—they supplied much of the personnel for the important German rap groups that began to develop in the late 1980s and early 90s. If these groups shared an enthusiasm for the new art form coming out of the U.S. ghetto, they were united by little else; indeed, the development of German hip hop can best be understood in terms of an overlapping series of oppositions: between the 'popular' and the 'political,' between the 'underground' and the 'commercial,' between notions of art-for-art's sake and art as a tool for defining one's identity and place in society. All of these debates revolve around a more fundamental question: The question of how to be authentic, or, in hip hop terms, how to 'keep it real.' In this sense, perhaps, German hip hop is little different than in the U.S. But these questions take on a special character in Germany because of the way in which they are linked to the broader issues of, on the one hand, how to put this 'foreign' art form to use—that is, how to use it in a *meaningful* way—and on the other, the particular (historical and contemporary) problems of the multicultural society in Germany.

The complexity of some of these seemingly simple oppositions is reflected in the history of two of Germany's most important rap groups, Die Fantastischen Vier (The Fantastic Four), and Advanced Chemistry. Die Fantastischen Vier, from Stuttgart, were one of the first groups to rap in the German language. Their move away from what they saw as mindless devotion to the surface elements of U.S. rap—member Smudo complained of groups whose entire program consisted of little more than repeating 'Yeah Boy' and 'Say Ho' over and over again—was completed by 1988–89.[19] It was influenced in part by a trip to Los Angeles that reinforced the band's growing realization of the lack of any real connection between the experience of poor Blacks in the U.S. and middle-class Whites in Germany.[20] The insight of Die Fantastischen Vier that much of German rap was simply 'too American'—i.e. too derivative—to have any meaning for Germans informed the group's attempt to rap in their own language.[21] This attempt met with huge commercial success from the beginning of the 1990s, but success (and the largely 'trite' lyrics that lay behind it) led to widespread charges that Die Fantastischen Vier were nothing more than a pop group—'the German *Salt'n'Peppa*' as one rap insider puts it—offering an uncritical and 'Whitebread' version of rap.[22]

The hit that made Die Fantastischen Vier pop stars—'Die da'—came out during a period of crisis in Germany. During 1992–93, a rising wave of anti-immigrant sentiment in the wake of reunification crested into acts of arson and murder against Turkish asylum seekers. A firebomb attack on the house of a Turkish family in Solingen in May 1993 killed two women and three girls, injuring seven other people. Three Turkish girls died in a similar attack in Mölln in November of the previous year. These attacks occurred in the wake of a number of non-fatal assaults on homes for refugees in 1991–92.[23] It was in this context that another group, the group that would come to be billed—and to a certain extent take on the roll of—Die Fantastischen Vier's antagonists, came to prominence. This was Advanced Chemistry, from

Heidelberg. Like Die Fantastischen Vier, Advanced Chemistry rapped in German, but unlike Die Fantastischen Vier, Advanced Chemistry was multi-ethnic in makeup and outspokenly multicultural. Their leader, Torch, was the product of the marriage of a Haitian mother and a German father. He was (and is) a hip hop activist, appointed by rap-godfather Afrika Bambaataa to head the first German chapter of Zulu Nation, and heavily involved with the 'Rap against the Right' initiative.[24] Advanced Chemistry burst onto the hip hop scene with a maxi-single released in November 1992. The song, 'Fremd in eigenem Land' (Foreign in Your Own Country), made a pointed statement about the position of immigrants in German society. In the video to the song, a band member brandishes a German passport in a symbolic challenge to traditional assumptions about what it means to be German. If the passport is not enough, the video implies, then what *is* required? German blood? This powerful critique of racism made Advanced Chemistry a sensation, and followed by the release of the *Advanced Chemistry* album, helped the group single-handedly create a strong German rap scene 'over night.'[25]

Mark Pennay argues that Advanced Chemistry and Die Fantastischen Vier can be seen as representative of two different traditions in German rap—one explicitly political or 'activist,' the other commercial and unpolitical.[26] But if the well-documented antagonism between the two groups does nothing to belie this assertion,[27] it might also be argued that it is less an attitude to politics *per se* than a basic disagreement about the relationship between art and commerce that separates them.[28] Die Fantastischen Vier made an all-out—and very successful—push for pop stardom, while Advanced Chemistry remained fiercely independent and 'underground' (by forming their own record label among other things). Thus, the tension between the two groups can been seen as part of a fundamental conflict between opposed productive approaches: 'major label' vs. 'Do it Yourself.'[29] Yet despite these differences, the two groups share something important in common: both are highly skeptical about 'Americanness'; that is, both have thought carefully about the problems inherent in adapting a foreign cultural form for use in Germany. A description of the problem by Torch of Advanced Chemistry could just as easily have been written by Smudo of Die Fantastischen Vier: 'What the Americans do is exotic for us because we don't live like they do. What they do seems to be more interesting and newer. But not for me. For me it's more exciting to experience my fellow Germans in new contexts … For me it's interesting to see what the kids try to do that's different from what I know.'[30]

Yet the basic difference between these two pioneering groups remains important. For Die Fantastischen Vier, hip hop—or rather rap music—is art and nothing more (even if their critics in the underground rap scene might sometimes, at least initially, question Die Fantastischen Vier's artistic credentials). 'In Germany,' writes Smudo, 'there is next-to-no relationship between social conditions and the creation of music.'[31] Implicit in this statement is the idea that the ethnic content of hip hop—its 'Blackness'—is important only inasmuch as it supplied the motive force for the original artistic innovation (in its U.S. setting). For Advanced Chemistry, on the other hand, rap music is not only art, but also—through its connection with hip hop culture—politics. It represents a *mode of resistance*; one perfectly suited to combating the radical right in Germany, perfectly suited to recognizing and strengthening the growth of a multicultural German society. In this context, the 'Blackness' of hip hop marks it as a vehicle of general human emancipation—the art produced out of the African-American experience carries an emancipatory charge applicable in settings other than the original. Here, hip hop does not entail any kind of ethnic separatism; on the contrary, groups like Advanced Chemistry, with their diverse ethnic makeup and overt opposition to right-wing xenophobia, speak, as Andy Bennett puts it, in 'the voice of the second-generation immigrant attempting to integrate into German society.'[32]

'ORIENTAL HIP HOP'

Advanced Chemistry thus represents not a rejection of the idea of 'Germanness,' but a vision of a multicultural type of 'Germanness.' Hip hop is important not just because it is art, but because it is a weapon against racial chauvinism and ethnic nationalism. But nationalism is not absent from the German rap scene; on the contrary, there is an implicit (and sometimes explicit) conflict over national identity that finds expression, on the one hand, in charges that the attempt to form a 'German' rap culture is inherently exclusionary, and on the other, in the growth of a counter-nationalism in the form of ethnic-Turkish or so-called 'Oriental hip hop.'[33] This conflict is in some ways a logical outgrowth of the fact that in Germany hip hop is an imported cultural form: taking the form over—making it 'German'—is not easy when there is basic disagreement about what being 'German' means in the first place. To some Turkish youngsters who don't feel particularly at home in Germany, taking an African-American art form and making it 'German' has little appeal. Is not the whole point of the art form resistance to racism and exclusion? Why take something African American and make it 'German' when you can just make it 'Turkish' instead? As one Turkish-German label owner interviewed by Andy Bennett put it: 'The point about a lot of this German rap is it's all about coloured guys saying look at us, we're like you, we're German. But I don't feel like that, I never have. I'm not German, I'm a Turk and I'm passionately proud of it.'[34]

'Oriental hip hop' was the product of two innovations, one having to do with language, one with choice of source material. Turkish language rap, which began with King Size Terror's 'The Life of the Stranger,' sprang from the same logic that produced German language rap, insofar as it represented an attempt to better employ hip hop for local effect. But the impact of Turkish language rap was quite different than that of German language rap; by using a foreign language as a marker of a 'nationalism' within a nationalism,' Turkish-German rappers were making a very different response to the challenges of multiculturalism in Germany than a group like Advanced Chemistry. With the second innovation—the introduction of samples drawn from Turkish folk music style of *Arabesk*, the genre of 'Oriental hip hop' was born. The first recording of the genre was the single 'My Melody'/'Istanbul' by Islamic Force, released in 1992.[35] It represented a flowering of the sort of cultural syncretism for which hip hop is famous. As Eric-E of the Oriental hip hop group Cartel says: '[James Brown] is not Turkish; he is Black. I thought samples should be from our own music.'[36]

Yet with or without James Brown, German hip hop in its 'Oriental' guise represented a powerful rallying point, not for ethnic integration into the dominant society, but for ethnic resistance against it. Dietmar Elflein and others have argued that the rise of 'Oriental hip hop' among German-Turks was a response to the national chauvinism implicit in the rise of German rap generally, and in particular in the release of a well-known compilation album in 1991: *Krauts with Attitude*. What was 'German' about the album was not language; 12 of the 15 acts featured rapped in English—what was 'German' was that the groups involved were trying to make an African-American art form their own by claiming a new geographical and cultural location for it (symbolized by the album title's play on the name of the U.S. group Niggaz With Attitude). This 'nationalization' of German hip hop was problematic, however, for as Dietmar Elflein has pointed out, with the release of *Krauts with Attitude*, 'an adopted musical style became grafted onto a national identity which de facto locked out many of its participants. Given hip-hop's special attractions for immigrant youngsters as a different, non-German cultural pattern ... this nationalist move was particularly problematic.'[37] The key, as Elflein notes, is that the adoption of African-American culture could not, in itself, classify as a meaningful act of resistance for Turkish-Germans. To do that, it would have to speak to their special situation in Germany, to respond to their particular needs as a group caught between worlds, neither fully Turkish nor fully German. But how could hip hop represent a solution to the contradictions of ethnic Turkish existence if it was also massively popular with ethnic Germans? It could not, unless it could somehow be transmuted into an expression of the real particulars of this existence, that is, be made to reflect the ambiguities of life in a diaspora. This was the real reason behind the rise of 'Oriental hip hop.'

That this is true is no surprise; the basic maneuver at the heart of 'Oriental hip hop' is the basic maneuver of rap everywhere it has traveled away from its point of origin—the act of using the art form as a way of creating a new and more useful identity. The globalization of Black culture is frequently spoken of in terms of the concept of 'diaspora'—diaspora as a scattering of peoples, and diaspora as a web of practices linking those peoples simultaneously to local places of origin and to the original African homeland. And it is precisely where immigrants face their own situations of diaspora—where, like the Turks in Germany, they can be said to make up 'diasporic communities'—that the 'Blackness' in hip hop resonates most strongly. Here, it supplies not only a connection to new and exciting currents of mass-mediated youth culture, but a ready-made model of ethnic solidarity and resistance against 'the powers that be.'[38]

In an in-depth study of 'hip hop youth' in Berlin's Kreuzberg district, Ayhan Kaya notes the way that this model of ethnic solidarity is made to resonate with the particular concerns and traditions of the Turkish-German community:

> What they call 'Oriental' hip-hop provides these youngsters with a ground where they can express their imaginary nostalgia towards 'home' ... as well as to manifest their attachment to the 'undiscovered country of the future.' In other words, 'Oriental' represents the symbolic dialogue undertaken ... between 'tradition' and 'translation,' between 'there' and 'here,' and between the local and the global.[39]

The appropriation of African-American culture occurs simultaneously with an appropriation of elements drawn from a mythic Turkish past, the latter expressed particularly through attachment to the folk music style of *Arabesk*. With its bittersweet longing for a homeland left behind—a homeland most Turkish-German youngsters could never have seen except perhaps on vacation—*Arabesk* expresses a nostalgia and cultural pessimism that dovetails perfectly with hip hop's invention of community through stories of displacement and loss. The central musical innovation in 'Oriental hip hop'—the rejection of African-American samples in favor of samples drawn from Turkish *Arabesk* and pop—is emblematic of the blending of diasporic Black culture and diasporic Turkish culture.

Oriental hip hop must also be seen as part of a broader rebellion of second- and third-generation Turks in Germany against what many see as a stifling policy of multiculturalism that privileges assimilation while glossing over the built-in disadvantages facing Turkish-German young people. Many Turkish-German artists and intellectuals express a growing militancy about the place of Turks in German society, drawing in many cases on the language, cadences, and sensibility of hip hop. Emblematic of this trend are the novels of one of Germany's leading literary figures, Feridun Zaimoglu, who in *Kanak Sprak* (1995), and *Kopfstuff* (1998), employs the creolized Turkish-German spoken by the disenfranchised youth of the hip hop generation. In naming this dialect using a racist German term—he dubs it 'Kanak Sprak,' or 'nigger speak'[40]—Zaimoglu claims respectability for a diasporic vernacular while making a pointed statement against the alleged racism of German society. This same project of reclamation also informs the sensibility of 'Kanak Attak,' a broad-based anti-racist project for which

Zaimoglu is a sort of 'spiritual leader.'[41] The sort of anti-assimilationist stance represented by 'Kanak Attak' is expressed with blunt elegance by another leading Turkish-German figure, rap impresario Cool Savas: 'We're no minority,' he says; 'We live here. It's that simple.'[42]

But the situation is, of course, far from simple. Turkish-German youngsters' embrace of imported visions of the 'thug life' represents a rebellion against the traditionalism of the parent generation, but it is a rebellion that simultaneously draws upon elements of the traditional culture, precisely because these elements *act as markers of difference in the German context.* Attachment to a mythical Turkish past—and to current expressions of Turkish culture like *Arabesk*—become part of a dual armament: on the one hand hip hop—the insurgent art form of the oppressed 'original man' *par excellence*; and on the other, Turkish tradition—above all Turkish language—with an element of foreignness that adds 'kick' to the rebellion already present in hip hop to begin with. The 'ethnic identity' that emerges out of this synthesis—even if it draws on 'authentic' elements of Turkish culture—is a pure construct. Dietmar Elflein emphasizes this artificiality in his discussion of the Turkish-German rap group Cartel, whose album, released in 1995, featured a Turkish flag on the cover in not-so-subtle imitation of the *Krauts with Attitude* album. What Cartel attempted to do, according to Elflein, was 'to gather up the excluded parts of the hip hop community under the banner of an artificially constructed ethnic minority which was supposedly "Turkish".'[43]

In adopting this 'symbolic ethnicity'[44] one did not necessarily have to be Turkish: 'The "Turkish" identity proposed was a mythological one.' As Elflein points out, one well-known group in the genre, Da Crime Posse, was composed of two Turks, one German, and a Cuban. The Turkishness of the Cartel album, and of 'Oriental hip hop' in general, Elflein concludes, was basically a marketing ploy.[45] Cartel was particularly successful in Turkey, where Cartel's flaunting of the Turkish flag not only made them big stars (their record sold 30,000 copies) but darlings of the radical right searching for militant expressions of Islamic identity (to the apparent dismay of the group's leader).[46] Cartel was successful in Germany, as well, in creating a vehicle for ethnic-Turkish militancy. As the rapper Fuat puts it: 'Until that time a Turk simply didn't glare at the camera and give the finger.'[47]

The made-up Turkish identity associated with groups like Cartel was not just an attempt to eke out a place in German society, nor simply to create an identity for themselves, but rather an attempt to set themselves up as an analog to the African-American community in the United States. It was an attempt, that is, to use the 'Blackness' in hip hop to form a sort of 'defensive ethnicity.' But, as the embrace of Cartel by the radical right in Turkey suggests, this move is far from unproblematic. Nor is it uncontroversial in the German hip hop community. One well-known German rapper in Kreuzberg complains, for example, of what he calls 'Turkish fascists' in the Kreuzberg hip hop scene, noting that a sizable minority 'identify themselves strongly with negative hip hop cliches. That's the problem, they see themselves as "White niggas," they think they are exactly like the Blacks in [the U.S.].'[48]

But if this Turkish 'resistance identity' is an artificial construct, that is, after all, the whole point: If Turkish-German hip hop kids in Kreuzberg were really Turkish they wouldn't need to construct an identity in the first place. It is precisely because they live in a situation of uncertainty that they need to resort to reinventing themselves—say, as 'gangstas.'[49] But because many of their White fellow-rap fans also want to be gangstas, Turkish-German youngsters have to become gangstas with a twist—a twist that both reifies and makes bearable their separateness in German society. And this underlines why rap music is such a perfect tool for the immigrant, post-colonial, or 'diasporic' community; in most youth subcultures, attachment to dominant culture is guaranteed by a common ethnic and cultural heritage, and therefore can be cast aside in search of new identities. With immigrants, connection with the dominant (White) society is insecure, and the cultural baggage of the parent culture is not so much a hindrance to be discarded as a resource to be utilized; it is needed as the *stuff* of a new identity that can be posed against White society. And with rap, images of a rebel 'ethnicity' are right there in the music: nationalisms, styles of dress, a radical otherness drawn on the one hand from the 'hood,' and on the other, from a mythic homeland free of the corrupting influences of the mean streets where the oppressed are put on ice by society.

The appeal of this synthesis to 'diasporic' Turkish-German youngsters is obvious. And it should also be obvious that scholars who emphasize the non-monolithic nature of cultural globalization—that is, who note the various ways in which meaning can be created by the receivers of globalized culture—are right on target. Following Andy Bennett's distinction between assimilationist and anti-assimilationist German hip hop[50] (his idea, my terms) and Dietmar Elflein's notion of competing 'nationalisms' within German hip hop,[51] I think it might be useful to think about three broad, overlapping categories of 'application' when talking of hip hop as an element of globalized Black culture. First, there is the importance of hip hop as a site on which to develop an oppositional stance toward society; this is something that it shares in common with other youth subcultures, and need not be explicitly political. Dietmar Elflein uses the term 'dissidence' to describe a world-wide community of young people who identify themselves naturally with the oppressed of the earth.[52] The groups on the *Krauts with Attitude* compilation, Elflein points out, make up part of this community, as do, I would add, Die Fantastischen Vier (their opinions about the social content of rap not withstanding). Here, the 'Blackness' of hip hop is less important for its ethnic nationalist charge than for its ability to stand in for various types of oppression. This brand of German rap, rooted in personal expression, and political only insofar as it connects with Elflein's 'dissidence,' carries the potential for massive mainstream appeal, as witnessed by the current success of Die Fantastischen Vier.

Second, there is the more explicitly political brand of hip hop that combines a *political* critique of existing social conditions with a celebration of a transplanted version of hip hop as a means of *cultural* resistance. In the German context this might be seen to correspond with groups like Advanced Chemistry—self-consciously multicultural rap that seeks to combat right-wing xenophobia. Both of these categories are consistent with membership in the dominant ethnicity, although more commonly they are associated with groups of mixed ethnicity (free interplay of races and cultures being the whole point of the enterprise). The third category would be rap that is explicitly put to use by youth of immigrant communities who, in response to what Ayhan Kaya calls 'structural outsiderism,' seek to create and embrace their own, exaggerated outsiderism as a means of self defense. In the German context, this category is represented by 'Oriental hip hop.' Hip hop is particularly suited to the last group for several reasons. First, as an art form that relies heavily on the spoken word, it is ideally suited to the telling of stories—a practice that is of great importance to groups whose story is left out of the dominant narrative. Second, as an art form that relies heavily on borrowing and appropriation through electronic sampling, rap music is ideally suited to the incorporation of diverse elements—like *Arabesk*—into a new synthesis. It is therefore of particular interest to groups—like the Kreuzberg Turks—who live an uneasy existence between and across cultures. Finally, as an art form that expresses a powerful spirit of resistance against oppression, especially the oppression of an ethnic minority by an ethnic majority, hip hop offers a ready-made model of underdog ethnic nationalism that is highly appealing to groups who have to deal with being 'strangers' in a strange land.[53]

NOTES

1. Between roughly 1961 and 1973, large numbers of Turkish workers were recruited to make up for Germany's post-war labor shortage. As of 2002 there were approximately 2.1 million Turks in Germany (3.4 percent of the population); *Britannica Book of the Year* (Chicago: Britannica, 2003). On Turkish immigration to Germany see Jenny B. White, 'Turks in Germany: Overview of the Literature,' *Middle Eastern Studies Bulletin*, July 1995.

2. *New York Times*, April 12, 2003.

3. On models of cultural imperialism see Dominic Strinati, *An Introduction to Theories of Popular Culture* (London; New York: Routledge, 1995), pp. 21ff; Keith Negus, *Popular Music in Theory. An Introduction* (Hanover and London: Wesleyan University Press and University Press of New England, 1996), pp. 164–5, 171–80, 205, 210.

4. Reinhold Wagnleitner, *Coca-colonization and the Cold War: The Cultural Mission of the United States in Austria after the Second World War* (Chapel Hill: University of North Carolina Press, 1994).

5. Tony Mitchell, *Global Noise: Rap and Hip-Hop Outside the USA* (Middletown, CT: Wesleyan University Press, 2001), p. 11.
6. Andy Bennett, 'Hip Hop am Main: The Localization of Rap Music and Hip Hop Culture,' *Media, Culture and Society*, Vol. 21 (1999), pp. 77–91, 86.
7. James Lull, *Media, Communication, Culture. A Global Approach* (Cambridge: Polity Press, 1995).
8. Andy Bennett, *Cultures of Popular Music* (Buckingham [England]; Philadelphia: Open University Press, 2001), p. 94.
9. Bennett, 'Hip Hop am Main.'
10. Mark Pennay, 'Rap in Germany,' in Mitchell (ed.), *Global Noise*, p. 111.
11. John Clarke, 'Style,' in Stuart Hall and Tony Jefferson (eds), *Resistance Through Rituals* (London: Routledge, 1975).
12. Andy Bennett summarizes the current state of the field nicely when he writes that 'it is no longer viable to speak in terms of rap and hip hop as being exclusively "Black" cultural forms'; Bennett, *Cultures of Popular Music*, p. 93. For a detailed discussion of the debate on essentialism see Tony Mitchell's introduction to Mitchell (ed.), *Global Noise*. See also Negus, *Popular Music in Theory*, pp. 100–13.
13. See Negus, *Popular Music in Theory*, p. 109; Mitchell, *Global Noise*, pp. 4–5, 10; Tricia Rose, *Black Noise: Rap and Black Culture in Contemporary America* (Middletown, CT: Wesleyan University Press, 1994), pp. 4–5.
14. Here 'ethnicity' is being used as a synonym for 'race'; 'ethnic German' refers in this context to White people of German heritage.
15. Sebastian Krekow and Jens Steiner (eds), *Bei uns geht einiges. Die deutsche HipHop-Szene* (Berlin: Schwarzkopf & Schwarzkopf Verlag, 2000).
16. 'Die Leipzig Story,' in Krekow and Steiner (eds), *Bei uns geht einiges*, p. 89; see also various accounts of the impact of *Beat Street* in the GDR, pp. 79, 246, 264, 346.
17. See comments of Smudo from Die Fantastischen Vier below.
18. 'Die Leipzig Story,' in Krekow and Steiner (eds), *Bei uns geht einiges*, p. 89.
19. Smudo, 'Ich sehe da nicht viel neues. Hoffentlich irre ich mich,' in Krekow and Steiner (eds), *Bei uns geht einiges*, pp. 31–2.
20. Pennay, 'Rap in Germany,' p. 127.
21. Smudo, 'Ich sehe da nicht viel neues,' in Krekow and Steiner (eds), *Bei uns geht einiges*, p. 34.
22. Marcus Staiger, 'Einleitung,' in Krekow and Steiner (eds), *Bei uns geht einiges*, p. 12.
23. Hoyerswerda, September 17–22, 1991; Schwedt, Eberswalde, Eisenhüttenstadt, Elsterwerda in October 1991; Rostock-Lichtenhagen August 23–27, 1993. In some of these attacks the assailants were cheered on by the local population. On neo-Nazism and anti-foreigner violence in post-war Germany see Christophe Butterwege, *Rechtsextremismus, Rassismus und Gewalt: Erklärungsmodelle in der Diskussion* (Darmstadt: Primus, 1996); Dieter Schüpp, Josef Kopperschmidt, Hans Pöttgens, Hrsg., *Rechsextremismus und Gewalt: Phänomene, Analysen, Antworten* (Mönchengladbach: Fachhochschule Niederrhein, 1994); Ulrich Wank (ed.), *The Resurgence of Right-Wing Radicalism in Germany* (Atlantic Highlands: Humanities Press, 1996); Hans-Gerd Jaschke, Birgit Ratsch, and Yury Winterberg, *Nach Hitler. Radikale Recht rüsten auf* (München: C. Bertelsmann, 2001); Diethelm Prowe, 'Fascism, Neo-fascism, New Radical Right?' in Roger Griffin (ed.), *International Fascism. Theories, Causes and the New Consensus* (London, Sydney, Auckland: Arnold, 1998).
24. The initiative started in 1993 as a response to the wave of right-wing violence against Turkish immigrants and asylum-seekers. Dietmar Elflein argues that Rap gegen Rechts was relatively short-lived and ineffectual, but a quick perusal of the world wide web suggests that RGR was still going strong as recently as 2001. Dietmar Elflein, 'From Krauts with Attitudes to Turks with Attitudes: Some Aspects of Hip-Hop History in Germany,' *Popular Music*, Vol. 17, No. 3 (1998), pp. 255–65, 258.

25. Pennay, 'Rap in Germany,' p. 120.
26. Ibid., p. 123.
27. See the dismissal of Advanced Chemistry's activist brand of rap in Smudo, 'Ich sehe da nicht viel neues,' in Krekow and Steiner eds, *Bei uns geht einiges*, pp. 41–6.
28. The question of hip hop's (or any art form's) connection to commerce is complex; on the commercial mediation of hip hop see Rose, *Black Noise*, chapter 1. For a discussion of some of the larger theoretical issues involved see Negus, *Popular Music in Theory*, chapter 2.
29. An interpretation shared by many members of the scene; see comments in 'Textor,' in Krekow and Steiner (eds), *Bei uns geht einiges*, p. 334. The idea of 'Do it Yourself' (DIY) first rose in association with punk rock in the 1970s and has underpinned subsequent grassroots music movements—above all rap—even if the term remains largely associated with punk. The basic elements and larger implications of the DIY approach are ably summarized in Ashley Dawson, '"Do Doc Martins Have a Special Smell?" Homocore, Skinhead Eroticism, and Queer Agency,' in Kevin J.H. Dettmar and William Richey (eds), *Reading Rock and Roll: Authenticity, Appropriation, Aesthetics* (New York: Columbia University Press, 1999), pp. 125–43.
30. Torch, 'Was mich and Hip Hop in Deutschland am meisten ankotzt, ist Deutschland,' in Krekow and Steiner (eds), *Bei uns geht einiges*, p. 52.
31. Smudo, 'Ich sehe da nicht viel neues,' in Krekow and Steiner (eds), *Bei uns geht einiges*, p. 41.
32. Bennett, *Cultures of Popular Music*, p. 145.
33. The term appears to have been coined by the group Cartel as part of the 'Oriental Hip Hop Project' announced in conjunction with the release of its first album in 1995; see Elflein, 'From Krauts with Attitudes,' p. 260. The term has since been picked up by other artists to denote their blending of Turkish ('Oriental') and African-American influences; see Ayhan Kaya, *'Sicher in Kreuzberg.' Constructing Diasporas: Turkish Hip-Hop Youth in Berlin* (Bielefeld: Transcript, 2001), p. 211.
34. Quoted in Bennett, 'Hip Hop am Main,' p. 84.
35. Interestingly, the lyrics on this recording were in English; see Elflein, 'From Krauts with Attitudes,' p. 262.
36. Quoted in Kaya, *'Sicher in Kreuzberg,'* p. 198.
37. Elflein, 'From Krauts with Attitudes,' p. 258. See also Kaya, *'Sicher in Kreuzberg,'* p. 185.
38. See Kaya, *'Sicher in Kreuzberg,'* especially chapters 2 and 6.
39. Ibid., p. 29.
40. The actual German word is 'Kanake'; shortening the word to 'Kanak' may be seen as analogous to American hip hop's reclaiming of the word 'nigger' by changing it to 'nigga'; Kaya, *'Sicher in Kreuzberg,'* p. 189.
41. Something of the flavor of the group's anti-multicultural anti-racism can be gleaned from the following passage from its website: 'Although Kanak Attak is a predominantly migrant movement it should not be seen as the "cool voice" of the ghetto. That's how they would like it, the commercial vultures of the cultural industries, who are searching for "authentic" and "exotic" human experiences to be sold to those living in the grey mainstream of everyday German society. Here the figure of the young, angry migrant fits perfectly; the person who endorses the "out of the ghetto" mythology that assures complacent liberals that German society is meritocratic after all, and which in turn is used to great commercial success by the German music and film industries in falsifying the "German Dream".' Available at <http://www.kanak-attak.de/ka/about/manif_eng.html>.
42. *Frankfurter Allgemeine Zeitung*, June 22, 2003, Nr. 25.
43. Elflein, 'From Krauts with Attitudes,' p. 260.

44. H. Gans, 'Symbolic Ethnicity: The Future of Ethnic Groups and Cultures in America,' *Ethnic and Racial Studies*, Vol. 2, No. 1 (January), pp. 1–20.
45. Elflein, 'From Krauts with Attitudes,' p. 260.
46. Kaya, '*Sicher in Kreuzberg*,' pp. 183–4.
47. Fuat, 'Der Letzte Bonobo Panzer,' in Krekow and Steiner (eds), *Bei uns geht einiges*, p. 262.
48. 'Das P-Pack-Interview Mit Danny,' in Krekow and Steiner (eds), *Bei uns geht einiges*, p. 213.
49. The unreflective adoption of the idea of the 'gangsta' by gang-oriented hip hop enthusiasts in Germany has been the subject of much criticism within the scene. See comments on the Kreuzberg 'gangstas' in 'Das P-Pack-Interview Mit Danny,' in Krekow and Steiner (eds), *Bei uns geht einiges*, p. 213.
50. Bennett, *Cultures of Popular Music*, p. 145.
51. Elflein, 'From Krauts with Attitudes,' pp. 258–60.
52. Ibid., p. 258.
53. Tony Mitchell, *Popular Music and Local Identity: Rock, Pop, and Rap in Europe and Oceania* (London; New York: Leicester University Press, 1996).

10
Africa on their Mind:
Rap, Blackness, and Citizenship in France

Veronique Helenon

When studying French hip hop, scholars rarely stress its connections to Africa.[1] However, rappers' ties to the continent are strong and expressed in many ways. A close look at lyrics as well as music clearly indicates an abundance of references to Africa. The lack of focus on this important characteristic of French hip hop may be explained by the fact that African bonds are not always expressed overtly but, to get a sense of the importance of Africa one should also consider featurings and samplings. Moreover, songs entirely dedicated to this theme are rarely among the most promoted by mainstream radio stations. Beyond a simple glance at songs and music, a full understanding of French rap requires a consideration of the political and social status of minorities in France. Indeed, the development of rap in this country is directly linked to the postcolonial relationships established with former colonies of Africa and the Caribbean. In this regard, the definition of the nation according to French standards, as well as the nature of racism in French society, is key to comprehending the reason for the success of hip hop and especially of rap in France. Addressing their lack of visibility, rappers, who are overwhelmingly of African descent, claim their origins, redefine their identity and challenge traditional French conceptions of race and citizenship.

While Afrika Bambaataa was central to the development of Afrocentric themes during the early 1980s, French rappers have since emancipated themselves from his patronage to define their own agenda, which sometimes overlaps themes developed in the U.S. French rap specifically has been a multi-dimensional expression of ties with Africa. One of the most direct ways to look at the Africanness of French rap is to consider lyrics. Indeed a number of songs address historical as well as contemporary issues directly linked to the African continent. Interestingly, 'Les tam-tam de l'Afrique,'[2] released in 1991 by IAM, was one of the very first hits of French rap and dealt expressly with slavery. Using a sample of 'Past Time Paradise' by Stevie Wonder, this track focused on the plunder of Africa, the abduction of its inhabitants, the Middle Passage, and the plantation system in the Americas. In fact, the theme of slavery has been addressed more than once by French rappers. For instance, 1998 marked the 150th anniversary of the abolition of slavery in France and several projects were organized to celebrate the date. On May 22, the official date of the abolition of slavery in Martinique,[3] a huge concert took place at the Olympia, one of the most famous and elegant theaters in Paris. The evening opened with a show by drummers chained together, and the concert went on with performances by rappers of African descent such as Doc Gynéco, Stomy Bugsy, Arsenik, and Hamed Daye, to name a few. That same year, Fabe recorded the title 'Code noir,'[4] in which he denounces slavery and the Black Code of the slave system as crimes against humanity. While preparing this album, Fabe made a trip to Martinique, his parents' home island, where he met with some local rappers, The Niggas,[5] who contributed to the writing of 'Code noir.' It was also in 1998 that several artists produced a video inspired by the writings of the Martinican poet Aimé Césaire. Among them were Ménélik, KDD, Bambi Cruz, MC Solaar, and Positive Black Soul, all of whom made an original contribution to rap music by using excerpts from the *Cahier d'un retour au pays natal* (Notebook of a Return to the Native Land) as their lyrics. In fact, narratives about Africa cover a great variety of issues related to the continent, including historical as well as current topics. As a counterbalance to the devastating impact of slavery, many songs take great pride in being Black. Rappers glorify the African past and extol its values which they often oppose to those of Western societies, considered to be on the wane politically as well as morally. In his song 'Les bords du fleuve,'[6] Dontcha, a rapper of Congolese descent, recalls scenes of his childhood:

> I grew up in the shade of the palm trees by the Zaire River
> Where diamond mines can be seen gushing by the hundreds
> I was floating on the pirogues while dabbling in the waters of
>   the sweet rivers
> Obsessed by the longing to see freshwater mermaids
> As a child with a catapult I could have killed a crocodile,
> Knocked down a wildcat by throwing coconuts
> The sorcerer's tales nourished my fragile childish mind
> I was cherished, beneath the straw roof covering the clay hut
> Dirt paths connected woods, fields and hills[7]

If some tend to idealize the African continent, it is critical to place this discourse within the context of the school system. Indeed, in spite of an extensive past of slave and colonial power, this underbelly of French history has been excluded from curricula and minorities are largely ignored. Many rappers protest the way history has been defined in France and their lyrics try to revise this blindness by emphasizing the participation of Black people in French history.[8] Indeed, curricula teach the history of the 'nation' exclusively as composed of White people, but the contribution of minorities, and especially Blacks, to the building of France is discarded. When their presence on national soil is acknowledged, it focuses on the most recent period, the last four decades. And here, the growing number of people of African descent has been constructed as the immigration problem.

In 'Le message,'[9] Teemour addresses this issue directly, stressing the fact that African figures have been deleted from French history. As an alternative, he offers his own reading of the past and names some of the heroes who inhabit his pantheon. Haile Selassie, Shakka, Sundjiata Keita,[10] and Behanzin[11] are mentioned along with ancient Egypt, Nubia, the Songhai empire, and Ethiopia, which he considers central to Black people's history. His selection of figures and locations clearly calls to mind the idea of a strong and glorious continent, the birthplace of humankind. It is also important to note that being a rapper of Senegalese descent living in France, Teemour is inclusive and addresses people from the continent as well as the diaspora. Furthermore, he celebrates the hybrid character of the diaspora when combining icons from both the anglophone and francophone worlds. Indeed, while figures such as Haile Selassie, Shakka and places such as Ethiopia, Egypt and Nubia are commonly mentioned in diasporic discourses, Teemour's contribution is to add francophone references such as to Sundjiata Keita or Behanzin.

MC Solaar's album *Cinquième as* also pays clear tribute to Africa, and especially to Senegal where he grew up. In 'Les colonies,'[12] he compares past colonial oppression to today's exploitation of the 'third world' and denounces the role of institutions such as the World Bank. Furthermore, he addresses the conditions under which Black people have migrated to and settled in France. In the piece 'Lève-toi et rap,'[13] he describes his Chadian parents' migration from Senegal to a Parisian suburb, the main stages of his teenage years and how he finally came to discover rap. The design of the album also carries Solaar's message. The front cover is a picture of a group of men including Solaar. All of them are stripped to the waist, and at first the image seems to evoke captives about to be taken aboard a slave ship. A closer look at other pictures inside the booklet makes it clear that these men are in fact, African wrestlers. The photo on the back of the album is a close-up of Solaar's body fully dressed in a wrestler's costume and wearing his mystical protections. Using the theme of wrestling and boxing, the album pays tribute to the African presence in France. The mythic Senegalese boxer Battling Siki is also present in the booklet. Siki, who was a veteran of World War I, made a career in France and became the world light heavyweight champion in 1922 after defeating Georges Carpentier in a memorable fight. However, Siki could not escape racism; journalists constantly compared him to a chimpanzee.

Another illustration of how Africa is made brought to the front Black revisionism as presented by the group IAM. Since its very first tape, the mythical 'Concept Tape,' the group has developed a unique identity largely, but not solely, centered on ancient Egypt. Their lyrics as well as in the names chosen by four of the six members of the group—Kheops, Akhenaton,

Imhotep, Kephren—indicate this influence. In fact, French rap's quest for history follows two main tracks, often intermingled. The first stresses Afrocentric themes and claims Africa as the cradle of mankind, while the other points to the contribution of Blacks to French history. The group La Brigade is a good example of this attempt to restore Black French history. In the title 'Partir ailleurs,'[14] they recount another chapter left out of French textbooks: the African participation in the French colonial armies during both World Wars.

> Now I realize, I fought in the trenches to liberate the borders, I dreamt of equality while my people were being killed, I thought I was serving the children by sacrificing myself and today what do I see? The daughters and sons of those who yesterday were at the front treated as pariahs, excluded, disparaged without dignity. We don't even have a right to respect. It's just as if we didn't exist anymore. Now I realize.[15]

Many rappers view their songs as a tool to respond to contemporary challenges and to address the present situation of African societies. Their message is clear: the condition of the Black minority in France today and the bankruptcy of the African continent are by no means a reflection of the continent's worth and potential. In fact, these problems are understood to have been generated by external causes, namely the slave trade and the subsequent plunder of the continent. However, the analysis goes well beyond this position. Current African leaders must also accept some of the blame. In 'Afrique tolérance,'[16] Démocrates D insists on the responsibility both of Western powers and African leaders for the spread of poverty and hunger over the continent. Similarly, with a great sense of humor, Bisso Na Bisso's 'Dans la peau d'un chef'[17] delivers a biting critique of corruption in contemporary Africa:

> I cash in my benefits, I don't leave a penny
> Time is so short, I swear, when you're a chief
> I've been appointed, I swear fidelity to my homeland
> I pray for the development of my country that is falling into decay
> Believe me I swear to gorge myself (…)
> My family is complicit
> Too bad we're ransacking the country, the elder that we respect
> My militia decapitated, then I negotiate
> What is worth 100 I sell for 10, I take the dough
> Bodyguards, fetish, the people is broke
> It's because of my democracy which is fucked up[18]

When considering the African component of French rap, group names are as eloquent as album and song titles. Indeed, some rappers have picked names that expressly refer to Africa. For instance, the members of Djoloff, a Senegalese posse, have called their group after the empire which existed in the region of present-day Senegal; Mafia K'1 Fry is slang for African Mafia; Ménélik, who is from Cameroon, chose his alias in memory of the Ethiopian emperor; and Bam's pseudonym is meant to remind us that she belongs to the Bamileke ethnic group. Similarly, the group Bisso Na Bisso[19] was composed of rappers of Congolese descent only, for the production of one album *Racines*, which quickly became a hit. By the same token, Liste Noire entitled their first album *Les damnés de la terre* and Franz Fanon's book is also referred to in songs such as 'Damnés'[20] by Minister A.M.E.R and 'Mourir debout' by Hamed Daye.[21] Other groups have chosen names that express their connection to Africa but primarily assert their identity as Blacks: 2 Bal 2 Neg, Afro Jazz, N.A.P. (New African Poets), Neg de la Peg.

Music is another way rappers have brought Africa into the French repertory. Largely computerized, as is standard practice in rap, soundtracks can be enhanced with recordings of acoustic African instruments such as the kora, the balafon, and the ngoni[22] as well as a great variety of drums played in Africa and the Caribbean (derbuka from North Africa, djembe from Senegal, bèlè drums from Martinique, gwoka drum from Guadeloupe, etc). These borrowings are not limited to traditional music; modern rhythms are used as well. In its album, *Salam*, the Senegalese rap group Djoloff includes some famous West African musicians such as the Malian griot, Moriba Koïta, on the ngoni and Yakhouba Sissokho on the kora. The Algerian rap group Intik has collaborated with various North African musicians such as Djamel Benyelles who usually accompanies the great Kabyle singer Idir on the violin. Likewise, on her album *Black mama*, Lady Laistee presents an interlude played solely on gwoka drums of Guadeloupe, her parents' native island. The Senegalese Wasis Diop, a big name in World Music, has contributed to many rap albums and participated in the composition of the song 'Le lion est mort' by the rap group Aktivist.[23] Likewise, Bisso Na Bisso's *Racines* features some of the most celebrated Soukous stars such as Papa Wemba, Lokua Kanza, and Koffi Olomide. This album also pays tribute to the talent of Franklin Boukaka, an icon of post-independence Congolese music. Conversely, some rappers are featured on albums by Caribbean and African artists. This is the case of Diziz La Peste, a rapper of Senegalese descent, who appears on the album of Sekouba Bambino, a Guinean griot; they co-star in the song 'Promesse.'[24] Since these African contributions are generally mixed with other types of music, they contribute to an atmosphere in which Africa is present but not necessarily predominant.

The African connection can also be explored from a more immediate standpoint since an overwhelming majority of French rappers have family in Africa and the Caribbean. For instance, Teemour's family came from Senegal, Stomy Bugsy's from the Cape Verde Islands; MC Solaar has his origins in Chad, Kool Freddy Jay in Martinique; Passi's parents are from Congo; Lady Laistee came from Guadeloupe, Hamed Daye from Mali;

Freeman's (of IAM) background is Algerian, and El Tunisiano's (of Sniper), as his name hints, Tunisian.

Their arrival in France is a direct consequence of a migration that has its roots in the French slave and colonial past. Indeed, a Black minority developed in continental France at least as early as the eighteenth century. However, it was during the two decades following World War II that migrations soared. The economic boom that followed this conflict generated a need for manpower which greatly exceeded the national potential, and the government's solution was immigration on a grand scale. Using its colonial ties to Africa and the Caribbean, the French government largely, but not solely, recruited from these regions and organized migration to continental France. As early as 1945, a public office, the ONI,[25] was created to supervise and encourage the arrival of new immigrant workers, while in 1961 another structure, the BUMIDOM[26] was set up for French overseas departments where migration was considered to be a solution to unemployment and social unrest.[27] Paralleling this policy and after the independence movements, agreements were negotiated with some of the newly formed African governments in order to secure the migration influx. Africans represented 42.8 percent of the immigrant population in 1982,[28] most of them coming from North Africa, and mainly Algeria.[29] The census of 1999 indicates that Africa continues to be the main source of immigration into France. However, although North Africa remains the main source, the number of migrants from sub-Saharan Africa increased by 43 percent between 1990 and 1999.[30]

Because of their difference in status, Caribbeans and Africans who arrived in the second half of the twentieth century were not appointed to the same type of positions. Caribbeans who were French citizens could therefore enter the public sector where they were employed at its lower levels while Africans were generally hired in the private sector. As a result, Blacks arriving in France constituted an important source of petty civil servants and menial employees. More often than not, they were severely exploited with little or no power to resist or protest their condition. As Hamed Daye puts it:

'My father came to France in the 60s. He was living in one of these ramshackle immigrant housings projects, with one shower per floor and over-crowded rooms. But he did not give up. My father was my hero: he personified authority and determination. My mother was much more sweetness. My father's generation would rather submit while wheeling and dealing on the side. I call it a moral imbalance. It's all these frustrations that made us so arrogant. Our generation doesn't want to shut up and we demand equality of treatment.'[31]

Immigration, racism, and the exploitation of immigrant workers have logically become some of the major themes of French rap. 'Ils ont,'[32] by Aktivist, gives a good summary of these realities:

Aktivist denounces intolerance towards all immigrant fathers
Exploited in France since the 50s–60s
30 years of building sites and factories
For the new era 2000, their bodies are falling apart
And their children are still being judged according to their origins.[33]

The economic growth of the second half of the twentieth century required the construction of large apartment projects to house the burgeoning population. Called *cités*, these huge projects are located on the outskirts of the major French cities and form what is called the *banlieue*, an agglomeration of *cités*, which is more often than not synonymous with urban poverty. While many poor White French live in the *cités* (unlike the situation in U.S. ghettoes), the percentage of immigrants of African descent is very high. With the oil crisis of the 1970s, the employment priority was given to French citizens and the situation in the *banlieues* rapidly deteriorated. Immigrants' living conditions worsened along with education, housing, and job opportunities. In addition to the precariousness of their economic life, they also endure daily racism, police brutality, and political disenfranchisement. Living in some of the poorest neighborhoods, children of Africans and Caribbeans as well as poor Whites attend the worst of schools, which for most of them means inability to access higher education, limited job prospects, and no possibility of social advancement. In response to this situation, riots regularly break out in the *banlieues* of Paris and other major French cities: Les Minguettes in 1981 and Vaulx-en-Velin in 1990 (both located in the *banlieue* of Lyon), Rouen and Avignon in 1994, Toulon in 1997, Toulouse in 1998, and Clichy-sous-Bois in 2005 are a few of a long list. Films such as *La haine* by Mathieu Kassovitz and *Ma cité va crack-er* by Jean-François Richet exemplify these explosive situations.

Directly addressing the condition of Blacks in France, rap brings to the forefront populations who are usually labeled dysfunctional. Hip hop and more especially rap has created an opportunity to speak in the first person and on a scale never attained before. To assert their identity and break free of the anonymity usually reserved for minorities, rappers report the reality of their presence in France. This is why lyrics contain countless references to the neighborhoods where they live. By means of rap lyrics, *cités* commonly considered to be among the worst, are proudly flaunted: Timide et Sans Complexe declare that they come from Vitry, while Démocrates D regularly refer to their *cité* of Les Bosquets in Montfermeil, both on the outskirts of Paris. Ministère A.M.E.R. entitled their second album *95200*, the Zip code for Sarcelles, a northern *banlieue* of Paris, where they grew up, whereas NTM definitely affirm their ties to Seine Saint-Denis.

In the huge complexes of the *banlieues*, the fight against dehumanization is accomplished through a variety of means including a validation of the family home, the first place where a proximity to Africa is expressed. In fact, it is in the parents' home that relatives and friends stay when arriving in France in search of employment or vacationing. The many trips back and forth, suitcases full of spices and minds packed with memories, have been additional ways to keep in touch with the homeland. Among other means, intimacy is maintained through food. Local dishes are not exotic but are part and parcel of the daily menu. Logically, culinary images punctuate many rap verses: mafé,[34] couscous, rum, and atay[35] are frequently referred to in lyrics even when Africa is not the main theme of the song.

It is also at home that many have learned to speak their parents' mother tongue, and thus, language has also become a very strong tool for rappers to assert their specific connections to Africa. Many write a chorus or even a whole song in their parents' language. For instance, the Senegalese of Positive Black Soul wrote many of their songs in Wolof, while the Algerian group Intik usually raps in Arabic, and the Martinicans of Les Neg' in Creole. However, French remains by far the most used language. Most of the time, words and expressions in Creole, Wolof, Arabic, Bambara, Lingala, etc, are inserted into lyrics written in highly distinctive French. Following the usage of the *banlieues*, this French is combined with various forms of slang, one of the best known being *Verlan*,[36] the slang of the *cités*. '*La langue de Molière*' is therefore deconstructed and redefined as to make the Black presence evident in the language itself. Distorted and remodeled, words gain different sonorities and new meanings, and rap lyrics directly challenge the very foundations of the dominant language. Unsurprisingly, critics claim not to understand 'a word of what they are saying.'

However, when considering their relationship to Africa, French rappers admit to being caught between two cultures. Groups such as La Rumeur or Bisso Na Bisso, among others, describe the ambivalence of their situation. Even when claiming their pride in Africa and their desire to promote solidarity among Blacks, rappers also acknowledge being deeply rooted in the French urban context. In spite of regular visits to their families, many feel disconnected when returning to their parents' native countries. In fact, some parents envisage these travels precisely as a way to counterbalance the influence of French society on their children and to pass on values that they themselves received in their own childhood. 'Tonton du bled'[37] by 113 recounts a summer vacation spent in Morocco. After reluctantly leaving the *cité* in the over-packed family car, K-Rim arrives in the village where he spends one month with his cousins. Nice meals and sweet idleness are tempered by his difficulties in speaking the Arabic slang used by his cousins, who keep heckling him with questions like 'how come we never see you on TV?' Back home, he tries to keep some of the village with him, eating the same meal for a month and above all admitting how powerless he feels when confronted by the political and economic situation there. The last chorus goes like this:

I wanted to stay in the *cité*, my father told me (no, no, no)
In that case, I'll bring all my friends with me (no, no, no)
Then in one week I'll be back in Vitry (no, no, no)
I will finish my days there (yeah, yeah, yeah)
Please let me take my scooter (no, no, no)
Well, in this case I'll bring my coat (no, no, no)
Ok, I take all my CDs and my tapes (no, no, no)
So, I take nothing? (yeah, yeah, yeah)
Then, I'll shave my head before we go (no, no, no)
I take the playstation (no, no, no)
The living room TV at least (no, no, no)
You really think I'm going there to get married or what?
    (yeah, yeah, yeah)[38]

When claiming their ties to Africa, rappers not only express an intricate proximity to their parents' homeland but above all they question their condition as Black in France. According to the official French conception of the nation, the Republic is one and indivisible and cannot admit any difference of race among its members. In theory this implies that all inhabitants, no matter what their origin may be, are offered equal opportunities. Of course, this model has proven to be limited and particularly inadequate to fight racism, and beyond the sympathetic imagery of a national soccer team winning the 1998 World Cup with numerous players of African descent, the visibility of minorities in general, and of Blacks in particular, remains very low. This situation can also be measured by the almost complete absence of Blacks in the film industry and on television. Ignoring the reality of the streets, the media depict a society where Whiteness is the standard and French Blacks receive very little exposure.

While rap has become a major means of addressing the condition of the youth of the *banlieue*, this is not merely a consequence of the Americanization of France. Actually, it has much more to do with the peculiar status of minorities in this society. When the idea of the nation does not allow any racially based claim, a U.S. detour has been instrumental in questioning the French model of multiculturalism. Indeed, the United States today offers to many the image of a society where Black people have successfully articulated their struggle. Their achievements, combined with the power of U.S. international policy as well as the impact of U.S. television and films, produce a sense of empowerment which has become easy to relate to. For young French Blacks, the identification-building process has been fueled by African-American figures such as Denzel Washington, Whoopi Goldberg, Wesley Snipes, Shaquille O'Neal, Michael Jordan, and Serena and Venus Williams who represent some of the new heroes coexisting with Martin Luther King Jr., Malcolm X, Angela Davis, Louis Armstrong, and Ella Fitzgerald in a very heterogeneous pantheon of Black role models.

In this context, it is no accident that rap has become so popular in the *banlieues* where the percentage of young French of African descent is high. Moreover, at least since the interwar period with the arrival of many African-American musicians to France, U.S. Black music has been an inspiration to many French, not just Blacks. By the early 1980s, following the growth of rap music in the U.S., budding French rappers have been following and reinterpreting the rhythms beating across the Atlantic. One good example is 'Le message' by Teemour, whose title clearly pays tribute to the mythical piece by Grandmaster Flash. Among other features, rap has been at the same time understood as a component of U.S. Black popular culture as well as a committed music which can be used to denounce the condition of minorities in France. It is in this context that rap has contributed to the recent, though still limited, visibility of minorities of African descent in France.

North Africans, Caribbeans, and sub-Saharan Africans often live side by side but generally without knowing each other. On the contrary, they come from different regions, have their own specific cultures, and, ultimately, do little to share with the other communities. In this regard, the situation of North Africans stands out. Since they are usually considered as a separate group with a specific culture and a distinctive historic connection with France, and even though they are stigmatized, they are not regarded and do not regard themselves as Black. Similarly, Caribbeans tend to dissociate themselves from sub-Saharan Africans as well as North Africans. Moreover, although Blacks are often considered by mainstream France as similar whatever their origin may be, in some contexts each is proud to claim a distinct local identity—Malian, Guadeloupean, Ivorian. Refusal to be associated in any way with one of the other groups' has also been a way to identify these other communities as the source of the problem. In this sense, racism is frequently seen as a legitimate response on the part of French society to the other group's so-called dysfunctional culture and identity.

Large scale migrations have led to some interesting evolutions. First, minorities of African descent have become more and more numerous in continental France. In addition, the new generations born on French soil now tend to share a common experience. The increasing number of citizens of African descent, combined with the economic crisis that began in the 1970s, has contributed to the development of different expectations, reactions, and ways of addressing the condition of the minorities on the part of the new generations. Living in the same neighborhoods and facing similar situations of discrimination many rappers of North African, sub-Saharan, and Caribbean origins have increased a community of interests. Though differences and rivalries are far from having disappeared, hip hop has often created a space where oppositions can fade when the possibility of developing new networks appears.

Progressively, rap music has become a way to articulate a new definition of Blackness, which transcends boundaries and includes references to North

Africa, the Caribbean, and sub-Saharan Africa. In this way, French rappers participate in the emergence of an identity that is all the more powerful that it does not follow traditional classifications. Indeed, many groups include North Africans, sub-Saharan Africans, and Caribbeans. For example, 113 comprises a Malian, a Guadeloupean, and a Moroccan while N.A.P.'s members come from Congo, Senegal, Mali, and Algeria. Fonky Family's members originate from the Comoros islands, Algeria, France, and Réunion while Lunatic's rappers are from Morocco and Mali.

Furthermore, while rap initially developed in the larger metropolises of France, it also spread to Africa and the West Indies, becoming a distinctive contemporary popular music for the Black French diaspora. Guadeloupe, Martinique, Senegal, Guinea, Congo, Ivory Coast, Algeria among many others, have their own rappers, such as Neg'Lyrical, Bill de Sam, Positive Black Soul, Intik. This profusion of groups is largely the result of images received via satellites but it also reflects migrants' travels between France and its former colonies. Whether in the Caribbean or Africa, rappers look at specific local issues but they also denounce their countries' historical and economic dependency on France. Thus, the Algerian group Intik criticizes the corruption of national leaders and the political situation in their home country. The Guinean, Bill de Sam, dedicated his album *Exile* to the two stowaways who died in 1999 in the landing gear of the Airbus where they were hiding in a desperate attempt to reach France. Some, such as the Senegalese group Djoloff, even claim that the foundations of rap lie in Africa, not in the United States. They claim a direct connection between rap and the art of the griot.[39] As the Senegalese group Positive Black Soul puts it, 'rap grew up in America, but its roots are in Africa.'[40] By tracing the origins of rap to Africa, these rappers also attempt to reverse the relationships between the center and the periphery, the Western powers and the former colonies.

Over time, many groups have come up with a meaning of Black that is not so much about color of skin as it is about asserting one's origins and heritage in a country where multiculturalism is in fact largely synonymous with Whiteness. From this perspective, Africa is redefined according to norms that refute its traditional definition. For instance, North Africans are traditionally considered to be closer to the Middle East than the rest of the African continent, but in the French context many rappers have shaped connections that go beyond those classifications. Thus, although Maghrebians are generally not regarded as and do not consider themselves as Black, they can be included in a common African identity which does not necessarily have to do with the color of skin. Interestingly, this identity can also include White French who represent a minority of the MCs. For instance, playing on the meaning of their name[41] which they interpret in many ways, the members of IAM have created an identity rooted in the thesis of Cheikh Anta Diop but also including other peoples and cultures. Though most members claim Egyptian names, one of the MCs of the group declares himself to be a martial art disciple and to believe in Taoism. Consequently, Asian culture has always coexisted with Afrocentric lyrics and concepts. Similarly many groups have used the term Black very broadly, as a synonym for minority. The members of Lunatic who are of Moroccan and Senegalese descent state that 'if you don't like Black, you don't listen and that's it.'[42]

Complex connections between France, the Caribbean, and Africa can also be comprehended through both lyrics and music. Rappers of various origins frequently include in their lyrics words in Arabic, Creole, or languages from sub-Saharan Africa. For instance, among the words that are regularly used, one will find the Arabic *sheitan* which means devil and is ascribed to Whites and the West. Another example is the Creole *bonda*, meaning one's behind, and refers to a woman's bottom. In 1990, the Caribbean Lionel D wrote 'For You the Arab,'[43] in which he denounced prejudices against Arabs, and invited the Tunisian singer Amina to perform background vocals. By the same token, the Congolese Mystik, in 'Le chant de l'exilé,'[44] used the traditional call and response of Caribbean storytellers as the rhythmic base of his chorus. Furthermore, although Bisso Na Bisso claimed to have been created only to gather rappers of Congolese descent, the album also includes a piece which mixes zouk and rap, and in which the Guadeloupean zouk stars Tanya St-Val and Jacob Desvarieux as well as the Martinican bass player Michel Alibo contributed. Similarly several albums present the fusion of dancehall and rap. One of the most prominent French dancehall groups is Neg' Marrons, and rappers such as Rhoff, Pit Baccardi or the Fonky Family are featured on their album *Le bilan*. Another collaboration of this type features NTM and the Martinican Lord Kossity, whose career reached national level following his participation in the piece 'Ma Benz,' on one of NTM's albums.[45]

The emergence of this new identity includes religion. Islam has become solid cement between North and sub-Saharan Africans and even Caribbean peoples. This religion is today the second most populous in France and some even claim that its followers now outnumber Catholics. Many rappers are Muslims. They have either been raised in this religion or have converted as adults. One of the most radical and striking conversions is certainly that of the Haitian Kery James, who has long belonged to the most hardcore form of rap as a member of Ideal J. However, when he became a Muslim, he decided to break with his former life and even envisaged abandoning rap. Instead he released an album in 2001, *Si c'était à refaire* in which he examines his past years, delivering a message of solidarity to rappers and the youth of the *banlieues*. Akhenaton, leader of IAM, is another good example of the connections established through Islam. Born Philippe Fragione, he represents the third generation of a family of Italian descent. After starting a career within IAM, he decided to convert to Islam and married the North African Aisha.

Far from demonstrating a strict interpretation of a Black consciousness, this heterogeneous African identity should be understood as an implement to make visible the presence of minorities in French society and presents an implicit critique of the nation according to official and popular French standards. As KDD puts it, there is a need 'to add one more color to the flag.' In their most recent album, *Une couleur de plus au drapeau*,[46] this group from the south of France gave a very personal interpretation of the *Marseillaise*, the French national anthem:

[Original lyrics of the *Marseillaise*, retained in the song, are in italics.]

One more color to the flag
Arise children of the fatherland and all the repatriates as well
The day of glory has arrived for those who are beginning to cry out
One more color to the flag, one more color to the flag
Against us stands tyranny, We've got to make it, bro
The bloody flag is raised to stop our sobs
One more color to the flag, one more color to the flag
Build for your descendants, build for your descendants, build for
    your descendants[47]

DISCOGRAPHY

113, *Les princes de la ville*, Double H (1999)
Ad'Hoc-1, *Musique du monde*, Sony (2000)
Aktivist Group, *Toujours actif*, Universal (2000)
Bisso Na Bisso, *Racines*, V2 (1999)
B-Love, *B-Love*, (1996)
Daara J, *Xalima*, Déclic (1998)
Démocrates D, *La voie du peuple*, Wotre Music (1995)
Dontcha, *Les bords du fleuve*, Sony (1999)
Fabe, *Détournement de son*, Small (1998)
Hamed Daye, *L'or noir*, Sony (2001)
IAM, *De la planète Mars*, Virgin (1991)
IAM, *Ombre est lumière*, Delabel (1993)
Ideal J, *Le combat continue*, Barclay (1998)
Intik, *Intik*, Columbia (2000)
KDD, *Une couleur de plus au drapeau*, Sony (2000)
Kery James, *Si c'était à refaire*, WEA (2001)
La Brigade, *Le testament*, Barclay (1991)
Lady Laistee, *Black mama*, Barclay (1999)
La Rumeur, *Poison d'Avril*, (2000)
Lionel D, *Y'a pas de problème*, CBS (1990)
Liste Noire, *Les damnés de la terre*, Artikal Production (1998)
Lunatic, *Mauvais œil*, 45 Scientific (2000)

MC Solaar, *Cinquième as*, Sentinel Ouest (2000)
Minister A.M.E.R., *Pourquoi tant de haine?* Musidisc (1992)
Mystik, *Le chant de l'exilé*, Sony (1999)
N.A.P., *La fin du monde*, BMG (1998)
Neg' Lyrical, *Kimannièoupédimwenanbagaykonsapéfet?!* Déclic (1996)
Neg' Marrons, *Le bilan*, Sony (2000)
Passi, *Genèse*, V2 (2000)
Positive Black Soul, *Salaam*, Island (1996)
Sekouba Bambino, *Sinikan*, Blue Jackel Entertainment (2002)
Sekta Vodoo, *Attitudes ... L'envers du décor*, Atmosphériques (1998)
Sniper, *Du rire aux larmes*, East West (2001)
Supreme NTM, *Supreme NTM*, (1998)
Teemour, *Don Blakka*, East West (1999)
Timide et Sans Complexe, *Dans Paris nocturne*, Night & Day (1995)
Tout Simplement Noir, *Dans Paris nocturne*, Night & Day (1995)

NOTES

1. See Manuel Boucher, *Le Rap. Expression des Lascars. Signification et enjeux du rap dans la société française* (L'Harmattan, 1998); Christian Béthune, *Le Rap: Une Esthétique Hors la Loi* (Autrement, 1999), André J.M. Prévos, 'Postcolonial Popular Music in France: Rap Music and Hip-Hop Culture in the 1980s and 1990s,' in Tony Mitchell (ed.), *Global Noise: Rap and Hip-Hop Outside the USA* (Middletown, CT: Wesleyan University Press, 2001), Ted Swedenburg, 'Islamic Hip-Hop vs. Islamophobia: Aki Nawaz, Natacha Atlas, Akhenaton,' in Mitchell (ed.), *Global Noise*.
2. 'African Drums' on the album *De la planète Mars*.
3. Since France had not yet developed its empire in Africa and Asia, the abolition of slavery mainly concerned the four colonies of Martinique, Guadeloupe, Guyane, and Réunion. Although was abolition decreed by the French state on March 4, 1848, in the twentieth century different official dates of commemoration have been chosen in order to recall the local slave rebellions that broke out in 1848.
4. 'Black Code' on the album *Détournement de son*.
5. Les Neg'.
6. 'The River's Banks' on the album *Les bords du fleuve*.
7. J'ai grandi sous l'ombre des palmiers au bord du fleuve Zaire
   Où les mines de diamants par centaines on voit jaillir
   Flottais sur les pirogues taquinant le courant des rivières douces
   Obnibulé par l'envie de voir des sirènes d'eau douce
   Petit muni d'une catapulte j'aurais tué un croco
   Assomé un félin par des lancers de noix de coco
   Les contes sorciers nourissaient mon esprit d'enfant fragile
   Couvé sous un toit de paille couvrant hutte en argile
   Des sentiers de terre reliaient forêts, champs et collines
8. It is only in May 2001 that a law was passed by the French Parliament recognizing slavery as a crime against humanity and ordering a revision of the textbook. However, it still remains to be fully implemented.
9. 'Le message' on the album *Don Blakka*.
10. Sundjiata is known as the founder of the empire of Mali.

11. Behanzin was the last king of Dahomey to resist the French in the late nineteenth century. He was captured in 1894 and was exiled to Martinique.

12. 'Les colonies' on the album *Cinquième As*.

13. 'Get Up and Rap.'

14. 'Going Elsewhere' on the album *Le testament*.

15. Maintenant j'me rends compte, j'ai combattu dans les tranchées pour libérer des frontières, j'ai rêvé d'égalité en voyant tomber les miens, j'ai pensé servir les enfants en m'sacrifiant et aujourd'hui qu'est-ce que je vois? Les filles et les fils de ceux qui étaient au front hier traités en parias, en exclus, rabaissés sans dignité, on a même plus le droit au respect. C'est comme si on existait plus. Maintenant je me rends compte.

16. 'Tolerance Africa' on the album *La voie du peuple*.

17. 'Being a Chief' on the album *Racines*.

18. Le benef j'encaisse, j'laisse rien dans la caisse
Le temps est si bref dans la peau d'un chef.
On m'a nommé, je jure fidélité à ma patrie, prie pour le développement de mon pays qui sombrait dans la décadence (ambiance).
Faites-moi confiance je jure de me bourrer la panse.
Complice est ma famille, tant pis on pille le pays
Le doyen qu'on repecte, ma milice coupe des têtes
Puis je négocie, ce qui vaut 100, je vends 10, je prends le pognon
Garde rapprochée, fétiche, peuple fauché, faute reprochée à ma démocratie à chier

19. Bisso Na Bisso means 'among us' in Lingala, one of the main Congolese languages.

20. 'Wretched' on the album *Pourquoi tant de haine?*

21. 'Dying Standing Up' on the album *L'or noir*.

22. The kora and the ngoni are two stringed instruments. Usually the kora is made with a calabash and the ngoni with wood. Another difference between the two is that the neck of the ngoni is inserted into the body of the instrument while the neck of the kora goes through its calabash resonator. The balafon is a xylophone usually made out of wood.

23. 'The Lion is Dead' on the album *Toujours aktif*.

24. 'Promise' on the album *Sinikan*.

25. Office national d'immigration (National Immigration Office).

26. Bureau pour les Migrations intéressant les départements d'outre-mer (Office of Migration for overseas French departments).

27. In 1946, the Caribbean islands of Guadeloupe and Martinique as well as Guyane and also Réunion in the Indian Ocean, went from colonial status to the status of French overseas departments, while the African colonies became independent in the late 1950s to early 60s.

28. Algerians were the majority with 21.6 percent in 1982 while migration from sub-Saharan Africa, mainly Senegal, Ivory Coast, and Mali, developed only later and multiplied by more than four between 1968 and 1982. (Statistics are from Milet Abou-Sada 1986.)

29. It is important to stress the fact that official data never include the Caribbean, since Martinique, Guadeloupe, and Guyane are French departments. As such the census does not separate them from the rest of the French population.

30. Julien Boëldieu and Catherine Borrel, 'La proportion d'immigrés est stable depuis 25 ans,' *Recensement de la population 1999*, INSEE, November 2000, #748.

31. Hamed Daye interviewed in *L'Affiche*, No. 89 (February 2001).

32. 'They Have' on the album *Toujours aktif*.

33. Aktivist dénonce l'intolérance sur tous les pères immigrés
Exploités en France depuis les années 50–60
30 ans de chantiers et d'usine
Pour la nouvelle ère de l'an 2000, leur corps est en ruine
Et leurs enfants sont encore jugés de par leurs origines

34. Senegalese dish made with a peanut sauce.
35. Mint tea.
36. *Verlan* consists of speaking backwards. The last syllables of the word are put in the front to build a new word in the reverse order of the syllables. *Verlan* is, in fact, the backward pronunciation of *l'envers*, which actually means backwards in French. It is similar to pig Latin.
37. 'Uncle of the Country' on the album *Princes de la ville*.
38. Je voulais rester à la cité, mon père m'a dit 'Lè, lè, la'
    Dans c'cas-là j'ramène tous mes amis, 'Lè, lè, la'
    Alors dans une semaine j'rentre à Vitry, 'Lè, lè, la'
    J'irais finir mes jours là-bas, 'Oua, oua, oua'
    S'te plait, vas-y laisse-moi ramener mon scooter, 'Lè, lè, la'
    Bon, ben dans c'cas-là j'ramène mon trois quart alors 'Lè, lè, la'
    Bon j'prends tous mes CD, toutes mes cassettes, 'Lè, lè, la'
    Bon ben j'prends rien alors 'Oua, oua, oua'
    Bon ben j'me fais la boule au moins avant d'partir, 'Lè, lè, la'
    J'ramène la playstation, bon la télé du salon alors, 'Lè, lè, la'
    Tu crois qu'j'vais aller là-bas pour m'marier ou quoi? 'Oua, oua, oua'
39. Griots use their ability to shape stories to the musical rhythm to praise and stir up their audience. Depending on the occasion, performances receive different names: for instance *labane* for the preparation of a wedding, *tage* before a fight, or *tassu* before a dance.
40. Interview in *Libération*, March 22, 1996.
41. IAM which is always pronounced with the English accent clearly implies the same meaning in English, but it can also be interpreted as 'Imperial Asiatic Men,' 'Indépendantistes Autonomes Marseillais' (Autonomous Independence Militants from Marseilles), or even 'Invasion Arrivant de Mars' (Invasion from Mars—Mars referring here to the planet as well as the city of Marseilles).
42. 'Si tu kiffes pas renoi, t'écoutes pas et c'est tout' in 'Si tu kiffes pas ...' on the album *Mauvais œil*.
43. On the album *Y'a pas de problème*.
44. 'The Song of the Expatriate' on the album *Le chant de l'exilé*.
45. 'My Mercedes' on the album *Supreme NTM*.
46. Album, *One More Color in the Flag*.
47. Une couleur de plus au drapeau
    Allons enfants de la patrie et de rapatriés
    Le jour de gloire est arrivé pour ceux qui semettent à crier
    Une couleur de plus au drapeau, une couleur de plus au drapeau
    Contre nous de la tyrannie, faut qu'on s'en tire mon gadjot
    L'étendard sanglant se lève pour stopper nos sanglots
    Une couleur de plus au drapeau, une couleur de plus au drapeau
    Contruis pour ta descendance, construis pour ta descendance, construis pour ta descendance

11
Cuban Hip Hop:
Making Space for New Voices of Dissent[1]

Annelise Wunderlich

It's a late Friday afternoon in downtown Havana and an old man in a worn-out tuxedo opens the doors under the flickering green and red neon of Club Las Vegas. A poster on the wall, its corners curling, advertises the usual cabaret fare: live salsa, banana daiquiris, and beautiful women. But the people standing outside with me are not tourists looking for an exotic thrill. They are mostly young, mostly Black, and dressed in the latest styles from Fubu and Tommy Hilfiger. And despite the $1 cover charge—steep for most Cubans—the line to get in is long.

Once inside, I see two young Afrocubans on a small stage in the back. One is tall and languid, the other is shorter and in constant motion. They wear baggy jeans, oversized T-shirts, and sprinkle their songs with 'c'mon now' and 'awww' ight.' But while it's clear they admire American hip hop style, Yosmel Sarrias and Maigel Entenza Jaramillo rap about a distinctly Cuban reality.

'It's time to break the silence/ This isn't what they teach in school/ In search of the American Dream/ Latinos suffer in the hands of others ...'[2]

'This music is not for dancing. It's for listening,' a young man wearing a Chicago Bulls jersey tells me. He waves his hand high in the air. 'And for Cubans, believe me, it takes a lot to keep us from dancing.'[3]

Jaramillo criss-crosses his arms as he moves across the stage, and the crowd follows him, word for word. Sarrias stands toward the back of the stage, delivering a steady flow of verse. The audience is enrapt.

Anonimo Consejo—Anonymous Advice—is one of Cuba's top rap groups, waiting for the next big break: a record contract and a living wage to do what they love.

They are not the only ones. Three girls, decked out in bright tank tops and spandex, sit on the sidelines and watch Jaramillo's every move. Yordanka, 20, Yaima 19, and Noiris 17, are cousins, and tell me that a year ago they started their own rap group, Explosión Femenina. So far they've only exploded in their living rooms or at school talent shows, but that could change. In a week, they will perform for the first time at Club Las Vegas. If Cuba's top rap producer likes them, he'll groom them just as he has Sarrias and Jaramillo.

Right now that producer—Pablo Herrera—is in the DJ's booth, looking down at the two rappers. 'What you're seeing is Cuba's underground. I'm talking about the empowerment of youth as a battle spear for a more conscious society,'[4] he says to me in English so flawless that he's sure he lived another life in Brooklyn. And he looks it—from the braids in his hair to the New York attitude.

Herrera and a fellow representative of Asociación de los Hermanos Saíz, the cultural arm of the Young Communist Party, put on the weekly hip hop show. With more than 250 rap groups in Havana alone, he chooses each Friday night's line-up carefully. 'I can't work with everybody, I'm not a machine,' Herrera says with a shrug. 'I mostly go with what I like.'

But even with Herrera's approval, the world for young rappers here is full of contradictions. They believe in Cuba, but they're not ideologues—they just want to make music from their own reality. Anonimo Consejo's lyrics are edgy, but getting too edgy could end their careers. The girls in Explosión Femenina try to be tough in the macho rap scene, but still rely on their sex appeal to get through the door. Each day is a political and social balancing act.

Cubans' fascination with hip hop is more than just a passing teenage fad. The Cuban government now sees rap music—long considered the music of American imperialism—as a road map to the hearts and minds of the young generation. Far more likely than their elders to complain about Castro, young Cubans are the question mark of the island's political future. Thousands took to the streets in 1994 to protest the regime, and polls in Havana and Miami often highlight youthful angst as a sign of potential upheaval. And in recent years, more and more have started voicing their discontent by rhyming—on buses, street corners, anywhere a crowd might gather to listen.

Young Cubans have long consumed American pop culture like junkies, waiting to watch the next smuggled hit from MTV or VH-1. For young Afrocubans in particular, the popular music of Black America is replacing salsa as their music of choice—especially hip hop. With its hard-driving beats and street smart message, rap often depicts a powerful and distinctive Black identity. In Cuba, where Castro's government promotes the idea of a 'color-blind' society, this idea has revolutionary potential.

But a full-scale hip hop rebellion hasn't happened yet. So far only one Cuban rap group has made it big—Orishas. The group was also a Pablo Herrera creation, back in the early 1990s. Then they were called 'Amenaza,' or 'Threat,' and Herrera says they were the first rappers to explore racial identity and challenge Castro's ideal of a colorless society. Tempted by an enticing record deal with a European label, the group traveled to Paris to perform in 1998 and stayed.

Sarrias and Jaramillo look at them with both awe and disappointment. Once abroad, Orishas made hits, but they did so by adding Cuba's beloved salsa and rumba beats to their music. As their singles climbed the foreign charts, Cuban rappers back home criticized them for selling out to commercial pressures to evoke Cuban nostalgia. 'Salsa makes it easier for older people to accept rap music. But it's not what Cuban youth are really listening to,' Sarrias says.[5] He and Jaramillo want Anonimo Consejo to succeed by sticking to rap, and not jumping onto the salsa fusion bandwagon. But they've been at it for four years and their parents—supportive up until now—are beginning to talk about 'real' jobs.

Orishas' success story reveals the dilemmas inherent in marketing the music of youthful dissent. On the one hand, many Cuban rappers claim to eschew the materialist nature of mainstream American rap music. But at the same time, foreign record producers often seduce them with stories of big contracts and lavish lifestyles abroad.

Kali Akuno, a Berkeley-based organizer for the Malcolm X Grassroots Movement who leads trips to Cuba, says the temptation to stray from revolutionary ideals is strong. 'There is the danger of people on [the foreign] side of the Cuban rap scene serving more as exploiters. When people come to Cuba to make records with rappers there, they want to sell a product. But where is the money going? That's a major concern.'[6]

All of these pressures bear down on a passion that began as a hobby. When they met nine years ago, Jaramillo, then 13, and Sarrias, 17, were just kids looking for fun on an island so depressed that scores of their countrymen were building rafts out of everything from styrofoam to old tubes to take their chance at sea. Jaramillo and Sarrias watched them from their homes in Cojímar, once a sleepy beach neighborhood on the outskirts of Havana. By the time they were adults, the government had built dozens of Soviet-style high-rise apartment buildings there, providing housing for hundreds of people—most of them Black.

For relief from the dog days of 1993, the two young men and their friends hung out at Alamar, a sprawling housing complex nearby. The kids entertained themselves in a big, empty pool improvising, breakdancing, and listening hard to the American music coming from antennas they rigged on their rooftops to catch Miami radio stations. They heard songs like this one:

''Cause I'm black and I'm proud/ I'm ready and hyped plus I'm amped/ Most of my heroes don't appear on no stamps,' rhymed Public Enemy in 'Fight the Power.' Sarrias was hooked. 'Their songs spoke to me in a new way. There was nothing in Cuba that sounded like it.' Or talked about issues that Afrocubans had only begun to face. Instead, Cubans have been taught to ignore race and the Revolution tried to blur color lines by opening all professions, universities, and government to Afrocubans. Officially, race all but disappeared as a part of national discourse.

But increasingly, race is an issue in Cuba. If Afrocubans benefited most from the Revolution, they've also suffered the most during its crisis. Every Cuban needs dollars to survive and the bulk of the easy money coming in remittances goes to the White Cubans because it was their relatives who left early on. Darker Cubans also face discrimination getting the island's best jobs in the tourism industry. Skin color—despite the Revolution's best intentions—has once again become the marker of a class divide.

Cubans of all shades are quick to deny the existence of racism on the island. They point to the many interracial couples walking the streets as proof that pre-Revolutionary hang-ups about skin color have all but vanished. But many will admit to a more subtle 'social prejudice' that takes the form of police harassment and racial profiling.

'Cuban racial categories are much more fluid than in the United States,' says Nadine Fernandez, an anthropologist at Florida International University. 'It's a question of facial features, hair texture, and skin tone that decides what category you belong to, and it depends who you talk to. Police harassment and discrimination are everyday experiences for many Black Cubans, but a vocabulary of Black oppression doesn't exist here.'[7]

That is changing. As more international academic research develops around race on the island, more Cubans have made contacts within the African-American intellectual community, and have begun to share their ideas. For years, Castro positioned racism as a problem outside of the country. But now a growing number of Afrocubans wonder if that was not just a way of displacing the racial question at home.

Kali Akuno has been involved with the hip hop scene in Cuba for more than six years. He first went to the island for the second annual Cuban rap festival, where he participated in round table discussions with Cuban artists and other African-American artists and scholars.

'The government response initially was not enthusiastic. There was this sense that both hip hop and rock music were coming from a gringo imperialist perspective,' Akuno says. 'Hip hop was very racialized there as it was here. The government's attitude was "we don't want this music to divide Cubans".'[8]

Politics, however, are not keeping pace with social reality. All Cubans are discouraged from visiting government-designated 'tourist zones,' such as the fancy restaurants and night clubs in Old Havana, and police will ask most who show up there for ID. But statistics show that the police arrest Afrocubans all over the island more often than Whites. Many Afrocubans say the government assumes Blacks are more likely to be involved in criminal activity.

Sarrias, Jaramillo, and others in Cojímar say they feel the weight of an old stigma. 'Because we are Black, wear baggy pants and have braids—which is strange in Cuba—on every block the police ask for our identification cards. There is this perception that all White people are saints and all Blacks are delinquents.'

The first Cuban exiles in Miami, most of them White, often accuse Blacks of being the pillar of Castro's regime. The social mobility Afrocubans enjoyed after 1959 did win Castro much support among the island's Black population, but the Special Period—not the Revolution—marks a turning point in the minds of most young Afrocubans.

Despite decades of improved living standards and educational achievement for Blacks, the poorest and most dilapidated neighborhoods are still home mainly to Afrocubans. Many of these areas are labeled *focos delectivos*— crime zones—where police regularly comb the run-down tenement housing and tourists are warned to stay away. Traditionally Black parts of the island—Granma, Santiago, and Guantanamo—are also the most poverty-stricken, and in recent years thousands of migrants from these cities have poured into Havana's slums, straining already scant resources.

'Social dangerousness,' an official crime in the Cuban criminal code, is broadly defined as any behavior deemed to be 'against the norms of socialist morality.' According to Alejandro de la Fuente, a history professor at the University of South Florida, most of those arrested for being socially dangerous are non-White, making it a crime 'essentially identified with the conduct of Blacks, and particularly young Blacks.'[9]

Sarrias and Jaramillo grew up in a neighborhood where few White Cubans were to be found. They too lived in substandard housing, with constant police presence. Like disaffected youth everywhere, they looked for role models that gave them a sense of pride. In school, when Sarrias tried to talk about his African ancestry, teachers called him 'unpatriotic' for thinking of himself as something other than Cuban. He turned to his mother to find out more about his African roots, and before long, her stories became his lyrics: 'In my poor bed/ I read my history/ Memories of Titans/ Africans kicking out the Spanish.'

She also taught him about *Santeria*, Cuba's African-derived religion that has outlasted any political regime. 'In school they taught him about slavery, but they didn't go into depth,' his mother says, standing in the dirt yard in front of their small, wooden clapboard house. Lines of laundry hang to dry in the hot sun. A single mother, she washes her neighbor's clothes in exchange for a few extra pesos each month. Sarrias weaves her lessons throughout songs like this one: 'If you don't know your history/ You won't know who you are/ There's a fortune under your dark skin/ The power is yours.'

He sought other teachers as well. He and Jaramillo often stop by the house of Nehanda Abiodun, an alleged member of the Republic of New Afrika living in exile on the island. There they receive informal sessions about African-American history, poetry, and world politics. The messages in their music, says 54-year-old Abiodun, come naturally. 'They were born in a revolutionary process where they were encouraged to ask questions and challenge the status quo,' she says. It also comes from their daily lives: '... their parents, their experiences on the street growing up, what's going on in the world.'[10]

If expatriots like Abiodun served as historical guides, African-American hip hop artists gave them their beat. 'It was amazing to hear rappers from another country worried about the same issues I was,' Sarrias notes. Alternative rap artists like Common [Sense] and Mos Def have been traveling to Cuba since 1998 as part of the Black August Collective, a group of African-American activists and musicians dedicated to promoting hip hop culture globally.

Even when unsure about the movement, the Cuban government welcomed American rappers because of their support for the Revolution, says Vera Abiodun, co-director of the Brooklyn branch of the Malcolm X Grassroots Movement, and part of the Collective. Cuban youth responded to the rhythm, but also to the visitors' obvious pride in being Black. 'We didn't know how huge this would become in the beginning,' she says.[11]

Just as Black Americans did in the 1960s, Afrocubans in the 1990s began to embrace their African heritage. Sarrias notes: 'Every time that the police harass me, I don't feel like being here anymore ... When that happens, the first place I think about is here,' he touches an African amulet hanging around his neck. 'When I feel African, I don't feel Black.' And for many young Afrocubans, rap music—not the syrupy lyrics of salsa—validates the ancestry they've been taught to overlook.

Sarrias and Jaramillo admire heroes of Cuban Revolutionary history like Jose Marti and Che Guevara. But they also look up to Malcolm X, Mumia Abu-Jamal, Nelson Mandela, and other Black icons. They and thousands of other young Cubans heard Mumia Abu-Jamal's son speak at an anti-imperialist rally two years ago. And when the young rappers talk about meeting American hip hop artists, their faces beam.

Their musical style reflects the love. Like that of their favorite American groups, Anonimo Consejo combines politically charged lyrics, most written by Sarrias, with Jaramillo's playful vocal delivery. Because of limited technology on the island, their sound is more 'old school' than the slickly engineered music produced by American rappers like P. Diddy and Jay-Z.

Perhaps because of this lack of pretension, Cuban hip hop has become the darling of the American underground rap scene. Socially conscious rappers and cultural exchange groups have come to the island in search of what many consider the pure essence of hip hop. Even when they can't understand Spanish, visitors to the island come away with a positive impression of *el rap cubano*.

Eli Jacobs-Fantauzzi, 23, is just one of a growing number of hip hop pilgrims who go to Cuba in search of the true 'underground': the more progressive element in hip hop culture that focuses on social justice and racial equality in its music. I met him back in Berkeley, after he had just returned from Havana. Since 1995, when rap musicians decided to hold a hip hop festival each August, more and more American and European hip hop devotees have showed up in Cuba—often with recording equipment and CDs in hand. The word in the close-knit underground community is that Cuba is where it's happening.

'It's been a dream of mine to go to Cuba for a long time,' Jacobs-Fantauzzi told me. His eyes lit up as he watched video footage he shot of the sixth annual hip hop festival in Havana.[12] He bounced his head up and down to the beat and sang along with Magia, the female MC of Obsesión, one on the long roster of Cuban rap groups to perform alongside some of the best known hip hop artists of the U.S. underground scene.

'My first impression of hip hop in Cuba is just that it's raw, like these people do it for the love of it,' he said, hitting his fist in his palm for emphasis. 'Right now I feel like hip hop out here in the States is really diluted and people like it for other reasons: money, girls, cars, whatever it is. But out there they do it for a love of the music, 'cause they're not really getting much from it. They're not getting the Bentleys or the big diamonds—that's not going to happen in Cuba.'[13]

Even in poverty, the frequent foreign visitors and word-of-mouth popularity give Anonimo Consejo a certain cachet in Cojímar.

'What bug crawled out of your hair and ran around all night?' A middle-aged woman yells at Jaramillo as he walks by her front porch, his long afro gently bobbing in the wind. 'People around here think we're a little crazy,' he grins. 'But they love us anyway.' But you can't live on love alone. That's where Pablo Herrera comes in. A former Havana University professor who taught English and hip hop culture, Herrera is both a devotee of African-American culture and passionate about Cuba. He has also emerged as Cuban rap's main spokesperson internationally and at home.

In a country where the government controls just about everything, rap is no exception. A few years ago, police regularly shut down hip hop shows and labeled rap as 'imperialist' music. But Herrera and other hip hop disciples waged a publicity campaign to revamp rap's troublemaker image. Writers like Ariel Fernandez published numerous articles on rap in state-run newspapers and cultural journals, while Herrera helped organize committees on its relevance for the Revolution.

Herrera reminded the old guard that the younger Cubans needed a voice— and rap music was their chosen form of expression. 'The purpose of hip hop is serving the country, not being an antagonistic tool,' he says. 'The idea is to improve what is already in place.' His efforts were rewarded—in 1998 Abel Prieto, the Minister of Culture, officially declared rap 'an authentic expression of *cubanidad*' and began nominally funding the annual rap festival. Even Fidel himself rapped along with the group Doble Filo at the national baseball championship three years ago. With Castro's blessing, Prieto recently funneled about $32,000 of audio equipment to rappers through the Young Communist Union's cultural arm, *Asociacion de los Hermanos Saiz*.

Although officially accepted, rap is still in its infancy. Herrera estimates that Havana alone now has around 250 rap groups. He is the producer with the most equipment to make them sound professional. Herrera, 34, works out of his sun-filled studio with a turn-table, a mixer, a drum machine, a sampler, and cartons of classic Cuban LPs. It's a simple set-up, but by Cuban standards, it's a soundman's paradise. As he notes, 'Since most music here is not really produced electronically, there's not many people who can do this.'

Now that Orishas' remake of Company Segundo's famous tune 'Chanchan' can be heard all over Havana, rap music is more popular than ever in Cuba. Herrera hopes Anonimo Consejo can achieve the same stardom—without defecting from *la patria*.

In a T-shirt with the words 'God is a DJ,' Herrera shuffles through a stack of CDs and smokes a cigarette while Sarrias and Jaramillo sit on his couch, intently studying every page of an old *Vibe* magazine. 'Yo, check this out,' Herrera finds what he's looking for. 'En la revolución, cada quien hace su parte.' In the Revolution, everyone must do his part. Fidel's unmistakable voice loops back and repeats the phrase again and again over a hard-driving beat. Herrera nods to Sarrias, who takes his cue: 'The solution is not leaving/ New days will be here soon/ We deserve and want to always go forward/ Solving problems is important work.'

Herrera may not be the only rap promoter on the island, but rappers say he is the best connected to the government. As a key member of the *Hermanos Saiz*, Herrera has rare access to music clubs like Las Vegas. Any rapper who hopes to be seen at a decent venue must first get the Association's approval, and that can only happen if their music is seen to serve the Revolution.

But having equipment doesn't necessarily mean an artist is a government puppet. According to Nina Menendez, a San Francisco-based music promoter, breaking into commercial distribution depends on personal connections within the industry more than towing the Party line. 'Many people whose politics seem outside of official discourse have no problems getting access and even receive a state salary,' Menendez says.[14]

In the Cuban hip hop world, there is a strong tradition of alternative distribution methods—mainly smuggling records on and off the island. The Cuban music industry has been slow to catch on to hip hop, especially because most Cubans—and foreigners—prefer more traditional music. Resources are limited for most rappers, particularly for those who are young and still unknown. But Menendez feels this will change naturally as Cuba's hip hop scene grows.

'Hip hop is emerging as a new genre of Cuban music, but it is still in the development stage,' she says.

Herrera's mission is to help speed that process along. He is the unofficial ambassador of Cuban hip hop for the recent flood of foreign reporters, musicians, and record producers coming to the island in search of the next big Cuban musical export. He discovered Anonimo Consejo at the first rap festival seven years ago. 'I work with them because their music is really authentic,' Herrera says. 'I like their flow, but what is really striking is what they say ... so mind-boggling.'

Up to a point. Cuban rap—and Anonimo Consejo is no exception—pushes the envelope, but not so far that it offends the government. The duo has become a favorite at state-sponsored shows, warning young Cubans against the temptations of American-style capitalism. In the song 'Appearances are Deceiving' they rap, 'Don't crush me/ I'm staying here/ Don't push me/ Let me live/ I would give anything for my Cuba/ I'm happy here.'

Their nationalist pride recently helped them land a contract with a state-run promotion company. All that means, though, is that their travel expenses are covered when they tour the island and they receive a modest paycheck, usually around 350 pesos each ($17.50), after each major show. That money doesn't go far in an economy increasingly dependent on U.S. dollars. And it's getting harder to convince their parents that a rap career is worthwhile.

Jaramillo quietly slips out of the recording session at Herrera's studio and doesn't return all afternoon. Later he says that he was upset and needed to cool off after an argument he had with his mother that morning. 'She says that I'm a grown man now and she's tired of supporting me. She thinks that I should get a real job,' he says, twisting the end of a braid between his fingers and looking at the ground. 'She doesn't understand that this is what I want to do—this is my job.'

Five years ago, both Jaramillo and Sarrias decided to forgo Cuba's legendary free university education and devote themselves to making music. They both still live at home with their mothers, depending on the state's meager ration cards to eat. Herrera is trying to help them pay the bills. 'They are already the top group in the country,' he says. 'They deserve a very good record deal, and they deserve to be working at a studio every day making their music.' But for now, when their session is over, and they still need to borrow a dollar to catch a bus back home.

BREAKING INTO THE BOYS' CLUB

Record deal or not, the girls from Explosión Femenina would do almost anything to be in Anonimo Consejo's place. A faded portrait of Fidel hangs on the dark walls of their tiny tenement apartment in central Havana. The girls fill up the entire space as they crank up the volume on their boom-box and rap about boy troubles over Eminem's hit song, 'Real Slim Shady.' Whatever they may lack in sophistication, the girls compensate with energy and charm.

'When they first started out, I thought it was just a fad,' their mother says. 'But then they wouldn't let me watch my soap opera because they were practicing all the time. We live like this,' she presses her palms close together, 'so I had no choice but to go next door to watch my show.'[15] All the practicing has paid off. At next Friday's Las Vegas show, Herrera will be listening.

On their rooftop, with the sun setting over the maze of narrow streets below them, they practice their one finished song. Yaima, born for the spotlight, undulates as all three harmonize about the hardships they've faced as women rappers: 'With my feminine appearance I've come to rival you/ If you want to compete, if you want to waste time trying to destroy me/ I'll get rowdy and impress you.' The song is a flirtatious challenge to the male rapper's ego. 'If you are a man, stop right there/ Don't hide, kneel before me/ Put your feet on the ground and come down from the sky.'[16]

Female rap groups are few and far between in Cuba. The most famous of them, Instinto, has yet to win much international attention, and like many American female performers, relies on their considerable sex appeal to win an audience. With revealing outfits and smooth, R&B inflected voices, Instinto has inspired Explosión Femenina's style—but they know they need more to impress Herrera.

The producer has about as much respect for female rappers who profit from a sexy image as he does for the flashy posturing of what he calls 'commercial rap.' Just as he coaches Anonimo Consejo to confront social problems in their songs, he is looking for a female act that is willing to tackle sexism. 'Too many women just let men get away with insulting them, insulting their dignity as women. I want to produce female rappers who speak up for the rights of women,' he says.

The girls in Explosión Femenina know their music needs a sharper edge to win over Herrera and they practice another song about prostitutes—referred to in Cuba as *jinateras*. 'We wrote this because so many guys we know assume we're *jinateras* just because we like to look good,' Yaima explains. 'Even though about 70 per cent of the girls we know do it, we don't, and we're sick of them judging us.'

Just as young Afrocuban males complain about being stopped for criminal activity, young Afrocuban women are quick to point out the injustices in their own lives. Job opportunities and salaries have plummeted since the Soviets pulled out, and women more often than men are responsible for holding households together financially in *la lucha*—the daily struggle for survival.

The only sector of the economy that is booming is tourism, and most of those highly coveted jobs go to lighter-skinned women. In the hotel industry, *buena presencia*—good appearance—is a job requirement often equated with Whiteness. The one area of tourism wide open to women of a darker tone is Cuba's thriving sex industry. Though officially frowned upon by the government, prostitution is widespread on the island, where in almost every restaurant older tourists can be seen dining with beautiful young women of color.

Once considered the 'brothel of the Caribbean,' the island has long appealed to American and European men looking for a good time. Visions of the sensual mulatta are a prime marketing tool for Cuban tourism—the government even invited *Playboy* magazine to run a feature on the 'Girls of Cuba' in exchange for free publicity for the island's tourist facilities. Nadine

Fernandez says the *jinatera* has become a racialized category. 'The allure for foreigners is the exotic mulatta image. Even women who are socially White in other contexts alter their appearance to be mulatta, trying to look more mixed by curling their hair or being very tan, because that is what sells.'[17]

Anonimo Consejo is one of many rap acts to criticize Cuban women for coveting material goods enough to sell their bodies to buy them. 'Men here have a hard time dating our own women because we can't afford to buy them the things tourists can,' said Jaramillo, with a roll of his eyes. 'That's not right. Our songs try to remind girls what's really important in life.' Herrera hopes to get more women rapping about these same issues. Explosión Femenina is eager to meet his expectations, but they say it takes more than just writing a song about prostitution to do it.

Their most pressing worry at the moment is how to pay for their outfits. 'It will be about $30 for each of us just to buy the clothes,' Yaima complains. 'It's also about $25 for a producer to make us original background music. That's impossible. We would have to give up going to the disco for about three months if we wanted to come up with that.' She laughs, but the danger to their budding career as rap artists is real. Without the right look or sound, they won't get much respect on stage. And without dollars, those essential elements are out of reach. The next Friday, outside Club Las Vegas, the girls are giddy. They excitedly snap photos of one another and different rapper friends, laughing to disguise their nervousness. They huddle with Magia, one of the few women rappers in Havana, and also their mentor. 'Remember to pay attention to where you are standing on stage. And sing in tune,' she warns, rubbing their backs in encouragement. Yaima frequently whispers to Papo Record, her rapper boyfriend, and looks worriedly around the crowd gathered out front. Papo, wearing a white Adidas headband and a spider tattoo, puts his arm around her and kisses her forehead. Time to go in.

Santuario, a group visiting from Venezuela, are the first on. Adorned with heavy gold chains, gold-capped teeth, and designer labels, they clearly come from a different economic situation than their Cuban hosts. Their manager films them with an expensive video camera, and their background music is sophisticated. Yaima, Noiris, and Yordanka look on. Unable to afford the outfits they wanted, they wear normal street clothes. '[Santuario] are so amazing,' Noiris whispers, biting her bottom lip. 'Do you really think we are good enough to be up there after them?'

Good enough or not, DJ Ariel soon calls out, 'Explosión Femenina!' The girls breathe deeply and take the stage, looking very young and decidedly unglamorous. Spare background beats boom out of the speakers, and they begin. Tentative at first, it doesn't take Yaima long to get into the groove, and soon all three are rapping and shaking their hips with confidence. Their one song is over fast, and the applause is friendly rather than deafening. Herrera takes Yaima off to a corner. When she returns, her eyes are moist. She forces a smile. 'Pablo says that he is used to strong rappers,' she says.

'He still sees us as very weak. He says that for our first time we sounded good.' But not good enough for Herrera to produce.

Nevertheless, the youth branch of the Communist Party schedules the girls for an early appointment to audition at the Ministry of Culture. They show up in their best clothes, with boom box in hand, but no one is there to greet them. They wait for an hour, and then leave. 'It's always hard for rappers just starting out,' Yordanka says. 'We just need to get some good background music and keep practicing.' But that will be difficult. Yaima will leave Havana for a six-month stint as a cabaret dancer at a beach resort, and Noiris and Yordanka have schoolwork to catch up on. 'I love rap, but I am also invested in my studies,' says Yordanka, who wants to be an orthodontist.

WAITING FOR THE DEAL

For Pablo Herrera, there's only one formula for success, in Cuba or anywhere. 'Write great lyrics, have dignity and be hard working,' he says. But it takes more. A week later, Club Las Vegas closes its Friday hip hop show to make room for a more traditional salsa crowd. 'That's the way it goes in Cuba,' Jaramillo says, bitterness in his voice. 'With salsa comes the money.'

For now that leaves them with Alamar, the first and last refuge of Cuban rap. Located on the eastern side of Havana, on the other side of a long tunnel, Alamar is home to more than 10,000 of Havana's poorest residents. Once billed as a shining example of communal living, in the 1970s, the giant housing complex was Fidel Castro's pet building project. Now, rows of crumbling white buildings look out over the sea, far from most jobs and services. Few White faces lean from the rows of windows, watching the action below. It is here in a giant empty pool where Cuban rap began and continues. Every Friday night, Havana's aspiring and already established rap groups pace the pool's concrete steps and strain to be heard over a lone speaker in a corner. For only five pesos, hip hop fans can make the long trek out here to hear what they won't hear on the radio: the music of their generation.

Anonimo Consejo has to pay the entrance fee like everyone else and mill with the crowd. Jaramillo sips from a small bottle of rum and greets his friends with high-fives, while Sarrias cuddles with his girlfriend off to the side of the pool. This is their territory—everyone knows them, and no one cares much if they have a record deal—here they are already famous. When the time comes to perform, the sound system fades and in the middle of one song the CD skips, leaving them with no background music. Sarrias glares angrily into the hard light coming from the DJ's booth. They start again, but their energy is low. Next, a group of five young rappers come out grabbing their crotches and doing a poor imitation of the American gangsta poses they've seen on TV. Jaramillo cheers them on, but Sarrias sulks on the sidelines. 'I'm tired of this place. There are always problems,' he mutters.

Despite their lyrics about staying put in Cuba, they want more. 'We are waiting around for an angel to come from abroad who recognizes our talent and is willing to invest a lot of attention and money in our project,' Jaramillo says. But celestial intervention moves slowly. In 2001, Anonimo Consejo appeared on a U.S.-produced compilation called 'Cuban Hip Hop All Stars' [Papaya Records] and they were featured in recent issues of *Source* and *Vibe* magazines. They got the chance to travel around the U.S., performing in various alternative hip hop shows. But so far, none of that has translated into a deal or dollars.

'Sometimes I think we're supposed to live on hope alone,' Jaramillo says, back at his mother's house where his bedroom is plastered with magazine photos of NBA basketball stars and his favorite rap musicians.

Then he hikes up his baggy pants and goes outside to wait for a crowded bus to Herrera's studio. A couple of British record producers were supposed to swing by to hear Anonimo Consejo lay down some beats. You never know, he says as he climbs aboard, this time it could be their big break.

NOTES

1. A shorter version of this chapter appeared as 'Underground Revolution,' in *ColorLines*, Vol. 4, No. 3 (Fall 2001), and as a chapter in *Capitalism, God, and a Good Cigar: Cuba Enters the Twenty-first Century* by Lydia Chávez (ed.) and Mimi Chakarova (photographer) (Durham, NC: Duke University Press, 2005).
2. Original lyrics by Anonimo Consejo, all copyrights reserved by Anonimo Consejo. Reprinted here with the authors' permission.
3. Interviewed by author, tape recording, Club Las Vegas, Havana, Cuba, April 2001.
4. Pablo Herrera, interview by author, tape recording, Club Las Vegas, Havana, Cuba, April 2001.
5. Yosmel Sarrias, interview by author, tape recording, Havana, Cuba, April 2001.
6. Kali Akuno, interview by author, tape recording, Berkeley, California, February 2001.
7. Nadine Fernandez, interview by author, telephone interview, March 2001.
8. Kali Akuno, interview by author, tape recording, Berkeley, California, February 2001.
9. Alejandro de la Fuente, 'Race Ideology, and Culture in Cuba: Recent Scholarship,' *Latin American Research Review*, 2000.
10. Nehanda Abiodun, interview by author, tape recording, Havana, Cuba, April 2001.
11. Vera Abiodun, interview by author, by telephone, December 2000.
12. Jacobs-Fantauzzi made the film *Inventos—Hip Hop Cubano* which provides a unique glimpse into music and politics of today's Cuba. This film features Anonimo Consejo, Grandes Ligas, and Obsesión; and highlights Havana's two most well-known hip hop producers, Pablo Herrera and Ariel Fernandez as well as U.S. rappers Dead Prez, Tony Touch, and others who offer encouragement to Cuban hip hop artists. [Editor's note]
13. Eli Jacobs-Fantuzzi, interview by author, tape recording, Berkeley, California, December 2000.
14. Nina Menendez, interview by author, by telephone, February 2001.
15. Interview by author, Havana, Cuba, April 2001.
16. Original lyrics by Explosión Femenina, all copyrights by Explosión Femenina. Reprinted here with the authors' permission.
17. Nadine Fernandez, interview by author, by telephone, March 2001.

12
Dancing Between Islands:
Hip Hop and the Samoan Diaspora

April K. Henderson

CULTURE MOVES: CALI TO CHRISTCHURCH

Christchurch

Two hands, chilled from the icy wind that sweeps across the square of this little town, a place priding itself on being more English than England; two hands, brown, deft, lifting dark and glossy vinyl onto turntables. The track starts, melodic, haunting. Strings and a woman's operatic soprano. She sounds like African-American coloratura Kathleen Battle, but a look in the liner notes would be fruitless—the sample goes unmarked. After two cycles through the strings, the soprano, the beat drops, but the rhyme dropping with it is not the original. In 1996, long before he was taken under the wing of super-producer Dr. Dre, Los Angeles MC Xzibit released this track as 'Paparazzi' on his album *At the Speed of Life.*

This is not 'Paparazzi,' however. And it is not Xzibit. And this is not Los Angeles. This is Christchurch, Aotearoa/New Zealand and the namesake cathedral rising prominently from the opposite end of the cobblestone square remains the city's most prominent official feature.[1] For the performers and many in the audience at today's outdoor concert—part of the scheduled events at the first ever Aotearoa Hip Hop Summit—this South Island city's other prominent feature is the gangs of racist skinheads rumored to roam the streets. The skinheads are the most salient representative image of a city understood by Aotearoa's largely Maori and Pacific hip hop community as overwhelmingly White and hostile.

Against this backdrop of gray cobblestones, gray skies, gray people, the Indigenous Footsouljahs—four Samoan performers from the capital city of Wellington—ascend the stage. The group is animated, colorful, a brilliant blur of red and 'Carolina blue' and the ever-present camouflage fatigues that echo their militaristic moniker. DJ Raw spins the 'Paparazzi' instrumental while lead lyricist K.O.S.-163 launches into the first verse of their crowd-pleasing anthem 'Always Represent':

Legacy/ Pasifikan styles/ Penetrate the mind
Vigorous blows from the brain/ No denyin'
Inflict the pain to your nervous system ...

Polynesian son causing friction
Perpetrators on the path/ Get evicted
What's the verdict?/ Emancipate the mental
Colonialistic fools got your mind in a shambles
Casualties of imperialism/ Submerge indigenous thoughts into oblivion/
Mind in prison

Fellow MC Flowz joins in the chorus: 'Always represent for my people/
Pacific Islanders on foreign soil/ Style lethal/ Take a look as we enter
the next chapter/ Flip the script.'[2] Back in Wellington, the notebook in
which K.O.S.-163 first scrawled these lyrics stands nestled on a shelf in his
bedroom, between a book on the U.S. Black Panther Party, a history of
the Samoan independence struggle, and Samoan novelist Albert Wendt's
classic migration narrative, *Sons For the Return Home*. Amidst these texts on
various *movements*, Kosmo's lyrics flow ably, nimbly, but not arbitrarily.

Cali

Some of the older members of Wellington's hip hop community still vividly
recall when a teenaged K.O.S.-163, more commonly known as Kosmo,
turned up on the scene in the early 1980s, fresh from a stay in Los Angeles
County and telling all who would listen about the world of the West Side
Piru.[3] Skepticism greeted Kosmo's gang talk, but his mastery of a dance
form called *popping* left deep impressions. Kosmo learned the dance while
staying with *'aiga* in the City of Carson, a community which drew large
numbers of Samoans relocating from the islands in the1950s–70s.[4] As Kosmo
discovered, popping and other 'street dance' forms thoroughly saturated the
lives of Samoan youth growing up in the late 1970s and early 80s in Carson
and neighboring Compton and Long Beach. As he vividly remembers, 'all
the coolest cats was poppin' down at [Carson's] Scott Park.'[5]

Many young Samoans growing up in Los Angeles County struggled in
school but excelled in athletics and dance. For Samoan males, in particular,
physical size and prowess as football players or dancers led to both status
and stereotype. As the narrator of a 1978 documentary on the Carson-based
Samoan community organization Omai Faatasi states, 'Lots of times, people
are afraid of us just because we're physically large.' Adds another Omai
Faatasi staff member, 'The only kind of publicity we would get would be
negative publicity, except for maybe football. Another stereotype was [as]
"dancers." So any time you need a dancer, you just call a Samoan and he'll
do a dance for you.'[6]

Reductive stereotypes based on Samoan physicality continue to exert
powerful pressure on Samoan communities in the U.S., contributing to a
history of overzealous and brutal assaults on Samoan men and women by
nervous law enforcement officers.[7] That street dance fed these stereotypes
does not negate the powerful ways it made meaning for Samoan youth.

Recently arrived from the islands and painfully aware of the accents that marked them as 'foreign,' young Samoans in multi-ethnic neighborhoods earned status and respect through mastering the physical vocabularies of dance or sport. For young men, dance skills also helped to attract the young women who were always present either as critical audience or as fellow dancers. As Kosmo recalls, 'All the poppers got the girls.'

In Los Angeles, Samoans are among the practitioners of such street dance forms as popping, locking and, in the San Francisco Bay Area and Sacramento, strutting. While female dancers had limited opportunities and scant encouragement to turn their art into a profession, and often remain at the level of neighborhood legend, a handful of male artists built successful professional careers as dancers, or parlayed dance into other opportunities in the music industry.[8] Among these, Suga Pop remains one of the most enigmatic.

Raised as the eldest son of Pasi Tunupopo, Suga Pop spent his childhood moving between the Samoan island of 'Upolu and the significantly Pacific Islander neighborhood of Newtown in Wellington, New Zealand, before crossing the Pacific to attend Kaimuki High School in Honolulu, Hawai'i. A talented dancer, Suga Pop had already built a local reputation in Hawai'i before moving to Los Angeles in the late 1970s and early 80s heyday of popping. There, on the weight of his hunger and enthusiasm, he began receiving formal instruction in popping from its African-American originators, the Electric Boogaloos. On a subsequent stay in New York, Suga Pop brought along the Boogaloos' popping techniques.[9] Prior to his arrival, East Coast dancers had attempted to learn the West Coast dance form by mimicking a 1979 televised appearance of the Boogaloos on *Soul Train*—a predicament they shared with countless others around the world who'd also seen the galvanizing broadcast.

While in New York, Suga Pop also expanded his own repertoire, dancing with the legendary Rock Steady Crew and learning the New York street dance form, called breaking, b-boying/b-girling, or breakdancing,[10] which made the Crew famous. Returning to California, Suga Pop cemented his prominent role in the bicoastal cross-fertilization of popular dance. As writer Raegan Kelly recounts, 'In 1980 a young Samoan dancer named SugarPop would move west from the streets of New York to bring breaking to the poplockers of South Central, Venice and Hollywood in Los Angeles.'[11]

While Suga Pop continues to be a key figure in international street-dance exhibition circuits and also remains active in the U.S. music industry, producing his own and other artists' material, it is the group he formerly managed that has done the most to shape public perceptions of Samoan involvement in hip hop. The Boo-Yaa T.R.I.B.E., formed around a nucleus of four brothers from Carson, gained their early musical experience playing instruments in their father's church. 'We would get to church early and would be playing P-funk,' recalls member Danny 'Monsta O' Devoux, referring to the music of Black American funk supergroup Parliament-Funkadelic, 'But as soon as that first car pulled up, we'd switch to 'Amazing Grace.'[12] Attuned to the funk rhythms that permeated their South Bay neighborhood, the Devoux brothers formed the dance crew Blue City Strutters and began performing professionally with their blend of popping, locking, and strutting.

As dancers, the Devoux brothers gained valuable experience in the entertainment industry and began honing one of the most memorable images in Los Angeles hip hop history. While touring Japan as professional dancers in the mid 1980s, the group turned again to making music. Paul 'Gangxta R.I.D.' Devoux began rapping as part of their show, building his microphone skills in front of Japanese audiences eager for live hip hop music and dance. When the Devouxs returned to Los Angeles as the Boo-Yaa T.R.I.B.E., much of their following was built on high-energy live performances that drew upon the brothers' wide-ranging talents. Boo-Yaa T.R.I.B.E. stage shows featured R.I.D.'s husky-throated rapping, live funk or funk-metal instrumentation from a full band, and the dancing of group leader Ted 'Godfather' Devoux and 'hype-man' Donald 'Kobra' Devoux.[13] Although they've never achieved the mainstream success associated with multi-platinum record sales, the Boo-Yaa T.R.I.B.E. remain prominent figures in the music industry and are, according to hip hop documentarian Brian Cross, 'synonymous with hip hop in Los Angeles.'[14]

Another prominent family of California Samoan performing artists, Jack and Charlie Hisatake ('Hekyll and Jekyll') were influenced by the Electric Boogaloos after moving to Los Angeles from the Bay Area. Utilizing popping techniques to add a harder edge to their strutting style, the Hisatakes built significant and enduring reputations as dancers, performing at clubs and competitions and choreographing and appearing in music videos. They later branched into other aspects of the music industry, singing with an R&B band, Boyz of Paradise, and providing production assistance for other recording artists. In 1999, their cousin Rodney Hisatake formed an independent record label in San Francisco and released a double-disc rap and R&B compilation featuring a variety of U.S.-based Samoan and other Pacific Islander artists along with internationally known African-American rap artists such as Snoop Dogg and Lord Tariq and Peter Gunz.[15]

Aotearoa

The nearly three decades of Samoan involvement in street dance and rap music in California has significantly impacted Samoan cultural production in other places where Samoans have settled, including New Zealand. During his stay in California in the early 1980s, Indigenous Footsouljah's Kosmo was deeply impressed by the California Samoan dancers he met and observed. He credits the Blue City Strutters, and especially Donald and Danny Devoux, as an original inspiration for his lifelong interest in street dance and eventual move into performing hip hop music.

Like many young Samoans, Kosmo picked up whatever dance styles he could in Carson—a little bit of strutting, a little boogaloo and popping, some tutting. Upon returning to New Zealand, Kosmo's movement vocabulary brought prestige among his peers, many of whom had attempted to learn moves from watching the recently released movie *Beat Street*. '[Kosmo] didn't consider himself any good until he came to New Zealand ... Here they were just doing the basics, [he explains] I knew more.'[16]

In 1990, Kosmo, fellow Samoan MC 'Khas the Fieldstyle Orator,' and DJ Rockit V created The Mau, a hip hop group that took its name from the organization that agitated for Samoan independence under both the German and New Zealand colonial administrations. Although the name was Samoa-specific, the decision to invoke Samoan colonial history demonstrates U.S. influences: 'There was a movement of Black consciousness in America at the time [involving such artists as] Paris, Ice Cube, X Clan, Public Enemy ... This was fuel for thought for [Kosmo's] crew whose motto became that of the Mau movement in Samoa—*Samoa Mo Samoa*, Samoa for Samoans.'[17]

Later reforming as Rough Opinion, Kosmo and Khas continued to cut-'n'-mix their multinational influences, articulating a diasporic Samoan cultural nationalism by drawing alternately upon their knowledge of Samoan history and the popular narratives of the U.S. Black Power movement circulating at the time in American hip hop. Although Rough Opinion never recorded their material, their potent blend of machete-waving Samoa-centricity, occasional Samoan language rhymes, and U.S. Black Power iconography in live performances were influential on acts that followed.[18] Kosmo, in his late thirties, has remained a dancer, MC, promoter, and youth worker in Wellington for nearly 20 years. With the full-length Footsouljahs album *Puttin' in Work* finally under his belt, Kosmo is, as he glibly puts it, 'H.F.I.C.,' Head Fob In Charge.[19]

The Two Samoas

That Samoans were present in urban California communities where street dance forms like popping and locking were first practiced, that they found these forms meaningful and actively participated in and contributed to them, and that their embodied knowledges were passed back to the islands of Samoa and out to Aotearoa, necessarily owes to the colonial and neo-colonial interdependencies that have shaped modern Samoan history. The Samoan Islands were divided between the United States and Germany at the close of the nineteenth century; the U.S. desired the deep water port of Pago Pago, on the eastern island of Tutuila, while Germany had significant plantation interests in the larger and more agriculturally productive western islands.[20]

Today, Tutuila and the eastern Manu'a islands remain an unincorporated territory of the United States. The territory lacks the Organic Act that would confer citizenship on American Samoans, but most American

Samoans appear content with the territory's status: as American nationals, they benefit from U.S. aid and the right to travel freely in the U.S. while retaining traditional custom and indigenous title to most of the land in the territory. Representatives from American Samoa recently lobbied to have the territory removed from the United Nations list of non-self-governing territories, arguing that the people of American Samoa are exercising their right to self-determination by choosing to retain their political relationship with the U.S.[21]

Since the 1950s, thousands of American Samoans have settled in predominantly urban environments in Hawai'i and the continental United States. U.S. military service has played a significant role as a conduit for Samoan migration; Samoan communities in the U.S. grew up first around military installations, but have since branched out significantly to include most major West Coast cities. In California, in particular, Samoans tend to share working-class African-American and Latino neighborhoods, sharing as well the economic and social vulnerabilities of their neighbors.[22]

German-governed Samoa transferred to a New Zealand administration in 1914 as a result of World War I. Western Samoa was subsequently governed by New Zealand for nearly 50 years, first under League of Nations mandate and later as a United Nations trusteeship, before achieving independence in 1962. In 1997, Western Samoa chose to change its name to the 'Independent State of Samoa,' or simply 'Samoa.' While Samoa is formally independent, the nation has maintained close political and economic ties with New Zealand. New Zealand's active recruitment of Samoan labor to meet post-World War II demands for industrial manufacturing workers resulted in rapidly expanding Samoan populations in New Zealand in the 1960s and early 70s. As in the U.S., Samoan migrants to New Zealand clustered in predominantly urban environments, and were similarly vulnerable to processes of urban economic restructuring. Many migrants who came for manufacturing work stayed on to eke out a tenuous existence during the global recession of the 1970s.[23] Today, Samoans form the third largest population in New Zealand, after Europeans and the indigenous Maori.

Nineteenth- and twentieth-century colonial histories continue to link the U.S. with the territory of American Samoa, and New Zealand with the independent nation of Samoa. Constant traffic between the urban centers of New Zealand, the United States, and the two political entities of the Samoan archipelago ensure the continuous circulation of people, commodities, cultural forms, and ideas. American Samoa and independent Samoa are, in a sense, 'out of the way places,'[24] but the unique political division of the archipelago and the two entities' respective links to the United States and the British commonwealth circuit, via New Zealand, position them also at an important center—a generative crossroads where people pick and choose from the cultural productions of two expansive empires.

Dancing Between Islands

For many hip hop artists in New Zealand, a small nation of just over 4 million people, the connections between Los Angeles and Wellington, or Auckland, or Christchurch, are not as direct as they are for Kosmo Fa'alogo. A more circuitous route brought locking, popping, breaking, and the music that accompanies these American street dance forms, from California to New Zealand via the islands of Hawai'i and Samoa. For a number of early poppers in New Zealand, new dance styles were learned not on a trip to Los Angeles, but on a trip to Samoa. The islands of Samoa, central both physically and psychically in a diasporic migrant Samoan matrix, were an important early node in transmitting and translating U.S. street dance south to Aotearoa.

Californian street dance forms traveled quickly; as soon as Samoans were locking and popping on the streets of Carson, Compton, and Long Beach, in California, their cousins were mimicking their moves in the public housing complexes of Honolulu and in the homes, garages, and yards of villages all across American Samoa. For dancers traveling to Hawai'i from California, the ubiquitous presence of dance crews in the islands, and their level of skill, came as something of a surprise. For young people traveling from Hawai'i or the continental U.S. to American Samoa, the prevalence of street dance forms across the largely rural main island of Tutuila was even more unexpected.

Numerous are the narratives of young Samoans raised in the continental United States or Hawai'i who, upon relocating to American Samoa when their fathers retired from military service, were shocked to hear the familiar strains of U.S. funk or early hip hop music and see their rural relatives popping and locking with skill and style. Tune Vaouli, a nighttime hip hop DJ with American Samoa radio station KSBS, recalls moving from Hawai'i to the village of Alofau on the east side of Tutuila:

> We moved down here in '80, and I was used to seein' breakdancers in Hawai'i ... [but] that summer when we moved down, you could tell by my amazement on my face—I walked into my house and I could hear Planet Rock and [see] people poppin'. I was like, 'What the hell?!'[25]

Christopher Seei, who spent his early childhood moving with his family between Hawai'i and the Los Angeles-area community of Norwalk, relocated to American Samoa with his parents and siblings in 1984. 'When I got there,' he recounts, 'I was quite shocked at the caliber of poppin' that was there. It was pretty much just like any place in the U.S where kids would do that. It was pretty competitive, just like how I seen it in the Mainland.'[26] Vaouli, Seei, and other young people who moved to American Samoa in the early 1980s had their conceptions of global/local, *here* and *there*, profoundly tweaked when they journeyed to a place they had envisioned as remote, isolated, even backward, only to find that place permeated by the sights and sounds they thought they had left behind. Not only were young people in American Samoa practicing street dance forms like popping, they had organized crews and were actively competing.

The saturation of American Samoa by street dance testifies to the transferability of the dance forms themselves. It testifies, as well, to the active diasporic networks through which Samoans circulate—the circuits through which people and all their embodied knowledge travel. In American Samoa, as in California, the mastery of new dance forms conferred prestige. But in American Samoa, dancing took on an additional valence; popping became a sort of diasporic currency where new dance styles, like new albums, cassettes, or items of clothing, signified a connectedness with the metropolitan communities 'over there.' While not commodities in the strict sense—lacking material form, and slipping in and out of processes of valuation and exchange—dance styles could be, and were, circulated through 'aiga networks.

When National Geographic published a 1985 article on contemporary issues in the Samoan Islands (they borrowed from Margaret Mead's famous ethnography to title the piece 'The Two Samoas: Still Coming of Age') the magazine's photo editors emblematically accompanied the article's written juxtaposition of 'tradition' and 'modernity' with two markedly different photographs of Samoan youth. The story's opening image is a two-page spread of a young boy on the island of Savai'i, then Western Samoa, sailing a handmade canoe along the shore. He is smiling, waist-deep in seawater, clad only in a floral wraparound lavalava. Below the picture, the caption reads:

United by culture, Western Samoa and American Samoa are separated by politics. U.S. aid pampers American Samoa, but the lure of the South Pacific emanates more strongly from Western Samoa's Savai'i, where a boy sails a double-hulled canoe reminiscent of those of his Polynesian ancestors. The H.M.S. Pandora sailed to the islands searching for Bounty mutineers, and here Margaret Mead made her famous observations of adolescents.[27]

The National Geographic article appears to make its own pointed observations of Samoan adolescents, moving quickly from the 'lure of the South Pacific' purportedly emanating from this first picture to a quite different depiction of Samoan youth. The very next photograph in the article shows young male dancers in the graffiti-tagged clubhouse of the American Samoan dance crew Famous Original Blood Brothers (a.k.a. Fagatogo Old Blood Brothers, or F.O.B.B.s). The dancers are clad head-to-toe in athletic gear—bandannas or hats on their heads, Adidas jackets or hooded sweatshirts, and Converse or Adidas brand shoes. One hand-lettered poster on the back wall announces the crew name and their dance specialties, 'breaking' and 'po[p]ping,' while a piece of graffiti on an adjacent wall references Carson Samoan dance crew Blue City Strutters (aka the Boo-Yaa T.R.I.B.E.). The picture is intended to illustrate, as its caption suggests, what happens when 'the Samoan way collides with fa'a America.'[28] Juxtaposed with the first photograph, the F.O.B.B. crew popping, locking, and breaking on the linoleum floor of their Fagatogo clubhouse are cast as U.S.-spawned hybrids, a new form of 'inauthentic' native less alluring to *National Geographic*'s orientalist readership than their more traditional cousins to the west.

Yet popping and locking didn't stop in the *nu'u* (villages) of American Samoa. A significant aspect of the 'transnational' connectedness of Samoan family networks is the deep ties that link Samoans in American Samoa to relatives in the independent nation of Samoa. However much *National Geographic* might suggest the absolute 'Americanization' of American Samoa and the contrasting conservative traditionalism of independent Samoa, the two political entities maintain a close, if sometimes contentious, relationship.[29] The vast majority of American Samoa's 'foreign' migrant population is in fact women and men from independent Samoa, laboring in Pago Pago's two tuna packing plants. A significant percentage of independent Samoa's 'tourists' are American Samoans visiting relatives or simply taking advantage of Apia's rich nightlife and the relative strength of their American dollars. Samoans frequently travel back and forth, visiting family, going to school, fulfilling kinship obligations, or going on shopping or recreational outings. People across the island chain share a common language, Samoan, and, as many researchers have found, a remarkably unified expressed commitment to the *faaSamoa*, a set of customs, practices and ideals symbolizing 'Samoanness' or more generally 'the Samoan way of life.'[30]

People in Samoa and American Samoa also share new ideas and new information about the peoples, places, and things encountered on the migrant periphery. These connections ensure that the transnational transfers of popular dance and music that filter down from Hawai'i and the continental U.S. do not simply stop in the U.S.-administered territory of American Samoa, but spill into its larger independent western neighbor. What filters to American Samoa from the U.S. filters to Samoa, and filters, in turn, to the Samoan populations dispersed to Aotearoa New Zealand and Australia. Conversely, what filters back to Samoa from New Zealand and Australia makes its way to American Samoa, Hawai'i, and to Samoan communities in the continental U.S. Hip hop dance, the movements of temporally and spatially situated human bodies, is inextricably tied to the movements of history.

Aotearoa Street Dance: 1980–2002

The 2000 Aotearoa Hip Hop Summit in Christchurch featured, among other events, popping competitions for both females and males. The venue was the Lumiere Theatre, the official Summit site just off Cathedral Square. On the day preceding the outdoor performance by Kosmo and his Indigenous Footsouljahs, Bonnie Tamati ('Phem1'), a young Samoan woman from the Christchurch-based all-female b-girl crew Anonamiss, took part in the female popping competition. Tamati had only been popping and b-girling for two months. She was a bit bashful and her sets were short, but she had strong support both on and off the Lumiere Theatre stage. Two sisters and one cousin joined Tamati at the Summit, a whole family of female hip hop artists undeterred by the pressures of negotiating the still strongly masculine public and private sites of hip hop production. Tamati's older sister, Sara ('SpexOne'), danced earlier in the day as part of the featured battle between Wellington's Time Bandits Crew and Christchurch's Blitz Crew. A cousin, Lili, and another sister, Karoline, performed with Bonnie in Anonamiss's b-girl showcase. As MC 'Ladi6,' Karoline would also perform formally in the Summit's Friday night concert and participate more informally in the various freestyle rhyme battles between local and visiting MCs taking place throughout the week. To round out the Tamati sisters' rich contributions to Aotearoa Hip Hop Summit 2000, Bonnie also completed two pieces on the communal wall officially sanctioned for Summit graffiti writers.

Tamati had significant encouragement going into the popping competition, both from family members and the larger audience. Throughout the week, in fact, participants of both sexes boasted of the support female performers in general were receiving at the Summit; some male participants even suggested, as a point of pride, that this was an aspect that distinguished Aotearoa hip hop communities from their American counterparts. Even with this enthusiastic reception, however, Tamati's nervousness was still apparent. She came out for two short dance sequences before moving quickly to the back of the stage. When she came forward for her third set, however, her style shifted and she was suddenly dancing Samoan *siva*, but slowly, exaggeratedly, alternately tensing and releasing her body to 'pop' each muscle group, reinterpreting the Samoan dance movements through a body tuned to bass-heavy funk. It was Tamati's longest set of the competition; by the time she had dropped to her knees, reminiscent of a *taupou* dancing a *taualuga*, the audience was screaming and pumping their fists with appreciation.[31]

The spontaneous enthusiasm that greeted Tamati's performance likely involved recognition and appreciation for the distinct elements upon which her dancing drew. The audience of hip hop artists and fans, overwhelmingly Polynesian, were uniquely situated to read in her dance sequence both the specific relationship between head, eye, and hand and foot gestures that characterize Samoan *siva* and the exaggerated muscle movements that mark the urban street dance form popping. Over and above that, however, the enthusiastic audience response bespoke recognition and appreciation for the artful way Tamati, contrary to 1985 *National Geographic* logic, brought those elements together—how the specific bodily relationships of *siva* could be preserved in an apparently contradictory form.

Tamati's artful marriage of apparently divergent dance forms was not without precedent. Fifteen years before Tamati took the stage in Christchurch, a young Samoan dancer in Wellington named Petelo Petelo articulated the links he understood between an imported dance form he called 'bop' and Samoan traditional dance:

> Me, I don't know enough about Samoan dance ... there are a lot of kids who are shy of their dance—but I reckon you can get over that shyness through bop. There are close links between islands dance and bop and now that we have broken through the confidence barrier with our bop we're starting to mix island culture in our dance and show off with pride. For a lot of our [dance] team, when we go to Samoan fiafias we actually do our Samoan dance and you won't be shy at all. Your relatives are surprised and afterwards they come up and they're proud. It's been a long time coming but bop is breaking down cultural barriers—people aren't ashamed of who they are, it's something inside you that makes you want to dance, to take your place.[32]

Rather than contradicting or opposing traditional forms, street dance was what, according to Petelo, enabled the children of migrants to have the confidence to learn and perform traditional dance at Samoan gatherings.[33] Petelo's reference to 'something inside you that makes you want to dance, to take your place,' locates in dance a potentially inarticulable power to render new conditions of possibility for the dancing body. For Petelo, engaging in one set of movements, 'bop,' among peers in the social environment of the street allowed for the performance of a different set of movements, Samoan *siva*, in the context of a traditional Samoan gathering.

While the change Petelo references is meaningful to him, personally, it is important that his dancing body is one among many. The form of his narrative begins at the level of the individual, 'Me, I don't know enough about Samoan dance,' but quickly moves to locate Petelo in a larger collective of Islander youth. As he acknowledges bop's ability to counter 'shyness,' Petelo's 'I' slips easily to a 'we.' The 'shyness' he references, what people in New Zealand frequently also call 'that old Polynesian shyness,' is not an individual psychological condition but rather a complex weave of psychologically conditioned fears and anxieties. On the one hand, Maori and Pacific Islander families and communities often censure members who give the impression that they are trying to stand out from the group. Samoans, in particular, have a range of expressions for other Samoans who act *fiapoto*, too smart, or *faamaualuga*, too uppity. On the other hand, Pacific Islanders and Maori in New Zealand are constantly aware of a White gaze that marks them as other and inferior, a 'coconut,' 'fob,' 'dirty hori,' or 'bunga.'[34] Young people are trapped between being too Polynesian and never Polynesian enough. Thus, what Petelo terms shyness is rather a feeling of vulnerability to critique from within and without the community that, at its worst, paralyzes expression. Street dance, for Petelo and others, is a means of negotiating out of this paralysis. It is a means of confidently and creatively living out the present in a way necessarily different from both Islander and Maori elders and New Zealand Whites.

On the day of the dance competitions at Aotearoa Hip Hop Summit 2000, Summit co-host Ritchie Mills had opened up the day's activities in the Lumiere Theatre with a recitation of street dance origin stories, briefly narrating the 20-year history of locking, popping, and breaking in Aotearoa New Zealand. Although Mills credited Kosmo for the information he told the audience, his version also significantly echoed the one detailed in Mark Scott's early history of New Zealand street dance, *Street Action Aotearoa.*[35] In Scott's text, Petelo Petelo returns to Wellington in the early 1980s from a stay in Samoa with a new dance form he'd been taught by family and friends:

> Petelo had just spent a bit of time back in Samoa where the whole island was filled to overflowing with the bop—not too much break, mostly bop. It had trickled down from America where about 40,000 Samoans live, through to American Samoa, and spilled across to Western Samoa where Petelo picked up on the excitement, and plunged into learning a few moves. [He] could hardly wait to show off the dance back home, inject a bit of that excitement into Wellington streets [but at first] it went down like a lead balloon … But in Auckland and around the country other Samoan kids were doing the same thing—bringing back a few moves, trying them out on homeground.[36]

Petelo and the other young dancers were most likely trying popping moves (perhaps locking, as well), but they referred to the dance as bop. Mills' year-2000 account, with a self-consciously comic hindsight, elaborated how this modified pronunciation occurred; filtered through numerous Samoan accents, the name of the dance sounded less like *pop* and more like *bop*. When other forms of hip hop dance became wildly popular and widely practiced in New Zealand, primarily by Maori and Pacific Islander youth, the word bop was used as the general term for a range of urban dance forms, including popping, locking, and b-boying/b-girling.

There is another important element to Scott's origin story. Along with the transmission of dance between bodies—continent to island, village to village, island to island—popping, locking, and breaking began to 'arrive' in Aotearoa via movies and music video. Suddenly, according to Scott, movies such as *Flashdance* (which featured a brief performance by members of the Rock Steady Crew), *Breakin'*, and *Beat Street* provided a wider context for the dance styles of individuals like Petelo, who had picked up his moves in Samoa, or Kosmo, who was just then returning from Los Angeles.[37]

Perhaps the most provocative catalyst referenced by Scott is the imported U.S. television program *That's Incredible*. Given its small population it has historically been more cost efficient for New Zealand television broadcasters to air a mix of American, Australian, and domestic programming, rather than attempt to entirely substitute domestic programming for slickly produced foreign products. Significant to Scott's narrative is the fact that in the 1970s, 80s, and 90s, this mix of imported and domestic television programming featured predominantly White actors, newscasters, talk show hosts, and commentators. Prior to the mid 1980s, shows featuring non-Whites were extremely rare, and domestic programs featuring Maori and Pacific Islanders virtually non-existent. As Scott notes, 'A Polynesian kid watching television in [New Zealand] can be excused for thinking he or she doesn't exist ... Not surprisingly, the television image of Black America is the one the kids identify with and given everything else it's often the only one they pick up from anywhere.'[38]

Much as with radio, where Maori and Pacific Island youth would wait through hours of EuroAmerican, British or *pakeha* (White New Zealander) artists, fingers hovering over the record-button for that rare Marvin Gaye, Bob Marley or James Brown tune, televised exceptions to the predominantly White norm have had significant impacts on Polynesian youth. Within the structured (lack of) media representation of non-Whites in New Zealand, even the most banal, the most formulaic, the most inane American programming involving people of color has had radically unforeseen effects.

> [H]alfway through 1983 and by complete accident, television at long last dished up something positive, alive, exciting that a Polynesian kid here could relate to ... something that said you can do it, go to it, you're incredible. It happened on a Saturday night about 7:30. In amongst all those people wrestling grizzly bears and water-skiing on their heads, the TV programme *That's Incredible* squeezed in a few minutes on some ghetto gangs who were dancing in the streets instead of fighting, were doing the bop. That five minutes out of a lifetime acted like a trigger—for hundreds of kids that Saturday night was the last they would spend staring blankly at the box. The forgotten kids got something at last.[39]

What Scott's 'forgotten kids' received was not simply an image of brown bodies on their television screen; it was an image of brown bodies engaged in something so mind-blowingly beautiful, so powerful, so catalytic, that it suggested to many Maori and Pacific Island youth alternative possibilities for the organization of their own daily lives. Some had already been dancing, of course, but the mediated American images of street dance granted a compelling legitimacy to their individual efforts. The brief segment of *That's Incredible* emphasized that those Samoans who had picked up a few moves in Samoa were part of a much larger dynamic youth culture. The same connection to the islands that those youth were used to being routinely insulted for was in fact giving them the advantage in what soon proved to be an international youth movement. 'Bop' was a realm where Islanders had legitimacy over and above *pakeha* youth, and legitimacy in relation to indigenous Maori youth, as well, translating into a potent confidence boost for the children of recent migrants. 'Bop'—American street dance forms such as popping, locking, and breaking—created a space of solace and comfort where Maori and Pacific Islander young people could seemingly fashion their own codes and conditions for acceptance and exercise a limited form of power.

Importantly, this space of refuge was not an absolute or final rejection of what was deemed Maori or Pacific Islands culture or tradition. It is critical to keep in mind Petelo Petelo's testimony to the role of bop in *enabling* his participation in Samoan cultural gatherings amidst a general New Zealand social environment that derided such 'fresh off the boat' behavior. In Petelo's case, the skills mastered in street dance instilled the pride and confidence necessary for him to (re)turn to Samoan *siva*. For many other Maori and Pacific Islander dancers, DJs, MCs, and graffiti artists, elements of cultural nationalism and cultural pride transferred through American hip hop forms frequently prompted a similar turn to local languages, local history, and local regimes of symbolic representation. Simultaneously, the multi-ethnic spaces of bop and hip hop music encouraged ways to think beyond destructive discourses of absolute ethnic difference between indigenous Maori and migrant Islanders, or between migrant communities of Tongans and Samoans, fostering current trends toward pan-Polynesian collaborative work and the counter-fertilization of activist discourses.

In July of 2000, nearly two decades after hip hop dance forms such as popping, locking, and breaking were carried to Aotearoa by both traveling Islanders and traveling television signals, Ritchie Mills circulated his version of these origin stories from the stage at the first annual Aotearoa Hip Hop Summit. These stories, 'forms of individual and collective narrative,' were 'not merely representations disconnected from "real" political life.' Neither were they 'transparent records' of social history.[40] Collective narrative-making at the Aotearoa Hip Hop Summit intently articulated local connections to global transnational phenomena.

Ritchie Mills' account was a history lesson for the youth in the audience, most of whom were participants of the post-1995 second wave of breaking popularity in New Zealand. Mills mentioned the momentous 1983 broadcast of *That's Incredible*, and he mentioned also the more intimate links Samoans and other Polynesians in the audience had to what otherwise might be construed as wholly American, or more specifically, wholly African-American or Latino, cultural imports. They were linked, through an expansive network of hip hop dance practitioners encompassing New Zealand, Samoa, American Samoa, and Hawai'i, to California Samoan dancers like Jack and Charlie Hisatake and the brothers of the Boo-Yaa T.R.I.B.E.

Even more specifically, Summit participants were linked to global street dancing legend Suga Pop. Some Summit participants recounted 20-year-old memories at the mention of Suga Pop's name; his history was their history, as well. Ritchie Mills' account at Aotearoa Hip Hop Summit 2000 didn't simply situate popular street dance forms in the history of Aotearoa or the Pacific Islands, it also situated Pacific Islands and Pacific Islanders in the history of those dance forms. His particular origin story testified to the transnational impact of American popular culture, but Mills also subtly emphasized the *a priori* transnationalisms that continue to contribute to American popular cultures.

Suga Pop

The Indigenous Footsouljahs are two verses into their signature song in Cathedral Square. A bitterly cold gust of wind momentarily catches the 'Paparazzi' instrumental on DJ Raw's turntable; the needle skips, a brief rupture, but the Footsouljahs press on undeterred. Kosmo's lyrics resound off the gray stone square, the gray stone cathedral, the gray stony faces of passersby. His is a 'travel story,' to be sure, linking pasts and futures to narrate a place of continuous arrival in the present. To be an Indigenous Footsouljah, to be a 'Pacific Islander on foreign soil,' is to draw on originary myths of a Samoan homeland alongside contemporary migrant histories, American Black Power rhetoric, Maori sovereignty struggles, and the culture of hip hop. The 'traveling native' performs, quite literally, from the stage in Cathedral Square, articulating indigeneity alongside diaspora over borrowed beats, envisioning possibilities for an alternative world.[41]

> Resurrection/ Emerge like a volcanic plateau
> Knowledge absorbed within the circle of travel
> Mythical lyrics to enhance the mental/ Invoke legendary myths of old/
> Reminiscing
> Extravaganza/ Catchin' wreck like cyclones
> Tropical Hamos[42]/ Outriggers on arrival
> Contemplate/ My mind's focused
> Approach revolution/ Panther power/ Check my ten-point platform!
> Words ravel to confuse the mind flow
> Demonstrate indigenous flavors on metallic chrome
> Apparatus of the trade/ Echoes
> Left for dead in my wrath/ Like Arnie, I'll be back

And again, the mantra-like chorus: 'Always represent for my people/ Pacific Islanders on foreign soil/ Style lethal/ Take a look as we enter the next chapter/ Flip the script.'[43]

Los Angeles, so figuratively and literally connected as a condition of possibility for the Footsouljahs' performance, was not, in the end, implicated in the way 'Represent For My People' was eventually, with the assistance of a Creative New Zealand arts grant, recorded in 2004. International copyright laws and artistic pride preempted the use of Xzibit's 'Paparazzi' in the official release, so Footsouljahs were faced with the task of composing a backing track equally as evocative but original enough to avoid copyright infringement. Kosmo briefly considered enlisting the legendary Suga Pop to lend production assistance—the two men have been friends for years.

Though Suga Pop did not have a hand in how 'Represent' was finally released, he was present in other ways, even in his absence, at the inaugural Hip Hop Summit in Christchurch. More intimate, even, then their connection to the Hisatakes or the Devouxs, the poppers, lockers, b-boys, and b-girls demonstrating their skills all week at the Aotearoa Hip Hop Summit were linked to the infamous Suga Pop, the enigmatic figure whose traveling body, dancing in and out of islands and continents, negotiating all sorts of mythic homelands, connects Samoa, Aotearoa, Hawai'i, Los Angeles, and New York City. Suga Pop is a progenitor, an Islander, a dance legend, and Maori dancer Swerv 1, one of the oldest b-boys in Aotearoa and possibly the first person to do a top-to-bottom graffiti piece on a train in the entire nation of New Zealand, can remember himself being a 'wee bub' in Newtown when Pop used to pass down to him his old skateboard decks.

Though Suga Pop would be the first to assert that 'fame, for us, is not measured by how many videos you've been in,' he 'arrived' in Aotearoa via video as well. He was featured in Topper Carew's dance documentary *Breakin and Entering*, which circulates from home to home in New Zealand via thrice-dubbed bootlegs. He helped choreograph and perform the popping sequences in Michael Jackson's epic *Thriller* video and prominently appears with Janet Jackson (as well as former Boo-Yaa T.R.I.B.E. member E.K.A.) in the clip for 'That's The Way Love Goes.' Though now based, again, in Los Angeles, Suga Pop continues to arrive in New Zealand; in the physical sense, he makes occasional trips for business and pleasure, maintaining close ties with family and old friends. But Suga Pop also continues to arrive in streams of mediated images and snatches of song, through the dance videos he edits and distributes from his Silverlake home.

Several months before the inaugural Aotearoa Hip Hop Summit, I finally caught up with the legendary Suga Pop at the 2000 B-boy Summit in Los Angeles, one of the premiere annual U.S. events dedicated to showcasing the street dance forms—locking, popping, and b-boying/b-girling—that have since come to be associated with hip hop culture. Suga Pop graciously agreed to an interview, and, seated in his Pasadena hotel room with Electric Boogaloo members Popin' Pete and Skeeter Rabbit between exhibitions, he answered my questions about 'back in the day,' about street dance and his connections to Pacific peoples and places. It was then that Suga Pop told me that, contrary to printed assertions and endlessly spiraling street discourses, he is not of Samoan ancestry. 'Me?' he has since written, 'Well I'm the original "half-breed-outcast"—always have been.'

Suga Pop, one of the first 'Samoan' hip hop stars, discovered that his biological father is not the Samoan man who raised him but a rather different

'Islander'—an itinerant sometimes-musician from St. Kitts, according to one version of the story, AWOL from the U.S. Army and traveling the Pacific with his band. 'At times my opinions may seem a lil' jaded,' Pop writes, '[after continually hearing] "You're not a real Samoan—your daddy's a nigger and your mom is White.'[44] I am reminded now of that passage from George Lipsitz's essay 'Cruising Around the Historical Bloc,' where Lipsitz reveals that the first commercially successful Chicano rock and roller in Los Angeles, L'il Julian Herrera, was in fact a Hungarian Jew raised by a Mexican woman in Boyle Heights.[45] What does such a revelation mean for the work I attempt here?

I end with Suga Pop precisely because his example provides a curious twist to the larger questions central to my work: what are the stakes of articulating a Samoan hip hop identity? How are such articulations situated within contested discourses of authenticity and fields of power? I end with Suga Pop precisely because it would be too easy to envision this chapter as simply an attempt to argue for the legitimacy of Samoan hip hop production and Samoan hip hop identity vis-à-vis the Black American referents that overwhelmingly determine understandings of hip hop culture. I am not solely concerned with trying to locate Samoans within the contested discourses of hip hop authenticity, or about maintaining the centrality of Blackness as the *only* pole around which Samoan hip hop identity must orbit. Suga Pop reminds me that there are multiple poles, and that they need to be held in tension. I end with the figure of Suga Pop because his example in fact provides the inverse of what many readers would expect this text to be about. Suga Pop; a person of both impeccable hip hop credentials and African ancestry who nevertheless has spent much of his life situating himself and being situated within discourses of what it means to be authentically Samoan. 'I used to really want to *belong*,' Suga Pop says. 'I used to hang with the fellas in Hawai'i, then in California with the Boo-Yaa T.R.I.B.E.—*shit*, I could speak better Samoan than they could. But I don't care anymore, I'm OK with it.'[46]

In May 2002, nearly two years after the first Aotearoa Hip Hop Summit where his name was so frequently invoked, Suga Pop was brought back to Aotearoa New Zealand to perform in a dance exhibition and teach two workshops on popping and locking. His trip, organized by local dancers and funded by the Wellington City Council, was billed as the triumphant return of a native son. Some of the predominantly Pacific Islander and Maori participants in the workshop learned that Suga Pop was not, in fact, Polynesian, but nobody really cared. They listened in rapt attention as he broke down the history of the dance forms that meant so much to them. They struggled, sweating and grinning, to master his impressive techniques. On the second day of the workshops, a Sunday, one young Samoan man brought him *to'ona'i*, the traditional Samoan Sunday meal. No matter his genealogy, Suga Pop was considered family to them. Suga Pop, 'the original half-breed outcast,' or perhaps just one of many border crossers, who despite this, or because of it, single-handedly embodies all of the complexity and connectedness and contradiction I seek to write about here.

NOTES

1. Note that the indigenous Maori term for New Zealand is Aotearoa. I use the terms alternately throughout the text.
2. 'Always Represent,' *Puttin' In Work*, 2Much Records 2004.
3. West Side Piru is an old and prominent set of the Los Angeles Blood gang organization.
4. *'Aiga* can mean 'family, descent group, or kinship in all its dimensions.' Malama Meleisea, *The Making of Modern Samoa* (Suva, Fiji: Institute of Pacific Studies of the University of the South Pacific, 1987), p. vii.
5. SpexOne, 'K.O.S.-163,' *Back2Basics* (September 2001), pp. 22–4.
6. Omai Faatasi, which translates as 'Come together as one,' served the South Bay Samoan community during the 1970s, offering educational outreach, job training, health care information, and agitating for greater social services for Samoans. The organization lost their community center and most of their funding as a result of California State Proposition 13. Visual Communications, *Omai Faatasi: Samoa Mo Samoa* (Los Angeles: 1978).
7. The 1989 beatings of female and male members of the Dole family in Cerritos, CA, the 1991 shooting deaths of the Tualaulelei brothers in Compton, CA, and the 1998 shooting death of Rodney Laulusa in Honolulu, HI, all by active duty law enforcement officials, are notable examples. In all cases, officers made statements after the incident about the physical size of the Samoans they beat or shot. Paul Feldman, 'County Ordered to Pay Extra $2.3 Million in Brutality Case,' *Los Angeles Times*, November 9, 1995; 'Deputies Used Excessive Force,' *Los Angeles Times*, June 20, 1995; Andrea Ford, 'Police Officer Charged in Two Killings,' *Los Angeles Times*, October 17, 1991; 'Jury Deadlocks in Compton Officer's Manslaughter Trial,' *Los Angeles Times*, May 20, 1992; Andrea Ford and Eric Malnic, 'Ex-Officer to Avoid Retrial in Slayings,' *Los Angeles Times*, June 4, 1992; Ed Rampell, 'Did This Man Have to Die? The Shooting of Rodney "Banks" Laulusa,' *Honolulu Weekly*, February 25–March 3, 1998.
8. Most male dancers I've interviewed will, when pressed, admit that some of the best poppers and/or lockers they've ever seen were female, but very few women have been able to travel or perform street dance professionally. Men typically attribute this to the fact that women have less ambition and/or bear the primary burden of childcare, therefore having less mobility and less desire to be frequently on the road. This projection, by men, of women's desires and motivations is frequently at odds with the stories given by women involved in street dance, who often emphasize gender discrimination and lack of opportunities and encouragement to continue performing.
9. Jorge 'Fabel' Pabón, 'Bicoastal Exchange Program: Breaks Pop the Lock of Cultural Confinement,' *Rap Pages*, Vol. 5, No. 8 (September 1996), p. 43.
10. The term 'b-boy,' or, alternately, 'b-girl,' refers to a male or female breaker. These terms, like many in hip hop, are constantly debated. Some practitioners insist on one term, while others vehemently disagree and insist on another. The terms 'b-boy' and 'b-girl' are said to refer to a 'break-boy' or 'break-girl,' a dancer who performs particular moves within the breaking repertoire. The 'break' in breaking refers to the extended instrumental break between stanzas in the funk or soul records critical to hip hop development. DJs experimented with these breaks, switching between two turntables playing identical or complementary records in order to extend the break indefinitely, and breakers performed to these expertly manipulated sonic subversions.
11. Kelly errs on the date here, as Suga Pop doesn't recall traveling to New York until 1981. Also, the question of Suga Pop's 'Samoan' ancestry will be returned to later in the chapter.

'Hip Hop Chicano,' in Brian Cross, *It's Not About a Salary ... Rap, Race and Resistance in Los Angeles* (London: Verso, 1993), p. 70.

12. Jeremy Miller, 'Tribal Scars: Certified OG's on the West Coast, Boo-Yaa T.R.I.B.E. Finally Seem on the Verge. What Took Samoa's First Family So Long?' *Source* (March 2001), pp. 158–61.

13. DJ Zen, 'Ready to Rock Hard: The Brothers of Boo-Yaa Tribe Come Back Swingin',' *Rap Pages* (April 1993).

14. Cross, *It's Not About a Salary*, p. 149.

15. This compilation, *Eyez on the Prize*, was planned as a soundtrack to an independent film of the same name which Rodney Hisatake intended to co-produce. The film was to follow the struggles of four fictional brothers migrating from American Samoa to California, illuminating in particular the hardships of two of the brothers who become enmeshed in illicit drug economies. Due to insufficient funding, the film has not, as yet, been made. It is interesting, given Paul Gilroy's remarks in *Against Race* on the changing category of freedom in Black popular culture, that the *Eyez on the Prize* compilation displays a marked trend towards the representations of the hyper-physical and commoditized body that Gilroy notes (although it substitutes a Samoan body for an African-American one), while retaining the title of a popular documentary series about the U.S. civil rights struggle. Paul Gilroy, *Against Race: Imagining Political Culture Beyond the Color Line* (Cambridge, MA: Harvard University Press, 2000).

16. SpexOne, 'K.O.S.-163,' p. 23.

17. Ibid., p. 24.

18. One memorable logo used on posters, flyers, T-shirts, and stage backdrops for both Rough Opinion and K.O.S.-163's current group, Indigenous Footsouljahs, features simply the band's name and a stark black-and-white representation of Black Panther Party member Huey Newton holding a machine gun.

19. A variation of the American Black vernacular expression 'Head Nigga In Charge,' the 'Fob' in this case referring to the sometimes derogatory shorthand for 'Fresh Off the Boat,' a reference to recent Pacific Islander migrants.

20. J.W. Davidson, *Samoa Mo Samoa* (London: Oxford University Press, 1967); Malama Meleisea (ed.), *Lagaga: A Short History of Western Samoa* (Suva, Fiji: University of the South Pacific Press, 1987).

21. Eni F.H. Faleomavaega, 'Statement Before the United Nations Special Committee on Decolonization (C-24),' Havana, Cuba; Caribbean Regional Seminar to Review the Political, Economic and Social Conditions in the Small Island Non-Self-Governing Territories, May 23, 2001; Fili Sagapolutele, 'American Samoa is Not a US Colony, Tauese Reiterates,' *Samoa News*, April 12, 2001. Critical voices have emerged to contest the dominant narrative of beneficent American administration of the territory, notably Dan Taulapapa McMullin. See, in particular, McMullin's chapter on American Samoa in the reader *Resistance in Paradise* (Philadelphia: American Friends Service Committee, 1999), pp. 87–107.

22. Cluny Macpherson, Bradd Shore, and Robert Franco (eds), *New Neighbors: Islanders in Adaptation* (Santa Cruz, CA: Center for South Pacific Studies, 1978).

23. Paul Spoonley, David Pearson, and Cluny Macpherson (eds), *Nga Take: Ethnic Relations and Racism in Aotearoa/New Zealand* (Palmerston North, NZ: Dunmore Press, 1991).

24. Anna Tsing, *In the Realm of the Diamond Queen* (Princeton, NJ: Princeton University Press, 1993).

25. Tune Vaouli, from tape-recorded interview. Alofau, American Samoa, August 6, 1998.

26. Christopher Seei, from tape-recorded interview. Honolulu, HI, October 17, 1997.

27. Robert Booth, 'The Two Samoas: Still Coming of Age,' *National Geographic* (October 1985), pp. 452–73.

28. Ibid., p. 455. 'Fa'a America' in this case is a play on the term *faaSamoa* intended to denote instead 'the American way.'

29. The contentiousness of the relationship between the governments of America and independent Samoa has deep historical layers, involving, among other things, pre-colonial chiefly hierarchies and present-day economic disparities. In general, there is a great deal of pride on both sides of the political dividing line, which translates into deeply felt concern that the Samoans on the other side of the political boundary might think that 'they,' for whatever reason, are better than 'us.'

30. Robert Franco, *Samoan Perceptions of Work: Moving Up and Moving Around* (New York: AMS Press, 1991); Lowell D. Holmes and Ellen Rhoades Holmes, *Samoan Village Then and Now* (Fort Worth, TX: Harcourt Brace Jovanovich, 1992); Bradd Shore, 'A Samoan Theory of Action,' Ph.D. Thesis, Department of Anthropology, University of Chicago, 1977.

31. The *taupou* is frequently referred to in anthropological literatures as the 'village maiden' or 'ceremonial virgin,' both terms that carry a dense accretion of gendered Western imaginings of Pacific Islands women. Today, the *taupou* is perhaps better understood as the young woman chosen to represent a Samoan village by performing particular duties in ceremonial matters. A *taualuga* is a type of *siva*, or dance, which features the *taupou*, and it is accorded a special place of status in Samoan performing repertoires. In the dispersed and adaptive Samoan communities which have formed in the United States and New Zealand, often a young woman functioning as a *taupou* and dancing a *taualuga* is not representing a village, per se, but another body of Samoans such as a church congregation, a school group, a cultural troupe, etc.

32. Mark Scott, *StreetAction Aotearoa* (Auckland, NZ: Arohanui Publications, 1985), p. 43.

33. A *fiafia* is a type of Samoan party or cultural gathering usually held to mark a special occasion, especially the arrival or departure of a visiting group. A *fiafia* typically involves a back-and-forth exchange of music and dance performances by the host and visiting group, and can extend for hours into the night.

34. This last slur is perhaps derived from the way Polynesian languages sound to an untrained ear.

35. Kosmo and a number of the other participants at the 2000 Aotearoa Hip Hop Summit actually appear in Scott's 1985 text—a testament to their enduring commitment to hip hop forms.

36. Scott, *StreetAction Aotearoa*, p. 54.

37. Ibid.

38. Ibid., p. 50.

39. Ibid.

40. Lisa Lowe, 'Work, Immigration, Gender: New Subjects of Cultural Politics,' in Lisa Lowe and David Lloyd (eds), *The Politics of Culture in the Shadow of Capital* (Durham, NC: Duke University Press, 1997), pp. 356.

41. My use of the term 'traveling native' borrows from Teresia Teaiwa, 'Between Traveler and Native: The Traveling Native as Performative/Informative Figure,' unpublished paper, University of California, Santa Cruz, 1993.

42. *Hamo* is a common slang term for a Samoan person.

43. 'Always Represent,' *Puttin' In Work*, 2Much Records 2004.

44. Suga Pop, from emailed communication received by author. May 8, 2001.

45. George Lipsitz, *Dangerous Crossroads: Popular Music, Postmodernism and the Poetics of Place* (London: Verso Press, 1994), p. 142.

46. Suga Pop, from conversation notes. Wellington, NZ, May 15, 2002.

13
Negotiating Ethnicity and Authenticity in Tokyo's Club Harlem

Rhiannon L. Fink

New York, Jersey, Philly, B-more, DC, Virginia, Atlanta, everybody rise!!! C'mon! N.C., L.A., Texas, Detroit, Chicago, Miami, N.O., Cleveland, rise!!! C'mon! Denver, Boston, Nashville, Seattle, Albany, Kansas City, everybody rise!!! C'mon! Buffalo, St. Louis, New Haven, Kentucky, Oakland, Phoenix, Vegas, everybody rise!!! C'mon!

Busta Rhymes in 'Everybody Rise,' from *Extinction Level Event*[1]

Busta Rhymes didn't specify Tokyo, but in Japan, too, everybody rose. Busta's third album hit the airwaves in 1998, and when I hit the Tokyo clubs in the spring of 1999,[2] this song was a crowd favorite. Standing in my favorite spot on the dance floor of Club Harlem, the largest hip hop club in Japan and one of the largest in Asia, I heard this track played nearly every week. On innumerable Friday nights at a party called 'Daddy's House,' I would be one of the few *gaijin* (foreigners) crammed onto the dance floor, all of us *gaijin* and *nihonjin* (Japanese nationals) bouncing in unison like a sweating rubber ball. When the DJ threw down this particular track, fans screamed, chanted the cities along with the MC, and threw their hands in the air when Busta commanded 'Rise!' While many of the Japanese b-boys and b-girls liked Busta's flow and energy, I believe that this song's prevalence bears great significance, and that its popularity is exceptionally relevant to an examination of hip hop culture in Japan. First, on an exterior level, the lyrics were widely comprehensible, which is fairly uncommon in Japanese consumption of U.S. hip hop. Second, on a more conceptual level, I propose that Busta's frenetic listing of cities, which both acknowledges individual hip hop scenes and marries them in a unified call to 'rise,' spoke to the hip hop diaspora in Tokyo—as if Busta was saying *dozo* (welcome!) to the distinct localities of the global hip hop community.

1982 marked the release of the classic hip hop film *Wild Style*, depicting the DJs, MCs, bombers, and breakers who pioneered the South Bronx hip hop scene. The subsequent promotion of this film by some of its featured dancers through appearances at Tokyo shopping malls infected Japan with its own hip hop boom. Since its inception, the Tokyo scene has been plagued with contentions of hollow imitation and inauthenticity.[3] Japan's hip hop scene has been undeniably 'Japanified' over the past two decades, yet two main challenges to the scene's perceived authenticity remain: first is the

200

language barrier, and second, the lack of shared experience between hip hop's originators and Japanese hip hop artists and fans.[4] In this chapter, I focus on the latter challenge and how it plays out in a site-specific, multi-ethnic interaction in the Tokyo hip hop scene. I chart the negotiations of ethnicity and authenticity between African-American and Japanese hip hop fans in Club Harlem. I present a diverse chorus of voices from both sides of the Pacific to discuss the question, *is Club Harlem authentic?*

Ian Condry, currently a professor of Japanese Cultural Studies at MIT and arguably the foremost U.S. scholar on hip hop in Japan, highlights the fact that Japanese artists and fans deem the *genba* (actual site) of Japanese hip hop to be the nightclub.[5] He explains:

Thanks to the huge sound (*dekai oto*), the physical intimacy of performers and audience, and the loosening effect of alcohol, clubs are a space where an ideal hip hop world can be given free play ... [they] represent a kind of crossroads, where foreign and local music mix and are remixed and where fans, musicians, and media and industry people keep in touch with each other.[6]

Condry's other works illustrate how hip hop, as a global phenomenon, is 'mediated through local language and key sites of performance, a perspective he calls "genba globalism".'[7] Condry argues that Japan has identified with particular elements of U.S. hip hop and fashioned those elements into something that is unequivocally Japanese. As popular rapper and Harlem MC 'Shiro' of Rhymester put it, 'If I were to say what hip hop is, it would be a "culture of the first person singular." In hip hop ... rappers are always yelling, "I'm this".'[8] In a culture that has historically emphasized a group mentality over the individualism of the West, an emphasis on 'me' in Japanese hip hop is socially and culturally significant. Furthermore, despite the myth of ethnic and social homogeneity in Japan, Japanese nationals are certainly no strangers to oppressive social mores and stratifications, and these issues are becoming more and more prevalent in Japanese hip hop. Specifically, lyrics protesting Japan's rigid age hierarchy have become common. And while the appropriation of English phrases by Japanese MCs was once prolific, it is significant that the use of English is now becoming less frequent, with many MCs using exclusively Japanese. In light of these illustrations, in which it is evident that in many ways Japanese hip hop artists have 'made hip hop their own,' Condry challenges allegations of cultural imitation and misappropriation by Japanese by asking, 'What if hip hop is used to express one's Japaneseness?'[9]

It's important to note that the mere act of clubbing in Japan is read by some as an indicator of authenticity. Going to Harlem for 'Daddy's House' on a Friday night is an invested decision. First, no trains run between midnight and 5:00 a.m., so the choice to 'come out to bounce' is a commitment to a sleepless night. The dedication required to stay out all night signifies, for the Japanese, a level of authenticity. Second, many of the 1,000 hip hop fans, both Japanese and foreign,[10] that the club regularly packs in on a weekend night have arrived on the same train line, at around the same time, meet around the same place, and make their way towards Harlem in a loose exodus-style.[11] This familiar, ritualized experience serves to unify hip hop fans. Third, clubbing in Tokyo isn't viewed as casually as it is in the West. Though it's becoming less stigmatized in Japanese culture, the act of clubbing remains a transgressive social statement. Club Harlem's location just off 'Love Hotel Hill' in Shibuya further adds to the hint of rebellion.[12] For these reasons, the emotional atmosphere of Tokyo clubs is more intense than anything I'd previously experienced in the United States.

Some Japanese do perceive a relationship between ethnicity and authenticity in hip hop. Many of the foreigners who frequent Club Harlem are African or African American. As I discovered in an interview I conducted with DC-based journalist Luciana Lopez, who was living and working in Japan at the same time as me, Blacks were guaranteed 'street cred' in the Japanese scene, regardless of their actual interests or background:

> Although I'm Latina, I was usually mistaken for Black in Japan, especially in hip hop clubs. And even though I've never primarily been a hip hop head, because I had darker skin and kinky hair, I was accorded an automatic legitimacy in Japanese clubs. I often saw people staring at me, watching what I was doing.[13]

Japanese hip hop fans have often been criticized for various appropriations of an 'authentic' hip hop look. In Club Harlem, expensive gear and jewelry are the norm, though often these 'clubbing' outfits are stripped off the next morning as clubbers don their school or work uniforms.[14] Also, tanning is a widespread hobby for Japanese youth. In a hip hop context, darker skin can indicate a desire to be 'authentic,' which is viewed favorably by some but seen by others as 'a mere superficial imitation that contradicts a key element of keeping hip hop real, namely, being true to who you are.'[15] Perhaps not insignificantly, the process of tanning is translated as *buraku naru* (to become Black). Additionally, it is not uncommon for Japanese hip hop fans to sport fake dreads (either synthetic dread accessories, or by perming their own hair into fake dreads). In one instance, Lopez had become friends with a very talented b-boy, 'Uta,' who practiced his moves three to five hours daily, five days per week, for all four years of college. While one might assume that such dedication would afford Uta a certain level of confidence in his own 'authenticity,' Lopez reveals that Uta wore fake dreads when he went to Tokyo clubs. As Lopez explains, 'he still felt compelled to use an accessory to give himself some kind of legitimacy in the scene.' While clearly not the case for Uta, Lopez suggests that for some fans at Harlem, hip hop *is* merely a skin they slip into on the weekends. In reference to Japanese 'poseurs,' whom she somewhat satirically differentiates from 'heads' who 'truly, truly care about the scene,' Lopez theorizes:

I think this goes to the heart of not just hip hop, but a number of culturally 'adopted' social movements in Japan. Because most of the kids don't have the language or the cultural context to understand so much of hip hop—the issues of racial separation, isolation, class/income stratification, social (dis)enfranchisement—they tend to go for the access road that's open to them and are heavily dependent on appearance.[16]

Last year *The Japan Times* featured an article by Eric Prideaux entitled 'Who Copped My Hip Hop?' that aptly illustrates that negotiations of ethnicity and cultural misunderstanding flow both ways.[17] The author, who is African American and describes himself as 'relatively new to Japan,' stood on the street in Shibuya, stopped Japanese wearing hip hop gear, and quizzed them about Malcolm X. He concedes that the consumerization of hip hop aesthetics (such as fashion marketing) took 'authentic' hip hop gear out of the Bronx and marketed it worldwide almost two decades ago but claims to have been curious as to whether the teen represented a 'growing awareness of Black America among Japanese youth.' Through methodology that he himself calls questionable, Prideaux learned that clearly some individuals had more interest in hip hop's roots than others. He was somewhat put-off by short answers and a diversion of eye contact, which he read as a lack of interest, though I suspect it had much more to do with the young people's terror at not only being *approached* but *interrogated* in (presumably) English by a foreigner on a topic about which young Japanese are clearly already feeling insecure. The author felt as if part of his culture had been misappropriated, yet his own cultural blinders further hindered understanding.

Prideaux's article lit a fire under the keyboards of a multitude of hip hop fans in both the U.S. and Japan, who responded on the message board of hiphopmusic.com.[18] In fact, this particular weblog continues to this date, 18 months after Prideaux's article was published, spanning over 40 pages. The varied responses interweave debates about the essence of hip hop, philosophical waxes on the meanings of culture and cultural relativity, laments about the commercialization of hip hop, and accusations of ignorance aimed in every direction. Critiques of Prideaux's methodology and argument are abundant and diverse. Fans problematize Prideaux's claim of ownership ('my hip hop') as well as his lack of acknowledgement of the cultural, economic, and linguistic differences that serve to emphasize the visual in the Japanese scene (fashion, b-boying, graf writing) over the text of the lyrics. Highlighting the significance of the language barrier, blogger 'Keiko' mentions that he writes an e-newsletter/magazine in Japanese called 'Hip hop generation,' which familiarizes Japanese fans with hip hop's culture, people, and history. He describes the poor English language education most

Japanese receive and attributes Japan's alleged hip hop ignorance to a lack of resources for understanding rather than a lack of interest.

Blogging from America, fan 'daikokubashira' uses Prideaux's own model of criticism to show the 'inauthenticity' of U.S. consumption of Japanese culture:

> It's become a cliché when writing about hip hop catching on in Japan, or Korea, or any other country except England maybe. The article always starts out as a question, 'do they really get it?' and then on it goes. There are always going to be people who love the fashion, the music, etc, of hip hop culture, but don't get the 'message,' or even want to hear it, or who even care about 'what's really going on' and a whole lot of them are going to be part of the group who are the so-called originators. There are way more young Black teens who know more about Nelly than they know about Malcolm. And hip hop here can be said to be 'devoid of meaning.' Being pissed at the kid in the article because he didn't know Malcolm X is akin to me being pissed at my nephew for not knowing about Hotei-sama. So now I have to call his love of anime 'not authentic' or something because he doesn't know what an Onsen is? I mean what nonsense.[19]

This blogger's line of reasoning problematizes accusations of inauthenticity, showing that that finger can usually be pointed in multiple directions. Further, he suggests that there likely are Black hip hop fans who couldn't pass Prideaux's Malcolm X Test, yet it's the non-Black hip hop fans who are accorded automatic skepticism and ridicule.

It is notable that this blog, rather than first and foremost a conversation between African Americans and Japanese, primarily illustrates a polemic within the African-American diasporic community. Some want to claim ownership of what is rightfully theirs. Others are frustrated by those claiming ownership of something owned by everyone. Blogger 'Michael' said, 'Hell yes hip hop is a Black culture, and hell yes Blacks have full ownership of Black culture.' Blogger 'Jon' quite eloquently retorted that 'hip hop is one of the greatest gifts Blacks have ever given society.' Blogger 'Unkown' emphasizing the universal potential of the hip hop experience, professed his 'deepest love and respect for all the Japanese and other peoples in the world who have felt the experience of hip hop and held on to it with respect and love.'

But ultimately, as Lopez asserts, 'it's hard for people who haven't experienced racial tension to really understand it.' In the spring of 2002, in a shocking confirmation of this lack of understanding, Club Harlem established a new entry requirement; no foreigner can enter the club without a Japanese escort.[20] Club representatives conceded that this move was harsh, but after reports of 'problems' with foreigners (problems left unidentified in this particular web forum), the club felt compelled to institute the rule to avoid further attention from the police. As the largest and most ethnically diverse hip hop club in Tokyo, with a steady stream of foreign DJs and MCs passing through its doors, the decision has been extremely controversial. On Blacktokyo.com, Black hip hop fans in Japan have unsurprisingly expressed outrage at Harlem's policy: 'They come to New York dye their skin, dance our dance, snub and imitate us, and have free reign … what's wrong here [sic]!?' In other posts, Harlem-goers have lamented the violence that seems to inevitably accompany hip hop wherever it roams. In an emotion-laden post by blogger 'Erick,' the writer reprimands the (presumably) Black Harlem-goers causing the alleged problems that incited the club to enforce the restriction. Erick chastises these unidentified men for disrespecting Japanese culture, imploring them to 'stop embarrassing the rest of us.' Ironically, through his tirade aimed at the 'immature low class,' he identifies their transgressive behavior as part of a history of internal struggle within the Black community.

Despite the multitude of inauthenticity and misappropriation charges lobbed at the Japanese hip hop scene, it seems paradoxical that many Blacks in Japan find its scene to be *more* authentic than the current hip hop environment in the U.S. American DJs and MCs are grateful for the respect and attentive interest (sometimes approaching unabashed worship) they receive from fans. As third-generation Japanese-American Key-Kool writes, 'the difference is that in Japan most fans don't let egos get in the way of expressing their enjoyment of a performance.'[21] Furthermore, the lack of misogyny and violence in Japanese hip hop is appreciated by U.S. fans who oppose these facets of contemporary commercial hip hop in America. Also, the aforementioned intensity of the Japanese club can foster a feeling of togetherness among the fans inside, a quality cherished by fans who are put-off by the hostile atmosphere that can surface in some U.S. clubs.

Moreover, the tension between Black and Japanese hip hop fans in Tokyo is often productive and serves the interests of mutual cultural understanding. More and more information is becoming available in the Japanese language that pays tribute to hip hop's origins. The Japanese underground is becoming more political—e.g. King Giddra's '911,' which reflects on the aftermath of tragedy in both August 1945 and September 2001.[22] Blacks in Japan are finding family in Japanese hip hop fans, and the mere acknowledgement of racial tension in Japan's hip hop scene is a progressive departure from Japan's long history of ignoring social difference.[23]

Hip hop is a site of cultural negotiations, and Club Harlem is a location of exceptionally complicated intersections of ethnic identity. Whether Japanese or African-American, Tokyo hip hop fans seem to be striving for the same experience of authenticity, but mutual cultural misunderstanding often functions to emphasize ethnic difference rather than unite all fans in Busta Rhymes' call to 'rise.' Then further, these cross-cultural negotiations often fuel an internal debate within the Black community. However, as observed by the proliferation of discussions of these tensions in scholarship, online web-boards, and face-to-face encounters in Japan, hip hop fans are actively negotiating the relationship between ethnicity and authenticity. Ultimately, as authenticity is globalized, genuineness will become relative to each *genba*, to each 'true site' in the hip hop diaspora. As Key-Kool puts it, 'true hip hop fans do exist in both countries, ... and dopeness is simply dopeness.'

NOTES

1. David E. Camon, Dominick Lamb, Busta Rhymes (Trevor Smith), 'Everybody Rise,' *Extinction Level Event*, Elektra Entertainment 1998.
2. The author spent 16 months in Tokyo between 1999 and 2001.
3. Accusers are those who consider themselves 'authentic' for any variety of reasons: their knowledge or opinions about hip hop, their age, their ethnicity, or their geographic location.
4. When I refer to Japan's hip hop music scene, I am including both Japanese consumption of American hip hop and Japanese-produced hip hop. Each distinction has its own history and bears its own scourge of problems. However, for the purposes of this chapter, as I will be concentrating on interactions at Club Harlem (a consumptive site of both American and Japanese hip hop), I will frequently use 'hip hop in Japan' to refer to both distinctions.
5. A renowned quote from rapper and Harlem MC 'Shiro' of the group Rhymester suggests that we can find authenticity in the club: '*Doko ga riaru? Sore wa genba. Tsumari koko ni aru.*' (Where is the 'real'? It's in the clubs. In other words, right here.) Yoyogi Park in central Tokyo is another critical spot for hip hop culture-building, particularly for breakers. Dancing is extremely common in the park, and weekend crowds know where to find b-boys and b-girls practicing and performing, especially on Sunday afternoons. After winning the world title multiple times, Japanese crews have gained considerable worldwide recognition.
6. Ian Condry, 'A History of Japanese Hip Hop: Street Dance, Club Scene, Pop Market,' in Tony Mitchell (ed.), *Global Noise: Rap and Hip-Hop Outside the USA* (Middletown, CT: Wesleyan University Press, 2001).
7. Ian Condry, 'Japanese Hip Hop and the Globalization of Popular Culture,' in G. Gmelch and Walter Zenner (eds), *Urban Life: Readings in the Anthropology of the City* (Prospect Heights, IL: Waveland Press), pp. 357–87.
8. Ibid., p. 383.
9. Ian Condry, 'Japanese Hip Hop,' available at <http://web.mit.edu/condry/www/jhh/>; accessed April 21, 2003.
10. In terms of club clientele, ethnic diversity is not unique to Harlem, but it's certainly not standard. I occasionally went to three other hip hop clubs (Family, Bed, Nuts), and Harlem was by far the most diverse. In fact, I caused a serious commotion when I went to Nuts, as I was the only female and the only foreigner. 'How did you find this place?!' I was asked incredulously, as I was invited to partake in a bottle of vodka being passed across the dance floor.
11. Most clubbers arrive via the Shibuya Station on the Yamanote Line, a convenient train that loops central Tokyo. Most reach Shibuya just before midnight, catching the last train before they stop running for the night. Just outside Shibuya Station is a famous statue of a faithful dog, 'Hachiko,' which serves as the area's most popular meeting place.
12. Shibuya is a dizzying youth shopping district peppered with love hotels. Advertising different prices for a 'rest' and a 'stay,' love hotels are frequently used exclusively for sex (more so than ordinary hotels) and are viewed as scandalous sites.
13. Luciana Lopez, interview by author, April 27, 2003.

14. However, in the current climate of Japan's changing economy, there is a widespread rejection among Japanese youth of the traditional 'salaryman' lifestyle. As a trend, young adults are choosing *arubaito* (part-time jobs) over traditional career paths, thus giving them more time and social allowance to be true to their interests.

15. Ian Condry, 'Social Production of Difference: Imitation and Authenticity in Japanese Rap Music,' in Heide Fehrenback and U.G. Poiger (eds), *Transactions, Transgressions, and Transformations* (New York: Berghan Books, 2000), pp. 175–6.

16. Ibid.

17. Eric Prideaux, 'Who Copped My Hip Hop?' *The Japan Times*. Online. April 21, 2003.

18. 'Comments: The Hip Hop Scene in Japan,' hiphopmusic.com. Online. October 20, 2004.

19. Prideaux, 'Who Copped.'

20. 'Re: Foreigners Need Japanese Escort to Enter Club Harlem,' Blacktokyo.com. Online. April 30, 2003. In Japan, restrictions against foreigners are not uncommon. Outside Tokyo, some clubs and bars prohibit foreigners entirely. Such a club may display a sign that says 'no foreigners,' or a doorman might simply state 'no foreigners' when one attempts to enter. Occasionally this rule is bendable, often as the result of a display of Japanese language competency by the foreigner. I cannot say with certainty, but I suspect that proof of Japanese language proficiency might suggest to a Japanese national that this particular *gaijin* has a certain respect for Japanese culture, perhaps a certain 'authenticity' as a respecter of Japan, and is not simply a drunken American voyeur who may cause 'problems.'

21. Key-Kool, 'Individuals,' Bombhiphop.com. Online. April 21, 2003.

22. Condry, 'A History of Japanese Hip Hop.'

23. Japanese society has historically ignored certain issues of social inequality. For example, the myth of ethnic homogeneity serves to deny the existence of the *bunrakumin* (the 'invisible' Japanese underclass), as well as Korean individuals born, raised, and living in Japan who are denied Japanese citizenship and cannot vote. In another example, sexual orientation is largely undiscussed. I was told by several Japanese male colleagues at my school in Tokyo that there are no homosexuals in Japan. Thus, the acknowledgement of social difference and tension is necessarily the first step in striving for social equality.

14
Globalization and Gangster Rap: Hip Hop in the Post-Apartheid City

Zine Magubane

INTRODUCTION

It has been argued that long playing records surpassed sea-going vessels as the most import conduits of Pan-African communication in the twentieth century.[1] This adage is an apt description of the mechanisms whereby a poly-lateral dialogue between African Americans and Black South Africans has been able to sustain itself for over a century. Since 1890 music has been one of the primary mechanisms through which Black South Africans have accessed African-American culture and used it as a vehicle for formulating and articulating critiques of and responses to the social forces that structure their lives.[2] This chapter examines the latest manifestation of this phenomenon, analyzing the various ways in which American rap music has been 'indigenized' or integrated into the symbolic framework of South African culture and society. My discussion is oriented around two levels of analysis that are critical for understanding the dynamics of 'globalized' or 'de-territorialized' cultures:

1. The political and economic conditions that shape the commodification and global dissemination of African-American culture.
2. The political and economic factors that shape how global cultures are received and used by local populations.

African-American cultural practices have held a unique place in the popular imagination of Black South Africans for over a century.[3] In the words of ethnomusicologist Christopher Ballantine: 'For several decades, urban Africans were held in thrall by American culture—but above all by the activities and achievements of Blacks in that society. Where American culture fascinated, *Black* American culture infatuated.'[4] Analyzing the dynamics of this historical linkage is theoretically illuminating because it requires a more rigorous accounting of what constitutes 'Western' or 'American' culture. Furthermore, because South Africa is composed of a mix of sharply differentiated ethnic, racial, and class formations, it also forces us to analytically engage with the question of *who* is consuming global culture, *what* aspects of that culture are being consumed, and how. I will thus begin my analysis with a brief discussion of the status of 'Blackness,' its complex relationship to Western modernity, and the implications this has for thinking about what we mean when we talk about the globalization of 'American' or 'Western' culture.

WHAT IS AMERICAN CULTURE?
BLACKNESS, MODERNITY, AND DOUBLE CONSCIOUSNESS

When assessing the impact of a globalized, de-territorialized economic system on local lived experience theorists have generally clustered around two theoretical poles. There are those who argue that globalization inevitably means 'Americanization' and/or 'cultural homogenization.' In this formulation, local cultures are, for the most part, powerless to ward off foreign incursions.[5] Yet another theoretical school exists which insists that local cultures exhibit a great deal of resilience in the face of 'cultural imperialism.' These analyses center on demonstrating that local cultures are able to assimilate and indigenize significant elements of Western culture, while still retaining a sense of cultural integrity.[6]

Far too often, however, these types of questions are posed in a strict either/or formulation that limits our abilities to think creatively and critically about the producers and consumers of American culture. Scholars on both sides of the theoretical divide have had the unfortunate tendency to homogenize both 'the West' and 'the Rest' in ways that not only flatten out the complexity of the world, but also close off important avenues of theoretical investigation. For example, George Ritzer asserts that 'while we will continue to see global diversity, many, most, perhaps eventually all of those cultures will be affected by American exports; America will become virtually everyone's "second culture".'[7] Writing from the opposite end of the theoretical spectrum, Arjun Appadurai argues that 'the United States is no longer the puppeteer of a world system of images but is only one node of a complex transnational construction of imaginary landscapes.'[8] Although Appadurai and Ritzer take opposing theoretical positions, neither gives much thought to what they mean by 'America' or 'American culture.' *Who* and *what* constitutes 'American culture'? *What* are the specific aspects of this culture that are being 'exported'? *Who* are the cultural agents that are producing these 'exportable elements' and under what historical and social conditions? *What* significance does any of the above hold for understanding how cultural products enter the global arena?

The fact that Black cultures represent what Paul Gilroy calls a 'counterculture of modernity'[9] is, thus, central to my analysis. Gilroy demonstrates that people of African descent have historically had to struggle with the fact that they are 'both inside and outside the West' because of the intimate association between slavery and the rise of modernity.[10] The experience of being enslaved fundamentally altered Black people's relationship to, and experience of, modernity because 'racial terror was not merely compatible with occidental rationality but cheerfully complicit with it.'[11] Slavery's historical legacy is one of the central reasons why the intellectual and cultural achievements of Black diaspora populations exist only partly inside the 'grand narrative' of the West. Although African Americans dominate the American culture industry, and the export of American culture is often tantamount to the export of African-American culture, the sometimes liminal status of African-American culture with respect to modernity and 'the West' complicates any simple definition of what we mean by the globalization of 'Western' or 'American' culture.

Rap music is a preeminent example of an art form that exhibits dual tendencies with respect to Western modernity. On the one hand, rap music celebrates individualism, racial chauvinism, consumerism, capitalism, and sexual dominance—core values that have shaped the trajectory of modernity and its bitter fruits, particularly for people of color. As cultural critic Michael Eric Dyson puts it:

> [G]angsta rap is often sexist and it reflects a vicious misogyny that has seized our nation with frightening intensity. ... The ethic of consumption that pervades our culture certainly supports the rapacious materialism shot through the narratives of gangsta rap. ... Equally troubling is the glamorization of violence and the romanticization of the culture of guns that pervades gangsta rap.[12]

On the other hand, rap music has also provided a powerful critique of Western modernity. The rap music produced by artists like Mos Def and KRS-One offers an alternative worldview that eschews violence and market values while promoting respect for the community and reverence for the historical struggles undertaken by communities of color around the globe. Female rappers like Queen Latifah and Monie Love have disparaged sexism and promoted sexual egalitarianism in their rhymes. As George Lipsitz observed:

> In contemporary culture, artists from aggrieved communities often subvert or invert the very instruments of domination necessary for the creation of the new global economy—its consumer goods, technologies, and images. Post colonial literature, Third cinema, and hip hop music all protest against conditions created by the oligopolies who distribute them as commodities for profit.[13]

The rap music that has become a major part of what is exported and consumed globally as American music culture is a complicated mix of both of the aforementioned tendencies. As a result, when it is 'indigenized' both elements become available for interpretation and incorporation. As will be shown below, South African rap artists have seized upon both traditions, shaping the values that inhere in American popular aesthetics to reflect local political, economic, and gender struggles.

THE POLITICAL ECONOMY OF BLACK MUSIC

In an insightful article on the political economy of Black music, Norman Kelley describes the relationship between the six major record firms (Warner, Polygram, MCA, BMG, Sony, and CEMA/UNI) and African-American artists as a 'postmodern form of colonialism.'[14] He notes that rap music, although it 'forms the very foundation of the $12 billion music industry in the United States,' exhibits an historic pattern typical of African-American aesthetic products like jazz and blues which, although created largely by Blacks, were under the corporate control of Whites. Black owned production companies like Uptown Records, Def Jam, and Bad Boy, Kelley explains, 'do not control a key component of the music-making nexus, namely distribution.' For example, the albums produced by Master P's No Limit Records as well as those by Roc-A-Fella Records (owned by Damon Dash) are distributed by Priority Records. Those produced by Cash Money Records are distributed by Universal, while Sean Combs' Bad Boy label is distributed by Arista. Thus, although young Black entrepreneurs have 'been able to swing the balance of power somewhat in their direction, they are still far from having complete dominion [because] in the music business distribution is the final battleground.'[15] Because African-American artists have virtually no control over the domestic distribution of their music, they likewise have no control over international distribution. Thus, White owned and controlled media conglomerates determine which African-American cultural products enter the global arena.

It is well known that the majority of rap music (perhaps as much as 70 percent) is purchased by the White youth consumer market, which is hungry for caricatured images of Black gangsters and pimps—a postmodern form of minstrelsy. As Kelley puts it: 'When Blacks react to their environment, it is taken up as a style by Whites who have gotten it from an intermediary source: rappers and music videos. This "style," particularly the music, is seen as having the desired effect of boosting sales.'[16] The major labels have invested their energies in signing, marketing, promoting, and distributing those genres of rap music that are most likely to appeal to White adolescent audiences. As Dyson explains:

> White record executives discourage the production of 'positive' rap and reinforce the desire for lewd expressions packaged as cultural and racial authenticity. ... [D]ie hard hip hop fans have long criticized how gangsta rap is eagerly embraced by White record companies while 'roots' hip hop is grossly under financed.[17]

As a result, so-called 'gangsta' rap, and its sometimes minstrelized images of Black suffering, is the genre of rap music that is most likely to enter transnational networks.

THE GLOBALIZATION OF THE GANGSTER IMAGE

Images of American gangsters have been part of the local Black South African imaginary for half a century. In Sophiatown, a slum area close to Johannesburg, the 1950s witnessed the explosive popularity of gangster images from the American silver screen. As South African cultural critic Rob Nixon explains:

> The *tsotsi* or gangster stood as a critical bridging figure between the criminal underworld of Hollywood fantasy and Sophiatown street life. ... It was they who were principally responsible for giving American style and slang a local subcultural look and accent. Paradoxically, the gangsters' adaptations of foreign style rendered Black urban culture all the more inimitable and thereby indisputably indigenous.[18]

In the twenty-first century, American manufactured gangster images are once again on the ascendant in South Africa. Music and music videos have simply replaced film as the preeminent vehicles whereby gangster images enter the circuits of global exchange. Gangster imagery, although it still provides a resource for articulating feelings of economic and social marginality, dislocation, and frustration, has undergone significant changes in the last 50 years. In the postmodern/postcolonial era *kwaito*, an indigenous form of rap music, has emerged as a key site for the indigenization of American gangster images and their associated musical idioms.

In her pioneering exposition on the emergence of rap in the United States, *Black Noise*, Tricia Rose makes the argument that rap music is an aesthetic response to the urban malaise that accompanied the trans-nationalization of the American economy: 'Life on the margins of postindustrial urban America is inscribed in hip hop style, sound, lyrics, and thematics.'[19] A similar argument can be made for the emergence of hip hop, rap, and kwaito as subcultures in South Africa as Black South Africans face many of the same economic problems as their counterparts in the West. When the African National Congress (ANC) assumed the mantle of power in 1994, the government inherited a state that was shedding employment in the manufacturing sectors and the majority of Africans were either unemployed or under-employed. Affordable housing was virtually non-existent while over-building and speculative construction of commercial property generated artificially high land prices in central business districts. The ANC's macro-economic framework, 'Growth, Employment and Redistribution' (GEAR), attempted to reverse these trends by embracing the economic orthodoxy of globalization—'outward oriented' growth. GEAR introduced a number of measures designed to lure foreign investment in the new global marketplace. 'Investor friendly' measures such as making the labor market more 'flexible,' reducing expenditure on wages, privatization of state assets, and cutting government spending were intended to increase foreign investment and thus create 400,000 new jobs by the turn of the century. In actuality, unemployment worsened considerably, with job losses totaling more than half a million during the ANC's first term.[20] Thus, low income Black South Africans are, like their African-American counterparts, suffering the devastating effects of economic globalization. As Chideya observed, 'South African youth and American youth live in parallel universes.'[21]

Kwaito is an indigenous form of rap music that emerged from the most economically depressed areas of South Africa. Levine aptly described it as 'the sound of the ghetto.'[22] Just as was the case in the United States during the 1970s, the reorganization of urban space that accompanied globalization had a perceptible impact on Black South African performance culture. Urban communities, marked by an absence of public space for recreation, cramped and overcrowded residential space, and sub-standard schools whose budgets did not allow for the funding of enrichment programs such as music, were responsible for pioneering a style of music which, in essence, is a form of rhymed story-telling accompanied by highly rhythmic, pre-recorded music. Making rhymes required practice and diligence but no formal musical training. Nor did it require expensive instruments, or access to a large space where a band or other large ensemble might practice. As Coetzer observed, 'the beauty of the form is its accessibility—essentially one person and a few pieces of equipment can produce a complete album.'[23]

Kwaito, which incorporates elements from rap, hip hop, reggae, soul, and traditional South African music, was pioneered by club and party DJs who mixed house music from the U.S. and UK with rap music, slowed down the beats, and adapted them to well known indigenous African songs. According to Coetzer:

> Although it has only recently become a familiar sound to the general SA music marketplace, kwaito has been in existence for more than five years. In essence it is the first genuine wave of post-apartheid expression in music, having its roots in the search by township youth for a homegrown sound. ... [T]aking its lead from the early '90s explosion of American 'house' music created by artists like Tony Humphries and Robert Owen, kwaito (or D'gong' as it is sometimes referred to) has as its musical base a slowed-down house beat or 'slow jam' that is overlaid with pared-down repetitive lyrics (in anything from township slang to Afrikaans) that are chanted or 'spoken.' Add a variety of electronic sounds, and the result is kwaito.[24]

Black South African youth have also been at the forefront of promoting local rap groups, modeled on American so-called 'gangsta' rap artists like Ice Cube or Snoop Doggy Dogg. According to Impey:

[C]oloured youth on the Cape flats were drawn to Black American rap and hip hop artist such as Ice-T, Public Enemy, and Niggers With Attitude. The music prompted the formation of local coloured rap groups ... [who] appropriated images of African-American hard-core rap: baseball caps, baggy pants, and gold jewellery, as well as their associated subcultures of break-dancing and spray-can art.[25]

Although kwaito and South African rap share the common musical ancestor of American hip hop, they not only have distinct sounds, but also were pioneered by different Black South African communities. As the quote from Impey suggests, American hip hop found particular favor among 'mixed race' or 'Coloured' performers in South Africa, and these communities were among the first to try their hand at making their own rap songs, many of which were sung in a vernacular form of Afrikaans. Kwaito, on the other hand, was pioneered by young African performers and most kwaito songs are sung in vernacular versions of the major indigenous languages of Zulu, Xhosa, Tswana, or Sotho. It would be a mistake, however, to rigidly separate kwaito as 'African' and South African rap as 'Coloured.' Such a rigid demarcation not only belies the common origins of both musical forms in American hip hop and hybrid South African musical styles that emerged from both Coloured and African communities, but also enforces too rigid a separation between Coloured and African people. This type of racial essentialism flies in the face of the Black nationalist ideology that informs much hip hop music in South Africa.

Many people whom the apartheid regime classified as Coloured have chosen to eschew the notion of 'mixed race' in favor of embracing a unified Black South African identity, which encompasses the varied histories and experiences of all groups classified as 'non-European.' Indeed this Black nationalist ideology has been promoted with particular vigor by Coloured hip hop artists like Black Noise whose 1998 song 'Black Thing' decries the divisive racial tactics of the apartheid regime and their cynical efforts to manipulate the identities and racial consciousness of Coloured people:

> The term 'coloured' is a desperate case
> Of how the devil's divided us by calling us a separate race
> ...
> But racism is a trap and the nation seems to lack knowledge of self
> But what it means, what it seems
> We're attracting anything but a Black thing

In South Africa, as in America, rap music has been an important vehicle for dispossessed communities to put forth an immanent critique of the local, national, and transnational forces that structure their lives. Rap lyrics, some of which can be brilliantly provocative, others of which are numbingly simplistic, sexist, violent, and consumerist, express the widely divergent attitudes about power and pleasure that exist in African-American communities. For this reason, American rap music has been able to effectively speak to the experiences of South African young people in urban communities. As a recent article on kwaito explained: 'the lyrics may not be literature, but when it comes down to what matters on the street, popular music has rarely been so candid and expressive.'[26]

Despite the ubiquity of groups with names like Prophets of Da City, which recall urban America, rather than urban South Africa, the relationship between South African rap artists and their American counterparts is best characterized as dialogic, rather than derivative. A 1997 survey of Soweto youth by the Alternative Consultancy revealed that African teenagers are profoundly ambivalent about the pervasive influence of American culture in South Africa. Thus, for artists to have legitimacy they must demonstrate their engagement with local communities and local conditions. Brasse Vannie Kaap, musicians from the 'Coloured' townships outside Cape Town, gave lyrical expression to popular sentiments about the ambivalence many South Africans feel about the ubiquity of African-American cultural forms in South Africa in their 1997 song 'Laat dat Rik':

> Yo man, what's up kid. Let's do this for the homeys.
> That's not the way we praat [speak] in the Cape.
> You must get with the program or scram
> Because your false accent doesn't make you cool
> You're not Chester Williams
> So don't even try
> Before I kick your butt like Popeye

Kwaito groups such as Skeem and Trompies routinely rap vernacular forms of the major indigenous languages, Xhosa, Sotho, Tswana, and Zulu. Their use of the vernacular is a conscious attempt to address the social, political, and economic issues that impact marginalized communities in ways that hold particular meaning for them. Language is critical for not only celebrating the uniqueness and legitimacy of local communities, but also for maintaining ties between artists and their audiences. As Dellios explains, 'Zulu may be the proud language of their parents, but it is proficiency in kwaito lingo, used in the new Black kwaito dance music, that puts urban youths on the cutting edge. Most Sowetans speak five or six languages, but there's more pride in being able to speak this street language.'[27] Thus, although South African musicians use American expressive culture as a point of reference and a source of images of Black subjectivity, the concerns of the artists, the source of their inspiration, and the content of their creations are firmly rooted in local conditions. As Levine explains, kwaito lyrics are 'dished up with such a local flavor, it'll be meaningless unless you're from hereabouts.'[28]

Although American rap music has been used as a vehicle for the creation of novel indigenous musical styles, it has come under heavy criticism from the older generation of South African musicians, some of whom have dismissed indigenous rap as hopelessly imitative of the worst excesses of American culture. In a speech before the Independent Broadcasting Authority (IBA), the well-known South African jazz musician Hugh Masekela complained that 'our children walk with a hip hop walk and they think they are Americans ... [they have] an African-American reject personality.'[29] Ironically, the jazz music Masekela and others of his generation pioneered owed an equal debt to American jazz artists as kwaito does to American rap. Furthermore, Black jazz musicians of the 1950s were subject to similar criticisms by the cultural elite. As Ballantine explains, jazz and its related subcultures were considered evil, 'associated with illegality, police raids, sex, and a desperately impoverished working class, it was vilified as a corrupting menace.'[30] Just as the musicians of Masekela's generation identified with the feelings of marginality African-American artists articulated through the jazz idiom, young African and Coloured youth also see hip hop and its subcultures as the art form that best expresses their feelings of economic marginality and social dislocation. As Chideya aptly put it, 'many African youths are looking to America to find ways to express their own hopes, fears, and frustrations.'[31]

The song 'Understand Where I'm Coming From,' recorded by Prophets of Da City in 1993 is typical in this regard. The song begins with a lament about poverty and social dislocation in the ghetto, questioning the wisdom of patriotism in a class stratified society:

> Why should I fight 4 a country's glory
> When it ignores me
> Besides, the township's already a war zone
> So why complain or moan
> ...
> A whole factory got laid off the other night
> Now unemployment makes men sell poison
> To boys and girls in your neighborhood
> But who's gonna pay for food
> Forget about a politician or a millionaire
> Thinking will he care about your ass in Soweto
> Or Mitchell's Plain
> And the bitch'll claim he sympathizes
> But the rich will blame the poor 4 the state of the townships

The final verses of the rap question the degree to which the 'new South Africa' is really new at all, given the racial and class inequalities that continue to plague its communities:

A new South Africa
I don't believe them
I see them with a new scheme, a scam
To set up the Black man

The aspects of American rap that are incorporated into South African music and the ways in which these frustrations are expressed are by no means uniformly progressive, however. Feelings of marginality and frustration and the associated desire for freedom are equally as likely to be expressed in ways that 'associate autonomous agency with sexual desire and promote the symbolic exercise of power in the special domain that sexuality provides' as they are in calls for the overthrow of capitalism.[32] Kwaito fans often express their desires for escape and empowerment through sexual identification with their favorite singers. For example, an enthusiastic young female fan of Arthur, a popular kwaito artist, expressed her desire to possess him sexually in a letter penned to a popular South African music magazine, *eVibe*: 'I want Arthur and I want him now—sexually of course. ... Doesn't he just drive you wild with sexual desire? Don't you just want to grab him and make passionate love to him right there and then? Don't you girls want to lick him all over?'[33] A 22-year-old kwaito fan interviewed by music critic Adam Levine agreed that 'you'll get these groups of girls at the bashes and ... they're heading straight for the front of the audience trying to get Arthur or M'du into bed.'[34]

Even a casual perusal of the lyrics of popular South African rap and kwaito songs make it clear how correct Gilroy was when he cautioned critics against 'moving too swiftly and too simplistically to either condemn or celebrate' vernacular cultural forms.[35] Masekela's condemnation of South African hip hop culture arose in response to songs like 'Bantwana,' recorded by Bob Mabena, a popular South African rap artist, whose lyrics marry consumerism and female objectification in ways that would be thoroughly familiar to any American rap artist or fan.

Bantwana niyangibona	Babes, do you see me
Awungitshele ungangtkhona	Tell me you can take me
Ungibize ngodollar	Call me dollar maker
Fuhi ngivaya nge Corolla	I drive a Corolla
And niphete iMotorola	I carry a Motorola
Yebo baby ungangithola	Baby you can get me
Kanti vele ngiyahola	I earn baby
Manje woze saphola	Come on now, let's chill

Just as is the case in American rap music, homosocial bonding takes place over and through the objectification and denigration of Black women, who are frequently targeted as lyrical objects of male abuse. Mabena, for example, refers to women as 'fat ugly bitches' in the song 'Isigaga.' 'Dallah Flet 2,' recorded by Prophets of Da City in 1993, expresses the same negative and mysogynistic attitudes towards single mothers that are ubiquitous in American rap music.

Ek issie vaakie 9 maaande geleede
was ekkie eens in die Kaapie dis 'n haatie
Jy't nie 'n saak nie hou jou mond, moenie eers praat nie want jy
Kan niks maak nie
Genoeg van daai ek praat van 'n meit wak dink sy kwaai

I'm not stupid. Nine months ago I wasn't even in Cape Town
It's a pity, you don't have a case.
Keep quiet because you can't do anything
Enough about that
I'm talking about a bitch who thinks she's slick

FEMALE SOUTH AFRICAN RAP MUSICIANS

Female South African rap musicians have been quick to respond to the sexism of the South African music scene and that of their musical peers. Impey points out that 'kwaito has offered women a new kind of agency in self-representation in post-apartheid South Africa. ... [T]his agency does not operate in isolation, but is produced within a variety of social discursive practices, and draws on globally circulated media images.'[36] For example, Boom Shaka, a popular kwaito group whose lead rappers, Lebo Mathosa and Thembi Seete have become role models for many young South African women, appear at first glance to simply be reinforcing stereotypes about the wanton nature of Black female sexuality. Some critics have argued, however, that Boom Shaka's female members have used 'the skimpy clothes, the gyrating hips and simulated sex on stage to promote a variety of socially apposite concerns.'[37] The title track on their debut album *Boom Shaka* entitled 'It's About Time' boldly demands that 'it's about time' women were heard:

I'm tired
Of people always asking me
What's happening, what's going on
They try to see what's in my head
Why can't they leave me alone
(Chorus)
It's about time
You listened to Boom Shaka
It's about time
You listened to Boom

...

My weapon is my voice and
I'm pissed like that, yo
What you think about that Lebo?
The way you tell me is the way it is Thembi

On their second album, *Words of Wisdom*, the women of Boom Shaka
continued to shock and defy the expectations of the largely male South
African political elite by recording their own version of the new South
African national anthem, 'Nkosi Sikelel' iAfrika,' composed in 1897 by a
Methodist missionary. The song, which was frequently sung at the opening
and closing of political meetings, became a mantra of the liberation struggle.
In their remake, Boom Shaka replaced the heavily gospel inflected choral
accompaniment with a funky, rap and reggae inflected back beat. In concert
the band opens their version of the song 'old-school struggle style,' complete
with bowed heads and clenched fists, but jazzes it up along the way with
hard-driving rap beats and sophisticated dance moves. As Lebo explained
in an interview in the South African *Sunday Times*, 'we wanted to enrich
and popularize the song for the broader youth, the majority of whom just
mumble the lyrics without understanding them.'[38]

Despite their ambition to be post-apartheid South Africa's first post-
feminist icons, Boom Shaka has not completely captured the hearts and
minds of the young South African female audience, however. As the
following letter in *eVibe* from a young woman in Soweto shows, not all
young South African women would agree with Impey that Boom Shaka
offers women 'a new kind of agency in self representation':[39]

I am so fed up hearing Boom Shaka go on about girl power when all they do is bounce
around singing really crap songs, flashing their boobs and knickers, and spouting
even more harp in dodgy interviews. ... I can imagine many men getting off on Boom
Shaka's boobs and lycra knickers, but I would prefer to make a difference with my
mind thus making men and women realize that girls have more than their bodies to
use powerfully.[40]

Gilroy could easily have been describing the politics of writing about
kwaito when he declared that 'where the un-seasonal fruits of counterculture
become popular and the marginal moves into the mainstream, it would be
absurd to expect to find politics programmatically constituted.'[41] Boom
Shaka is typical of many South African kwaito and rap groups in that it is
impossible to classify them as either 'progressive/feminist' or 'reactionary/
commercial'—they are both and neither. Indeed, Gilroy's assertion that
'those who assert the marginality of Hip Hop should be obliged to say where
they imagine the centre might now be. Hop hop's marginality is as official,
as routinized, as its overblown defiance' is particularly apt in the South
African case because kwaito and rap quickly moved from the ghetto to the

corporate boardroom. It didn't take advertisers long to see the potential of using urban music as a vehicle for selling everything from soft drinks to school supplies.

SELLING SOAP AND SOFT DRINKS 'SOWETO STYLE'

A number of analyses of culture in the transnational world have argued that universal consumerism 'offers a powerful allurement for homogenization. Thus, there is always a theoretical possibility that regional cultures everywhere may be obliterated before long.'[42] The South African example demonstrates that transnational corporations (TNCs) do not always see homogenization as the surest route to profitability. Indeed, TNCs actually enact a range of varying responses. A number of them have not responded by attempting to impose a monolithic American culture. Rather, their focus has been on managing their images in ways that seek to emphasize their engagement with the local. In other words, they have attempted to reproduce certain features of local cultures in order to facilitate their easy accommodation to global imperatives. As the director of Fingerprint Advertising explained,

> US marketers, and the clients we represent, are threatened. ... The marketing strategies we are using are also threatened with extinction. Everyone knows the 'mass' in mass marketing has been eroding for quite a while now. Instead we must define ourselves emotively if we want to be different from the rest. We can only become a brand through a relationship, an emotional link between a customer and a brand.[43]

Transnational corporations thus operate on the principle that 'the quickest way to access South African Black youth is through subcultures.'[44]

Transnational corporations are much less interested in homogenizing or Americanizing the 'Other,' than they are in assessing whether local attitudes towards consumption are in line with American attitudes. For example, Research International, a marketing research firm, undertook a series of studies aimed at demonstrating whether or not consumer trends documented amongst Americans also held true for South Africa. They found that South Africans and Americans had almost identical attitudes to consumerism: they were brand oriented, led by peer pressure, had a strong desire to fit in, based their self-esteem on what they were able to buy, and would manipulate friends and relatives to procure income for purchases. As a result, the study concluded that 'there is a segment of Black South African children who demonstrate many of the consumer characteristics displayed by their American counterparts, and they are therefore definitely worth targeting as primary consumers.'[45]

There is no question that kwaito and rap were born in the townships. Adam Levine aptly described the manner in which residential segregation shaped the kwaito aesthetic in a recent article in South Africa's *Elle* magazine:

One thing you should know about kwaito: it's the sound of the ghetto ... that's the sound of Soweto you are hearing. Fresh from the street, into your ears and looping around between them. True as the thump of a takkie [sneaker] on the tarmac. Or the screech of taxi tyres in the dawn dust. ... About a year before Madiba became the main man, you could hear the kwaito baby screaming to be born. On bad, bootlegged cassettes. Outta stolen Toyota boots. Through blown out taxi speakers.[46]

Paradoxically, rap and kwaito's ghetto roots are precisely what makes them so attractive to advertisers. In the post-apartheid era advertisers are anxious to know about and appeal to young Black South Africans because 75 percent of the Black population in South Africa is under the age of 25.[47] As Maria McCloy explained in an article aptly titled 'Kangols, Kwaito and Ads' these are statistics that 'no marketeer can ignore.'[48] Soweto youth between the ages of 14 and 20 are of particular interest to advertisers because they are seen as trendsetters. Market researchers have thus devised a variety of methods, ranging from focus groups to sending young Black account executives to live with Black families in the townships, to get a feel for what young people find appealing so as to better design their ads. According to Gill Mkhasibe, publisher of *Focus on Soweto Youth*, a biennial report that is considered one of the most important sources of background information for market researchers, advertisers 'want to know about the young Black consumer, what products they use, what language they use, what to do in promotions, how to sponsor events, find out what interests them ... from there they look at evolving advertising from that.'[49]

In the past five years advertisers have sought to capitalize on the identification that exists between African and African-American youth. In-depth interviews with South African youth confirmed market researchers' suspicions that Black consumer habits are strongly oriented towards American products. According to South Africa's *Business Day*, 'Soweto's youths favour expensive, imported brand names despite a pervasive environment of poverty, unemployment, and crime.'[50] Research done by the Alternative Consultancy likewise showed that young people identified advertisements from Coke and Pepsi, the latter featuring NBA star Shaquille O'Neal, as well as commercials that 'featured rap music and dance sequences' as being amongst their favorites.

Marketers have identified three subcultures that, according to their estimates, as many as 60 percent of African youth identify strongly with. Two of the three, rappers and Italians, incorporate strong elements from African-American aesthetics. Advertisers have thus moved towards using images, models, and vernacular speech that recall very specific elements of these subcultures.[51] According to Lee Kotze of Research International:

some marketers seem to have a negative image of Black children, associating them with *poverty, violence, and AK-47s*. This stereotype disguises the fact that they are very much consumers in their own right, and as such are driven by a need to establish their own identity and belong to the group. This is why they are keen followers of Afro-American fashion trends, and accordingly they look to the USA to provide role models ... . [Y]outh strongly identify with all that is Afro-American. ... [S]imilarity between Black South African children and American children is extremely strong, especially in the context of popular Afro-American culture.[52]

Market research also confirmed that radio is the medium with the most loyal following amongst African youth and music is the preeminent form of transatlantic, inter-cultural communication. Long playing records simply gave way to compact discs, music videos, advertising jingles, and movie soundtracks. The Jupiter Drawing Room, a South African market research firm, determined that 'the major influence is African-American. ... The only White group that stylistically corresponds with a Black group is the "Homeboys," with both having based their style on American rap culture.'[53] Lee Kotze of Research International agreed that 'Snoop Doggy Dogg is, for example, more popular than Luckey Dube.'[54]

Despite the immense enthusiasm for American products and American culture, South African youth have an exceptionally strong commitment to local music. The Alternative Consultancy (1997), which interviewed 1,500 Black South Africans, found that 78 percent listed kwaito, an indigenous form of rap music, as their favorite form of music.[55] Research done by the Jupiter Drawing Room (1996) and the South African Advertising Research Association (1997) confirms their findings. Their loyalty has not deterred advertisers in any way, however. As media critic Robert McChesney explains,

the notion that corporate media firms are merely purveyors of US culture is ever less plausible as the media system becomes increasingly concentrated, commercialized and globalized. The global media system is better understood as one that advances corporate and commercial interests and values and denigrates or ignores that which cannot be incorporated into its mission.[56]

Thus, when South African slang, once the sole province of inner city youth became popularized in kwaito lyrics, advertisers quickly seized on its potential. Hugh Dellios explains:

What was the slang of rebellion in apartheid Soweto, known as 'tsotsitaal' or 'iscamtho,' now is the 'kwaito lingo' or 'ringas' by which youths searching for an identity in a new era of freedom judge each other's status. Speak it and prove yourself authentic, proud of your township roots. The dialect, frowned upon by some guardians of grammar and speech, nevertheless appears on advertisers' billboards. ... The roadside billboards that blare kwaito terms may be the best indication that the street tongue has become more acceptable. Over the last two years, advertisers have tried to reach out to Soweto youths as they recognized the consumptive potential of the new generation.[57]

The peaceful coexistence of a thriving local performance culture, which is strongly supported by local people, and a firm commitment to American consumerism highlights the inadequacy of trying to understand these processes using simple categories like 'cultural imperialism' vs. 'local resistance.' Rather, understanding these dynamics requires that we analytically separate the notion of culture as the 'lifeways of a people' from the notion of culture as an ideology (i.e. the culture of consumerism). The post-apartheid state has played an active role in protecting and advancing culture in the former sense, yet it has been powerless to halt the hegemony of the latter ideology. As will be discussed in the final section, the existence of a strong commitment to local music is no guarantee against colonization by global media firms. Indeed, in what might be the ultimate irony of globalization, so-called 'third world' audiences' preferences for locally made fare, rather than sounding a death knell for global media conglomerates, just might be the key to securing their ultimate hegemony.

CLASS, CULTURE, AND THE POLITICAL ECONOMY OF CONSUMPTION

It should be obvious from the above that South Africans have a strong commitment to locally produced music. Amongst young people, this commitment owes a great deal to the aggressive stance taken by the ANC after assuming the mantle of power in 1994. One of their first legislative acts was to dramatically increase the number of private radio stations from 30 to 115. Many of the new stations were community service oriented and broadcast in local languages. Section 53(c) of the Independent Broadcast Authority (IBA) Act put into law what constituted South African music. Music could only be considered local if the lyrics were written and performed by a South African. In the interest of promoting local music cultures, the state has imposed 'local music quotas' of 20–40 percent, depending upon the type of radio broadcaster (ICASA 2000). Local Content Regulations required radio stations to submit regular logs detailing all the music broadcast on a daily basis. As a result, local Black artists' music sales rose 215 percent in the first three months of 1999 as compared to 1998 (ICASA 2000). The commercial music industry has cooperated by markedly expanding its production of local music, while simultaneously re-releasing previously recorded songs.[58]

Most critiques of cultural globalization focus on the ways in which economic inequalities between nations, in particular American economic dominance vis-à-vis most nations, threaten the cultural integrity and independence of developing nations. The argument made by Jameson is typical:

American mass culture, associated as it is with money and commodities, enjoys a prestige that is perilous for most forms of domestic cultural production, which either find themselves wiped out—as with local film and television production—or co-opted and transformed beyond recognition, as with local music. We do not here sufficiently notice—because we do not have to notice—the significance, in the GATT and NAFTA negotiations, of the cultural clauses, and of the struggle between immense US cultural interests, who want to open up foreign borders to American film, television, music, and the like, and foreign nation-states who still place a premium on the preservation and development of their national languages and cultures and attempt to limit the damages—both material and social—caused by the leveling power of American mass culture.[59]

Jameson's analysis, though absolutely correct, fails to consider what impact local class dynamics might have on this process. Specifically, it fails to consider the ways in which class inequalities within developing nations influence consumption patterns such that the hegemony of global media is strengthened precisely *because* of the ways in which class inequality predisposes certain forms of consumption. Paradoxically, it is precisely the strong commitment of African people to local music that has been instrumental in helping global media conglomerates make strong inroads into the local market.

The South African entertainment industry is marked by a curious paradox, likely to be found in any developing nation. Although local cultures are extremely popular, they are not necessarily economically profitable because their core constituency tends to consume them in ways that evade the market. Simply put, most local people have limited incomes and can only afford to buy pirated cassettes. People who do not have high incomes are the primary purchasers of local music, thus making piracy particularly damaging to the local music market. According to the Recording Industry of South Africa (RISA), 'piracy has devastated the local music market.'

Profit margins in the industry dictate that record companies must sell a sizable number of local recordings to cover the increased costs associated with local recording and video production. Because South Africans' appreciation for local music is not expressed in ways that are captured by the market, however, local South African labels are hard pressed to compete with international labels, who have the resources to withstand losing a much larger portion of their profits to piracy. Thus it is precisely because the most enthusiastic supporters of local music are local people, and because they consume local music in ways that reflect their marginal economic status, that local music may ultimately fall entirely under the control of global conglomerates—a cruel paradox indeed.

Thus, the issue of cultural resilience in the face of globalization also must engage with the question of how to define cultural resilience and survival. Is it enough that local musicians are given the ability to write, perform, and produce music, which in turn is enthusiastically consumed by local communities if, as in South Africa, transnational corporations are able to take over the production and distribution of local music, thus eliminating the local recording industry? If a song is written and performed by local artists, but produced and owned by foreign conglomerates, to what degree is it still 'local'? Sony Music, for example, 'is hoping that a powerful thrust into the local market will boost its fortunes.'[60] Cultural resilience and survival does not in any way guarantee that the ownership and control of the commercial aspects of the local music industry will remain in local hands.

Likewise, the fact that artists from disenfranchised communities have pioneered profitable new musical genres is no guarantee that they or the communities they represent will reap the material benefits. Kelley could easily have been describing South Africa when he observed that 'Black music is cultural capital that has been turned into a valuable commodity outside Black control.'[61] Black South African cultural workers have, from time immemorial, been subject to the same exploitative conditions as other South African workers, despite the more glamorous nature of their profession. Many African singing sensations from the 1940s, 50s, and 60s have little or nothing to show for their fame. A 1998 article in the *Star* entitled 'From 60s Stars to 90s Beggars' detailed how record companies systematically exploited Black performers.[62] To their credit the current generation of South African performers is, unlike their predecessors, aware of this history and has taken active steps to avoid repeating it. Skeem, a popular kwaito group, burnt their contract in the street outside Sony's Johannesburg headqurters in 1998, claiming that the company had misled them and capitalized on their ignorance. In an interview with the *Sowetan* in November of 1997, Doc Shebelezza, a South African musician, specifically referenced this history as having motivated him to start his own production company that year. 'Having taken a good look at myself and the music industry, I realized that our old music greats almost died as paupers because of exploitation. I do not want to fall into that trap, and I do not want to see our young acts falling prey to unscrupulous companies.'[63]

Kwaito artists like Arthur Mafokate and M'Du, owners of the production companies 999 Records and M'Du Productions, have established themselves as producers. Young Black entrepreneurs have also made inroads as owners of independent record companies like Kalawa Records and Ghetto Ruff. 'The presence of independent companies is a hallmark of kwaito's evolution, signifying, in the case of people like Mafokate and M'Du, a growing Black economic empowerment within the music industry.'[64] However, like their African-American counterparts, they do not control distribution, a key component of the music industry. The American and South African music industries operate using similar models, Black producers recruit and produce talent, while the major labels control distribution. Robert McChesney described how the major media players have been able to facilitate their domination of music markets the world over, even where strong traditions of protection for domestic media and cultural industries exist.

> When audiences prefer locally made fare, the global media corporations, rather than flee in despair, globalize their production. This is perhaps most visible in the music industry. ... The five media TNCs that dominate the world's recorded music market are busy establishing local subsidiaries in places where people are totally committed to local music. ... Sony has led the way in establishing distribution deals with independent music companies from around the world.[65]

EMI's strategy in South Africa typifies this trend. EMI has signed partnership deals with several Black artists who have established themselves both as major artists and as producers of new stars. According to Goldstuck this production strategy is 'fast becoming a model for operating in the township music market.'[66] Levine agrees that 'all the major record companies have taken an unprecedented interest in small, independent companies, buying them out ... in a bid to stake their ground.'[67] Thus, although kwaito and rap music were aptly described by Madondo as 'everything that gets under the skin of the Black youth—their hope for life in a hopeless situation, their zeal, their aspirations for fun and the good life, and, perhaps most significantly, their craving to announce their presence in the worldwide scheme of things,'[68] whether these postcolonial Black artists will be able to finally end the 'neo-colonial' relationship that has historically existed between Black artists and the global music industry remains to be seen.

CONCLUSION

The last three decades have witnessed renewed interest in the study of cultural formations that transcend specific territorial boundaries. It is now commonly accepted that the 'local' is no longer the principal staging ground for culture. Because the globalization of American culture is so frequently conflated with the spread of a monolithic consumer culture, however, the class and ethnic differences within core nations that influence the dynamics of how cultural products are produced, and their subsequent global dissemination, are given short theoretical shrift. Likewise, the class and ethnic differences within periphery nations, which structure the dynamics of how cultural products for the 'core' are assimilated and indigenized, are given scant theoretical attention. My analysis of the incorporation of African-American culture into the South African symbolic order has, thus, delineated two levels of analysis that are critical for understanding the dynamics of cultural globalization. First, we must delineate the socio-political and socio-economic relations that inform the development of national cultures. Second, we must look at the socio-political and socio-economic factors that enable and influence the global dissemination of culture. The South African example likewise points to the necessity of taking our analyses beyond simply looking at whether or not local cultures are thriving in the face of American imports, turning instead to consider the extent to which local cultures are being put in the service of global objectives. This type of multi-dimensional analysis allows us to connect symbolic themes to socio-structural and socio-relational matters without reducing the former to the latter or vice versa.

DISCOGRAPHY

Black Noise, 'Black Thing,' on *Pumping Loose da Juice* [compact disc]. Johannesburg: Tusk (1992)

Boom Shaka, 'It's About Time,' on *Boom Shaka* [compact disc]. Johannesburg: Tusk (1994)

Boom Shaka, 'Nkosi Sikelel' iAfrica,' on *Words of Wisdom* [compact disc]. Johannesburg: Polygram (1998)

Brasse Vannie Kaap, 'Laat dat Rik,' on *BVK* [compact disc]. Johannesburg: Ghetto Ruff (1997)

Prophets of Da City, 'Understand Where I'm Coming From,' on *Age of Truth* [compact disc]. Johannesburg: Ghetto Ruff (1993)

Prophets of Da City, 'Dallah Flet 2,' on *Age of Truth* [compact disc]. Johannesburg: Ghetto Ruff (1993)

NOTES

1. George Lipsitz, *Dangerous Crossroads: Popular Music, Postmodernism, and the Poetics of Place* (London: Verso, 1994).
2. Veit Erlmann, *African Stars: Studies in Black South African Performance* (Chicago: University of Chicago Press, 1991); Charles Hamm, *Afro-American Music, South Africa, and Apartheid* (New York: Institute for Studies in American Music, 1988).
3. David B. Coplan, *In Township Tonight: South Africa's Black City Music and Theatre* (Johannesburg: Raven Press, 1985); Zine Magubane, 'The Impact of African-American Cultural Practices on South Africa,' in Paul Zeleza (ed.), *Leisure in Urban Africa* (Trenton: Africa World Press, 2002), pp. 297–319; Ntongela Masilela, 'New Negroism and New Africanism: The Influence of United States Modernity on South African Modernity,' *Black Renaissance/Renaissance Noir*, Vol. 2, No. 2 (Summer 1999), pp. 46–59; Rob Nixon, *Homelands, Harlem, and Hollywood: South African Culture and the World Beyond* (London: Routledge, 1994).
4. Christopher Ballantine, *Marabi Nights: Early South African Jazz and Vaudeville* (Johannesburg: Raven Press, 1993), p. 13.
5. Benjamin Barber, *Jihad vs. McWorld* (New York: Ballantine, 1995); Robert Goldman and Stephen Papson, *Nike Culture* (London: Sage, 1998); George Ritzer, *The McDonaldization Thesis* (London: Sage, 1998); Ziauddin Sardar, *Postmodernism and the Other* (London: Pluto, 1998); O. Seda, 'Understanding Popular Culture in Post-Colonial Africa,' *Southern Africa Political and Economic Monthly* (April 1998), pp. 19–22.
6. Arjun Appadurai, *Modernity at Large: Cultural Dimensions of Globalization* (New York: Routledge, 1996); Homi Bhabha, *The Location of Culture* (London: Verso, 1994); Stuart Hall, 'The Local and the Global: Globalization and Ethnicity,' in Anthony King (ed.),

Culture, Globalization, and the World System (Minneapolis: University of Minnesota Press, 1997), pp. 19–39; Lipsitz, *Dangerous Crossroads*.

7. Ritzer, *McDonaldization*, p. 89.
8. Appadurai, *Modernity at Large*, p. 31.
9. Paul Gilroy, *The Black Atlantic* (Cambridge: Harvard University Press, 1993), p. 1.
10. David Brion Davis, *The Problem of Slavery in the Age of Revolution* (Ithaca: Cornell University Press, 1975); Orlando Patterson, *Slavery and Social Death* (Cambridge: Harvard University Press, 1982).
11. Gilroy, *Black Atlantic*, p. 56.
12. Michael Eric Dyson, *Between God and Gangsta Rap* (New York: Oxford University Press, 1996), p. 178.
13. Lipsitz, *Dangerous Crossroads*, p. 34.
14. Norman Kelley, 'Rhythm Nation: The Political Economy of Black Music,' *Black Renaissance/Renaissance Noir*, Vol. 2, No. 2 (Summer 1999), p. 10.
15. Tariq Muhammad, 'Hip Hop Moguls: Beyond the Hype,' *Black Enterprise*, Vol. 30, No. 5 (December 1999), p. 78.
16. Kelley, 'Rhythm Nation,' p. 16.
17. Dyson, *Between God*, p. 181.
18. Nixon, *Homelands, Harlem, and Hollywood*, p. 32.
19. Tricia Rose, *Black Noise: Rap Music and Black Culture in Contemporary America* (Middletown, CT: Wesleyan University, 1994), p. 21.
20. Patrick Bond, *Elite Transition: From Apartheid to Neoliberalism in South Africa* (London: Pluto, 2000); Ian Goldin and Chris Heymans, 'Moulding a New Society: The RDP in Perspective,' in Gitanjali Maharaj (ed.), *Between Unity and Diversity: Essays on Nation-Building in Post-Apartheid South Africa* (Cape Town: David Philip, 1999), pp. 109–22.
21. Farai Chideya, 'Africa's Hip Hop Generation,' *Vibe* (April 1997), p. 67.
22. Adam Levine, 'A Tribe Called Kwaito,' *Elle*, Vol. 3, No. 4 (July 1998), p. 53.
23. Diane Coetzer, 'Kwaito Shakes the Nation,' *Business Day*, July 17, 1998.
24. Ibid.
25. Angela Impey, 'Resurrecting the Flesh? Reflections on Women in Kwaito,' *Agenda*, No. 49 (2001), p. 45.
26. Levine, 'A Tribe Called Kwaito,' p. 53.
27. Hugh Dellios, 'Multilingual South Africa Taking up a New Dialect: Evolving Fruit Salad Called Kwaito Lingo Rooted in Rebellion,' *Chicago Tribune*, February 9, 1998.
28. Levine, 'A Tribe Called Kwaito,' p. 53.
29. Gary Baines, 'Catalyst or Detonator? Local Music Quotas and the Current South African Music Explosion,' *Social Dynamics*, Vol. 24, No. 1 (Winter 1998), p. 83.
30. Ballantine, *Marabi Nights*, p. 6.
31. Chideya, 'Africa's Hip Hop,' p. 67.
32. Gilroy, *Black Atlantic*, p. 71.
33. *eVibe* (October/November 1997), p. 64.
34. Levine, 'A Tribe Called Kwaito,' p. 55.
35. Gilroy, *Black Atlantic*, p. 54.
36. Impey, 'Resurrecting the Flesh,' p. 47.
37. Ibid., p. 48.
38. B. Madondo, 'Nkosi Sikelei' Boom Shaka,' *Sunday Life Magazine*, May 31, 1998, p. 5.
39. Impey, 'Resurrecting the Flesh,' p. 46.
40. *eVibe* (October/November 1997), p. 64.
41. Gilroy, *Black Atlantic*, p. 54.
42. Masao Miyoshi, 'Globalization, Culture, and the University,' in Frederic Jameson and Masao Miyoshi (eds), *The Cultures of Globalization* (Durham, NC: Duke University Press, 1998), p. 239.

43. M. Ebersohn, 'Facing a One-To-One Future,' paper presented at *Marketing to Kids and Youth in South Africa*, Braamfontein, South Africa (April 23–24, 1996), p. 2.
44. J. Pearce, 'Targeting the Xpresser Generation,' *Mail and Guardian*, October 13, 1997, available at <http://www.mg.co.za/mg/news/oct13xpress.html>.
45. Lee Kotze, 'Identifying the Emerging Black Children's Market,' paper presented at *Marketing to Kids and Youth in South Africa*, Braamfontein, South Africa (April 23–24, 1996), p. 2.
46. Levine, 'A Tribe Called Kwaito,' p. 53.
47. Tony Koenderman, Understanding the Youth Market, *Financial Mail*, November 21, 1997, available at <http://www.fm.co.za/97/1121/admark/ad4.htm>.
48. Maria McCloy, 'Kangols, Kwaito and Ads,' *Mail and Guardian*, November 21–27, 1997, p. 8.
49. Ibid.
50. J. Lieb, 'Young Sowetans Still Aiming High,' *Business Day*, October 12, 2000, available at <http://www.bdfm.co.za>.
51. Dellios, 'Multilingual South Africa'; McCloy, 'Kangols.'
52. Kotze, 'Black Children's Market,' p. 13.
53. Pearce, 'Xpresser Generation.'
54. Kotze, 'Black Children's Market,' p. 13.
55. McCloy, 'Kangols.'
56. Robert McChesney, 'The New Global Media,' *The Nation*, Vol. 269, No. 18 (November 29, 1999), p. 11.
57. Dellios, 'Multilingual South Africa.'
58. Arthur Goldstuck, 'They Can See Clearly Now,' *Billboard*, Vol. 108, No. 14 (1996) pp. 60–5.
59. Frederic Jameson, 'Notes on Globalization as a Philosophical Issue,' in Jameson and Miyoshi (eds), *The Cultures of Globalization*, p. 59.
60. Goldstuck, 'They Can See,' p. 63.
61. Kelley, 'Rhythm Nation,' p. 19.
62. Aurelia Dyantyi, 'From 60s Stars to 90s Beggars,' *Saturday Star*, January 3, 1998.
63. E. Makhaya, 'Doc Shebelezza Grows,' *Sowetan* [Weekend pullout edition], November 7, 1997, p. 1.
64. Coetzer, 'Kwaito Shakes the Nation.'
65. McChesney, 'The New Global Media,' p. 11.
66. Goldstuck, 'They Can See,' p. 63.
67. Levine, 'A Tribe Called Kwaito,' p. 54.
68. Madondo, 'Nkosi Sikelei' Boom Shaka,' p. 4.

15

'Ni Wapi Tunakwenda': Hip Hop Culture and the Children of Arusha

Sidney J. Lemelle[1]

I want to know where I will go/I know where I come from
Where I'll go, I don't know/Let me tell you:
I'm looking for a passport now/I am going to stow away on a boat
Whereever I'll arrive/I will forget this African condition
I'm tired of home/I continue to be harassed

2 Proud[2]

On February 5, 1967, President Julius K. Nyerere of Tanzania announced that a new political ideology, *ujamaa* ('familyhood' or less poetically, socialism), would henceforth become the cornerstone of the country's national consciousness. This pronouncement, known as the Arusha Declaration, nationalized the economy's key financial, manufacturing, and trading sectors, and along with the *Mwongozo* or party guidelines of 1971, promised to halt political corruption and the private accumulation of wealth by party and government leaders.[3] The Declaration also held out the promise that all Tanzanians, no matter what their background, would share the fruits of the freedom struggle, while being protected against neo-colonialism and exploitation at the hands of global imperialism.[4] Years later, when cynical politicians had all but abandoned the principles of *ujamaa*, the spirit embodied in Nyerere's ideas would be reproduced by an unlikely source: rappers and hip hop artists in the streets of Tanzania. Nyerere, affectionately called *Mwalimu*, or teacher by the people, might not have appreciated this popular art form, especially with its slang-laced language and caustic political indictments, but would have recognized the spirit of their message: *uhuru, umoja na ujamaa* (freedom, unity and familyhood). Indeed, his concept of *ujamaa* created the social environment for the development of hip hop culture by the children of Arusha.

In 2000, over 30 years after the Arusha Declaration, the ethnomusicologist Werner Graebner described a scene in Dar es Salaam that captured the significance of hip hop culture and the cultural struggles of the time:

Around Dar streets there are many sign-writer kiosks sporting larger-than-life portraits of American rappers and hip hop artists like Tupac Shakur and Ice Cube. Young sign-painters use these images to advertise their trade and talents, identifying the role models of Tanzanian youth. The new Proposition points beyond Tanzania or Africa, as does one of the anthems of the new generation '*Ni Wapi Tunakwenda*,' (Where are we heading?) by Swahili rap star 2 Proud. 'I want to know where I will go/I know where I come from,/Where I'll go, I don't know/Let me tell you:/I'm looking for a passport now/I'm going to stow away on a boat/Where even I'll arrive,/I will forget this African condition/I'm tired of home/I continue to he harassed.'[5]

Woven together into this scene and the lyrics are a sense of anger and alienation, as well as a clear desire to seek a better life—whether inside the country or without. For years Tanzanians have traveled either as migrant laborers or merchant marines seeking a brighter future for themselves and their families. Today, despite the promises of politicians for a better life, individuals still tend to look to the outside—to Kenya, to Oman, to Europe—for hope. Indeed, borrowing directly from Swahili lore, Dar hip hop culture employs the concept of *msafiri* (the traveler) as a classic and reoccurring theme. However, what is needed to make sense of this complex metaphor of change and movement is a more nuanced understanding of Tanzanian society in the new millennium and how global complexities have compounded the contradictions of life. A key element, therefore, in deciphering how the society has reacted can be gained through an analysis of globalization and its effect on Tanzanian culture.[6]

In recent years scholars have written a great deal about the effects of globalization on world culture. In the older literature on Africa, the focus was primarily on U.S. imperialism, hegemony and the dissemination of its values, lifestyles and commodities. U.S. economic imperialism was inevitably accompanied by 'cultural imperialism' which scholars and activists saw as insidious because it threatened to completely subsume cultural differences throughout the Western world, not just in the third world 'economic periphery' but in Western Europe and Asia as well—creating the 'Coca Cola-ization' of world culture.[7] In contrast, postmodern theorists of today argue that cultural imperialism is not a monolithic force and that local cultures are able to absorb and 'indigenize' Western culture.[8] John Tomlinson, with Arjun Appadurai, J. Lull, and John B. Thompson, among others, notes the interaction between cultures and regions and how they typically involve active appropriation on the part of the affected group as it 'brings its own cultural resources to bear, in dialectical fashion, upon "cultural imports".' This 'indigenizing' process is of particular importance to cultural self-definition in an age of globalization, and Tomlinson acknowledges the power of 'indigenous' cultures to engage in 'intercultural negotiation.'[9]

This chapter will not repeat these debates on globalization since they are discussed extensively elsewhere. Instead, I will make use of the notion of the reformulation of global cultures within sets of specific localisms. More specifically, I will analyze how hip hop culture as a representation or signifier of 'Blackness' is played out in the African nation of Tanzania at a time when it was in the throes of creating a post-colonial nation-state. The study will illustrate that U.S. popular culture (in this case hip hop) has played a crucial role in influencing Tanzania since independence. Moreover, it will demonstrate that hip hop culture was not only a driving force behind the transformation of Black culture per se, but was a key element in informing the project of how to construct a nation, with all its incumbent considerations around ethnicity, gender, and class. As I hope to show, hip hop should not be underestimated as a force that helps to shape contemporary public debate and discourse on the political and economic landscape of Tanzania. In the process, this chapter will also help fill a lacuna in the scholarship on music and popular culture, which has neglected the global effects of hip hop on Africa when so much has been said about Europe and the U.S.

To grasp properly both the origins of Tanzanian hip hop culture, and the importance of its message, we must contextualize it within the historical contradictions of Tanzania's colonial and post-colonial society. Tanzania has a history of adopting and adapting cultural elements and incorporating them into its identity. In a colonial context this cultural dynamic contributed to its rich and diverse cultures, but also reflected contradictions of class, ethnicity, language, and gender.

In that regard hip hop and rap music are part of a historical continuum. Like other cultural forms and manifestations before them, both have been localized and indigenized to fit the political economic and social cultural realities of post-colonial/neo-colonial struggles, and both have served as avenues for artistic expression and political protest. Nationalism and the post-colonial state have, from the 1960s, played crucial roles in nurturing artistic expression and political protest. At the same time they have not been able to control its development, despite influencing it substantially. Likewise, the process of globalization has not meant a complete subsumption of hip hop to 'Americanization.' Imitation is a key element of hip hop culture and rap music, and by the 1990s innovation with Kiswahili and vernacular languages began the evolution of an independent and indigenous genre of music that typified the young descendants of the Arusha promise of *ujamaa*.

FROM RUMBA TO RAP

A bicycle has no say in front of a motorbike
A motorbike has no say in front of a car
A motorcar has no say in front of a train
The poor person has no rights
I am poor; I have no right to speak
Poor and weak before the powerful
Weak as long as the powerful likes
Remmy Ongala[10]

Prior to the advent of German and then later British colonialism, the musical traditions of Tanzania were a blend of many cultures.[11] The people of the East African coastal region had a long history of contact with the Persian Gulf, India, and Indonesia. Indigenous peoples blended these musical traditions with older Bantu and Khoisan traditions.[12] The European colonists introduced other cultural influences such as military band music and Christian church hymns. By the end of World War II, returning African soldiers also brought Cuban music to Tanzania and within a short time groups began to reproduce the sounds of the rumba beats.[13] Even after independence the fusion of African and Latin-American styles, called 'Swahili Jazz,' continued to be extremely influential and popular.[14]

In addition to musical changes, political and cultural issues began shifting at a dizzying pace in the early 1960s. In 1961, the former colony of Tanganyika declared independence from Britain; and within three years, in a show of Pan-African solidarity, mainland Tanganyika united with the island republic of Zanzibar creating the United Republic of Tanzania. After an uncertain beginning, *uhuru* (freedom) in Tanzania moved forward under the Tanganyika African National Union (TANU) and Nyerere's leadership. The government established the socialist policy of *ujamaa* as the means of building and solidifying a national identity. *Ujamaa* policy had several key components. First, as a way of uniting the more than 120 ethnic groups, Nyerere established Kiswahili as the lingua franca, and English as the second official language. Developing a nation-state *and* a 'national' culture became a major imperative for *Mwalimu* Nyerere. In 1962 he wrote: '... I believe culture is the essence and spirit of any nation. A country which lacks its own culture is no more than a collection of people without the spirit which makes them a nation. Of all the crimes of colonialism there is none worse than the attempt to make us believe we had no indigenous culture of our own.'[15] *Mwalimu* was adamant about recognizing the complex nature of what he viewed as cultural imperialism.[16]

In order to deal with some of the challenges and contradictions of building a nation-state and a national culture after 70 years of colonialism, Nyerere and TANU created the Ministry of National Culture and Youth. The new ministry, as imagined by Nyerere, would seek to create a new public space where Tanzanian popular culture could develop and flower. He intended to do this by promoting a sense of pride in 'Tanzanian' culture and incorporating the varied traditions and customs of *all* peoples of Tanzania, thus creating a national culture. This was a pragmatic approach. Nyerere understood that it would be impossible to distill out the 'indigenous' cultures after centuries of outside influence. He recognized that 'A nation which refuses to learn from foreign cultures is nothing but a nation of idiots and lunatics ... [but] To learn from other cultures does not mean we should abandon our own.'[17]

Besides establishing *ujamaa* and enacting various cultural policies, the government banned most foreign music on national programs in 1973.[18] In addition, Radio Tanzania Dar Es Salaam (RTD) became critical to the cultural life of the country by nurturing Tanzania's music scene. Since there was a chronic shortage of studio space and production equipment, RTD became the main advocate of the country's musicians, by default. In 1974 the government also created a national music council BAMAUTA (*Baraza la Muzikila Taifa*) which coordinated official national music policies, controlling musical instrument imports and issuing club and discotheque licenses.[19] Out of this regulated cultural atmosphere many bands emerged and a live entertainment scene thrived. With the Tanzanian government promoting live entertainment, Dar es Salaam became the incubator for new African popular music styles. Here musicians from the Congo imbibed Swahili coastal and local music, mixed with Taarab from Zanzibar, and local versions of 'AfroJazz' developed.[20]

The evolution of RTD and BAMAUTA, as imagined by Nyerere, required strict government planning and controls of popular culture. This over-determined relationship was a hallmark of *ujamaa* and its Maoist influences. For Nyerere, it was necessary to build a 'people's culture' for the workers and peasants; primarily as a safeguard against the reemergence of bourgeois culture that served the interests of imperialism and neo-colonialism.[21] Therefore matters of class proved an important issue even if Nyerere's concept of class in Tanzanian society was somewhat idealized.[22]

Throughout its evolution in the post-colonial era, Swahili culture, particularly its musical culture, was adoptive and practical, taking ideas and institutions and adapting them for its own use.[23] In the case of Tanzania, we can at best speak of Swahili 'cultures,' never just a single culture, and within those cultures there were class divisions. In early post-colonial Tanzania class divisions were prominent, while ethnic and gender divisions were secondary, yet all played a part in the rise of rap and hip hop culture.[24]

RAP MUSIC AND HIP HOP CULTURE IN TANZANIA

'In Kenya, man eats man. In Tanzania, man eats nothing.'
Street saying[25]

By the late 1980s few politicians thought or spoke of *ujamaa*, or the principles of African socialism anymore. In post-Nyerere years, young Tanzanians had no concrete conception of these ideas, they only knew that their leaders had failed to create a 'modern independent nation-state' out of a former colony.[26] The promise of economic development and complete political independence gave way to unemployment, empty shelves in stores and people standing in bread lines. With the abandonment of *ujamaa*, Tanzania passed through years of severe hardship. Under instruction from the International Monetary

Fund (IMF) and World Bank, government officials introduced austerity measures in the form of so-called Structural Adjustment Programs (SAPs).[27] The period of 'liberalization' opened the country to the same neo-colonial practices Nyerere and his parties TANU and *Chama cha Mapinduzi* (CCM) had fought against. With the societal 'safety net' of *ujamaa* withdrawn, many Tanzanians fell through the cracks in society.[28] Millions of young Tanzanians faced an uncertain future: unemployment, lack of education, malnutrition and disease, in particular diseases of poverty: cholera and HIV. The streets of Dar es Salaam suddenly became '*Kama Nairobi*' ('like Nairobi').[29] The increased number of *wahuni* (criminals or thugs) threatened the balance in society in new ways. It is not surprising that most Tanzanians viewed these conditions, especially the rise in crime, and the almost simultaneous rise of rap music, as a single phenomenon. The political establishment and older generation did not accept rap music or *uhuni* music—since it became synonymous with disruption and anti-social behavior. Yet for the younger generation, traditional Swahili music did not address contradictions of the 'liberalized' Tanzanian economy.

The early to mid 1980s also witnessed the 'mythological birth' of hip hop culture and rap music in Tanzania, although there is no consensus about when hip hop culture arrived in Tanzania or when rap music began to gain the attention of Dar es Salaam youth.[30] Writing about this early period, journalist Ramadhani Mponjika (aka rapper 'Chief' Rhymson) detailed the four rudiments of hip hop culture in Tanzania: breakdancing (or b-boying), graffiti art, Djing, and rapping.[31] According to Mponjika, rap music was by far the greatest influence of hip hop culture in Tanzania, particularly DJ competitions, which he believes provided the main stimulus for the birth of hip hop culture.[32] This was particularly popular in Zanzibar because unlike the mainland, which had no local TV, the island had television that broadcast these competitions. Early MCs Young Millionaire, Conway Francis, and Fresh-XE united to form 3-Power Crew, one of the first crews. In the early days of Dar es Salaam hip hop, rappers displayed their skills in rather informal public spaces: at school graduations, house parties, and picnics along the beaches at Oyster Bay and Bahari.[33] Thus hip hop culture in Tanzania, not unlike the U.S., began chiefly as an underground movement, meaning no radio exposure or nightclub engagements. Often promoters and artists recorded and copied music in makeshift studios using rudimentary equipment.[34]

Many early Tanzanian rappers actually began their careers outside the country. Dolasoul or 'Balozi' (Ahmed Dola), for example, was introduced to hip hop while living and studying in Nigeria. For young rappers like him, who had the support of his family, 'it was just for the fun, no money was involved.'[35] To them education came first, because it was the key to their achieving a better life. After returning from the UK with an advanced diploma in computer studies, Dolasoul 'got married to the rap game.'[36] He joined the Deplowmatz, whose other members Saigon and Tripp Dogg were all the sons of Tanzanian diplomats. Another example was Master J, an electronics engineer, who produced many of the early rap tapes.[37]

One of the earliest and most recognizable of the Tanzanian rappers was Saleh Jaber, who was born and raised in Dar es Salaam. In the early 1980s famous African-American rappers like LL Cool J, Big Daddy Kane and others, influenced Saleh J—as he began to call himself. By 1986, he knew and competed against artists like Eazy-B and Nigga One; both top Tanzanian rappers associated with the big annual rap battles 'Yo Rap Bonanza'—a talent show sponsored by local Indian merchants. The YRB competition, as it became known, marked a new era in the Swahili rap scene because many rappers from regions outside Dar es Salaam took part, indicating the spread of this genre. It is significant that most of these early MCs were not only urban dwellers, but gained fame rapping in English, a language they understood. Indeed artists like Saleh J added his own touch by taking English rhymes and translating them, however roughly, into Kiswahili.[38]

Rap music and hip hop culture arrived in Tanzania via African America through various filtered borrowings, adaptations, and transmissions. The early Tanzanian rappers included individuals who often 'studied and learned from' African-American rappers, sampled their popular rap beats and substituted Swahili lyrics for English rhymes.[39] Within a generation these rappers began to make innovations in style and content that would reflect Tanzanian culture and history. According to 'Chief' Rhymson of Kwanza Unit (KU), '... back then everyone was trying to copy the Americans, Run DMC, Public Enemy, those [sic] stuff. All I wanted was to have our own style, based on our own living, so I suggested that people should start rhyming in Swahili.'[40] He goes on to say, 'When we started in Kiswahili it was more like experimental, experimenting if we could rhyme in Kiswahili. More like a fusion.'[41]

Ironically, underground rap began, not in the poorer working-class areas of Dar, but in slightly better off parts of the city among those with access to the Western world through friends, family, and travel opportunities. They were the students who knew English and/or had relatives in the United Kingdom or Dubai who could buy them cassettes. These connections and linkages allowed them more access to rap music than the working class. But it should be kept in mind that the 'middle class' in Tanzania was not the same, in either its makeup or its access to means of production, as the middle class in the U.S. These were not the White middle-class youths of the U.S. suburbs who became the main consumers of rap music. While this may have been the case for some individuals, we should be careful with such generalizations not to characterize early rappers in terms of the class categories and structures of advanced capitalist nations.[42] Krister Malm, a Dutch ethnomusicologist, remarked that 'the rappers in Dar are no slum kids,' and that '[M]ost of them have secondary school education and a middle class background with access to recordings from the US.' In the early 1990s 'the fans of most Dar rap groups were mainly secondary school, college and university students.'[43]

From the beginning these 'middle-class' rappers and their fans transcended certain class and ethnic divisions. They spoke to the disappointment and anger of the younger generation, but increasingly of others too. One of the most famous rappers, Rhymson, denies that his group KU represents the middle- to upper-class Dar es Salaam residents, claiming to have come from the working-class areas of Dar es Salaam himself: 'It's all wrong. I, for one come from Temeke, we call it TMK.'[44] As K Singo, another member of KU, commented: '… It's a stereotype that rap was from middle-class kids.'[45] Likewise, their music was supported by different strata of the society and was no longer viewed as *'uhuni'* or 'gangsta' music and, therefore, undesirable and dangerous. This change took place in the early to mid 1990s, during the transition from underground to commercial acceptance, which also reflected major political-economic, social, and cultural shifts in Tanzanian society.

'SWAH RAP' AND ITS CONTRADICTIONS

By the end of 1992, three major hip hop crews—Villain Gangsters, Riders Posse, and Tribe-X—joined with some solo artists to form the powerful mega group (similar to the Wu-Tang Clan in the U.S.) Kwanza Unit. The idea of a joint venture group originated with Rhymson, the founding member of the group Villain Gangsters. Like Saleh J, these crews had heard, and were heavily influenced by, the latest underground hip hop songs by artists such as Gang Star, Big Daddy Kane, and N.W.A.[46] KU's plan was to follow in the footsteps of Afrika Bambaataa, the African-American hip hop innovator who built the universal Zulu Nation. The idea of 'Chief' Rhymson was to be the first group in Tanzania to establish its own 'hip hop nation.' Not unlike the Afrika Bambaataa model in the U.S., which had introduced youth to both rap music and hip hop culture in the ghettoes and barrios of New York, KU wanted to promote 'Kwanzanian nation' and ideals. According to one publication, 'Kwanza Unit [has] moved from a family to a tribe or rather an ethnic group called Kwanzania. Kwanzania is not made up of performing artists only but also fans, supporters and everyone who is down with KU ideas, within and outside Tanzania.'[47]

In an interview, KU's rapper K Singo explained: 'Kwanzania is a hypothetical country where Kwanzanians live. Everyone who is down with Kwanzanian living in Kwanzania.'[48] Accordingly, the biggest achievement for Rhymson, K Singo, and others would be 'the realisation of the Kwanzanian nation, a nation whose cementing force is hip hop culture. It is hip hop that will bind together the members of this nation. A unique nation with its own way of life, own culture, own values, own goals.'[49]

KU represented a form of hip hop nationalism, complete with an 'imagined community,' invented ideologies, and code of ethics. According to George Lipsitz, '[Bambaataa] used [the Zulu] example to inspire his efforts to respond to racism and class oppression in the U.S.A.' Like Bambaataa's Zulus, Kwanzanians would be 'heroic warriors resisting oppression.'[50] Metaphorically, members of the group distanced themselves from the harsh reality of Tanzania, with its widening contradictions, and instead set about constructing Kwanzania as a hip hop nation. Their emphasis was not so much on fighting racism, but recognizing and resisting class oppression—in particular working-class oppression; echoes of *ujamaa*.

The early 1990s marked the beginning of Swahili rap or what some called 'Swah' rap.[51] The struggling Tanzanian economy and the rise of 'hip hop nationalism' served as a broader socio-economic backdrop for the expansion of what MC Rhymson termed the 'Kiswacentric' concept. The group pioneered the idea of making sure that Kiswahili meanings were at the center of their rhymes. Even if their raps were in English they should never lose meaning when translated.[52] Kiswacentric aimed to give hip hop a politically charged cultural image, relating hip hop with the Tanzanian environment.

The use of Kiswahili in rapping is grounded in a historical and cultural context. Many of the signature aspects of rap music, including wordplay, risqué or suggestive puns and lyrical rhyme, are deeply inscribed in Swahili culture, in the form of Swahili parables, proverbs, and allegory called *mithali*. Shaaban Robert, a Muslim civil servant who wrote verse during the interwar period, remains the most famous Swahili poet.

> He was remarkably sensitive to contemporary issues [depression, war and colonialism] and could dramatize them in a literary form which established him as unofficial poet laureate and made his work a major historical source ... [He] seems to have inherited many coastal values, notably pride of race, love of Islam and the Swahili language, and delight in moralizing and verbal elaboration ... he valued rhyme above abstract principle.[53]

Swahili rap can be seen as a continuation of this tradition, combining essentials of observation, lamentation, and protest, as well as more modern elements of boasting and 'diss-ing.'

The Kiswacentric concept is important for understanding both the language and the meanings of Kiswahili rhymes as well as the complicated issue of tropes and their use in 'Swah' rap.[54] Their rhymes often include words and ideas borrowed from U.S. 'gangsta rappers,' though many of the ideas were foreign to Swahili culture. Their lyrics try to use Swahili ideas rather than simply reproducing African-American popular culture, or at least what music directors have promoted as African-American popular culture on Independent Television (ITV) and radio, i.e. full of manufactured and commodified tropes. Their hybridity challenges tradition, but also re-inscribes it. The challenge for Swahili musicians has been to balance tradition and originality, a particularly difficult proposition when considering rap as a diasporic idiom—even in its commodified form.

Unfortunately, Swahili rappers still fell prey on the one hand to many of the old commodified tropes of African-Americans,[55] and on the other challenges to their authenticity as rappers based on lingering stereotypes associated with African-American rap.[56] The group Jungle Crewz Posse has said in its own defense: 'Nowadays most rappers in third world countries are just copying from abroad. Rap is not copying from abroad ... we are not talking gun. If you show me a gun it would be hard for me to tell you which is the trigger. I know gun in movies, pictures. We are talking things that we know and see and understand.'[57] Likewise rapper Sam Stigillydaa has said, 'American rappers talk about crazy things—drinking, drugs, violence against women, American blacks killing blacks. I hope African rap stays African and doesn't turn crazy.'[58]

Much of the problem has been that Tanzanians, both artists and fans, have been experiencing 'gangsta rap' outside its historical context. Based on their sense of 'American music,' Tanzanians see the United States as a notoriously aggressive country that romanticizes both violence and crime. And while Tanzania is not without violence and crime, it does not have the same romantic notions. They see crime as caused by economic need, not greed or cupidity, and those who become criminals risk having people brand them as social outcasts or *wezi* (thieves) or, even worst risk their lives to 'instant justice' on the streets. Also, while there are several large gangs in Dar es Salaam, they bear little resemblance to the organized and well-armed drug dealing gangs in inner city America.[59] The popularity of the 'gangsta' style in the U.S. has not spread wholesale into the Swahili rap repertoire, because the circumstances that African-American rappers address remain rare in Tanzania. Nevertheless, Swahili rap continues to use the same stereotypical references that are endemic in global rap culture; the same discourse that dominant White U.S. society recognizes and perpetuates, which characterizes African Americans as symbols of deviance, dysfunction, and violent excessive behavior. These stereotypes also serve as constraints on wholesale acceptance of Western or diasporic rap and vulnerability to cultural imperialism. As Bourdieu has noted, 'Like ethnic or gender domination, cultural imperialism is a form of symbolic violence that relies on a relationship of constrained communication to extort submission.'[60] In this instance it consists of universalizing the 'particularisms' of one aspect of African Americans' historical experience of violence and making it 'misrecognized' and thus recognized as universal. According to rapper Abbas Maunda:

Most of the hip hoppers in America they talk violence. Me personally violence, I don't
take it. So I talk the way we live in Tanzania. Hip hop the way we live in Tanzania. This
hip hop can change by the way you're living. In America they live in violence. But we
live in an African way, hip hop in an African way. Just because Americans live in that
kind of way it should mean that we should live in that kind of way? No. We can live
the same hip hop, but in an African way.[61]

With regard to hip hop culture, Tanzanians have both recognized and
rejected most aspects of this hegemonic relationship, especially with regard
to accepting African-American 'particularisms' as universal—but have also
'indigenized' the artform.

Another set of 'particularisms' not addressed in Swahili raps have to do
with gendered language, specifically related to women. In African-American
'gangsta rap' these tropes—the so-called 'Booty/Bitch/Ho' narrative—are all
too prevalent and rappers, promoters, and record executives see these tropes as
the ticket to market viability. In Tanzania, where religion (particularly Islam)
is such a major part of the Swahili culture, such degrading characterizations
of women present difficulties. Swahili rappers face a critical problem: on the
one hand trying to fix 'authenticity' as gangsta rappers, while on the other
hand wanting to avoid being typecast with many African hip hop groups as
'gangsta wannabes,' simply mimicking their Western counterparts. Positive
Black Soul (PBS), a rap group from Senegal who perform throughout Africa,
summed this problem up best:

[Many] African crews will dress like, behave like, talk like and try to sound like the
African-American rap artists. Some now go to the extent of talking trash, calling
women b*****s and h*s, claiming how they have all these women they sleep with
etc etc ... Most of these albums covers always seem to have the rapper(s) frowning
into the camera, the gold and diamond chains, bracelets and teeth, the pit bulls or
alligators on leashes and maybe the big booty women in bikini/thongs ... common
[sic], who are we kidding, you know exactly what the music will sound like, you know
that that CD is not worth jack![62]

But this resistance to mimicry has been eroded now that rap groups from
Europe, South Africa and the Congo (formerly Zaire), often imitating
African-American rappers, have been receiving significant radio and TV
airplay in Tanzania. In their songs and rap videos, particularly those
from the Congo and South Africa, such characteristic language tropes
and lewd depictions of women are more common. But increasingly (since
the Tanzanian state deregulated the airwaves), the proliferation of such
representations has increased—even amongst Swahili rappers.[63]

In 2001 the rapper Dully Sykes released a recording entitled 'Nyambizi'
(slang for a large voluptuous woman), which contained explicitly sexual
references:

Because she was drunk, she wasn't shy anymore, this is what she said:
'Dully why don't you get a room for us' (Hidaya/female voice)
I went to the receptionist and paid for the room
Then *Nyambizi* and I went to the room, we started with the foreplay
I felt like it was time for us to have sex, I asked her if she was ready for it,
She said 'little kid have you eaten already?' (Hidaya)
Aah! *Nyambizi* can't you feel sorry for me? I'm tired of jackin' off.
Please give it to me.
'Dully I feel sorry for you, OK go turn off the light and come and eat me'
    (Hidaya)
I did what she told me just to get what I wanted. Oh *Nyambizi*, a big
    mama from Tanga, she was wearing beads around her waist.
Though she was big, she was very flexible, she was so good I don't know
Where she got that from. I couldn't tell that much because her eyes were
    shut
We did it till dawn, she didn't want me to stop, we did it without a
    condom.[64]

Shortly thereafter, both public and private stations refused to air the song. Private capitalists like ITV and Clouds FM recognized the historical and cultural norms related to cursing and 'vulgar' lyrics, particularly in the age of HIV/AIDS awareness.[65] Ironically, the song continued to be requested and sold. In 2004 the rapper Crazy GK released the album *Nitakufaje* and simultaneously launched the group East Coast Team. Their video *Ama Zangu, Ama Zao* (featuring Lady JD) was so provocative that it was almost censored by the government.[66]

At the same time, Tanzanian media were slow to embrace the female rappers who might offer a gendered voice and a counter-narrative in the public sphere. Not surprisingly, there are only a few female Kiswahili rappers in East Africa. Among the early popular Tanzanian female hip hop artists are Dataz, Lady Lou, Bad Gear, SJ and Aunt Su (formerly of Da Struggling Islanders) and Bad G with younger rappers like Dineh of Fortune Tellers, Sist-fedap, G-Dry, Sister P and Zey B, as well as artists who mix genres like Unique Sisters, Ray C (Taarab/R&B) Farida, Pauline Zongo, Lady JD (R&B/Rap), and K-Lyinn (R&B/Zouk). Among Kenya's most notable female Kiswahili rappers are Nazizi, Ffyonna, and the Nubian Motown Crew, Necessary Noise. The most obvious difficulty facing female rappers is the notion that MCing and DJing are directly associated with 'hooliganism' and 'masculinity.' Tuni of the Nubian Motown Crew noted that while females were encouraged by the group, they 'were too surprised at our entry into a male dominated field.' She added that 'many girls shy away from engaging in rap due to the attitude that rap is a male thing and is associated with gangs, violence and all manner of evil, though such is not so much in countries like Kenya.'[67]

In East Africa, Swahili rappers, especially women have traditionally avoided issues dealing directly with sexuality. However, this is changing. Some groups like Nubian Motown have 'advised husbands to refrain from extra-marital affairs'—an obvious reference to AIDS awareness and prevention. Likewise, the Bongo rapper Bad Gear (Witness Mwaijaga) deals with 'love, about how we can help out the women, about how we deal with HIV.' In her most popular song 'Demu Akijileta' (Women Are Coming On When Women Offer Themselves) she says, 'If she's coming on, but she don't want to eat sugar in a plastic bag, you'd better put your pants on, because the disease is the bad one' (i.e. if a woman is coming on to you, but does not want you to use a condom, you'd better stop because AIDS is deadly). In another one of her hits, 'Unanisuuza' (You Are Cleaning Me Up, slang for you are BS'ing me), she raps first in Kiswahili, then Kinyakyusa, the language of her ethnic group, and sings the chorus in both. The song asserts there are three kinds of man—those who love you, those who beat you, and those who only 'open your beer'—and it has struck a chord with the women who are beginning to question these social relationships. Bad Gear sees her work as a positive force. She believes hip hop can help educate the naive kids, particularly the young girls, who are migrating to the city with few opportunities other than as barmaids or prostitutes.[68] But female rappers and performers remain the exception even in this era of transition in Tanzania's hip hop culture.

By the late 1990s, hardcore 'gangsta' type groups such as G.W.M (Gangstaz With Matatizo), Hardblasters, N.W.P. (Niggaz With Power), Rough Niggaz, Bantu Pound Gangster, and Hardcore Unit were continuing to use Swahili or 'Kiswacentric' slang to stress street knowledge and self-awareness. But they, along with other groups, have started to move away from 'gangsta rap' and towards more politically cognizant themes that criticize class and gender oppression/exploitation, misuse of political power, and neo-colonialism.[69] Even though the names of Tanzanian rap groups appear similar to African-American 'gangsta rap' groups, their themes are defined by local urgencies. In short, the Tanzanian music industry as a whole, not unlike the U.S. and global market, is replete with contradictions within and between the different genres of rap.[70]

NI WAPI TUNAKWENDA? ... UTAONE (WHERE ARE WE HEADED? ... YOU WILL SEE)

In songs by Tanzanian rappers in the late 1990s, a number of artists developed an oppositional discourse, using themes and ideas that draw directly on the African-American experience and Black popular culture, but localized to fit the Tanzanian situation. This period saw the development of 'reality' rap or 'Bongo Flava' rap. 'Bongo' (Swahili for smart or clever) was the slang name for Dar es Salaam, the implication being that individuals have to be smart to survive in the city.[71] Many Bongo rappers expressed opposition to the social, political, and economic system supported by the Tanzanian government. In particular, they questioned the sincerity of post-*ujamaa* Tanzanian politicians and their anti-imperialist rhetoric.

In 1995, while Tanzania was still undergoing political, economic, and socio-cultural changes, international finance threw another element into the mix.[72] As mentioned earlier, in that year government officials allowed television broadcasting, which had been available on Zanzibar for a decade, to develop on the Tanzanian mainland. With the encouragement and support of World Bank policies, a local entrepreneur named Reginald Abraham Mengi founded IPP and its subsidiaries Independent Television (ITV) and Radio One.[73] In essence the government had relinquished partial control of the airwaves, thereby 'liberalizing' and 'privatizing' the public sphere by local corporate capitalists in Tanzania.[74] Yet, unlike the United States where rap music is used to commercialize everything from soft drinks to batteries, in 1990s Tanzania the voices of dissent had not yet been marketed 'and manipulated' over the airwaves. Thus for most Bongo Flava rap artists it was essential that their message remained 'meaningful and socially useful.'[75]

One of the most popular voices of dissent to rise in Tanzanian rap was an MC named 2 Proud, aka Mr. II or, as he is referred to today, Sugu. He began life as Joseph Mbilinyi, and, until 1997, was a clerk for British Petroleum in Dar es Salaam. He gave up his job to become one of the most streetwise Swahili lyricists in Bongo Flava. In a relatively short period of time, his posse track, 'Ndani ya Bongo' (Inside the Bongo/Hood), became a youth anthem with its use of Swahili slang to promote pride in the emerging urban culture.[76] The lyric for his wildly popular song 'Hali Halisi' graphically explained this sense. In this rap he points out that politicians are aware that life is painfully difficult in Tanzania, '... even the president knows.' He goes on to show the unfair and oppressive nature of the nation's police, penal, and judicial systems:

> Everyday is us against the police and the police against us
> The judge at the court is waiting for us
> The prison officer is waiting for us

Meanwhile this 'Hali Halisi,' or real situation, is waiting for them. But the real question is how much longer will people keep 'smiling all the way.' People are getting fed up with the same old self-serving and 'fake' politicians:

> I see same faces, same political leaders
> From the time I was at school to now
> Don't play with politics, politics is a dirty game
> They want to be famous, many of politicians in Bongo are fake

Increasingly, Tanzanian society is tattered and torn, and while politicians say 'Don't worry, no problem' the real situation, is:

> Many friends of mine are in a jail cell for they don't have work
> Some of my sisters don't like to be prostitutes
> They don't like to be hookers
> So many educated people but no employment
> No more allowance to teachers, we kill education
> I'm saying it's alright for the youths to go crazy it's alright
> This is the real situation[77]

For many Tanzanians these words rang true, capturing their anger and disaffection.

Mr. II's 'Chini ya Miaka Kumi na Nane' (Under the Age of 18) also carried a powerful message to Tanzanian youth, as did Daznundaz rap 'Maji ya Shingo' (Up to One's Neck) and John Mjema's 'Mimi Sio Mwizi' (I am Not a Thief).

In each of these songs, and hundreds others like them, the social and political message to the people of Tanzania is strong. The youth, even those who feel most marginalized either because of lack of education or their social status, are given a sense of legitimacy through rapping and are able to present their viewpoint to the public.[78]

One thing all these rappers share is a desire, through music, to contest the system—one of the few possible ways of challenging its authority. Asked why he raps, G'sann of the rap group X Plastaz responds: 'There have always been problems in our lives ... My father spent all his money on alcohol and women. He forgot to take care of his family.' But Tanzanians find it difficult to defy authority directly, thus G'sann expressed his experiences in an alternative fashion. 'I see those problems throughout society. Many people recognize themselves in our rap music.'[79] Rap groups like X Plastaz, perform for a reason: to get their political message across to the people. In this way, rap groups like X Plastaz have to be understood within the broader context of hip hop culture as a voice for public debate and political action.

In their song 'Haleluya' X Plastaz rap about 'the misfortunes in Tanzania,' referring to several tragic incidents including the 500–600 people who drowned in Lake Nyanza (1996) and the death of *Mwalimu* Nyerere (1999). 'We talk about things that happen in everyday life, good and bad things like war and disease. We also talk about human rights. We rap about these matters to educate others to come to the rescue of the destitute. Another topic we've addressed is AIDS,' said Ziggy-Lah.[80] Younger Tanzanians hear their message loud and clear, and older people, particularly those in positions of power, are increasingly being forced to recognize their importance.

Since many lyrics are performed in local languages, the importance of rap music increases as an alternative medium in the public sphere to newspapers, radio, and television. Rap has become a medium, with roots in the oral tradition of Africa. This can be seen in a more indigenous 'rap style' of street entertainment known as *mchiriku*, which is popular in Dar es Salaam. *Mchiriku* grew out of the traditional wedding *ngoma* (dance) of the local Zaramo people. 'The songs are not unlike ... the young rappers', talking about the plight of the youth trying to make a decent living, or commenting on large political or social issues.'[81] In the mid 1990s government officials banned *mchiriku* public performances ostensibly because of the prevalence of illegal liquor and drugs as well as 'unruly lyrics and licentious dancing.'[82] The political nature of the songs undoubtedly also played a role.

Another powerful and poignant example of the importance of rap and oral traditions occurred in 2002. A team of WaterAid project specialists touring Zamcargo community of Dar, observed the health and sanitation problems. One of the workers noted, 'As we walked around, I noticed a lot of young people hanging around the streets. We were introduced to a group of youths one of whom gave us a rendition of a rap song he had written. The lyrics were about the inadequate water supply in the community, illnesses and the need for the government to help them.'[83] This incident speaks volumes about the use of popular culture as a means of political expression, but not without contradictions.

Members of the hip hop community are also organizing themselves. The best example is 'PREACH/SEMA,' an 'organization promoting the discussion of social issues among youth. They have started organizing weekly rap concerts in which young people are free to present their raps, and have held rap festivals focusing on raising AIDS awareness.'[84] In 2002, the Tanzanian Arts Council recognized rap as an official genre within Tanzanian popular music, urging young rappers to use their lyrics to discuss society's problems, such as drugs, sexual abuse, and lack of education.[85]

Rappers have worked with both governmental and non-governmental organizations (NGOs) to get across the message. Rough Nigga, a group from Tanga, performs an anti-drug song in the Tanzanian movie *Unga Adui* that deals with 'a cocaine gang vs the police, Pulp Fiction style.'[86] Another group, Bantu Pound Gangster (Nigger Pure and Kassie) rap about their culture: 'We are talking about drugs. To tell people not to use drugs. To advise people about HIV.' Population Services International hired Soggy Doggy Anter to do public service promotions for condom use among secondary school students.[87] In more recent years several popular artists have recorded raps about these topics; among them are Mwanafalsafa / Mwana FA ('First Philosopher') who in 2003, was voted best hip hop artist for his track 'Alikufa Kwa Ngoma'—an anti-AIDS song. He also has album releases: *Mwanafalsafa* and *Toleo Lijalo*—both of which include songs discussing

AIDS. Solo Thang is another artist who's lyrics tell 'real' life stories about issues such as poverty and HIV/AIDS.[88]

First among the organizations working with Tanzanian rappers is Madunia, a young non-profit NGO, based in the Netherlands. It was founded to promote African music. In 2001, the Madunia foundation helped organize a Dar es Salaam conference that brought together rappers from South Africa, Holland, and Tanzania. The foundation worked with NiZA (Netherlands Institute for Southern Africa) to involve themselves in what they call 'Edutainment' (i.e. mixing entertainment with education through popular culture).[89] They use rap music as a medium to present messages about topics like domestic violence, HIV/AIDS, or drug abuse.[90]

According to George Lipsitz, 'It is no accident that the state so often involves itself in questions of culture. Governments sustain or suppress artistic expression out of self-interest, out of recognition of the complex connections linking "the nation" with the imagi-nation.'[91] Such was the case of Nyerere and TANU in the early period of *uhuru* and *ujamaa*. Until the day he died Julius Nyerere believed in a form of socialist humanism, although modified by years of dealing with the failures of his vision of *ujamaa* and the contradictions of structurally adjusted neo-colonialism. His humanism, similar to, but distinct from, that espoused by Nkrumah and Senghor, remained grounded in traditional notions of *ujamaa* or familyhood.[92] Seeing the extended family as the basic structure of African society, he articulated a vision of socialism as 'an attitude of mind,' a culture of avoiding domination and fostering hospitality.

As Gesthuizen has noted, 'The revolutionary politics of *Ujamaa*, or African socialism, in the 1970s did much to create a feeling of national unity and equality, and some of its ethics seem to echo in the local rap lyrics of the new century.'[93] But there is dialectic involved in this process. Rap artists and musicians have been manipulated and have manipulated; they have used their celebrity status 'to advance their interests as citizens and subjects. Popular music can play a complicated role in politics. It helps to construct the nation-state while at the same time being constructed by it.'[94] Thus even though hip hop culture and rap music (like the society in general) continues to change and evolve, the children of Arusha go on sampling Nyerere's dream of *uhuru*, *umoja* and *ujamaa*, but with a new attitude of mind, new rhymes, and new Bongo Flava.

NOTES

1. The author would like to thank a number of people who provided information and insight for this chapter. In particular Nasir Mbwana, Lafunyo Mvungi, K Singo (aka K Single and KBC), John Mahundi, Isaac Siwingwa, and Gardner Habash—all of whom gave valuable interviews. Also, one of the leading experts on Tanzanian hip hop is Thomas Gesthuizen aka Juma4 of the African Hip Hop Foundation. He has written about, and been involved with the industry for many years. Others who have written extensively on

Tanzanian hip hop are Professor Alex Perulla and more recently Dr. Jose Arturo Saavedra Casco. I have learned from each, although the interpretations in this chapter are strictly those of the author.

2. Werner Graebner, 'Tanzania Popular Music,' in Simon Broughton, Mark Ellington, and Richard Trillo (eds), *World Music: The Rough Guide, Volume 1: Africa, Europe and the Middle East* (London, 1999), p. 686.

3. Goran Hyden, *Beyond Ujamaa in Tanzania* (Berkeley: University of California Press, 1980), p. 97. Also see Issa G. Shivji, *Class Struggles in Tanzania* (London: Heinemann, 1976), chapter 8.

4. *Mwalimu* Nyerere would subsequently articulate these principles in his tomes *Uhuru na Umoja* (Freedom and Unity) and *Uhuru na Ujamaa* (Freedom and Socialism). Julius K. Nyerere, *Uhuru na Umoja: Freedom and Unity: A Selection From Writings and Speeches 1952–65*. Also see by same author *Uhuru na Ujamaa: Freedom and Socialism: A Selection From Writings and Speeches 1965–67*.

5. Graebner, 'Tanzania Popular Music,' p. 686.

6. John Tomlinson, *Globalization and Culture* (Chicago: University of Chicago Press 1999), p. 1.

7. J. Freidman, 'Globalization as Awareness,' in John Benyon and David Dunkerley (eds), *Globalization: The Reader* (New York: Routledge, 2000), p. 44. See also I. Wallerstein, 'Culture as the Ideological Battleground of the Modern World System,' in Mike Featherstone (ed.), *Global Culture* (Beverly Hills: Sage, 1990).

8. Today, with the evolution of cultural studies and global studies the theme of cultural processes and globalization has been given a more complex understanding, if not always more accurate. As Bourdieu and Wacquant have noted about the new language of 'newspeak,' much of its vocabulary most particularly terms like 'globalization … not to mention their so-called postmodern cousins, "minority," "ethnicity," "identity," "fragmentation." Etc. The diffusion of this new planetary vulgate—from which the terms "capitalism," "class," "exploitation," "domination," and "inequality" are conspicuous by their absence, having been peremptorily dismissed under the pretext that they are obsolete and non-pertinent—is the result of a new type of imperialism …' See Pierre Bourdieu and Loïc Wacquant, 'Neoliberal Newspeak: Notes on the New Planetary Vulgate.' This is the expanded translation (by David Macey and Loïc Wacquant) of an article that originally appeared in French in *Le Monde Diplomatique*, 554 (May 2000), pp. 6–7, in a special dossier on 'America in Everyone's Head.' Available from <http://www.globalanthropology. com/ BOURDIEU,%20Planetary%20vulgateneoliberal.pdf>; accessed August 18, 2003. My thanks to Mr. Gary Wilder for pointing this article out to me. See also George Lipsitz, *Dangerous Crossroads: Popular Music, Postmodernism, and the Poetics of Place* (London: Verso, 1994). Arjun Appadurai, *Modernity at Large: Cultural Dimensions of Globalization* (New York: Routledge, 1996). Arjun Appadurai (ed.), *Globalization* (Durham, NC: Duke University Press, 2001). Arjun Appaduri, 'Globalization,' *Public Culture*, Vol. 12, No. 1 (Winter 2000).

9. Tomlinson, *Globalization and Culture*, chapter 3.

10. Lyrics to 'Mnyonge hana haki' (The Poor Person Has No Rights), Remmy Ongala, in Graebner, 'Tanzania Popular Music,' p. 685. Remmy Ongala, who as of 2004 still lived in Mikocheni area of Dar es Salaam, introduced the music of Tanzania to the World Music scene. Ironically, many of his local albums were censored because of his 'straight talk about corruption, AIDS and the problems of the poor,' which were in many ways ahead of their time. See Banning Eyre and Sean Barlow, 'On the Scene in Dar es Salaam' (2004), *Afropop Worldwide*, available at <http://www.afropop.org/multi/feature/ID/411/ On+the+Scene+in+Dar+es+Salaam+(2004)>; accessed April 29, 2005.

11. In colonial times Tanzania was called German East Africa and later Tanganyika by the British.

12. John Iliffe, *A Modern History of Tanganyika* (Cambridge: Cambridge University Press, 1979), pp. 33–5.

13. Banning Eyre, *Tanzania* (Tanserve).

14. Graebner, 'Tanzania Popular Music,' p. 682. *Also* Africa Online.com Correspondent, 'Tanzanian music—an introduction'; available at <http://www.africaonline.com/site/Articles/1,10,751.jsp>; accessed July 24, 2003.

15. Nyerere, *Uhuru na Umoja*, p. 186. See also Benedict Anderson, *Imagined Communities* (London: Verso, 1983).

16. Nyerere, *Uhuru na Umoja*, p. 186. Nyerere said: 'When we were at school we were taught to sing the songs of Europeans. How many of us were taught the songs of the Wanyamwezi or the Wahehe? Many of us have learnt to dance the "rumba," or the "chachacha" to "rock'n'roll" and to "twist" and even to dance the "waltz" and the "foxtrot." But how many of us can dance or have even heard of, the *Gombe Sugu*, the *Mangala*, the *Konge*, *Nyang'umumi*, *Kiduo* or *Lele Mama*? ... It is hard for any man to get much real excitement from dances and music that are not in his own blood.'

17. Ibid., p. 187.

18. The only exception was music from Zaire.

19. AOL Correspondent, p. 2.

20. Krister Malm and Monika Sarstad, 'Rap, Ragga and Reggae in East Africa,' part of the Music–Media–Multiculture research project, available from <http://www.Musikmuseet.se/mmm/Africa/mission.html>; accessed June 21, 2002.

21. Graebner, 'Tanzania Popular Music,' p. 682. As an example, one of the oldest and most popular of the new 'Jazz Bands' was the NUTA Jazz, named after the National Union of Tanzanian Workers. Also other bands formed under the umbrellas of the police, army, national service, party youth wing, the Dar es Salaam city council and bus service. The names clearly showed a connection between music and working-class culture. At the same time these musicians were not simply 'paid lackeys,' they were talented and innovative artists who believed in socialist nation building. As with earlier musical forms, in subsequent eras there was an amalgamation or blending of traditions. This happened when local musicians absorbed the U.S. and European inspired Disco wave of the 1970s and 80s, and took disco songs and improvised a 'Swahili' rhythm.

22. See Shivji, *Class Struggles in Tanzania*, parts three and four.

23. At a general level it defined how people made sense and gave meaning to their world, as Stuart Hall has noted. Culture reflects a collective set of beliefs, styles, values, and symbols. See Stuart Hall, *Representation and the Media*, Video lecture 1997. Also Stuart Hall (ed.), *Representation: Cultural Representations and Signifying Practices: Culture, Media and Identities*, Vol. 2 (London: Sage, 1997).

24. As we will see momentarily, 'Race,' as understood and preformed in Western capitalist nation-states, did not appear as an issue in the construction of hip hop culture among Tanzanian youth.

25. Eyre and Barlow, 'On the Scene in Dar,' p. 2.

26. Claude Ake, *Democracy and Development in Africa* (Washington, D.C.: Brookings Institution, 1996), p. 61.

27. Claude G. Mung'ong'o and Vesa-Matti Loiske, 'Structural Adjustment Programmes and Peasant Responses in Tanzania,' in David Simon et al. (eds), *Structurally Adjusted Africa* (London: Pluto Press, 1995). Generally speaking, the SAPs in Tanzania are formally divided into three main phases: the National Economic Survival Programme (1981–82), Structural Adjustment Programme (SAP/1982–85), and The Economic Recovery Programme (ERP/1986 onward). Also see C.S.L. Chachage, 'Forms of Accumulation, Agriculture and Structural Adjustment in Tanzania,' in Peter Gibbon (ed.), *Social Change and Economic Reform in Africa* (Sweden: Uppsala, 1993).

28. Mung'ong'o and Loiske, 'Structural Adjustment Programmes,' pp. 162–3. 'The policies adopted included the partial devaluation of the shilling, the partial liberalization of

internal and external trade and partial liberalization of agriculture, especially through formulation of the national agricultural policy which, for the first time, allowed private ownership of land.' The ERP continued the SAP '... policies have involved the removal of all subsidies on agricultural inputs and urban food supply, reintroduction of direct taxation and further cuts in social services expenditure.' According to Chachage, 'other knowledgeable observers of Tanzanian socio-political scene, however, believe that these programs have only benefited local and international private capital at the expense of the less endowed social groups in the country.' On February 5, 1977 Nyerere created the Chama cha Mapinduzi (CCM/ Party of the Revolution) by combining the old TANU and the Afro-Shirazi Party of Zanzibar.

29. To Tanzanians Nairobi was long known for its prostitution and street crime. 'The Stereotype was that Kenyans are tough and direct while Tanzanians are polite and ineffectual.' Eyre and Barlow, 'On the Scene in Dar,' p. 2.

30. Thomas Gesthuizen, 'Bongo Flava: Hip Hop in Tanzania,' *Waxpoetics*, No. 2 (spring 2002), p. 68. Graebner, 'Tanzania Popular Music,' p. 686.

31. Mack D, the leader of the rap group Ugly Faces, was one of Dar es Salaam's earliest breakdancers. Dolasoul report, 'New Generation MC: Mack D,' available at <http://www.africanhiphop.com/interviews/mack-d.htm>; accessed July 4, 2002. Ramadhani Mponjika, 'Swahili Coast Hip Hop,' available at <http://www.africanperspective.com/html37/mam37.html>. Rhymson, for the purposes of this article, uses his original name Ramadhani. This adds an interesting authenticity knowing he was involved in the events he is describing. Another famous b-boy of his day was a dancer known as Digga Digga. K-Singo, interview by author and Nasir Mbwana, tape recording of phone conversation, Claremont, CA, July 17, 2004. Also see Malm and Sarstad, 'Rap, Ragga and Reggae.' On the website 'Rap, Ragga, Reggae in East Africa' there are several instances of Hip Hop Art, in one particular illustration there is a bus with the words 'HIP HOP' written in bold colorful letters and the word 'Niggers' etched at the bottom (with the caption: 'Niggers in Dar?'). In Tanzania this bus graffiti was not as common as in Nairobi where many of the local *daladalas* displayed aerosol art. Also see Mponjika, 'Swahili Coast Hip Hop.' See Alicia Rebensdorf, 'Representing the Real: Exploring Appropriations of Hip-Hop Culture in the Internet and Nairobi,' online project; available from <http://lclark.edu/~soan/alicia/rebensdorf.101.html>; accessed July 7, 2002.

32. Mponjika, 'Swahili Coast Hip Hop,' African Perspective.com. In 1992, early promoters like Kusaga and Kim organized dance and DJ competitions like the big annual rap battles 'Yo Rap Bonanza'—a talent show sponsored by a local Indian businessperson. In addition, producers like Ted Osiah from Nairobi, Halfani aka Paul, Master J and DJ Boni Luv (Bonni love) of Dar es Salaam put much effort into creating the unique East African underground rap sound.

33. Mponjika, 'Swahili Coast Hip Hop.' In addition, one informant remembers that there was a very popular show called 'the Beach Party,' that was held at Oyster Bay Beach in Dar es Salaam. This particular show later became known as 'The Summer Jam' and later 'The Fiesta.' Another interesting connection between the early introduction of African-American hip hop and Tanzanian culture was basketball. It seems that basketball courts were not numerous and could only be found at secondary schools or in a few locations like Upanga, Masaki, Chang'ombe, and Mikocheni. Many early freestyle rappers like K Singo and Fresh XE were also basketball players and fans of African-American ball players. Thus they shared a love of two Black American artforms: rap and basketball. Isaac Siwingwa, interview by author and Nasir Mbwana, email typescript, May 26, 2004. Also indirectly confirmed by K Singo interview.

34. Malm and Sarstad, 'Rap, Ragga and Reggae.' Indeed, Master J (Joachim Kimario) ran one of the earliest studios, which he built out of a freight container. Also see *Rockers Magazine*, 'Kwanza Unit Marathon,' December 15, 1998, 'Rockers meet K Single [K Singo],' p. 14.

Underground pirated tapes popped up everywhere. According to one observer, 'Taking a short trip on the public transport (daladala) in Dar Es Salaam, it is not rare for passengers to have the privilege to hear an entire album from a local artist.'

35. 'Balozi Wenu,' the new Dolasoul 'dolasolo,' in *Nubian Underground: The Home of African Hip-hop.* Available from <http://www.nubianunderground.com/nu/indexx.php?chmbr= h&ctnt=true&link=hype/dolawenu.htm>; accessed July 4, 2002.

36. Ibid.

37. One informant, while agreeing that many of the early rappers like Saigon and Dolasoul of the Deplowmatz and MC Arthur Luhigo came from schools like Tambaza Secondary School, others came from places like Temeke and thought of themselves as 'authentic' because of their poor neighborhoods and schools.

38. In 1992 Saleh Jaber won the YRB competition with his own rendition of 'Ice Ice Baby.' Thereafter, in the small hip hop circles he was known as 'Ice Ice Baby—King of Swahili Rap.' Like several other rappers of his day he eventually left Tanzania to join relatives in UAE. Thomas Gesthuizen, 'King of Swahili Rap,' Africanhiphop.com, October 2001. Ken Gibbs, 'MC: Man of the Community?' available at <http://www.africana.com/daily/ article/index/20000912.htm>; accessed September 12, 2000. Gesthuizen, 'Bongo Flava,' p. 68.

39. Ibid. K Singo puts great stress on the point that early Tanzanian rappers like Adam Tui and Rhymson did not 'mimic' African Americans but learned from them 'how to talk to their communities.'

40. *Rockers Magazine*, 'Kwanza Unit Marathon.'

41. Ibid. Malm and Sarstad, 'Rap, Ragga and Reggae.' 'Kwanza Unit.'

42. Ibid. While Tanzania does not have the wide-ranging income or class hierarchy of some other 'third world' countries, it does have class differences. Under *ujamaa*, the main distinction was between the combined working class, peasantry and lumpen-proletariat (mostly unemployed and poor) elements in the city, a small commercial petite bourgeoisie (mostly Asian), and a class referred to as the 'bureaucratic bourgeoisie.' See note 20 above.

43. Malm and Sarstad, 'Rap, Ragga and Reggae,' 'GWM.'

44. *Rockers Magazine*, 'Kwanza Unit Marathon,' December 15, 1998, 'Kwanzania, A New Nation is Born.'

45. K Singo, interview by author and Nasir Mbwana, tape recording of telephone interview, Claremont, CA, October 11, 2003.

46. Mponjika, 'Swahili Coast Hip Hop.' In 1998, before several members including Rhymson left Tanzania, the group consisted of Rhymson (alias Ramahani Mponjika), KBC (Kiba Cha Singo), D-Rob (the late Robert Mwingita), Eazy-B (Bernard Luanda), Bugzy Malone (Edward Margat), Papa Sav (Makanga Lugoe), Abbas Maunda, Fresh-G and Y-Tang and K Single. There was also a wider circle of affiliated members referred to as Kwanza Unit Foundation or Kwanzonians. Malm and Sarstad, 'Rap, Ragga and Reggae,' 'Kwanza Unit,' p. 68.

47. *Rockers Magazine*, 'Kwanza Unit Marathon,' 'Background.'

48. Ibid.

49. Ibid.

50. George Lipsitz, *Dangerous Crossroads*, p. 26. See also 'Official site of the Universal Zulu Nation,' available from <http://www.zulunation.com/hip_hop_history_2.htm>; accessed July 3, 2002.

51. Gregory Barz, *Kwayas, Kandas, Kiosks: Tanzanian Popular Choir Music*, p. 2. Available from <http://research.umbc.edu/eol/2/barz/barz2.html>; accessed July 4, 2002. Historically Swahili has included expressions and meanings which simply could not be expressed in English, and vice versa.

52. *Rockers Magazine*, 'Kwanza Unit Marathon,' December 15, 1998, 'Kiswacentric Concept.' As Rhymson once mused: 'When I say my rhymes are fat like an elephant, this is definitely Kiswacentric, you can't have something like this from New York. Back in the days there was a local DJ who used to translate the chant Ice Ice Baby into meaningless *Barafu barafu mtoto.*'

53. Iliffe, *A Modern History of Tanganyika*, p. 379.

54. Gesthuizen, 'Bongo Flava,' p. 70. According to Thomas Gesthuizen: in its early years '... hip hop's core concepts and expressions had to be translated by these exponents. The first Swahili rap releases relied on the artist's sole interpretation, where curses and references to sexuality were left out in accordance with local culture.' But when they began to write raps direct in Swahili, language and tropes became critical.

55. Ibid. Dolasoul, member of the rap group the Deplowmatz, explained it this way: 'Tanzanians don't go out there and do crazy stuff. They are really respectful people. If you do that everybody would say "Hey what's wrong with him. He's a Tanzanian, why is he doing that?" It's a matter of different values [i.e. different from African Americans].'

56. Ibid. 'There is this conception here in Tanzania that rap music is just for dropouts, people who smoke marijuana. Tanzanians think that we're just copying Americans, we steal their rap stuff, the instrumentals. There are people out there who still think some of the songs we've make that they are American and we just changed the words a little bit. But that is not the case actually.'

57. Malm and Sarstad, 'Rap, Ragga and Reggae,' 'Jungle Crewz Posse.'

58. James Astill, 'Tanzanian rap breaks free of past,' *Guardian* (London), February 3, 2001, p. 18.

59. A similar point is made about Kenya by Rebensdorf, 'Representing the Real,' p. 47.

60. Bourdieu and Wacquant, 'Neoliberal Newspeak,' p. 1. This article gives primacy to the notion of cultural imperialism as a subsumptive device, with little hope of indigenous societies being able to resist this domination.

61. Malm and Sarstad, 'Rap, Ragga and Reggae,' 'Dar es Salaam High Class: Abbas Maunda.'

62. 'Positive Black Soul hit Seattle,' *Nubian Underground*, available from <http://www.nubianunderground.com/nu/indexx.php?chmbr=h&ctnt=true&link=hype/pbswmd.html>; accessed July 7, 2002.

63. Lufunyo Mvungi, interview by author and Nasir Mbwana, tape recording of telephone interview, Claremont, CA, October 11, 2003.

64. Dully Sykes lyrics to 'Nyambizi' available from <http://www.geocities.com/getphatkenya/nyambizi.htm>. Lyrics translated by Nasir Mbwana from an interview by the author, Claremont, CA, October 12, 2003.
Kwa ajili yo pombe ilimtoka aibu ilibidi aniambie;
Dully chukua chumba ukanienzi! (Hidaya)
Nikaenda mapokezi kulipia chumba cha mapenzi
Mimi na nyambizi mpenzi, tukaingia ndani, tukaanza na romans, pole pole
tena kwa pozi.
Ukawadia ule muda wa dozz, nikamuuliza, Nyambizi tunaweza kulala? King'asti
unataka kulala ushakula? (Hidaya)
Aah! Nyambizi, nionee huruma mi sio kuchu, nipe japo kiduchu, mi
n'shachoka kupiga puchu!
Dully nakuonea huruma usije ukadata, haya kazime taa uje kupata! (Hidaya)Huwii!
Nikaenda kuzima taa ili nipate n'nachotaka. Nyambizi mama lakitanga, kiuno kizima
kajaza shanga.
Huwezi kuamini kwa jinsi alivyozipanga, kala mkorogo unaweza kujua nimmanga!
Jimama kote anacheza, hadi sodoma. Japo kanimeza lakini mchezo anauweza.
Na sijui wapi mchezo huu aliupokeza. Sababu macho anafumba na kiunoanakilegeza.
Semenimeni, semenimeni mpaka morning, nyambizi haniachi, hasikii walahaoni.

Nami sitoweza kumuacha, usiku huo ilikuwa bila zana. Ngoma dry ajalikazini mpaka kunakucha, Wwaaa! 'Bongo Lyrics,' available from <http://www.darhotwire.com/v2/go/tafuta/muziki/ explosions/lyrics/dullySykes/nyambizi.html>; accessed October 12, 2003.

65. Alex Perulla, 'Expectations in the Tanzanian Hip Hop Community,' *Tanzanian Affairs*, No. 73 (September–December 2002), pp. 35–6. It is known that FM stations like Clouds FM, Radio 1, East Africa Radio, Radio Tanzania, Radio Tumaini (a Catholic station), and Radio Zanzibar share promotions and can, ostensibly, ban a song from the airwaves if it is deemed offensive. As one Bongo Flava artist, Mr. Nice, put it: 'Clouds FM is a station that "kills artists".' Eyre and Barlow, 'On the Scene in Dar,' p. 5.

66. Birgit Quade and Lydia Martin, 'Who's Who in Bongo Flava,' Fly Global Music Culture, October 13, 2004, available from <http://www.fly.co.uk/fly/archives/2004/10/whos_who_ in_bongo_flava.html>; accessed April 30, 2005.

67. Eric Toroka, 'Tanzanian Female Hip Hop Artists,' Africanhiphop.com, 2000. Also Ken Anyama (Nairobi), Africanhiphop.com, 2001.

68. Astill, 'Tanzanian rap breaks free of past,' p. 18. Witness Mwaijaga, who along with Sam Stigillydaa formed Bad Gear, has had a rough life to base her lyrics on; after her mother kicked her out she moved to a rough area of Dar and began rapping in beer-joints for a few shillings. According to her, 'If I had not been strong I could have sold myself: been a bitch, But I dislike that.' However, in June 2004 Witness Mwaijaga joined with two other young Tanzanian female musicians, Langa Kileo and Sarah Kaisi, to form the group Wakilisha. Thereafter they won a ten-week-long talent search sponsored by Coca-Cola company; they were chosen from among hundreds of talented youngsters throughout Kenya, Uganda, and Tanzania. Eric Toroka, 'Coca-Cola Popstars to Perform in Dar,' *East African Times*, Friday, June 25, 2004.

69. Gesthuizen, 'Bongo Flava,' p. 70. See also Malm and Sarstad, 'Rap, Ragga and Reggae,' 'GWM.'

70. See Rebensdorf, 'Representing the Real,' p. 21.

71. Malm and Sarstad, 'Rap, Ragga and Reggae,' 'GWM.' Also note that according to Hashim, aka Dogo, '*Bongo Psychological depicts* a state of mind ... Bongo people are people with a lot of problems—Bongo people use their brains a lot to survive. The Psychological Part is the mental derived from the state you live in, Bongo—So Bongo Psychological. It is the psychology of a typical Bongo person, the way he thinks and acts.' Dolasoul, 'Meet HASHIM a.k.a. Dogo: The Bongo Psychological,' <Africanhiphop. com/interviews/hashim.htm>. Another version of the origins of Bongo Flava comes from rapper Afande Sele, 'The word came from the word "ubongo." It means brain. It was made "Bongo" because you have to use your head. If you want to survive, you rely on the brain, Bongo.' Eyre and Barlow, 'On the Scene in Dar,' p. 6.

72. Gesthuizen, 'Bongo Flava,' p. 68. According to Thomas Gesthuizen, 'Tanzanian rap existed for a decade without much backing by the music industry. Between 1985, when, reportedly, the first local kids took up a mic, and 1995, when the newly introduced commercial radio started out with a regular rap show, only three tapes were made commercially available.'

73. Ibid., p. 61. According to its website, 'IPP Limited is one of the largest private sector companies in Tanzania. The history of IPP dates back to the mid 1980s, when Mr. Reginald Abraham Mengi started a small scale, hand operated ball point assembly at his Dar es Salaam residence. From this humble beginning, the company has progressively mushroomed into diversified manufacturing business and service industries which play a major role in the social and economic development of Tanzania.' IPP's major subsidiary companies include the following: IPP Consult (provides financial and general consultancy services); Bodycare Limited (manufacturers of soaps and tooth paste in Tanzania); Bonite Bottlers Limited (bottlers of Coca-Cola range of soft drinks in Northern Tanzania); ITV-Independent Television Limited (the largest and most popular private television station in Tanzania);

Radio One Limited (the most popular private FM and AM Radio broadcasting station in Tanzania); The Guardian Limited (publishers of several daily and weekly newspapers which include *The Guardian, The Sunday Observer, The Daily Mail, Sun Set* and *Financial Times* in English; and *Nipashe, Nipashe Jumapili, Alasiri, Kasheshe, Lete Raha* and *Taifa Letu* in Kiswahili (the national language); Printa Afrique Limited (printers of newspapers and general publications); Press Services (PST) Tanzania Ltd. (a news agency company). IPP Limited and Coca-Cola Sabco (South Africa) jointly own Coca-Cola Kwanza Limited currently with bottling plants in Dar es Salaam, Mbeya, and Zanzibar.

74. Radio One is considered by many to be the most popular station in Dar es Salaam, but Clouds FM and Radio Free Africa (RFA) are probably more popular with rap audiences.

75. Perulla, 'Expectations in the Tanzanian Hip Hop Community,' p. 36.

76. Ibid., p. 69. Also Africanhiphop.com, 'Hip Hop in Tanzania—All the crews and the updates: Mr. II.' The political criticism of 2 Proud's songs caught on with the radio listeners, and soon his name was familiar even in the smallest upcountry villages in Tanzania. His conscious lyrics refer to street life, the everyday life in Tanzania, politics and, more than anyone else, he is responsible for having rap taken more seriously in Tanzania. Not surprisingly, 2 Proud's musical and ideological inspirations were Ice Cube, N.W.A., and above all Tupac Shakur. According to 2 Proud, '[Shakur] was a man of reality,' and his lyrics were not as important as his intense sense of freedom. Says 2 Proud, 'What I liked from Tupac, was his way of expressing himself without caring whether what he said was good or bad. It was the freedom to say anything ... Even though in my society we don't have gunshots, we don't say, "——you," we have problems, lack of employment, poor education, misusing of power. I talk about what is happening.'

In another interview, when asked what was typical for his style Mr. II replied, 'In a country like this the low standard people get tired of what is going on and the way they are being led by the African politicians.' At least one researcher, Thomas Gesthuizen, claims that 2 Proud was unique 'in that never before did any musician talk about politics in such a direct way.' While this point is probably overstated to make a point, it is certain that these same politicians listen to and talk about his music and debate exactly what was touching people's hearts.

77. Lyrics to 'Hali Halisi,' are available at *State of Bongo Hip Hop/Hali Ya Bongo Flava*: <http://www.kwetuentertainment.com/listen/Lyrics.html>; accessed December 12, 2004.

78. Perulla, 'Expectations in the Tanzanian Hip Hop Community,' p. 36.

79. Koen Van Wijk, 'Rapping for a reason,' available at <http://www.niza.nl/media/Ea.hivhop/Ea4.xplastaz.html>; accessed July 4, 2002, p. 2.

80. Kwaku, 'Words and Deeds,' *Billboard Magazine*, October 27, 2001.

81. Graebner, 'Tanzania Popular Music,' p. 687.

82. Ibid.

83. 'Visit to WaterAid Projects in Dar es Salaam, Tanzania,' available at <http://www.cycletothesummit.org.uk/wateraiddar.htm>; accessed May 21, 2002.

84. Ibid. *Rockers Magazine*, 'Kwanza Unit Marathon,' December 15, 1998. As of 1998 *Rockers Magazine* undertook a number of projects. These projects had a common sociological foundation. PREACH Education (Promote Righteous Environmetal And Community Health Education) Project / Swahili Version: SEMA (Saidia Elimu ya Mazingira na Afya) kupitia Rockers. This was Rockers' project on AIDS, health, and environment. It was an awareness campaign against AIDS, drug abuse, and environmental degradation.

85. Ibid.

86. 'Hip Hop in Tanzania,' available at <http://www.africanhiphop.com>; accessed July 4, 2002.

87. Malm and Sarstad, 'Rap, Ragga and Reggae,' 'Bantu Pound Gangster.' Also 'Swahili Poetry and Hip Hop Culture,' available at <http://www.tanserve.com/culture/Local_hiphop.html>; accessed June 21, 2002.

88. Quade and Martin, 'Who's Who in Bongo Flava.'

89. 'Swahili Poetry and Hip Hop Culture,' available at <http://www.tanserve.com/culture/Local_hiphop.html>; accessed June 21, 2002. Also Thomas Gesthuizen 'HIVhop: an informed decision saves lives,' available at <http://www.niza.nl/media/Ea.hivhop/>; accessed June 21, 2002.

90. Ibid. They sponsored the HIVhop campaign which included ten hip hop tracks by local artists dealing with key issues in the campaign. The HIVhop team chose to actively involve students in the shows and was open to creative contributions by rappers in the audience. The HIVhop CD mixed discussion, hip hop instrumentals, and the HIVhop lyrics in a creative way; radio stations rebroadcast the mixture several times and made it available. Although initially only scheduled in South Africa, in March 2001, organizers expanded the program to include Tanzania, with two Dutch rappers and two South Africans traveling to Dar es Salaam.

91. Lipsitz, *Dangerous Crossroads*, p. 137.

92. Fred Lee Hord and Jonathan Scott Lee, *I Am Because We Are: Readings in Black Philosophy* (Amherst: University of Massachusetts Press, 1995), p. 19.

93. Gesthuizen, 'Bongo Flava,' p. 68.

94. Lipsitz, *Dangerous Crossroads*, p. 138.

Contributors

Mumia Abu-Jamal is a legendary political prisoner and renowned journalist from Philadelphia who has been on death row since 1981 for allegedly shooting a Philadelphia police officer. Over the years Mumia has received national and international support in his efforts to overturn his dubious sentence. Mumia Abu-Jamal has been on Pennsylvania's death row for over 20 years and during that time his essays have reached a global audience. His books *Live From Death Row*, *Death Blossoms*, *All Things Censored*, *Faith of Our Fathers*, and the recently released *We Want Freedom* have sold over 150,000 copies and been translated into nine languages. For a list of his radio broadcasts see <http://www.prisonradio.org/mumia.htm>.

Eric K. Arnold grew up in the Bay Area, and attended college at UC Santa Cruz, where he wrote his thesis on hip hop's cultural roots in 1990 for the American Studies Department. After graduation, he served as the Editorial Director of *4080* magazine during the 'Golden Age' of Bay Area hip hop, from 1993 to 1997. After leaving *4080*, he wrote the 'In the Hood' column for *Source* magazine for several years, writing about regional scenes from Halifax to Tokyo. He has also written extensively for *XLR8R*, *Rap Pages*, *SF Bay Guardian*, *Raygun*, *Murder Dog*, *P.S.*, *SF Examiner*, and the *East Bay Express*, for whom he currently writes a column, 'Close 2 tha Edge.' In 2002, he collaborated with Cecil Brown and the African American Studies Department at UC Berkeley to present 'Hip Hop and Beyond', a conference bridging urban culture and academia, and is (still) in the process of writing his first book, on the history of Bay Area hip hop.

Dipannita Basu is associate professor of Sociology and Black Studies at Pitzer College (Claremont, CA). She specializes in urban sociology, popular culture, ethnic entrepreneurship, and race and ethnicity. Recent publications include chapters in *Sociology, the State and Social Change* and *African Americans in the US Economy*, as well as journal articles in *Post Colonial Studies*, *Psych Discourse*, *Ethnic and Racial Studies*, and *Left Curve*.

Umar Bin Hassan was an original member of the legendary group The Last Poets, who recorded such classic poems as 'Niggers are Scared of Revolution,' 'This is Madness,' 'When the Revolution Comes,' and 'Gashman' on their two record albums *Last Poets* (1970) and *This is Madness* (1971). Umar Bin Hassan grew up in a tough public housing project in Akron Ohio and overcame a broken home, child abuse, an imprisoned musician-father, and his own drug addiction to become one of the spokespersons of his generation. Today only Bin Hassan and Abiodun Oyewole remain of the original Last Poets group. He continues the tradition of defiant spoken verse to promote unity and pride amongst Black folks in their struggle against racism and disenfranchisement.

Timothy S. Brown, who is from Oakland, California, has lived in Berlin, Germany, where he was a Fulbright Fellow affiliated with the Free University. Currently he is an assistant professor of German History at Northeastern University. He is the author of *Bolsheviks, 'Beefsteaks' and Brownshirts: A Cultural History of the Radical Extremes in the Weimar Republic*, and has taught at the University of California Berkeley and at Pomona College. He is working on a new book on the protest movements of '1968' in West Germany.

Sohail Daulatzai is an assistant professor in African American Studies and Film and Media Studies at the University of California, Irvine. He has published articles on race, politics, and popular culture in various journals and books including *Spectator, Basketball Jones, SAMAR*, and *Amer-Asia* and has written the DVD liner notes to Kevin Fitzgerald's award winning documentary *Freestyle: The Art of Rhyme* on Palm Pictures. His current book projects include *Born To Use Mics: Reading Nas' Illmatic* (with Michael Eric Dyson) as well as *Return of the Mecca*, which explores the history of Islam and Black radicalism through jazz, sports, literature, and hip hop culture. He is currently the executive producer of *Free Rap*, a hip hop album inspired by the prison writings of Imam Jamil Al-Amin.

Rhiannon L. Fink is a graduate of the theatre-dance department at the College of Wooster and holds an MA in Performance Studies from New York University. She has lived and taught in Japan. Ms Fink has also worked as a choreographer and is currently teaching yoga in Manhattan.

Laura Alexandra Harris is an associate professor of English, World Literature and Black Studies at Pitzer College (Claremont, CA). She received her PhD from the University of California, San Diego. Dr. Harris publishes in the areas of literary criticism, feminist and queer studies, Black studies, African diasporic studies, and fiction and poetry. Her publications are featured in the *Journal of Lesbian Studies* and *African American Review*. She has co-edited *Femme: Feminists, Lesbians, and Bad Girls* with Elizabeth Crocker (1997) and published *Notes from a Welfare Queen in the Ivory Tower* (2002).

Veronique Helenon is a historian of Africa and the African diaspora. She is currently an assistant professor at Florida International University and has previously taught at the University of Massachusetts, Dartmouth and at the Institute for Research in African American Affairs at Columbia University. Her research interests focus on the francophone African diaspora, the Caribbean, colonization, and Black popular culture in France, especially hip hop.

April K. Henderson is a lecturer in Pacific Studies at Victoria University of Wellington, in Aotearoa / New Zealand. Ms. Henderson earned her MA in Pacific Island Studies at the University of Hawai'i at Manoa. Her writings on Pacific hip hop music and dances have appeared in *Back2Basics* (New Zealand), *DANZ* (Dance New Zealand), and *Out4Fame* (Australia). She is currently at work on a doctoral dissertation and book project titled *Gifted Flows: Hip Hop and Samoan Diaspora*, for the History of Consciousness program at University of California, Santa Cruz. Her postgraduate work focuses on Pacific participation in hip hop culture, with an emphasis on the circulation of cultural forms between communities in the continental United States, Hawai'i, American Samoa, Samoa, and Aotearoa New Zealand.

John Hutnyk is a senior lecturer at the Centre for Cultural Studies at Goldsmiths College, University of London. His main research areas are: urban anthropology, music, and politics, and specifically on institutions and the various connections between state and racism, knowledge industry restructuring, marxist critique, and post-structuralist theory. He is the author of *Critique of Exotica: Music, Politics and the Culture Industry* (2000) and *The Rumour of Calcutta: Tourism Charity and the Poverty of Representation* (1996). He was a co-editor of *Dis-Orienting Rhythms: The Politics of the New Asian Dance Music* (with Sanjay and Ashwari Sharma) and of 'Travel Worlds: Journeys in Contemporary Cultural Politics' (with Raminder Kaur), as well as special sections on 'Music and Politics' in the journals *Theory, Culture and Society* and *Postcolonial Studies*. His most recent publication is *Bad Marxism: Capitalism and Cultural Studies* (2004).

Adria L. Imada received her PhD in the American Studies Program (as well as a certificate in the Culture and Media Program) at New York University. Born and raised in Honolulu, Hawai'i, Imada is currently an assistant professor in the Departments of Ethnic Studies and Anthropology, University of Oregon. She has written on the circulation of Hawaiian entertainment and culture in the U.S. empire, from 1876–1959. She also has directed a short documentary, *Aunty Betty*, a portrait of an 85-year-old former hula dancer in New York City. Her current research is on Hawaiian Hula Performance circuits.

Robin D.G. Kelley is professor of Anthropology, African American Studies and Jazz Studies at Columbia University. Before arriving at Columbia, Kelley served as professor of history and Africana studies and chair of the history department at New York University. He also taught as a distinguished visiting professor in African-American studies, at Columbia in 1996 and served as the Louis Armstrong Professor of Jazz Studies 2000–01. Kelley is author of numerous prize-winning books including *Hammer and Hoe: Alabama Communists During the Great Depression* (1990); *Race Rebels: Culture Politics and the Black Working Class* (1994); *Yo' Mama's DisFunktional!: Fighting the Culture Wars in Urban America* (1997), and *Three Strikes: Miners, Musicians,*

Salesgirls, and the Fighting Spirit of Labor's Last Century, written with Dana Frank and Howard Zinn (2001). His most recent book is *Freedom Dreams: The Black Radical Imagination* (2002). Kelley also co-edited with Sidney J. Lemelle *Imagining Home: Class, Culture, and Nationalism in the African Diaspora* (1994). Currently, Kelley is completing a biography of musician Thelonious Monk, tentatively titled *Thelonious: A Life*.

Sidney J. Lemelle is professor of History and Black Studies at Pomona College (Claremont, CA). He has also been a lecturer at the University of Dar es Salaam, Tanzania and visiting associate professor Center for African American Studies at UCLA. He has written widely on topics related to Africa and African diasporan history. With Robin D.G. Kelley he has co-edited *Imagining Home: Class, Culture and Nationalism in the African Diaspora* (1994). Lemelle has also published chapters in *Black Modernity: Discourses Between the United States and South Africa* and *Black Protest Thought and Education*. He is currently working on several projects related to the African diaspora, and the circum-Caribbean.

Zine Magubane is an associate professor of Sociology at Boston College. She is the author of *Bringing the Empire Home: Imagining Race, Class, and Gender in Britain and Colonial South Africa* (2003) and *Posmodernism, Postcoloniality, and African Studies* (2002). She has also co-edited *Hear Our Voices: Race, Gender and Black South African Women in the Academy* with Reitumetse Mabokela (2004) as well as having published numerous other articles on gender, the body and embodiment, globalization, race, class and identity, and social policy.

Rachel Raimist is a Feminist Studies PhD student at the University of Minnesota in the Deptartment of Women's Studies, minoring in American Studies. She has a BA and MFA in Film Directing from UCLA. She has taught Feminist Film Studies at the University of Minnesota, Twin Cities, and Video Production at UC Irvine and has taught third wave Feminist Theory and Practice at Macalester College. She is a mother, filmmaker, hip hop feminist scholar, activist, and educator.

Annelise Wunderlich has a dual masters degree in journalism and Latin American studies at UC Berkeley, with a focus on documentary film and human rights. As a documentary filmmaker Wunderlich won the Golden Gate Award for best Bay Area documentary short at the San Francisco International Film Festival (2004).

Her film, *Crystal Harvest*, focuses on Modesto's methamphetamine problem and how it connects the lives of various residents. Wunderlich was also a reporter for the *Modesto Bee* and has published in several venues including *Colorlines* magazine and a chapter in *Capitalism, God, and a Good Cigar: Cuba Enters the Twenty-first Century* by Lydia Chávez (editor), Mimi Chakarova (photographer) (2005).

Index

Compiled by Sue Carlton